CHINA'S TIBET?
Autonomy or Assimilation

Warren W. Smith Jr.

ROWMAN & LITTLEFIELD PUBLISHERS, INC.
Lanham • Boulder • New York • Toronto • Plymouth, UK

ROWMAN & LITTLEFIELD PUBLISHERS, INC.

Published in the United States of America
by Rowman & Littlefield Publishers, Inc.
A wholly owned subsidiary of The Rowman & Littlefield Publishing Group, Inc.
4501 Forbes Boulevard, Suite 200, Lanham, Maryland 20706
www.rowmanlittlefield.com

Estover Road, Plymouth PL6 7PY, United Kingdom

British Library Cataloguing in Publication Information Available

Library of Congress Cataloging-in-Publication Data
Smith, Warren W.
    China's Tibet? : autonomy or assimilation / Warren W. Smith Jr.
        p.   cm.
    Includes bibliographical references and index.
    ISBN-13: 978-0-7425-3989-1 (cloth : alk. paper)
    ISBN-10: 0-7425-3989-X (cloth : alk. paper)
        1. Tibet (China)—Politics and government—1951– 2. Tibet (China)—Relations—
China. 3. China—Relations—China—Tibet. 4. Tibet (China)—Foreign public opinion. 5.
Tibet (China)—International status. I. Title.
    DS786.S557 2008
    951'.506—dc22

                                                                    2007049626

Printed in the United States of America

∞™ The paper used in this publication meets the minimum requirements of American
National Standard for Information Sciences—Permanence of Paper for Printed Library
Materials, ANSI/NISO Z39.48-1992.

Tibetans are betrayed by their hopefulness, the Chinese by their suspiciousness.

—Tibetan saying

Contents

The appendixes can be found on the book's website at http://www.rowman
.com/isbn/074253989X. They comprise the author's assessments of *The
Timely Rain* by Stuart and Roma Gelder, which describes their trip to Tibet in
1962; *Lhasa, the Open City* by Han Suyin, which describes her trip to Tibet in
1976; and *The Historical Status of China's Tibet*, which presents the Chinese
government's version of Tibetan history.

Introduction

WILL CHINA NEGOTIATE WITH THE DALAI LAMA in order to finally resolve the historical and political issue of Tibet, allow cultural autonomy sufficient to preserve Tibetan cultural and national identity, and allow the Dalai Lama to return and receive international acclaim for doing so? The thesis of this book is that China will not, because having successfully achieved the conquest of Tibet, China now fears jeopardizing that conquest by allowing Tibetan cultural and national identity, and thus Tibetan separatism, to survive. China is neither willing nor able to change its policies in Tibet. The legitimacy of Chinese sovereignty over Tibet is so sensitive for China that it cannot be flexible on any issue relevant to that legitimacy, including the nature of Tibetan autonomy within the Chinese state.

The title of this book is meant to expose the possessiveness of China's claim to Tibet, not to affirm the legitimacy of that claim. After several friends, especially Tibetans, expressed distaste for the original title, *China's Tibet*, the question mark was added in order to remove any appearance of approval for China's claim that Tibet belongs to the People's Republic of China (PRC). Chinese official statements and propaganda in English invariably refer to Tibet as "China's Tibet," or sometimes as "Tibet, China," an equally awkward locution. The PRC's foremost state-sponsored academic journal on Tibet is titled *China's Tibet*. A recent (1997) official Chinese version of Tibet's history is titled *The Historical Status of China's Tibet*. Recent Chinese propaganda about Tibet includes a CD called *China's Tibet* and two books, *Social History of Tibet, China*, and *China's Tibet: Facts and Figures*. The PRC's official website on Tibet is *China's Tibet Information Center*. The possessiveness revealed by Chinese terminology about Tibet is most obvious in the title of the PRC's 1992 State Council White Paper on Tibet: "Tibet: Its Ownership and Human Rights Situation." China even insisted that the Chinese version of the classic Belgian comic *Tintin in Tibet* be retitled *Tintin in China's Tibet*, until the original publisher objected.

The Chinese terminology is intended to inculcate the idea that Tibet and China are inseparable, or more specifically that Tibet belongs to China. It is meant to meld the concept of Tibet with that of China so that Tibet cannot be thought of other than as a part of China. It is meant to eliminate the concept of Tibet as a separate or independent national or political entity or as a "country" in any way separate or separable from China. Nevertheless, the possessiveness revealed by the terminology undermines China's purpose. The expression "China's Tibet" identifies Tibet as a thing, an entity, or a polity possessed by China. This entity has an identity that China wants to eradicate, but the possessiveness implied serves to emphasize that identity rather than obscure it.

In China, this terminology may be persuasive, since all Chinese are taught that Tibet has always been a part of China. However, outside China it is surely less effective. Tibet has a non-Chinese identity that predates the PRC and its annexation of Tibet in 1950–1951. Pre-1950, Tibet may have been generally thought of as in some way dominated by China, but it was also acknowledged as having a very strong identity based upon its territory, culture, and religion, all of which were very distinct from China's. Tibet was and is known as the "Roof of the World" due to its high altitude. And its "Shangri-La" image based on the unique Tibetan culture and religion was well established. Tibet was also known as one of the most exotic countries on Earth due to its remoteness, inaccessibility, and Buddhist culture. It was usually thought of as a country, a very large country, adjacent to China, India, and Turkestan, perhaps in some way dominated by China, but not part of China.

The unintentional consequences of Chinese nomenclature for Tibet are typical of Chinese propaganda. Just as "China's Tibet" highlights what it is intended to obscure, the strident repetition of propaganda phrases and themes usually elicits more doubt than certainty about the issues addressed. Since its takeover of Tibet in 1950–1951, China has created a tremendous amount of propaganda about Tibet in every conceivable medium, all calculated to justify Chinese rule over Tibet. Yet the very volume and intensity of Chinese propaganda raises questions about that which it seeks to establish as clear and undeniable. If Chinese sovereignty over Tibet is uncontroversial, then why the need for so much justification? If China's role in Tibet has been so benign and beneficial, then why the need to constantly defend it? Much of China's propaganda about Tibet has a simplistic and repetitive quality that is more characteristic of political indoctrination and thought control than reasoned argument.

Chinese propaganda sources provide valuable insight into Chinese cultural attitudes and political ideologies as applied in Tibet. This is fortunate, since propaganda articles were practically the only source available to the outside world for information about Tibet for the first thirty years of the Chinese occupation. Although many facts about the reality of Tibet are intentionally obscured by such sources, many more are unintentionally revealed. Chinese propaganda reveals doubts about the legitimacy of Chinese rule over the non-Chinese Tibetans and defensiveness about the lack of Tibetan acceptance of the legitimacy of Chinese rule. Much Chinese frustration is also revealed about the persistence of Tibetan resistance to the Chinese transformation of Tibet and China's inability to convince the world of the legitimacy and nobility of the Chinese mission in Tibet.

Chinese propaganda about Tibet has several primary themes. It claims that there is no political issue over Tibet's status because Tibet has "always" been part of China. Chinese Communist ideology maintains that there is no national issue of Tibet, only a class or social issue. Old Tibet before "liberation" was a feudal "Hell on Earth" from which Tibetans are said to be grateful to have been liberated by the Chinese Communist Party (CCP). An independent Tibet would mean an inevitable return to feudalism. Tibet since liberation has experienced social transformation and economic development. Tibetans enjoy self-rule, bestowed upon them by the party. All Tibetans—with the exception of a few malcontents deluded by the "Dalai clique"—prefer the present benevolent rule of China rather than the past, when Tibetans suffered under the misrule of the "government of serf-owners." Tibetans now have human rights for the first time in their history and enjoy ethnic harmony as one of China's minority nationalities.

The fundamental theme of Chinese propaganda is that there is no national issue of Tibet since Tibet was never a nation or country independent of China. Therefore, the only issue is Tibetans' liberation by the CCP from the abuse of their own feudal system and exploitative upper class. According to this version of reality, most Tibetans have welcomed Chinese rule over their homeland. Only a few of the former exploitative class have resisted the overturning of the class system by the "liberated serfs."

China was initially successful in cultivating many of the lower classes to this Marxist version of Tibetan reality, but many Tibetans stubbornly held on to the belief that they were an independent country and should have the right to national self-determination. Chinese propaganda could not obscure the reality that many thousands of Tibetans were killed during the revolt, or imprisoned in labor camps, or forced into exile, not because of their class status but because of their nationalist resistance to Chinese rule.

This book focuses upon Tibet under Chinese rule since 1951, and it relies heavily upon Chinese propaganda materials as well as the writings of some foreign sympathizers. (For a more complete and detailed history of Tibet, please refer to my earlier work, *Tibetan Nation: A History of Tibetan Nationalism and Sino-Tibetan Relations.*)[1] Propaganda materials provide an insight into Chinese cultural attitudes and political ideologies that cannot be gained or understood as well from any other source. Official Chinese publications of the 1950s tell the story of the consolidation of China's military and logistical control over Tibet and the initial steps taken to secure political control.

The PRC achieved political control over Tibet by means of the coerced 1951 Seventeen-Point Agreement for the Peaceful Liberation of Tibet. The Seventeen-Point Agreement theoretically granted to Tibet extensive autonomy, including the preservation of existing social, political, and religious systems. However, it also called for certain unspecified reforms and the eventual achievement of "national regional autonomy." The PRC's system of national regional autonomy was based upon Marxist-Leninist nationalities doctrine and assumed that Tibet would undergo "democratic reforms" and "socialist transformation" along with all the other national minorities within the PRC. The CCP assumed that it could persuade the Tibetans, or at least the lower classes and some upper-class collaborators, to voluntarily undertake reforms, thus superseding the provision of the Seventeen-Point Agreement that called for the social and political systems in Tibet to remain unchanged.

China began the political transformation of the territory that was to become the Tibet Autonomous Region (TAR) with negotiations about a preparatory committee for the TAR in 1954 and the committee's formal creation in 1956. However, China made the mistake of treating Tibetan areas outside the TAR as if they were not a part of Tibet. The implementation of "democratic reforms" and the beginnings of collectivization in those areas aroused resistance and revolt that eventually spread to central Tibet. In 1957, the CCP began to renege on the promises of its national regional autonomy system after minority nationality cadres took the opportunity of the Hundred Flowers liberalization to criticize nationality policies and to demand the type of autonomy that had actually been promised. Many nationality cadres, including some Tibetans, were purged in the subsequent Anti-Rightist and Anti-Local Nationalist campaign of late 1957.

China's "reforms" in eastern Tibet eventually led to the Lhasa revolt of March 1959. After that, China assumed direct rule over Tibet, while at the same time proclaiming that Tibetans had achieved self-rule by means of the suppression of the revolt and democratic reforms. The period after the rebellion is one of the most obscure in modern Tibetan history. The key to this period is an understanding of the techniques and purposes of the Democratic

Reforms campaign. This campaign was ostensibly intended to liberate the Tibetan serfs and slaves from the feudal serf society, but in actuality it was used to identify and repress the Tibetan opposition and to gain complete social and political control over Tibetans' lives.

There are now several Tibetan accounts that describe the process of democratic reforms. Much more information is also now available about the systematic depopulation and looting of Tibet's monasteries that took place between 1959 and the beginning of the Cultural Revolution, when the process was completed with the actual destruction of most temples and monasteries.

There is fortunately one extraordinary document that has recently come to light that paints a full picture of the results of the democratic reform process in the TAR. This is the Panchen Lama's famous 70,000-character petition submitted in May 1962 to Zhou Enlai and the CCP.[2] The Panchen Lama described the disastrous results of democratic reforms on Tibetan religion and society and the famine in Tibet that resulted from the Great Leap Forward of 1959–1962. Even though he addressed his petition to Zhou with the greatest respect and temerity, he was rewarded with public denunciation and imprisonment in Beijing for the next fourteen years. His petition was a closely held secret in China for many years until it was finally smuggled to the outside world in 1996. It provides a treasure trove of information about Tibet in the three years after the 1959 revolt.

Another very important resource for understanding the situation in Tibet after the revolt, especially the Chinese attitude toward Tibet, is provided by a prominent piece of Chinese Communist propaganda. The film *Serf* is about the miserable life of a serf in Tibet and his and all the other serfs' final liberation by the People's Liberation Army (PLA) and the CCP. This film reveals not the reality of life in Tibet before and after China's liberation of the Tibetans, but the Chinese conception of that life and those events. *Serf* was reportedly very popular in China and was seen by large numbers of Chinese in the early 1960s. It was almost the only source of information about Tibet for many ordinary Chinese and was therefore tremendously significant in forming the typical Chinese conception of the reality of Tibet. The film's depiction of the absolutely miserable life of the Tibetan "serfs and slaves" contributed greatly to the popular Chinese sense of legitimacy in regard to the supposed liberation of the Tibetans.

There are also two foreign sources that are valuable for their information about the period immediately after the revolt during which almost no outside observers were allowed into Tibet. Those few who were admitted into Tibet at this time were invariably journalists from other Communist countries or socialist sympathizers from Western countries. They usually had long relationships with the CCP leaders, as did the American communist Anna Louise

Strong, or were journalists with known socialist leanings, like the English couple Stuart and Roma Gelder. These particular foreigners were taken on tours of Tibet at a time of intense transformation, late 1959 for Strong and late 1962 for the Gelders, and were given extraordinary access to Chinese and Tibetan officials. Their privileged treatment was based upon the premise that they would promote the Chinese Communists' cause by writing highly sympathetic books about their Tibet tours, which indeed they did. Strong's *When Serfs Stood Up in Tibet* and the Gelders' *The Timely Rain* were the only eyewitness accounts in English of Tibet after the revolt and were therefore very influential with Western audiences.[3]

Both Strong and the Gelders fall into the category of what Paul Hollander has labeled "political pilgrims," idealists who visited the Communist regimes of China, Cuba, and the Soviet Union and wrote glorifying accounts of these societies' achievements.[4] Political pilgrims of this type were generally Western intellectuals who were alienated from their own societies—because they felt their achievements were not sufficiently appreciated or utilized at home—and sought to find within Communist countries the utopian social organization that they desired and that those countries claimed to be creating.

Like Strong and the Gelders, political pilgrims enjoyed in their travels to Communist countries a privileged status, VIP treatment, and access to high-level officials. This treatment, along with their own utopian ideologies, often influenced their reporting. They tended to believe that these governments had actually achieved the ideals to which they nominally aspired, one of which was that intellectuals like themselves should be far more influential in social and political administration. They often reported what they were told without question and even altered their own observations in order to portray a reality that did not in fact exist. They, along with their hosts, tended to hope that the reality they claimed for the present would actually exist at some time in the future when the socialist ideal was achieved. The end—the socialist and communist ideal—was considered to justify the means used to promote those ideals, including overly optimistic, unrealistically idealistic reporting and even intentionally deceptive propaganda.

One value of the political pilgrims' writings derives from their exclusive access to Communist societies during critical periods, such as Tibet during the democratic reforms. Strong was in Lhasa just six months after the revolt, when the repression of Tibetan resistance was still going on (although she saw none of this) and democratic reforms had barely begun. The Gelders were there three years later, when democratic reforms had been completed and the beneficial results supposedly achieved, to which they testified. Both Strong and the Gelders portrayed themselves as objective and incorruptible observers of social reality, and sometimes this ideal led them, despite their efforts to uncritically repeat their hosts' claims, to reveal some of the actual situation in Tibet at the time. Their accounts are also valuable in that they clearly expose the Chinese mentality about their role in Tibet and repeat almost verbatim the major propaganda themes. Foremost among these themes was the Chinese Communists' class-based version of Tibetan history and reality, which the Western political pilgrims were all too ready to believe.

Strong and the Gelders readily accepted the Chinese ideology that there was no national issue in regard to Tibet, no issue of China exploiting or oppressing Tibetans, nor any question about the legitimacy of Chinese rule over the non-Chinese Tibetans. They accepted Chinese assurances that Tibetans themselves had overthrown the feudal serf system and that they now enjoyed a true autonomy created and exercised by themselves. For the political pilgrims, as for the Chinese Communists, the only issue was the exploitation and oppression of the "serfs and slaves" by the former political and social system, a system characterized as a "dark, barbaric, savage, feudal Hell on Earth."

The pilgrims, like the Chinese Communists, adhered to the Marxist doctrine that nationalism was a remnant of the former bourgeois-democratic period that would be transformed into proletarian internationalism when the communist society was achieved. Marxist-Leninist nationality policy required the repression of the national sentiments of peoples who had not yet experienced capitalism or democracy so that they could "leap the stages of history" directly into communism. The theory, of course, justified the repression of the national ideal of self-determination in order to quickly transition to the communist ideal of a classless society and a world without nationalism or nationalist conflict.

The Communists' class ideology, as reflected in the political pilgrims' writings, was and is their most successful propaganda theme in regard to Tibet. The Chinese Communists and their socialist-leaning sympathizers have been most successful in disguising, obscuring, and confusing the real political issue of Tibet by means of this class argument. This argument still influences some who believe China's propaganda about the evils of old Tibet and therefore tend to approve of China's civilizing mission there. However, despite their usual socialist or populist pretensions, the pilgrims unwittingly adopted the most typical justification used by imperialists of all types, who claim to have rescued their colonial subjects from the abuses of their own misrule.

The Cultural Revolution in Tibet, beginning in 1966, is nearly as obscure as the previous period of democratic reforms. During this period, Tibet was closed off even to foreign socialists. Perhaps this was because of the undeniable destruction of cultural monuments taking place. Almost all Tibetan monasteries, emptied of their monks and valuables during democratic reforms, were physically destroyed, usually by Tibetans prompted and coerced by Chinese and Tibetan cadres. Almost all aspects of Tibetan culture, especially the Buddhist religion, were subjected to repression during the campaign against old habits, customs, traditions, and beliefs, all of which Tibetan culture epitomized. During the Cultural Revolution, there was not even the pretense of respect for Tibetan autonomy, which had been achieved, in theory, a year earlier, in 1965, with the inauguration of the Tibet Autonomous Region. During this period, from 1966 to 1976, China also achieved, by means of collectivization, the greatest degree of control over and regimentation of Tibetan lives and access to their economic production.

The Cultural Revolution saw an intensification of Chinese propaganda, mostly directed at Tibetans. Included were the "speaking bitterness" campaigns, in which Tibetans were encouraged to pour out the stories of their sufferings in the old society in contrast to their happy lives in the present. Some former serfs, especially those who had been mutilated by rapacious serf-owners, became semiprofessional witnesses of the evils of the past society and were exhibited in every city and town. In 1965, as a part of the inauguration of the TAR, a great gathering of these former serfs was held, during which they recounted their experiences for Tibetans and visiting Chinese and foreign dignitaries. At the inauguration, a Museum of the Tibetan Revolution was opened in Lhasa, displaying exhibits of torture instruments used by the serf-owners on the former serfs. In the early 1970s, an exhibit was added with more than a hundred life-size clay sculptures, created by Chinese art students, depicting the sufferings of the Tibetan serfs. This exhibition, titled "Wrath of the Serfs," was required viewing by Tibetan schoolchildren and the few foreign visitors, usually from Communist countries, during that time. The statues were so impressively sculpted that some Tibetans report they were influenced in their beliefs about the nature of traditional Tibetan society.

Two foreigners' accounts are also useful for this period, although neither Han Suyin nor Israel Epstein was quite a foreigner. They both wrote in English, so their influence was primarily outside China, but Han was a Chinese national, and Epstein was a Polish Jew who had lived in China most of his life and had taken Chinese citizenship. Han Suyin was a Chinese Communist sympathizer who wrote biographies of Mao Zedong and Zhou Enlai. Her impressions of Tibet, in *Lhasa, the Open City*, are infused with Chinese chauvinism.[5] Far more valuable is Epstein's account, *Tibet Transformed*. Epstein had been the editor since the early 1950s of the PRC's primary propaganda publication for foreign audiences, "China Reconstructs." His account covers a twenty-year period of Tibetan history, from 1955 to 1976, based upon lengthy visits in 1955, 1965, and 1976. Epstein's book is the most detailed and authoritative account of the supposedly liberating effects of the Chinese revolution upon Tibet and the social and economic development achieved in Tibet with

China's benevolent assistance. His book provides a wealth of information about the timing and intentions of the Chinese Communists' many political campaigns in Tibet.

After the death of Mao in 1976 and the end of the Cultural Revolution, both China and Tibet experienced a liberalization of CCP policies. Communes were dissolved, and in Tibet, a modicum of cultural autonomy was allowed. Monasteries were rebuilt, mostly by Tibetans themselves, and the Buddhist religion was allowed to revive. However, the rebuilt monasteries became a sanctuary for the revival of Tibetan nationalism, and by 1987, Lhasa was the scene of several anti-Chinese demonstrations. The revival of Tibetan culture, religion, and nationalism was a surprise to the Chinese, who had imagined that thirty years of repression and propaganda would have eliminated Tibetan separatism. After the declaration of martial law in Tibet in March 1989, as well as the June incident at Tiananmen Square in Beijing, China reversed its relatively liberal policies in Tibet. The government intensified its repression of all manifestations of Tibetan separatism, including Tibetans' loyalty to the Dalai Lama. Colonization was increased, supported by a policy of economic development. China's experience of the negative effects of actual Tibetan autonomy in the 1980s has presumably informed the debate about the advisability of autonomy ever since.

China's post-1989 Tibet policy was accompanied by a renewed emphasis on propaganda as a solution to the Tibet problem. Chinese propaganda was directed internally at Tibetans and externally toward China's international critics. It was supported by the employment of academic Tibetan studies for propaganda purposes. Within Tibet, China launched the Patriotic Education Campaign, aimed primarily at monks and nuns but later expanded to schoolchildren and then to the whole community. The themes of this campaign were China's version of Tibetan history, the patriotic role expected of religion, and anti–Dalai Lama propaganda, including a requirement that all participants declare their opposition to the Dalai Lama's separatism. The purpose of the campaign was to transform Tibetan national identity and loyalty to the Dalai Lama into Chinese national identity and loyalty to China. The Patriotic Education Campaign began in 1996 and has been expanded and periodically revived by the Chinese authorities in Tibet since that time.

External propaganda on Tibet was intensified with a series of official White Papers and numerous other propaganda publications. Between 1991 and late 2006, China published forty-nine State Council White Papers, the highest-level official publications of the Chinese government. Of these documents, six were on Tibet, the most on any single subject except human rights, which was the subject of seven—all of which also dealt with minority nationality rights, including Tibet. Another two papers were on China's National Regional

Autonomy system for national minorities, now known as Regional Ethnic Autonomy, both of which extensively covered Tibet. The White Papers provide China's most complete argument in favor of the legitimacy and positive achievements of its rule over Tibet.

In 1996, the Chinese government published a full-length book on the history of Tibet, in Chinese, and widely distributed it within China. The next year, the book was published in English, with the title *The Historical Status of China's Tibet*. The volume attempts to substantiate China's claim to sovereignty over Tibet since the Yuan dynasty, to refute the idea that Tibet was ever independent, and to establish that Tibet is now an inalienable part of China.[6]

The goals and techniques of China's external propaganda campaign on Tibet were revealed by two internal Propaganda Department documents that surfaced outside China. The first was from the 1993 meeting of the Central Government External Propaganda Department. This conference was described as the third annual meeting in Beijing to coordinate China's external propaganda on Tibet. It was attended by officials of the Propaganda Department and the State Council Information Office, the New China News Agency (Xinhua), and officials from the Tibet Autonomous Region and Tibetan autonomous districts in Sichuan, Qinghai, Yunnan, and Gansu. The speeches at this meeting revealed much about propaganda efforts up to that point, particularly the publication of the first White Paper, "Tibet: Its Ownership and Human Rights Situation," to which the assembled officials had devoted much effort and for which they had high hopes. They revealed that the White Paper had been distributed worldwide and that they believed it had been very successful in refuting critics of China's Tibet policy.

The 1993 meeting also introduced the strategy of using academic Tibet studies for propaganda purposes, an idea that was formalized in June 2000 at another conference that included both propaganda officials and Chinese and Tibetan academic Tibetologists. This conference was organized by the Central Government Propaganda Department and the State Council Information Office and was titled "Tibet-Related External Propaganda and Tibetology Work in the New Era." The stated aim of the 2000 conference was "to make our Tibetology work more effective for external propaganda on Tibet." This was said to be the first meeting intended to discuss ways of "improving Tibetology work from the point of view of external publicity" and "improving our external publicity on Tibet from the perspective of Tibetology."

Both these documents revealed plans to use international Tibet Cultural Festivals to promote China's propaganda on Tibet. From 2001 to 2006, China held six such exhibitions of Tibetan culture, the first in Australia and New Zealand in 2001 and the latest in Austria in October 2006. In North America, one such festival was held in Toronto in September 2002. It was sponsored by Chinese-

Canadian organizations and was billed as a "China Tibetan Culture Week," intended "to expose Canadians to the history, diversity and development of Tibet, highlighting traditional and modern Tibetan art, language, dance, theater and spirituality." The festival included ten song and dance performances, five exhibitions of *thankas* and photographs, two films, and a presentation by four Tibetan academics. The organizers passed out a large amount of Chinese government propaganda about Tibet at every event, including a glossy festival brochure, a CD entitled "China's Tibet," three books on Tibetan society and history, a tourist map of Tibet, and several pamphlets on various Tibetan subjects. The propaganda festival was protested by Tibetan-Canadians and received much publicity for that reason, thus significantly defeating the purpose of the Chinese government and the Chinese-Canadian organizers.

Since 1979, the PRC and the Tibetan government-in-exile based in Dharamsala, India, have engaged in a dialogue about Tibetan autonomy and a possible return of the Dalai Lama to Tibet. For the Tibetan side, this dialogue has been about the political issue of Tibet and the nature of Tibetan autonomy. Dharamsala and the Dalai Lama base their understanding about the potential for dialogue on a statement made in 1978 by Deng Xiaoping to the Dalai Lama's brother, Gyalo Thondup, that "anything but independence can be discussed." However, subsequent events have called the Tibetan interpretation of Deng's statement into question. The Chinese side has consistently denied that there are any unresolved political issues with regard to Tibet, including the nature of Tibetan autonomy, and has insisted upon confining the issue to the personal future of the Dalai Lama. The first series of official talks and delegation visits lasted from 1979 to 1984, with no results. This was followed by a period of little or no communication between the two sides. Talks were revived in 2002 and have continued through 2007 but have so far proven equally fruitless.

While China continues to profess its willingness to talk with the Dalai Lama, its preconditions essentially preclude any meaningful dialogue. China demands that the Dalai Lama give up independence, which seems to include his claim that Tibet was once independent. The Chinese also seem to believe that the Dalai Lama's demand for increased autonomy is based on his claim that Tibet was or is less than an integral part of China; therefore, the system of autonomy is also not open to discussion. China demands that the Dalai Lama give up his "splittist activities," presumably including all his international activities and even possibly the very existence of his government-in-exile. If the Dalai Lama will adhere to these conditions, then China will talk to him—but not about Tibet, only about his personal status. China's conditions make it apparent that it sees the "dialogue" with the Dalai Lama's representatives as a part of its propaganda strategy in regard to Tibet rather than as signifying any willingness to actually address the issue or alter its policies in Tibet.

The Dalai Lama and the Tibetan exiles continue to pursue the dialogue despite the lack of any progress. Tibet's international sympathizers continue to support the dialogue process, mostly because it is the only policy toward Tibet that foreign governments can support given their recognition of Chinese sovereignty over Tibet. The Dalai Lama's "Middle Way Approach" and his acceptance of Tibetan autonomy within China is dictated by the lack of international support for independence and is founded upon his belief that "genuine autonomy" is capable of preserving Tibetan culture, religion, and national identity. However, many Tibetans in exile prefer a policy in favor of Tibetan independence, given their belief that genuine autonomy within China is no less impossible than independence. They maintain that the Dalai Lama's Middle Way policy has confused and demoralized many Tibetans, who regret the abandonment of their fight for independence.

The conclusion of this study is that China has never been sincere in its promise to allow meaningful autonomy in Tibet. Autonomy was always assumed to be a temporary policy, while the ultimate goal was assimilation. China's experience with its actual policy in Tibet has been that it cannot allow any real autonomy without arousing Tibetan separatism. Almost all aspects of Tibetan culture have been demonstrated to have nationalist implications, which means that China cannot allow any real cultural autonomy. Chinese leaders cannot allow autonomy because the survival of a separate Tibetan national identity is a threat to China's territorial integrity and national security. China is not sincere in its dialogue with Dharamsala and is using it only for propaganda purposes. The Dalai Lama's Middle Way policy is not capable of achieving real dialogue with China or genuine Tibetan autonomy. In the absence of any solution to the Tibet issue, a policy of self-determination is most capable of pressuring China to improve its treatment of Tibetans within Tibet, as well as for sustaining the international issue of Tibet and maintaining the most essential elements of Tibetan national identity.

Notes

1. Warren W. Smith Jr., *Tibetan Nation: A History of Tibetan Nationalism and Sino-Tibetan Relations* (Boulder, CO: Westview Press, 1996).

2. See Panchen Lama, *A Poisoned Arrow: The Secret Report of the 10th Panchen Lama* (London: Tibet Information Network, 1997).

3. Anna Louise Strong, *When Serfs Stood Up in Tibet* (Beijing: New World Press, 1960); Stuart Gelder and Roma Gelder, *The Timely Rain: Travels in New Tibet* (Lon-

don: Hutchinson, 1962). An account of the Gelders' trip is available at http://www.rowman.com/isbn/074253989X.

4. Paul Hollander, *Political Pilgrims: Travels of Western Intellectuals to the Soviet Union, China, and Cuba, 1928–1978* (New York: Harper Colophon Books, 1983).

5. Han Suyin, *Lhasa, the Open City: A Journey to Tibet* (New York: G. P. Putnam's Sons, 1977); Israel Epstein, *Tibet Transformed* (Beijing: New World Press, 1983). An account of Han's visit is available at http://www.rowman.com/isbn/074253989X.

6. Wang Jiawei and Nyima Gyaincain, *The Historical Status of China's Tibet* (Beijing: China Intercontinental Press, 2000). An analysis of this book is available at http://www.rowman.com/isbn/074253989X.

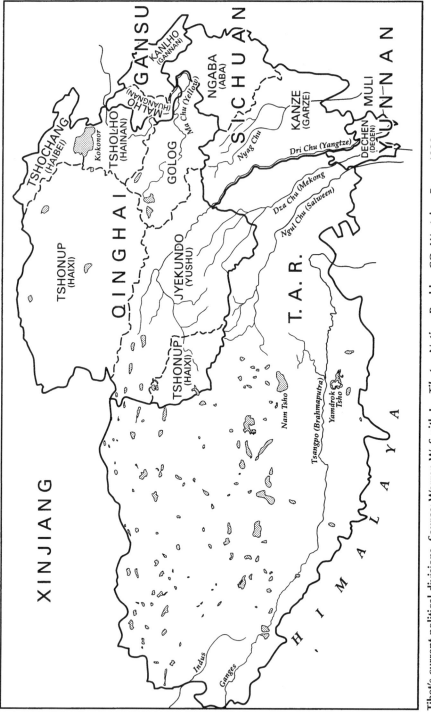

Tibet's current political divisions. *Source:* Warren W. Smith Jr., *Tibetan Nation.* Boulder, CO: Westview Press, 1998.

1

Historical and Political Background

Tibetan Ethnic Origins

HISTORICAL AND MYTHOLOGICAL SOURCES indicate that a primary component of the Tibetan ethnic group was the tribes originating on the Sino-
Tibetan border known to the Chinese as Qiang (Ch'iang).[1] Other probable
components are the Mon, who were perhaps the original inhabitants of Tibet,
and early Indo-European migrants from the north. The ethnic identity of the
plateau has also been significantly influenced by relatively modern migrations
of peoples of Mongolian ethnicity. Substantial migrations of Mongol tribes to
the northeastern plateau began during the period of the Mongol Empire in
the thirteenth century and increased upon the fall of the Mongol dynasty in
China in the fourteenth century. Later conflicts between Mongol tribes forced
many to seek refuge in the Kokonor area of northeastern Tibet. These Mongols, with a few exceptions, have been Tibetanized in language and culture.

The name *Qiang* is composed of the characters for "sheep" and "man,"
meaning "shepherd." The Qiang seem to have evolved out of early Neolithic
cultures in the Gansu area by a process of ecological differentiation between
agriculturalists and pastoralists. The pastoralists may have had some early cultural association with the agriculturalists, but cultural differentiation began at
a very early time due to ecological adaptation as well as outside cultural influences. The Qiang and the Chinese were in conflict from the time of the earliest records, as is typical of relations between pastoral and agricultural peoples.
The Chinese of the former and later Han dynasty (206 B.C.–A.D. 220) persecuted the Qiang and forced many of them to seek refuge in the heights of the
Tibetan Plateau.

Tibetan mythological sources speak of four or six original tribes of Tibet. The four tribes that appear in most sources, and to whom precedence is usually given, are the Don (lDon), Ton (sTon), Se, and Mu (rMu).[2] The mythological "original tribes" of Tibet can all be identified as being of eastern Sino-Tibetan border area origins, and most, if not all, can be identified as those same people known as Qiang.[3] The evidence of this comes from linguistic connections, similarities in the myths of origin of the Qiang and Tibetans, and the evidence from Tibetan history that the Tibetan population evolved by assimilation of groups who may be identified with the Qiang. The Qiang and Tibetans are definitely related, although R. A. Stein has concluded that "these two groups are not identical, though the latter are one of the principal elements which contributed to the formation of the former."[4]

The Don, Ton, Se, and Mu and their ethnic affiliates were very likely nomadic hunter-gatherers and primitive agriculturalists-pastoralists who migrated along a margin of similar ecological character on the eastern and southeastern edges of the Tibetan Plateau. Some of these groups gravitated to the grasslands, where they adopted pastoral nomadism, while others settled as agriculturalists in the valleys of central Tibet. Even though these tribes are referred to as the "original" tribes, they are also spoken of as "foreign," implying that they were not the indigenous populations of central Tibet, but rather groups that migrated there and absorbed the indigenous peoples.[5] Thus while the Qiang may be identified as an early component of the Tibetan ethnic mixture, it appears that they prevailed over the original inhabitants to the extent that only remnants of the indigenous people's mythology survived to identify the Qiang as immigrants.[6]

Tibetan legends indicate that the Mon were an indigenous people of the central valleys of Tibet who regarded the Qiang as foreigners. The Mon are linked with the Mon population of Assam and Burma and with the Mon-Khmer.[7] The extent of settlement of the Mon in Tibet is not known. However, based on what is known of their very early inhabitation of Himalayan areas, it is possible that they were the earliest inhabitants of the southeastern and southern Tibetan Plateau. In some sources, the Mon are described as carpenters and smiths who served the Qiang as craftsmen.[8] Their specialty as carpenters may be evidence that they were inhabitants of the forested areas on the fringes of the Tibetan Plateau. They are known from such areas in Sichuan. Tibetan scholars associate the Mon with the earliest Tibetan states of Kongpo, Pobo, and Dakpo.[9] The Mon can reliably be identified as a population who were encountered, displaced, and to some extent absorbed by those migrants from the north who were to become the Tibetans.

Early Indo-European additions to the population of Tibet are also probable. The Tocharians, or Yueh-chih, were on the borders of the Tibetan Plateau from as early as the beginning of the second millennium B.C., and their penetration into the northern and northeastern regions of the plateau is very possible. The plateau is most accessible at the northeastern corner; migration of nomads with their animals is easily accomplished from the Tarim via the Dunhuang area, and from the Qilian (Ch'i-lian) mountain region via the Kokonor Lake area. The Yueh-chih may have had an important ethnic influence on the Qiang. Chinese sources indicate that some of the Yueh-chih, the "Little Yueh-chih," migrated into the Qilian area in the second century B.C. and "settled among the Ch'iang."[10]

Ethnic affiliations between the Qiang and the Chinese, and consequently between the Chinese and the Tibetans, are possible given the territorial proximity of their areas of origin. Ethnic differences between the Chinese and the Qiang are also possible, due to original ethnic differences between the Qiang and the proto-Chinese or later Indo-European influences upon the Qiang. Tibetan assimilation of the Mon is not a source of ethnic differences between Tibetans and Chinese, since the southern Chinese also assimilated Mon peoples.

Whatever their original connections, the Chinese and Tibetans have differentiated to an extent that they formed two distinctly different ethnic groups from a relatively early time. This differentiation may date from the period when early pastoralists became separated from agriculturalists at the end of the third or beginning of the second millennium B.C., or when the Qiang began to be influenced by Indo-Europeans from the steppes to the north during the second millennium B.C., or at least from the former and later Han dynasties, when conflict between the Qiang and the Han resulted in large-scale Qiang migrations to the plateau. Adaptation to vastly different environments resulted in populations of significantly different cultural ecology, which is a primary component of the subjective sense of ethnic identity. A history of conflict between the two groups has also greatly contributed to this differentiation.

Tibetan Empire

Tibet became a unified state between 600 and 630, when the small independent states of central Tibet were unified under the king of Yarlung. The nature of the political alliance established by Yarlung may be best described as a feudal confederation. The union of clans under Yarlung also exhibited some of the characteristics of a confederation of the nomadic type in which tribes unite for the purpose of further conquests afield. The political union achieved by Yarlung, like nomadic confederations, was dependent upon rewards as a means of maintaining political unity.

In some of its characteristics, the early Tibetan state fit the nomadic state pattern, but in other aspects it was significantly different. The early Tibetan polity was not dependent upon exploiting surrounding sedentary societies, since central Tibet was an area of mixed economy and a sedentary style of life. In fact, the central Tibetan state expanded to include surrounding nomadic tribes, the reverse of the usual model of nomadic conquest of sedentary states. The political state that coalesced around the central agricultural base eventually united both the sedentary and nomadic populations of the plateau and combined the material strengths of both economies. Within a period of little more than a decade, the Yarlung confederation expanded to include all the peoples of the Tibetan Plateau, creating in the process a centralized Tibetan state. The high Tibetan Plateau physically delimits Tibet as a culture and as a nation. Common ecological adaptation to the conditions of high altitude has been one of the most fundamental cohesive factors of Tibetan national identity.

Although the Tibetan Yarlung state incorporated the surrounding nomadic tribes by force, their relations had much of a confederative character. Some of the large nomadic tribes of the northern plateau may have bargained their military strength for a degree of equal treatment by the central Tibetans and for a share in further territorial conquests. The nomadic tribes of the plateau were politically disorganized but powerful in terms of men and animal resources. These resources shared the characteristics of nomadic mobility and were therefore ideal for military campaigning. The nomadic tribes provided mounted warriors, porterage by means of man and animal, and food on the hoof.

Once the consolidation of the tribes of the plateau was accomplished, about 630 by the Yarlung king Srongtsan Gampo, the Tibetan state almost immediately came into conflict with Tang-dynasty China in the northeastern plateau area. This conflict with China was to continue throughout the empire period (630–840). Tibetan armies penetrated far into Chinese territory and at one time even briefly placed a Tibetan choice upon the Chinese throne at Changan (Xian). Tibet also expanded into Lhadak, Gilgit, and Hunza to the west and into East Turkestan to the north. During the empire period, Tibet was an important military force in Inner Asia, engaging in conflict with the Arabs, Turks, and Chinese and exercising influence over Nepal, Inner Asia, and western China.

Buddhism, which later would become a defining characteristic of Tibetan culture, was introduced during the empire. Srongtsan Gampo married Nepalese and Chinese princesses, both of whom were Buddhists, and allowed the introduction of Buddhism into Tibet. Tibet became a center of Buddhist culture, and Buddhist monks came to Tibet from India, Nepal, East Turkestan, and China.

Tibetan relations with China during the empire period offer ample evidence of Tibetan independence. Tibetan national identity was substantially defined by conflict with China. Sino-Tibetan military conflicts finally ended in 822 with a treaty that clearly defined Tibet and China as separate countries and delimited the border between them. In the treaty, China and Tibet agreed to "unite their kingdoms," but this was clearly in the sense of a union only in agreement. The treaty speaks of China and Tibet each guarding the borders of their separate territories and notes, "All to the east of the boundary is the domain of Great China. All to the west is surely the domain of Great Tibet." The treaty also says that "Tibetans shall be happy in the land of Tibet and Chinese shall be happy in the land of China."

The characteristics that define Tibet as a nation—a shared ethnicity, territory, culture, language, and religion—were all consolidated by the shared historical experiences of the empire. The subjective sense of common ethnicity of already affiliated tribes was strengthened by their association for collective military and political purposes during the expansion of the empire. A national cultural and political identity corresponding to the territorial extent of the plateau was created by the empire and survived its collapse. Tibetan territory was defined, defended, and administered from central Tibet and thus became a national and state territory. A script for the Tibetan language was acquired from India primarily for the purposes of administering an empire, not, as was later claimed by Buddhist historians, for translating Buddhist texts. The Tibetan written language was standardized and became the national language.

Tibetan Buddhist State

The Tibetan Empire collapsed in 842. For the next four hundred years, Tibet knew no central authority. This political vacuum was gradually filled by monastic Buddhism. Tibetan religious orders grew up around lineages of teachers and disciples. As Buddhist orders founded monasteries throughout the country, their temporal as well as spiritual power increased. By the beginning of the thirteenth century, Buddhist sects had become the dominant economic, political, and spiritual authorities in Tibet, but Tibet remained disunited because no sect was powerful enough to dominate the others. This situation was transformed with the rise of the Mongol Empire, under whose patronage one sect achieved predominance and Tibet achieved political unity but became dependent upon a foreign empire.

By 1234, the Mongol Empire had conquered all of northern China. In 1247, the head of the Sakya sect of Tibetan Buddhism, Sakya Pandita, submitted to Godan Khan on behalf of all of Tibet in order to avoid a Mongol conquest. He was then appointed as the representative of Mongol authority in Tibet. In 1254 Sakya Pandita's nephew, Phagspa, made a similar arrangement with Khubilai Khan, then khan of all the Mongols. Phagspa became Khubilai's teacher of Buddhism, while Khubilai became overlord of Tibet. This relationship between Mongol patron and Tibetan lama became the pattern for Tibetan relations with the Mongol Yuan dynasty of China established by Khubilai Khan in 1271.

Tibetan relations with the Mongols predate the Mongol conquest of China. Tibet's relationship with the Mongol Empire was established by Sakya Pandita in 1247 and by Phagspa in 1254 long before the establishment of the Yuan dynasty in 1271. Phagspa became administrator of Buddhist affairs in the Yuan Empire in 1260 and Khubilai's representative in Tibet. Tibet was treated as a special territory of the Mongol Empire due to the nature of Mongol khans' personal relations with Tibetan lamas. Tibet was allowed a great degree of autonomy, at least under Khubilai, due to the influence of Phagspa at the Mongol court. In the later Yuan, Tibet was integrated into the administration of the Mongol Empire, although not as part of China but as a separate subjugated country. Tibetan relations with the Mongol emperors were unique, based upon the theory developed by Phagspa of *cho–yon*, usually translated as "priest–patron," a relationship between spiritual and political leaders in which the spiritual master was theoretically equal to his political patron. The idealized cho–yon relationship of Buddhist lama to Mongol khan became the pattern for Tibet's foreign relations, especially in its relations with China. Phagspa's cho–yon principle was extremely sophisticated in its understanding of the cultural and political needs of the Mongols, but extremely naive in anticipating political implications for Tibet.

Mongol patronage of the Sakya sect of Tibetan Buddhism was instrumental in establishing the political dominance of Buddhist sects in Tibet. Because Buddhism was a universalistic doctrine, its exponents were willing to accept foreign patronage for the purpose of the propagation of the religion. Phagspa's theory of the equality of the spiritual and political realms obscured the Sakyapas' dependence upon foreign patrons and its implication for Tibet's political status. The Sakyapas' submission to the Mongols avoided a Mongol invasion of Tibet and created Tibetan political unity under a Buddhist sect, but it also established religious rule, with its fatal reliance on foreign political patronage, as the political system of Tibet. Furthermore, although the Mongol administration of Tibet created political unity in central Tibet, eastern Tibet was administered separately, a division that set the precedent for later divisions of Tibet along the same lines.

The Mongol Yuan dynasty fell in 1368 and was succeeded by the Ming (1368–1644). The Ming continued to confirm Tibetan officials' titles that had existed under the Yuan as if the Ming had inherited the Yuan relationship with Tibet. They continued to patronize Tibetan lamas and awarded new honors and titles to them. The early Ming emperors may have hoped that their patronage of Tibetan lamas could be transformed into political influence in Tibet equivalent to that enjoyed by the Mongol Yuan. However, the Ming had no real interest in Tibet beyond Tibet's role in Ming relations with the Mongols, who still remained a powerful threat outside the borders of China. Once the Mongol threat passed, the Ming were no longer concerned with Tibet and did little to substantiate their claim to authority there.

Tibet's continuing relations with the Mongols were much more politically significant than Tibetan relations with the Ming. Various Mongol khans continued to play the role of political patron to Tibet. In 1577, Altan Khan, leader of the Mongols outside the Ming domains in what is now Inner Mongolia, intending to "follow the example of Phagspa and Kublai," invited a Tibetan lama, Sonam Gyatso, to his camp. Altan awarded Sonam Gyatso the name *Dalai*, a Mongol translation of the lama's name *Gyatso*, both with the meaning of "oceanic." Sonam Gyatso thereafter became known as the Dalai Lama (the third, since two of his predecessors were posthumously recognized as the first and second Dalai Lamas). In exchange, Sonam Gyatso recognized Altan as a reincarnation of Genghis Khan, which allowed Altan to claim authority over all Mongols. Altan's grandson was subsequently recognized as the Fourth Dalai Lama, thus cementing relations between Tibetans and Mongols.

In 1642, Gushri Khan of the Kokonor Mongols unified Tibet on behalf of the Fifth Dalai Lama, the first time that a Dalai Lama had attained both temporal and spiritual rule. Regional and sectarian conflicts were suppressed, and Tibet was politically unified. The Dalai Lama established relations with the Manchu shortly after they conquered China in 1644. Tibet was important to the early Manchu Qing dynasty (1644–1912) due to the Fifth Dalai Lama's influence with the remaining independent Mongols. In 1652, the Dalai Lama visited the Manchu emperor in Beijing in the hopes of reestablishing the cho–yon relationship that had existed with the Mongol Yuan. However, the Manchu court interpreted the Dalai Lama's visit as signifying the nominal submission of the Dalai Lama to the emperor and the inclusion of Tibet within the Manchu Empire.

In 1682, the Fifth Dalai Lama died. In 1720, a Qing army invaded Tibet to expel the Dzungar Mongols who had invaded Tibet from the area north of the Tian Shan in what is now Xinjiang. This event marks the beginning of actual Qing control over Tibet. Five years later, the Qing reorganized the administration of Tibet under the Tibetan secular nobility, supervised by a Qing representative or *amban*, who was always a Mongol or Manchu. The Qing followed the example of the Yuan in administratively separating the eastern

Tibetan provinces of Kham and Amdo from central Tibet. The eastern part of Kham was administered by native chiefs under the supervision of the governor of Sichuan. The Tibetans and Mongols of Amdo were supervised by a Qing amban in Sining. After the murder of a Lhasa amban in 1750, the Qing again reorganized the Tibetan administration and put it under the overall authority of the amban.

In 1792, the Qing sent an army to Tibet to repel an invasion by the Gurkhas of Nepal, after which the Tibetan administration was again reorganized. The Qing amban took control of Tibetan frontier defense and foreign affairs. The Tibetan currency, which had been the source of trouble with Nepal, was also taken under Qing supervision. The Qing required that the incarnations of the Panchen and Dalai Lamas and other high lamas be approved by a process of choosing of lots from a golden urn. This procedure, despite later Chinese claims, was not meant to establish Chinese sovereignty over Tibet, but was rather a means that the Qing employed in both Mongolia and Tibet to limit the power of the aristocracy by limiting the discovery of reincarnations among them.

The measures undertaken in 1792 represent the height of Qing influence in Tibet. Thereafter, the Qing dynasty began to decline and, with it, Qing control in Tibet. In fact, most of the Qing reforms of 1792 were never fully implemented or quickly fell into disuse. The right to approve reincarnations, the most significant reform in terms of its implications for Tibet's sovereignty, became essentially symbolic or was even ignored by the Tibetans. During the nineteenth century, the Qing were preoccupied with foreign imperialism and were unable to pay much attention to Tibet. In 1847, the Lhasa amban abandoned financial and military powers to the Tibetan government, representing the effective end of direct Qing administration in Tibet.

During the long reign of the Qing, Tibet was placed, in the Chinese mind, in the category of Chinese territory. Nevertheless, Tibetan cultural, ethnic, and national identity was essentially unaffected. Although the Qing Empire was transformed into a Chinese ruling dynasty, Tibet did not thereby become a part of China. The nature of the Qing relationship with Tibet was one between states, or between an empire and a semiautonomous state, not a relationship between a central government and an outlying province. The Qing dynasty, like the previous conquest dynasty, the Yuan, distinguished Inner Asia from China. Inner Asian tribes and states were treated as dependent allies during the early Qing. Tibet was a dependent state of the Qing, much like Mongolia. Its inaccessibility and the difficulties involved in imposing direct administration contributed to the Qing preference to maintain Tibet's semiautonomous status within the empire.

British Patronage for Tibetan Autonomy

The Thirteenth Dalai Lama was born in 1876 and confirmed as the reincarnation in 1879 without the use of the Qing lottery system. He assumed temporal authority in 1895.

At the turn of the twentieth century, the British government of India, suspicious of Russian influence in Tibet, attempted to gain trade privileges in Tibet through negotiations with the Chinese. However, the Chinese, despite their claim to authority over Tibet, were proven powerless to make the Tibetans respect agreements made between China and the British. In 1904, the British invaded Tibet. Before the British expedition reached Lhasa, the Dalai Lama fled to Mongolia. In Lhasa, the British concluded a treaty that granted Great Britain trade privileges in Tibet.

The 1904 British expedition to Tibet ended Tibet's international isolation and exposed the myth of China's claimed authority in Tibet, but it also resulted in the flight of the Dalai Lama from Lhasa and led to an inevitable attempt by China to recover its position in Tibet. The British invasion served notice upon the Chinese that their claim to possession of Tibet was no longer safe from challenge by foreign rivals. The Chinese were compelled to either establish direct control and administration over Tibet or risk losing Tibet to British influence or to an independent status.

During the Dalai Lama's absence, the Chinese sent an expeditionary force into Kham in eastern Tibet in an attempt to convert that part of Tibet into a Chinese province, to be known as Xikang. In 1908, the Dalai Lama visited Beijing, where he was forced to accept a reduction in his status in Lhasa in favor of the amban. The Dalai Lama was able to return to Lhasa in 1910, but Chinese forces soon thereafter reached Lhasa from Kham and the Dalai Lama once again fled, this time to India.

The Qing dynasty was overthrown in 1911. In 1912, the Dalai Lama returned to Lhasa, refused the titles offered by the Chinese Republic, and repudiated China's claim to authority over Tibet. These acts are considered by Tibetans as a declaration of Tibet's independence. Mongolia also proclaimed its independence from China in 1912, and the next year, Mongolia and Tibet concluded a treaty of mutual recognition.[11]

In 1914, Britain attempted to secure Chinese recognition of Tibetan autonomy in tripartite negotiations at Simla in India between Great Britain, China, and Tibet. China claimed sovereignty over all Tibet and direct administration of eastern Tibet, but was willing to allow central Tibet some autonomous status. For their part, the Tibetans sought to have all Tibetan cultural areas included within the Tibetan state. They arrived at the conference with tax records demonstrating Tibetan administration over almost all the territory of Tibetan inhabitation and denied that the previous relationship between Tibetan Dalai Lamas and Chinese emperors implied Tibetan subordination to China.

The Tibetan position was essentially a claim to self-determination for all areas of Tibetan inhabitation, although the term *self-determination* was not used. A border between "Inner Tibet" under Chinese control and an autonomous "Outer Tibet" at the divide between the Mekong and Yangtze rivers was ultimately agreed upon. Britain and Tibet agreed to the final Simla Convention, but the Chinese government refused to ratify it. Britain and Tibet thereafter made a bilateral agreement on the border between British India and Tibet.

Because China did not ratify the Simla Convention, Tibet did not consider itself bound by its acknowledgment of any degree of Chinese authority over Tibet. By its refusal to ratify the convention, China lost its chance for British recognition of Chinese authority over Tibet, which the British had defined as suzerainty. However, at the same time, China avoided acknowledging Tibet's right to enter into an international treaty or any limitation on China's authority over Tibet. China reserved the right to settle with Tibet unilaterally at a time of its own choosing.[12]

In 1921, the British presented the Chinese with an ultimatum: if China refused to renegotiate the Simla Convention, the British would treat Tibet as an autonomous state under Chinese suzerainty. However, with the lack of any Chinese response, the British found themselves having effectively recognized Chinese suzerainty over Tibet without any corresponding Chinese admission of Tibet's right to autonomy. The British compounded this error during the following years by continuing to acknowledge Chinese suzerainty while never securing any Chinese recognition of Tibetan autonomy.[13]

After the 1914 Simla Convention, British influence in Tibet increased, including providing Tibet with military assistance that enabled the Tibetans to push the Chinese out of most of Kham. The Thirteenth Dalai Lama attempted to strengthen Tibet's ability to defend itself by raising taxes for the support of the army. However, these measures created resistance from the large estate holders, particularly from the Panchen Lama's estate in Shigatse. Relations between Lhasa and the Panchen Lama deteriorated to the point that in 1924 he fled to China, disrupting the Dalai Lama's attempt to create Tibetan unity and providing China with a means to create divisions within Tibet. In order to keep Chinese influence out of Tibet, the Tibetan government did not allow the Panchen Lama to return during his lifetime. He died at Jyekundo in eastern Tibet in 1937.

British support for Tibet was helpful to the Tibetans in maintaining their autonomy, but Britain's continuing recognition of China's suzerainty over

Tibet allowed the Chinese to maintain their claims even when their actual authority was nonexistent. Despite the lack of any Chinese control over Tibet, China's claim to sovereignty over Tibet was generally accepted by the outside world. Even Britain, which knew that Tibet was de facto independent, continued to recognize China's overlordship of Tibet because Britain was unwilling to go to the extent of becoming Tibet's protector against China.

In 1933, the Thirteenth Dalai Lama died, and four years later, the reincarnation of the Dalai Lama was discovered in Amdo. In 1939, the boy was brought to Lhasa and installed as the Fourteenth Dalai Lama. The Chinese government was invited to send a representative to observe the ceremonies of installation, as were the governments of India, Nepal, Sikkim, and Bhutan. However, the Chinese construed the participation of its representative as the official recognition and installation of the reincarnation, a version of events denied by Tibetans and other participants.

Tibet maintained its claim to independence from China throughout the 1930s and 1940s. It also demanded the return to Tibetan administration of Chinese-controlled areas of eastern Tibet. Tibet maintained its neutrality during World War II even though China was a combatant. This position occasioned the first Tibetan diplomatic contacts with the United States, when Tibet refused permission to transport war supplies across Tibet from India to China. An American mission to Tibet in 1943 was informed of the Tibetan claim to independence, in response to which it was suggested that Tibet might attempt to achieve recognition of its independence in a postwar peace conference.

In 1945, at the conclusion of the war, Chiang Kai-shek, in the anticolonialist spirit of the time, promised Tibet and other nationalities self-determination ranging from "a very high degree of autonomy" to independence.[14] Chiang's statement undoubtedly reflected the Western Allies' influence on China during the war and immediately after. Since China had been forced by the Soviet Union to recognize the independence of Mongolia after the war, Chiang may have been trying to prevent Tibet's case from being brought up by Great Britain or the United States.

Tibet attempted to establish diplomatic recognition of its independence after the end of the war by sending a "Victory Congratulations Mission" to India, China, the United States, and the United Kingdom. The Tibetans had been led to believe that a 1945 Chinese constitutional convention would confirm Chiang's promise to Tibet of the right to national self-determination. However, the Chinese falsely portrayed Tibetan attendance at that convention as Tibetan participation as a part of China in drafting the constitution. In 1947, Tibet participated in a nongovernmental Asian Relations Conference in India despite Chinese protests. In 1948, a Tibetan trade mission was received in India, China, the United States, and Britain.

Coincident with Indian independence in 1947, the British gave up their interest in and involvement in Tibetan affairs. By this time, some of the British officials involved with Tibet had realized the futility of their policy there. The British attempted to define *suzerainty* as "nominal sovereignty over a semi-independent or internally autonomous state." However, Hugh Richardson, the last British representative in Lhasa, admitted that suzerainty "has never been defined and, indeed, appears to be incapable of absolute definition."[15] The British were unable to give any substance to Tibetan autonomy, nor could they convince the Chinese to respect Tibetan autonomy or to confine their ambitions in Tibet to the British concept of suzerainty. The Chinese regarded British attempts to limit Chinese control over Tibet as an attempt to separate Tibet from China.

The British invasion of Tibet in 1904 had come at the end of an era for the British Empire as well as for China and Tibet. The British were intent upon protecting British India from imperial rivals, but they were unwilling and unable to extend their empire to include Tibet. The British hoped to establish an autonomous, but not independent, Tibetan state—one that would recognize Chinese suzerainty and would not require direct British administration of Tibet, but that would serve as a buffer state between British India and Russia and China. Rather than pursue a traditional colonialist approach in Tibet, the British attempted to preserve an archaic model of Tibet's traditional relationship with China at a time when that relationship had been changed forever by the very fact of the British entry onto the scene. This strategy by the British also affected Tibet's future status. Tibet might have emerged as an independent country if it had been definitely detached from China under a British colonial administration, as Outer Mongolia did after a period of Russian and then Soviet domination.

The British difficulty in defining and achieving Tibetan autonomy under Chinese suzerainty was due to more than just China's rejection of British interference in what it considered its internal affairs. The British were trying to define and perpetuate a political status of an era that had already passed. Tibet's traditional autonomy had existed only because the pre-twentieth-century Chinese dynasties had perceived no threat to their claim to sovereignty over Tibet, either from foreign rivals or from Tibetan nationalism. British interference in Tibet, especially British support for Tibetan autonomy, changed the situation entirely from the Chinese perspective. Chinese nationalism of the twentieth century arose in response to the Chinese perception of foreign interference, and once Chinese nationalism became a factor, there was little chance that China would willingly accept anything less than full sovereignty over Tibet.

Until this time, most countries, the United States included, had followed the British lead in recognizing Tibetan autonomy under Chinese suzerainty. The Americans, less aware than the British of the realities of Tibet, attempted to further perpetuate this status because of U.S. opposition to Chinese Communism. Thus was Tibet's role in the "Great Game" transformed into a similar role in the Cold War.

Tibetan National Identity

By the middle of the twentieth century, Tibet had established, if not de jure independence and international recognition of such, at least de facto independence and the corresponding right as a distinct nation to national self-determination. Tibet's national identity, based upon nationality, territory, culture, and government, had been established during the empire period and had not been lost during the subsequent periods of dominance by Chinese dynasties of non-Chinese origin. In the first half of the twentieth century, Tibet had, under British patronage, demonstrated its unequivocal desire for independence. Tibet also occasionally indicated its willingness to accept a nominal Chinese authority, similar to the traditional cho–yon relationship, but this was primarily due to the British policy of supporting Tibetan autonomy but not independence. Tibet during the early 1900s experienced a growth of national identity and nationalist sentiment due to both British and Chinese colonial interests in Tibet. After the end of World War II, it expressed a desire for national self-determination contemporaneous with the codification of that right in international human rights conventions.

Since its annexation of Tibet in 1950–1951, the People's Republic of China (PRC) has denied the validity of Tibet's right to national self-determination by construing the issue of Tibet as one entirely about class rather than nationhood. The PRC claimed that Tibet was already a part of China, so there was no issue of Tibet being a nation separate from China worthy of the right of national self-determination. The Chinese defined the issue of Tibet as the Tibetan people's need for liberation from the class exploitation of its own feudal serf system, and once that system was overthrown, they proclaimed the achievement of Tibetan "self-determination" by the Tibetans themselves. Since then, China has justified its liberation of the Tibetans with much propaganda about the evils of the dark, barbaric, cruel, feudal serf system that supposedly existed before liberation. Yet China's portrayal of pre-1950 Tibet does not accord with the testimony of Tibetans, Chinese, or other foreign visitors of the time.

The Tibetan government administered most of Tibet indirectly through traditional princes, nomadic chieftains, monasteries, or monastic sects. In addition, Tibetans who had served the government were often compensated with estates, from which they were allowed to collect labor and taxes, rather than being paid directly by the government. This indirect type of political administration is the real meaning of feudalism and, as Karl Marx said, represented a natural evolution of human political organization. Indirect rule obviated the need for central government administration, or police and military authority, while at the same time providing some social security within the feudal framework. Feudal estates provided their tenants with protection against bandits and other deprivations. Because estate lords and monasteries stored grain and gave it to the people in times of shortage, and Tibetans always gave generously to the poor and beggars, Tibet before 1950 was not recorded to have experienced famine.

Traditional leaders and estate lords had juridical authority over their areas and estates, but, by all accounts, abuses of authority were not pervasive. From neither Tibetan, Chinese, nor foreign accounts of traditional Tibet is one able to find evidence of widespread discontent due to the abuses of the social system. Instead, all accounts speak of the peaceful nature of Tibetan society and the happiness of the Tibetan people, primarily due to the influence of Buddhism. Traditional leaders and estate lords were generally restrained in their treatment of their tenants for religious reasons, but also because estate owners were dependent upon the labor of their tenants. The labor and produce required by landlords as payment from tenants was typically no more than the taxes required of citizens of any country. The Chinese would later claim that Tibetan society had been characterized by extreme inequality, but every society has its inequalities, not least of all Communist Chinese society.

The Chinese Communists defined Tibet as a serf society—which is accurate—but their depiction of the nature of this society was darkened by the need to justify the legitimacy of Chinese rule over Tibet. Serfdom is defined as a condition of hereditary bondage to an estate or, more rarely, directly to an estate lord. Though bound to their estates, agricultural serfs in Tibet had title to their own plots of land and contractual obligations for labor to the estate that could not be arbitrarily altered. They had rights to private possessions and physical mobility, except when their labor was required by the estate. Serfs could, by private trade or business, become relatively wealthy and were sometimes even in the position of loaning money or grain to the estate. They also had the right to initiate legal action against the estate owner. The final arbiter in such cases was the Dalai Lama himself. The worst aspect of the system was that estate owners had broad adjudicative rights over their serfs, the only escape from which was to flee or to become a monk. There was no system for returning serfs to the estates from which they had escaped, so some serfs were able to achieve personal freedom as petty merchants or hired labor in this way.

While estates were hereditary, they were held as grants from the state and could be revoked at the state's discretion. The two main types of property were agricultural estates, held by noble families or monastic institutions, and villages, held by the central government in the hands of district administrators. The agricultural serfs (*du-chung*, "small smoke") were bound to estates to which they had labor but not tax obligations. Village serfs (*tralpa*) basically had only tax obligations. Approximately half of the village serfs were *mi-bog*, or "man-lease" serfs, that is, those who had bought their own physical freedom. These two classes of village serfs can probably more accurately be characterized as tenants, as there was no legal means of enforcement of their bondage.

Although all Tibetans outside the nobility and the monasteries were classed as serfs, only the agricultural serfs were bound to the land. Usually only one member of each family was required to perform labor for the estate, and for only part of the year. Estate lords had no power to expropriate the serfs so long as they fulfilled their tax and labor obligations. Village serfs were theoretically bound to their villages, but only by tax and labor (usually *ula*, or road transport) obligations, and otherwise had physical freedom of movement. They could also fairly easily acquire mi-bog status, which gave them total freedom of movement. This status was considered lower and more precarious, however, not having the security of the tie to the estate. They usually had tax obligations, although less than those of the tralpa, but were not bound to any estate or locality.

Only rarely were serfs bound directly to a lord rather than to an estate. Household servants (*nangzen*) and estate administrators sometimes owed loyalty directly to the lord, but these people were usually the lord's favorites and enjoyed the highest status and greatest security of all. It is likely that slavery did not exist in central Tibet in 1950, although the institution may have survived in some border areas. Reforms of the serf system were instituted by the Thirteenth Dalai Lama in the first decade of the twentieth century. Any serf absent from his estate for more than three years was automatically granted *chi-mi* (common man) or central government serf status. The Fourteenth Dalai Lama had planned a reform in the 1950s whereby taxing and judiciary power of the nobility would have reverted to the government.

Eastern Tibet was not directly governed by the Lhasa government, although local chieftains might owe a certain allegiance to Lhasa. Monasteries, which were also large estate owners, had allegiances and obligations to the central monastery of their sect, which were all in central Tibet. Some small states of Kham also had relations of indirect rule with the Chinese administrations or warlords of Sichuan. At times of Chinese political disintegration, the small states of eastern Tibet were functionally independent. The same may be said of many nomadic tribes, which often were governed only by their own chieftains and tribal traditions. Many villages were in a similar status if they owed tax obligations directly to the Lhasa government or a local chieftain and not to an estate owner. Under these conditions, they were often able to exist with considerable autonomy.

Although Tibet was governed by a system of indirect rule that became increasingly autonomous toward the periphery, all Tibetans looked to Lhasa as the center of Tibetan culture, and they all recognized to a greater or lesser degree the authority of the Dalai Lama. Tibetans also had a sense, deriving from the history of the empire and from the reign of the Fifth Dalai Lama when Tibet was unified under his authority, that all Tibet rightly should come under one political administration, even if only loosely defined. This sentiment was demonstrated by the claim of the Lhasa government at the Simla Convention to authority over all Tibetans. It was also demonstrated by Tibetans' sense of national identity expressed by their resistance to Chinese rule after 1950.

Notes

1. Modern Chinese studies based on surveys of blood antigens have indicated that Tibetan origins were in the northeastern Tibetan Plateau area: "The Tibetans are descendants of people from southern Gansu and Qinghai provinces who moved south to the Himalayas." This evidence was cited to prove that "the Tibetan people are inseparable members of the Chinese family" ("Tibetans Related to Northern Chinese," *Beijing Review*, 6 August 1990, 30).

2. R. A. Stein, *Les Tribus Anciennes des Marches Sino-Tibetaines* (Paris: Imprimerie Nationale, 1959), 4; Erik Haarh, *The Yar-Lun Dynasty* (Copenhagen: Gads Forlag, 1969), 281.

3. Stein, *Les Tribus*, 84; Haarh, *Yar-Lun Dynasty*, 281.

4. Stein, *Les Tribus*, 84.

5. Stein, *Les Tribus*, 28, 40.

6. Ibid.

7. Gordon T. Bowles, *The People of Asia* (New York: Charles Scribner's Sons, 1977), 190.

8. F. W. Thomas, *Nam: An Ancient Language of the Sino-Tibetan Borderland*, Publications of the Philological Society, no. 14 (London: Oxford University Press, 1948), 151.

9. Tashi Tsering, personal communication, Dharamsala, 1990.

10. F. W. Thomas, *Ancient Folk Literature from North-Eastern Tibet*, Abhandlungen der Deutschen Akademie der Wissenschaften zu Berlin (Berlin: Akademie Verlag, 1957), 6.

11. Warren W. Smith Jr., *Tibetan Nation: A History of Tibetan Nationalism and Sino-Tibetan Relations* (Boulder, CO: Westview Press, 1996), 185.

12. Alastair Lamb, *The McMahon Line: A Study in the Relations between India, China and Tibet, 1904–1914*, 2 vols. (London: Routledge & Kegan Paul, 1966).

13. Hugh Richardson, "Tibetan Précis," in *High Peaks, Pure Earth: Collected Writings on Tibetan History and Culture* (London: Serindia, 1998), 626.

14. Chiang Kai-shek, "National Independence and Racial Equality," in *The Collected Wartime Messages of Generalissimo Chiang Kai-shek, 1937–1945*, comp. Chinese Ministry of Information (New York: John Day, 1949), 854.

15. Richardson, "Tibetan Précis," 625.

2

Tibet under Chinese Communist Rule

Seventeen-Point Agreement

IN EARLY 1950, THE CHINESE COMMUNIST PARTY (CCP) began sending the People's Liberation Army (PLA) into eastern Tibet in preparation for an invasion of central Tibet. Chinese troops encountered little resistance in Amdo or Kham since they scrupulously adhered to the CCP's policy on treatment of nationalities, which required respectful treatment of local people. Local Tibetan leaders were bought off with new positions and high salaries. The Chinese Communists also took advantage of the traditional hostility of the *Khampas* (people of Kham) to Lhasa by promising to help them create their own autonomous region independent of Lhasa's control.

By the summer of 1950, the PLA was in position all along the Yangtze River, the border between autonomous or Chinese-administered eastern Kham and Lhasa-administered western Kham (Chamdo district). The Chinese at this point called on the Tibetan government to send delegates to Beijing to negotiate Tibet's "peaceful liberation." However, the Tibetans refused and sent an appeal to the United Nations warning that China was threatening Tibetan independence.

On 7 October 1950, the PLA began its invasion across the Yangtze from eastern Kham and south from Amdo (Qinghai). Tibetan forces were rapidly overwhelmed. The PLA then stopped its advance and again called upon the Tibetan government to negotiate Tibet's peaceful liberation. The Tibetan government removed the Dalai Lama to the Indian border for safety and sent another appeal to the United Nations.

The Chinese maintained that they had not invaded Tibet proper, since they claimed the Chamdo region as Chinese territory based upon the Chinese conquests of the area in the period after the 1904 British invasion. China's influence in the area had ceased after 1912, but in 1939 the Kuomintang had nevertheless proclaimed the area to be part of a new Chinese province, Xikang, despite the lack of any actual Chinese administration there. In fact, the Chamdo area was entirely Tibetan and was administered by the Tibetan government at Lhasa, and the Chinese had to defeat the Tibetan Army in order to occupy it. Still, the Chinese tried to convince the world that the PLA had not actually invaded Tibet and insisted that the issue of Tibet could still be peacefully resolved if the Tibetan government would send delegates to Beijing to negotiate.

China's claim that it had not invaded Tibet confused many who thought that the issue could therefore be peacefully negotiated. Based upon this misperception, the United Nations decided not to take up Tibet's appeal. Receiving no UN support, Tibet was compelled to send delegates to Beijing to negotiate with the Chinese. There, the Tibetan delegates were forced to accept Chinese conditions under the threat that the PLA would be ordered to advance to Lhasa. The Tibetan delegates were finally coerced into signing the Seventeen-Point Agreement for the Peaceful Liberation of Tibet.

Because the Seventeen-Point Agreement had not been approved by the Tibetan government, it required that government's ratification. However, the Chinese denied this, claiming that the Tibetan delegates had had full powers to sign the agreement on Tibet's behalf. The Tibetan delegates knew that this was not true, but China nevertheless announced to the world that the agreement had been concluded. Again, this deluded international opinion and led Tibet's supporters to think that the Tibetan government had voluntarily accepted the agreement and that the issue was now resolved. Tibet thus found it impossible to garner UN support. Despite some U.S. offers of mostly clandestine support, the Tibetan government was finally forced to accept the accord.

The Seventeen-Point Agreement promised what was essentially a continuation of the traditional Tibetan social and political system, including the monastic system, the estate system, and even the unique system of religious-political rule by the Dalai Lama's government. The only change specified was that Tibet would "return to the big family of the Motherland" and would accept a small Chinese official and military presence. In addition, there were certain unspecified "reforms" mentioned in the agreement, but these were to be carried out only with the approval of Tibetans and, theoretically, by Tibetans themselves. Mao Zedong and other Chinese Communist leaders even assured the Dalai Lama and the Tibetan people that the Chinese were entering Tibet only to assist Tibetans in their economic development and that they would leave when that development was achieved. The Dalai Lama quotes the Chinese PLA commander in Tibet, Chang Chingwu, as saying, "When you can stand on your own feet, we will not stay here even if you ask us to."[1]

In the annexation of Tibet, the CCP underestimated the strength of Tibetan national identity and overestimated the efficacy of Marxist nationality theory and policy in defusing Tibetan resistance. Chinese Communist leaders may have believed that they could eventually persuade Tibetans to undertake certain reforms of their own free will. However, given that the reforms they had in mind entailed the virtual dismantling of the Tibetan political, social, and cultural systems, they must have expected some resistance. The Chinese Communists assumed that some of the Tibetan upper class might temporarily resist Tibet's incorporation into China but that they could be co-opted by the United Front or marginalized by class struggle. The lower classes were thought to be natural allies of the Chinese since they were supposedly being repressed and exploited by the upper classes.

Certain statements by Mao reveal that he did expect resistance. In the early 1950s, Mao recognized that the Chinese position in Tibet was precarious and that a Tibetan revolt was a possibility:

> We must do our best and take the proper steps to win over the Dalai Lama and the majority of his top echelon and to isolate the handful of bad elements in order to achieve a gradual, bloodless transformation of the Tibetan economic and political system over a number of years; on the other hand we must be prepared for the eventuality of the bad elements leading the Tibetan troops in rebellion and attacking us.[2]

Despite promises to Tibetans that there would be no changes to their social, economic, and political systems—or at least the option to "preserve or reform" their customs at their own will—Mao spoke only of an inevitable transformation, hopefully without Tibetan resistance but against it if necessary.

In 1952, in an address to a group of visiting Tibetans, Mao made a rather cryptic statement in regard to planned population increases in Tibet: "Tibet covers a large area but is thinly populated. Its population should be increased from the present two or three million to five or six million, and then to over ten million."[3] The Chinese Communists were at that time practicing a policy of colonization in Inner Mongolia and Xinjiang, and the Dalai Lama understood that Mao meant Chinese colonization: "It was clearly stated to me while I was in Beijing in 1955 that Tibet was a vast country with scarce population and China has a large population with insufficient land, so land and population should be exchanged."[4] Mao's statements, along with actual Chinese policies in Tibet, indicate that the promises of the Seventeen-Point Agreement of virtually total autonomy and no social or political changes were at best temporary and at worst duplicitous. Such promises were intended to deter Tibetan resistance to the imposition of Chinese control until it could be consolidated.

In Mao's comment above, he gives Tibet's population as "two to three million." This was indeed the Chinese estimate of the Tibetan population of the PRC at the time (2.77 million).[5] However, China later referred only to the Tibet Autonomous Region (TAR) as "Tibet," whereas Mao here clearly refers to the entire Tibetan Plateau, populated by two to three million Tibetans, as "Tibet."[6] Thus, Mao's words reveal that he, presumably along with many other Chinese, thought of *all* of the Tibetan-inhabited areas as Tibet. The Chinese name for Tibet, *Xizang* ("Western Treasure House"), demonstrates a Chinese perception of Tibet as a territory exploitable for its resources rather than as a nation, a country, or a people.

Mao and other Chinese leaders portrayed the colonization plan as a bargain for Tibetans as well as for China since land and natural resources, which Tibet had and China lacked, would be exchanged for population, which China had and Tibet lacked. Most Chinese, apparently including Mao, tended to think of Tibetan territory as practically empty, the number of Tibetans as negligible, and Tibetan land and resources as essentially unused. They also imagined that Chinese colonization would benefit Tibetans by raising their cultural level and improving economic development in Tibet.

The Chinese Communists were careful to characterize the 1951 Seventeen-Point Agreement for the Peaceful Liberation of Tibet as an internal agreement between the Chinese central government and a regional government within China. Nevertheless, the document has many of the characteristics of an international treaty. No other region of the PRC required such an instrument of incorporation. The Seventeen-Point Agreement disguised the forceful nature of the Chinese invasion of Tibet. Even though the agreement is the means by which China eliminated Tibet's independence and incorporated Tibet within China, it is also evidence of Tibet's legitimate separate status.

The Seventeen-Point Agreement promised to preserve Tibet's culture, religion, social system, and government practically unchanged, except that Tibet was now part of China. Article 3 of the agreement said: "The Tibetan people have the right of exercising national regional autonomy under the unified leadership of the Central People's Government." Article 4 declared: "The central authorities will not alter the existing political system in Tibet. The central authorities also will not alter the established status, functions and powers of the Dalai Lama. Officials of various ranks shall hold office as usual." The key to Chinese intentions was revealed in Article 11, which said:

> In matters related to various reforms in Tibet, there will be no compulsion on the part of the central authorities. The Local Government of Tibet should carry

out reforms of its own accord, and when the people raise demands for reform, they shall be settled by means of consultation with the leading personnel of Tibet.[7]

In fact, the Seventeen-Point Agreement was a contradictory document, guaranteeing on the one hand no alteration of Tibetan political and religious systems, while on the other hand imposing Chinese sovereignty over Tibet and providing for Tibet to be governed by the system of "national regional autonomy." The Tibetans took solace in Chinese guarantees that no changes would be made to Tibet's religious and political systems, but the Chinese intended to eventually subject Tibet to the CCP's program for "democratic reforms and socialist transformation."

The key to Chinese intentions was the provision in Article 11 that said that unspecified reforms might be undertaken if the Tibetan people should demand them. The Tibetans did not find this particularly alarming, because they thought that this was unlikely, and in any case the agreement promised that any such reforms would be voluntary and would be carried out only by the Tibetan government. However, the critical element to the provision on reforms, as well as all other provisions of the Seventeen-Point Agreement, was Chinese military and political control in Tibet. The agreement provided for the PLA to enter Tibet and establish a "military and administrative committee and a military area headquarters"—a provision that seemed to contradict the promise that the existing political system would not be altered. Under Chinese control, the Tibetan government's powers and functions could be, and gradually were, limited as the Chinese took over more and more of the political functions in Tibet.

The Seventeen-Point Agreement did not address the issue of Tibetan territorial boundaries. Many Tibetans assumed that all Tibetan cultural areas were to be treated alike under the provisions of the accord. Tibetans never made the distinction that eastern Tibet was not "Tibet" because it was not directly administered by the Tibetan government at Lhasa. The Chinese, however, defined "Tibet" as only that territory of central Tibet under the direct authority of the Dalai Lama's government and decreed that the Seventeen-Point Agreement would apply only to that area. They justified this division on historical and practical grounds. Amdo and Kham had been administratively separated from central Tibet since 1725; in 1950, Amdo was under the jurisdiction of Qinghai and Kham was theoretically under Xikang.

The CCP nationalities doctrine prescribed that autonomous territorial units should correspond to areas where minority nationalities were in compact and contiguous occupation. Autonomous territorial status was thus theoretically granted to nationalities according to their current patterns of settlement, not according to former political divisions. However, the CCP attempted to obscure the fact that all Tibetan territories were contiguous with the argument that Tibetans lived not only in what the Chinese called Tibet but also in the Chinese provinces of Qinghai, Gansu, Sichuan, and Yunnan. In truth, these areas of eastern Tibet were separated from the rest of Tibet only by arbitrary political divisions made by former Chinese administrations (Mongol Yuan and Manchu Qing). These Chinese rationalizations denied the reality that all Tibetan cultural areas were contiguous and formed a single nationality territory that should have been eligible for autonomous territorial status. Instead, only central Tibet (U-Tsang) was to be constituted as the Tibet Autonomous Region, while Kham and Amdo were to be divided into several autonomous districts within Qinghai, Sichuan, Gansu, and Yunnan.

With the exception of the city of Sining and the Sining Valley, Qinghai was a province made up of autonomous districts of a majority Tibetan population, all of which were contiguous to the TAR. Two additional Tibetan autonomous districts contiguous to the Tibetan territory of Qinghai were created in Gansu. The Ngaba area of southeastern Amdo became the Apa (Ngaba) Autonomous District of Sichuan; Ngaba is contiguous to the Tibetan areas of Kham and Amdo. The area the Chinese had designated as Xikang Province was made a separate Xikang Autonomous Region until 1956, when western Kham was incorporated into the TAR and eastern Kham was brought under Sichuan as the Kanze Autonomous District. A portion of southern Kham became Dechen Autonomous District of Yunnan. Only Muli Tibetan Autonomous Prefecture, within the Yi Autonomous District of Yunnan, is not contiguous to other Tibetan nationality areas. The only other significant nationality within Tibetan autonomous districts of Qinghai, Gansu, Sichuan, and Yunnan was the Mongols, most of whom were Tibetanized in culture and were almost indistinguishable from Tibetans.

Within what was to become the Tibet Autonomous Region, further territorial divisions were created. The Panchen Lama's domains in Tsang were constituted as a separate area of administration, as if deriving from a previously separate local government. Until 1956, the Chamdo region of Kham, from the Yangtze to the town of Giamda, was theoretically under the authority of the Chamdo Liberation Committee, but was actually administered by the PLA. Western Tibet, or Ngari, was put under the control of the PLA of the Xinjiang Military District and was thus effectively removed from Tibetan government authority. The Chamdo district, the Panchen Lama's domain, and Ngari were reintegrated into the TAR in 1956 after their exclusion from the Tibetan government's domains had been made unnecessary by the elimination of most of that government's authority.

By excluding eastern Kham and all of Amdo from the Chinese territorial definition of Tibet, more than half of Tibetan nationality territory and two-thirds of its population were excluded from the provisions of the Seventeen-Point Agreement. The Chinese nevertheless claimed that they had not in any way altered the political system in "Tibet" nor the authority of the Tibetan government. The PRC's policy of treating Tibetan nationality areas of eastern Tibet as parts of Chinese provinces, where the restrictions of the Seventeen-Point Agreement would not apply, was to be a significant factor in the eventual Tibetan uprising against Chinese rule.

National Regional Autonomy

Chinese Communist Party doctrine on minority nationalities claimed to "combine the universal truths of Marxism-Leninism with the concrete conditions of China." The Chinese Communists, like the Nationalists, assumed that equality within the Chinese state was the equivalent of self-determination for minority nationalities. Both Leninist dialectical self-determination and traditional Chinese assimilationism are evident in the assumption that these nations, or "nationalities" in CCP parlance, would voluntarily choose to unite with China because they would realize that their cultural and economic interest lay in a union with the more advanced state. The fate of China's minority nationalities was said to be historically determined to be assimilation within the Chinese multinational state. Should there be any question that this union was voluntary, the Han Chinese were defined as but one of China's nationalities, all of whom had collectively decided upon union.[8]

CCP nationalities policy was little different from typical Chinese frontier assimilationism. Imperial China, Republican China, and Communist China all had a common policy toward minority nationalities, derived from traditional Chinese ideologies of cultural supremacy and policies of frontier assimilationism. Both the Nationalist and Communist Chinese promised equality to all nationalities—but only to be equally Chinese. Republican nationalities policy was based upon the need to ideologically rationalize the incorporation of the imperial possessions of the Qing Empire into a Chinese national state. Sun Yat-sen acknowledged that there were non-Chinese peoples in the territory claimed by Republican China, but he said that their numbers were insignificant in relation to the Han and therefore China was essentially one nationality.

Sun's policy of national equality within a Han Chinese state derived from a typical Chinese conception that the only reason frontier peoples were reluctant to be civilized by assimilation to Chinese culture was their past or present mistreatment by the Han Chinese. That any uncivilized peoples should choose to remain unassimilated to Chinese culture was credited to their barbarism and ignorance, which had to be overcome by patient education in order to bestow upon them the enlightenment and benefits of Chinese civilization. Resistance to the civilizing efforts of the Chinese was also believed to have been encouraged—even created where no native resistance actually existed, as in Tibet—by the intrigues of foreign imperialists. The Chinese Nationalists interpreted self-determination for China's nationalities not as a right to independence but only as a right to form a free alliance of nationalities within China.

The Chinese Communists, like the Nationalists before them, maintained that Tibet was already a part of China and therefore that there was no issue of Tibetan independence except as invented and fostered by foreign imperialism. Almost all Chinese who had attended public schools had been taught that Tibet was a part of China. Many Chinese thought of Tibetans as uncultured barbarians and could imagine no basis for an independent Tibetan cultural and political existence. In their anti-imperialist zeal, the Chinese Communists could not see themselves as imperialists. They could see only the threat of foreign imperialism in frontier areas like Tibet and the need—even the duty—to liberate the Tibetans, along with all the Chinese people, from that threat. Many Chinese were convinced that not only was the idea of Tibetan independence an invention of foreign imperialists, but that Tibetan independence was an illusion, since if Tibet separated from China, it would not remain independent but instead would immediately come under the domination of foreign imperialists.

Upon its victory over the Kuomintang, the CCP declared that the liberation of Tibetans and all other "minority nationalities" had been achieved along with that of the Han Chinese. According to Marxist doctrine, national oppression could exist only under capitalism and colonialism. Since prerevolutionary China had been in the precapitalist stage of development, it could not have been in a colonialist relationship with any of its minority nationalities. With the liberation of all China's nationalities from foreign imperialism and the achievement of a socialist system in China (skipping the capitalist system and the capitalist period of development), national oppression would be abolished and the self-determination of all nationalities automatically achieved. The fate of China's minority nationalities was said to have been "historically determined" to be assimilation within the Chinese "multinational state."[9]

The CCP nationalities policy combined traditional Chinese frontier assimilationism with an ideology that promised to grant autonomy to minority nationalities. This was based upon the Marxist-Leninist theory that the promise of autonomy could be employed to facilitate the ultimate goal of assimilation. The Chinese Communists derived this policy from Leninist doctrine and Stalinist practice. Lenin defined self-determination as a right not of nations but only of the proletariat of those nations. Since, by Marxist definition, proletarian consciousness was non-nationalist, the proletariat of any nation would naturally choose union with a socialist state, in which national oppression was nonexistent. In the absence of a proletariat in a nationality, the decision about union with the larger state was to be made by the proletariat of the larger state, represented by the Communist Party. In order to prevent any nationality from exercising its theoretical right to self-determination, any such tendencies were categorized as "bourgeois" and therefore illegitimate.[10]

The goal of the CCP nationalities policy was to convince minority nationalities that class consciousness was more important than national consciousness and that they should therefore ally with the united nationality working classes in opposition to their own exploitative upper classes. As the socialist system eliminated exploitation within and between nationalities, local nationalism would also be eliminated and nationalities would voluntarily abandon their backward cultures in favor of Chinese socialist culture. This process would be facilitated by a strategy employing "national forms," or national language and traditions, to propagate the socialist message. The idea was that minority nationals would accept the socialist message if it came wrapped in familiar language and cultural attire, hence the slogan "Nationalist in form, socialist in content."[11] The autonomous rights temporarily promised to minority nationalities were not intended to develop and preserve their cultures but rather to facilitate their acceptance of socialist culture.

The Chinese Communists assumed, based on traditional Chinese attitudes toward frontier nationalities and on Marxist-Leninist theory, that minorities would voluntarily abandon their own backward cultures once they were convinced of the superiority and benefits of Chinese socialist culture. Cultural autonomy would therefore be necessary only temporarily, during the transition period, in order to win the confidence of the nationalities. All of China's minority nationalities were intended to eventually undergo socialist transformation along with the Han Chinese. The transformation to socialist culture would theoretically happen only when the minorities were ready and would therefore be voluntary. However, the impatience of the Chinese Communists and the resistance of minority nationalities, especially the Tibetans, led the party to abandon voluntarism and to impose its reforms by force.

The PRC adopted a system of "national regional autonomy" instead of a federal system like the Soviet Union's. China's nationalities were said to have undergone a historical process of ethnic mixing to the extent that none were now in exclusive possession of contiguous territories free of other minorities or Han Chinese. Even Tibetans, seemingly an exception to the latter characterization, were deemed to live in a compact community only in central Tibet—the area later designated the TAR—while many more Tibetans, like other nationalities in China, were "dispersed in different areas of the country," in particular, in Sichuan, Qinghai, Gansu, and Yunnan.[12] The CCP justified its system of national regional autonomy on the basis that it allowed for the exercise of autonomy by scattered nationality populations wherever they were found, rather than only in a single region as in a federal system, or as individual members of a minority nationality as in a system of national autonomy where members of minorities would exercise individual autonomous rights independent of their territorial location within the state.

The assumptions behind the CCP's regional autonomy system may have applied to China's internal minorities, but they did not at all apply to the nationalities on China's frontier in East Turkestan, Inner Mongolia, and Tibet. These were distinct nations with a history not of assimilation with the Chinese but of resistance to Chinese assimilation. The Inner Asian nations were further denied the status of federation, which would have preserved their national political identity. The national regional autonomy system was intended to divide the frontier nations into numerous separate territorial political units and to prevent any from having a unified territory or united political representation. The PRC's national regional autonomy system intentionally divided and obscured Tibet's national territorial integrity and identity. The divisions of Tibetan territory allowed the Chinese to argue that Tibetans were a minority, like other minorities, "mixed with Han and other nationalities" and scattered among several provinces.

Autonomy in Practice: Political Integration

Both when they entered eastern Tibet in preparation for the invasion of central Tibet and when they arrived in Lhasa after the signing of the Seventeen-Point Agreement, People's Liberation Army troops strictly adhered to their rules of conduct that required them to treat local people with respect. As in eastern Tibet, the Chinese ingratiated themselves by paying generously for all their provisions with Chinese silver dollars minted especially for use in Tibet. However, their presence in Lhasa almost immediately created shortages of food and fuel and caused inflation in prices that aroused local resentment. The Chinese also began acquiring land in the Lhasa Valley for their camps and bought houses for their offices from some of the Lhasa aristocrats.

Popular Tibetan resentment against the Chinese resulted in 1952 in the creation of an organization known as the Mimang Tsongdu (People's Assembly). It was supported by the two Tibetan prime ministers, Lukhangwa and Lobsang Tashi, who resisted all Chinese attempts to eliminate the powers and functions of the Tibetan government. They also insisted that the number of

Chinese troops in Lhasa be reduced because of the strain on Tibetan resources. On 31 March 1952, members of the Mimang Tsongdu surrounded the house of the Chinese commander in Lhasa and demanded that the number of Chinese troops be decreased and that the Chinese not reduce the status and power of the Dalai Lama. The commander, Chang Kuohua, complained to the Tibetan government that the demonstration was illegal and was intended to sabotage the Seventeen-Point Agreement and disrupt the relations between nationalities. The Chinese demanded that such demonstrations not be allowed in the future and blamed the two prime ministers for sympathizing with the Mimang Tsongdu. They mounted a campaign against the prime ministers, insisting that they be dismissed from their posts. The Chinese also moved additional troops to Lhasa. Under this pressure, the Dalai Lama was finally forced to remove the two prime ministers.

The removal of the prime ministers severely undermined the power of the Tibetan government and set the pattern for the future in Tibet. Whenever the Chinese encountered Tibetan opposition, they complained that Tibetans were spoiling the relations between nationalities and demanded that the opposition be curtailed, under threat of force. The Tibetan government was unable to resist the Chinese demands due to the preponderance of force available to the Chinese and their constant threats to use military means to achieve their demands. After this time, Tibetans were unable to mount either an official or a popular opposition to the Chinese. In addition, Chinese United Front policies succeeded in recruiting a number of Tibetan collaborators, who were rewarded with high positions in new governing bodies and whose children were sent for education in China. In many cases, especially for Tibetan officials, collaboration was unavoidable since the Tibetan government was bound by the Seventeen-Point Agreement to cooperate with the Chinese.

In early 1954, an agreement was reached with India, known in India as the Panchshila or "Five Principles of Peaceful Coexistence," that regulated and restricted Tibetan trade with India. The actual title of the treaty was "Agreement between the Republic of India and the People's Republic of China on Trade and Intercourse between Tibet Region of China and India." By this agreement, India recognized China's complete control over Tibet. This treaty ended any hope that Tibet might have had that India would support Tibet in its attempt to maintain its autonomy from China.

Since then, China has promoted these five principles—mutual respect for territorial integrity and sovereignty, mutual nonaggression, mutual noninterference in internal affairs, equality and mutual benefit, and peaceful coexistence—as its doctrine in all its international relations. However, each of the principles can be said to have been violated by China with regard to Tibet.

The Chinese also began to gain control of Tibetan trade by purchasing wool that would usually have been bought by India and by further restricting trade with India in favor of trade with China. Chinese policies in Tibet in the early 1950s were careful and cautious because the Chinese position was precarious. Chinese leaders were afraid of a Tibetan revolt occurring before China had sufficient means to suppress it. Chinese activities before the end of 1954 were primarily aimed at gaining control without arousing Tibetan resistance. In general, the Chinese confined themselves to programs that were more like foreign aid than foreign conquest and were intended to win Tibetans' support or at least to prevent their active or organized resistance.

At the end of 1954, China completed two roads from China to Tibet, one from Sichuan and the other from Qinghai. These routes increased China's control over Tibet, allowing China to rapidly move troops to Tibet in case of a Tibetan uprising. The roads also allowed the Chinese to supply their own needs in Tibet to a greater extent, thus relieving the pressure on Tibetan resources and alleviating Tibetan discontent to some extent.

The completion of the roads and the conclusion of the Panchshila agreement with India allowed the Chinese to begin to alter the Tibetan political and social systems. The first step in this process was to supersede the powers and functions of the Tibetan government by the creation of an alternative governing structure.

In late 1954, the Chinese persuaded the nineteen-year-old Dalai Lama to attend the inaugural meeting of the National People's Congress (NPC) in Beijing, at which the new constitution of the People's Republic of China was to be approved. The Panchen Lama was also invited to attend. The Dalai Lama, along with all of the high officials of the Tibetan government, traveled to China via the almost-completed road that ran through Kham to Sichuan.

Tibetan leaders in exile later claimed that the Chinese convinced the Dalai Lama to attend under false pretenses. They claimed that the Chinese had given the Dalai Lama and the Tibetans the impression that the meeting was intended to discuss Tibet's status and that Tibet might be granted autonomy practically equivalent to internal independence.

At Beijing, the Tibetan government representatives found that the NPC meeting was not intended to discuss Tibet at all but was simply meant to approve the new Chinese constitution. The Tibetans therefore found themselves participating as representatives of Tibet in the creation of the new Chinese state. The Chinese wanted the Dalai Lama and most of the Tibetan government present at the NPC session in order to create the impression that Tibet was an integral part of China and a willing participant in the creation of the new Chinese administrative system. Their presence was also intended to signify Tibetan approval of the system of national regional autonomy that was to govern Tibet as well as all other national minorities. As at the negotiations for the Seventeen-Point Agreement, the Tibetan representatives at the NPC meeting were divided between the Tibetan government, the Panchen Lama's government, and the still-existent Chamdo Liberation Committee. The Chinese once again managed to convey the impression that Tibet was divided politically, even though the Panchen Lama's separate government and the Chamdo Liberation Committee were entirely Chinese creations.

Tibetan participation in the NPC assembly and the preparation of the 1954 Constitution was portrayed by the Chinese as constituting Tibetan consent that the "no changes in the Tibetan political system" provision of Article 4 of the Seventeen-Point Agreement could be superseded by the "reforms" provision of Article 11. In addition, the Seventeen-Point Agreement itself would be superseded by changes in the political administration of Tibet made by mutual agreement with the Dalai Lama and his government. Tibet thus was to lose some of its special status entailed in the Seventeen-Point Agreement and come under the same system of national regional autonomy that was to govern all the national minorities in the PRC.

Both the Dalai and Panchen Lamas remained in Beijing after the National People's Congress. In January 1955, the Chinese announced that the two lamas had reached a historic agreement resolving all of their previous disputes. The disputes in question derived from the time of the previous Panchen Lama's 1924 flight to China. China was thus able to pose as the overall sovereign authority under which the different regions and local governments in Tibet could achieve unity. The agreement between the Dalai Lama and the Panchen Lama was portrayed as providing the basis for a unification of their previously separate governments within a new governing body.

The Chinese considered Tibet's participation in the NPC meeting as signifying Tibetan approval for the creation of a new administration for Tibet, to be known as the Preparatory Committee for the Tibet Autonomous Region (PCTAR). The Chamdo Liberation Committee was also to be included under the Preparatory Committee and therefore as part of the territory of the future Tibet Autonomous Region. This was portrayed as a magnanimous gift of the Chamdo territory to Tibet, but its actual significance was that eastern Kham was included within the Chinese province of Sichuan.

The PCTAR was intended to be the first step to Tibetan autonomy, under the system of national regional autonomy, and was apparently what the Chinese meant when they promised the Dalai Lama that Tibet would be granted a higher degree of autonomy. The committee was also presented as a unification of previously separate Tibetan political entities, which would expand the territory within which Tibetans would theoretically exercise self-rule. However, while purporting to guarantee Tibetan autonomy, the PCTAR actually transferred effective governing authority to the Chinese and secured Chinese political control over Tibet. It was thus perceived by Tibetans not as a grant of greater autonomy but as a violation of the promise of the Seventeen-Point Agreement not to alter the Tibetan political system.

The committee was not formally established until 1956, reportedly due to Tibetan resistance. Although the majority of the members of the PCTAR were Tibetan, all actual governing power was transferred from the Tibetan government to the CCP's Tibet Work Committee, composed exclusively of Chinese. In this way, the creation of the PCTAR altered the political system in Tibet and abolished the authority and functions of the traditional Tibetan government. Furthermore, the Chinese could maintain that Tibetans themselves had agreed to these changes. The creation of the PCTAR illustrates the transitory nature of the situation within Tibet in the 1950s. The Chinese Communists did not intend to tolerate the uneasy coexistence of the CCP and the Dalai Lama's government as a permanent system of Tibetan autonomy.

The Dalai Lama agreed to the establishment of the Preparatory Committee, apparently hoping that it might be able to function as an actual autonomous governing body. After he left Tibet in 1959, the Dalai Lama wrote that he was soon disillusioned that the committee was actually intended to function as an autonomous government of Tibet. He described obstruction by Tibetan members representing the Panchen Lama and the Chamdo Liberation Committee, both of whom owed their positions entirely to Chinese support and in return had to support any Chinese proposition. With these controlled votes and those of the five Chinese members, the PCTAR was powerless, he said, a mere façade of Tibetan representation behind which all effective power was exercised by the Chinese. The Dalai Lama said that it was almost laughable sometimes to see how the proceedings were controlled and regulated, so that plans already decided upon by the Chinese received a pointless and empty discussion and then were passed.[13]

On the occasion of the inauguration of the Preparatory Committee, a visiting representative of the Chinese government, Chen Yi, announced that Tibet would eventually undergo reforms, although he admitted that similar reforms in Kham and Amdo had already created resistance there. No reforms would be undertaken in the TAR without Tibetans' consent, he said, and therefore Tibetans should not be alarmed. However, he warned that "the Tibetan nationality must, in common with the other nationalities, pursue the road to Socialism." Chen promised that the political status and living standard of the aristocracy and lamas would be protected during reforms, and that the livelihood of the monasteries would be guaranteed by the state. He also promised that there would be no interference in the affairs of religion.[14]

In response, the Dalai Lama expressed his hope that reforms would really be carried out only at the wish of the Tibetans themselves. Tibetans in the TAR still had little idea of what the Chinese meant by "democratic reforms," and they could not anticipate the methods by which the Chinese would implement them.

Besides the political integration of Tibet with China, the Chinese Communists pursued a program of ideological indoctrination and ideological and cultural assimilation of Tibet within China. The ideological assimilation involved a redefinition of political and geographical terminology, a redefinition of national identity, and the creation of new social and political organizations within which ideological indoctrination would be pursued.

The first step in the ideological transformation and assimilation of Tibet was the designation of Tibet as a part of China and the introduction of terminology such as "China's Tibet" and "Tibet, China." CCP nationalities policy redefined the Tibetan nation as a minority nationality of China. Tibetans were taught that they were actually Chinese and that they were a part of the "Great Family of the Motherland." Tibetans were designated as "Chinese of the Tibetan nationality" (*Zangzu*), and the Chinese themselves as "Chinese of Han nationality" (*Hanzu*). Central Tibet was to become the Tibet Autonomous Region; eastern Tibet outside the TAR would no longer be referred to as Tibet at all. Chinese names or Chinese mispronunciations of Tibetan names were given to other places, things, or people in Tibet. A new political terminology was introduced to describe newly created political and social organizations and to define the terms of the party's political ideology.

The ideological redefinition of Tibet included not only the designation of Tibetans as Chinese but also the transformation of Tibetan national identity and the redirection of Tibetan loyalty from Tibet to China. The primary tool in this attempted conversion was class theory and class struggle. Chinese Communist class theory held that Tibetans' loyalty should be based upon class rather than nationality—that ordinary Tibetans had more in common with those of the same class of other nationalities than they did with the Tibetan upper class. The upper class was denounced as the enemy of ordinary Tibetans, while the CCP was proclaimed as their natural ally. Ordinary Tibetans were encouraged to redefine and redirect their loyalties from nationality to class and from their own exploitative upper class to their class's natural representative, the CCP. They were encouraged to denounce their own upper class and to replace their leadership with the leadership of the party. Tibetan independence was denigrated as an imperialist scheme to detach Tibet from China, and the Tibetan upper class that had collaborated with foreign imperialists was characterized as not only anti-Chinese but anti-Tibetan as well. Tibet's liberation by China was portrayed as Tibetans having become masters of their own affairs and of their own fate.

The Chinese People's Political Consultative Conference (CPPCC) was created as an aspect of the United Front policy. The United Front supposedly gave non-Communist political parties and national minorities a voice in political affairs. Its philosophy was to "unite from above and below," meaning that alliances should be made both with lower-class allies and upper-class collaborators. A variety of social organizations were created, such as youth and women's organizations, that served as a recruiting ground for educational tours to China and scholarships for schooling in China. Minority nationalist institutes were created for Tibetans at Xianyang near Xian and for Tibetans and other minorities at the National Minorities Institute in Beijing and at provincial nationalities institutes in Sichuan, Gansu, and Qinghai. At these schools, Tibetans were indoctrinated with Communist ideology and taught Chinese, while Tibetan language was deemphasized and Tibetan culture was denigrated. Schools were also created within Tibet where Tibetans were similarly indoctrinated. Political organizations were created that replaced Tibetan political institutions and within which Tibetans were instructed in CCP ideology. Tibetans were taught to accept the reality of CCP authority in Tibet. Chinese ideological indoctrination of Tibetans was enforced with the promise that conformity and cooperation would be rewarded, while resistance would be repressed.

The new Chinese-created social and political organizations were a critical part of the Chinese plan for the social transformation of Tibet. It was these new organizations that, they said, represented "the people," and it was these organizations that would promote Chinese "reforms." By means of these organizations, the Chinese were able to transcend the limitations of the Seventeen-Point Agreement, which specified that reforms would be undertaken only if Tibetans themselves demanded them. By having these entities demand reforms, the Chinese could claim that Tibetan representatives wanted reforms. The Chinese-created political administration of the PCTAR would carry out such reforms, thus transcending the limitation of the Seventeen-Point Agreement that any reforms had to be carried out by the Tibetan government.

A major tool of the Chinese Communists for the ideological transformation of Tibet was indoctrination in Communist propaganda. One major purpose of this propaganda in Tibet was to explain the CCP nationalities policy. Another primary purpose was to justify Chinese rule over Tibet. China's justification for its control over Tibet has three main themes: that Tibet has always been a part of China, that old Tibet was a feudal Hell on Earth from which Tibetans should be grateful to have been liberated, and that China's intention was only to help develop Tibet socially and economically while taking nothing from Tibet and allowing Tibetans to rule themselves under the PRC's system of national regional autonomy.

The PLA's advance into Tibet was accompanied by propaganda units whose purpose it was to defuse resistance by explaining CCP nationalities policies.

These PLA units put on dances and dramas of the same type that the Communists had used to cultivate support within China. The dances and dramas illustrated the Communists' themes of class liberation, and in nationality areas, of equal treatment of minorities. The PLA was depicted as a disciplined force that would liberate the people while refraining from taking "even a needle or thread" from them. The dance and drama troupes not only performed Chinese songs and dances but also attempted to incorporate Tibetan songs and dances as a demonstration of their respect for local traditions and culture. After the Chinese became established in Tibet, they formed Tibetan opera companies intended to convey respect for Tibetan culture while at the same time altering the traditional Tibetan repertoire to convey Communist themes.

The Chinese Communists also made use of a variety of media for propaganda, including newspapers, magazines, books, posters, film, and radio. Newspapers, magazines, and books were published in Chinese and in Tibetan explaining CCP nationalities policy and conveying Chinese propaganda about Tibet. Public readings were held for those who could not read. Posters and even signs made of rocks on hillsides were used to propagate Chinese slogans. Film was also used to impress Tibetans and to convey CCP propaganda. Movies were shown by PLA propaganda units even in remote areas where most Tibetans had never before seen motion pictures. In the absence of theaters, films were shown outdoors on the whitewashed sides of large buildings. Most of these pictures were in Chinese, but even though the Tibetans could not understand the dialogue, they were able to grasp the main themes. Radio was also extensively broadcast by means of loudspeakers in every street and public place in every town and village in Tibet.

Chinese use of propaganda in Tibet was very sophisticated, even if the propaganda itself was very simplistic. Every conceivable method, medium, and format was used to convey Chinese Communist propaganda. Many of the methods employed, especially opera and public ceremonies, combined entertainment with propaganda in order to more subtly convey CCP themes. While the methods used to convey Chinese propaganda in Tibet were pervasive and sometimes even subtle, the inescapable and often simplistic nature of propaganda made it overbearing and offensive and therefore often counterproductive. Some Tibetans, especially those chosen for schooling in China and eventually for leadership roles, may have truly come to believe in Marxism and CCP nationalities policies. Ultimately, however, the themes of Chinese propaganda were difficult for many Tibetans to accept. It was difficult to convince Tibetans that the issue of Tibet was one of class rather than nation, or of the inequality of class exploitation, rather than the illegitimacy of China's rule over Tibet. Most Tibetans did not agree that Tibet was historically a part of China. Tibetans knew very well that old Tibet had not been the Hell on Earth that the Chinese claimed. And China's claim that it had taken control over Tibet solely in order to liberate Tibetans, without any ulterior motives, seemed unlikely.

Democratic Reforms in Eastern Tibet

In 1956, Mao Zedong initiated a rapid acceleration of the socialist transformation process known as the "High Tide of Socialist Transformation." Because the Chinese Communists thought that minority nationalities' opposition to Chinese rule had already been essentially eliminated, most minority nationalities, with the exception of Tibetans within the TAR, were included in the High Tide. Mao himself decided that minorities should be included, since to deny them the benefits of democratic reforms and socialist transformation based upon the belief that they were not sufficiently socially or culturally prepared was equivalent to "looking down on the minority nationalities."[15] Mao's opinion set the stage for later criticism of nationality autonomy, especially the preservation of minority cultures and traditions, as rightist and not in the best interests of the minorities themselves.

The Tibetan autonomous districts of Qinghai, Gansu, and Sichuan had already achieved regional autonomous status and were therefore considered ready for democratic reforms. Democratic reforms consisted of land redistribution, suppression of landlords and "counterrevolutionaries," and initiation of class divisions and class struggle. In Chinese areas, democratic reforms were intended to overthrow the rule of the upper classes and substitute the rule of the workers, represented by the CCP. In nationality areas such as Tibet, however, democratic reforms had not only class but also national implications. The Chinese claimed that democratic reforms were implemented voluntarily by the Tibetans themselves in order to overthrow the feudal serf system. According to the party, Tibetan serfs stood up to become masters of their own fate by means of democratic reforms. In practice, democratic reforms enabled the Chinese to expose and eliminate all Tibetan opponents to Chinese rule. Democratic reforms facilitated not only Chinese political control over Tibet but social control over Tibetans as well.

The first step in preparation for democratic reforms was the cultivation of lower-class activists, who were promised an overturning of society in which they would become the new ruling class. Activists were rewarded with increased status and material goods. Coercion also played a role in gaining collaborators; reluctant members of the lower classes were threatened with denunciation as reactionaries if they refused to cooperate. Lower-class activists assisted the Chinese in gathering data upon which class divisions would later be based. Democratic reforms were initiated by making class divisions and stimulating conflict between classes. In eastern Tibet, Chinese and Tibetan officials, accompanied by Chinese PLA, traveled from village to village redistributing property and holding "struggle sessions" for those of the upper class accused of exploiting the people. Tibetans report that property of the upper classes was confiscated with much propaganda and fanfare, but when the redistribution took place, they found that the activists and the Chinese had taken the best of everything for themselves, including land and livestock.

Land and property redistribution was accompanied by struggle of landowners and traditional leaders. An essential element of the Chinese Communist class categorization was that political criteria were also applied; thus, a person of any economic category could be classified as an "enemy of the people" because of a "reactionary" attitude—evidence of which, in Tibet, included any opposition to Chinese rule. Many traditional leaders identified as opponents to the Chinese, even if they had not been large property owners, were subjected to "struggle"—*thamzing* in Tibetan—as exploiters in order to eliminate any potential leadership for resistance. Thamzing was a process that served to intimidate and repress not only the person being subjected to it but all participants as well. Everyone present had to condemn the accused, since even silence would identify one as an opponent and a possible target for thamzing. Lamas, *tulkus*, and other traditional leaders were subjected to thamzing, public humiliation, and arrests. Democratic reforms and thamzing allowed the Chinese to indoctrinate, identify, and eliminate all actual or potential opposition and to create an atmosphere of fear and conformity.

Religion was ostensibly protected during democratic reforms, but the Chinese intended that the Tibetan masses should realize that they were exploited by the monks and lamas and should cease to support them. Monasteries were deprived of their estates during land reforms, thus depriving them of their subsistence. In fact, religion was singled out for attack because the religious establishment was considered one of the main institutional obstacles to Chinese control, and Buddhism was regarded as the primary ideological competitor to communism. Lamas were denounced both as landlords and as political leaders. High lamas were often publicly humiliated, beaten, and even tortured to death. Lamas were tormented and tortured as a demonstration of their inability to summon divine assistance, the powerlessness of their gods, and therefore the falsity of their religion.

As the Chinese Communists were well aware, nationalist consciousness among the minorities resided predominantly in the ruling classes; therefore, nationality resistance could be reduced by the repression or co-option of a single class, under the guise of liberation from upper-class exploitation. However, the imposition of Chinese rule over peoples previously ruled only loosely even by indigenous authorities aroused a popular nationalist opposition in response. Although most of the former ruling class were co-opted or repressed, and many of the lower class were induced to collaborate by a variety of means, many others of all classes experienced an arousal of nationalist consciousness. The repression of local leaders under the guise of democratic reforms was more successful in creating resistance to the Chinese than it was in creating "proletarian class consciousness." Many local social, political, and religious leaders subjected to humiliation and suppression during democratic reforms were not regarded as class exploiters, but as respected, even revered, figures who represented that nationality's cultural, religious, or national identity. While the CCP astutely co-opted those of the upper classes who were willing to cooperate in the United Front, it miscalculated in thinking that it could repress uncooperative members of the upper classes without arousing national resistance.

In April 1956, shortly after the ceremonies in Lhasa inaugurating the Preparatory Committee, Tibetan leaders of Kham were propagandized to "request" that democratic reforms be introduced. This attempt to force the introduction of democratic reforms was the beginning of the Tibetan uprising in Kham. One reason for this was that reforms included confiscation of weapons, which were a part of the normal attire of the Khampas. The revolt soon became widespread in Kham due to the Khampas' resistance to democratic reforms.

Tibetan attacks on the Chinese were initially successful due to the Khampas' familiarity with the terrain and their martial skills, but the Chinese held out in their fortresses and began a massive introduction of troops to quell the rebellion. Large numbers of Chinese troops were introduced into Kham to suppress the revolt and to prevent it from spreading to the TAR. Soon, many Khampas were forced to leave their villages and take to the mountains to wage a guerrilla campaign.

Chinese attempts to arrest local lay and religious leaders in Lithang in the spring of 1956 led to two or three thousand Tibetans being surrounded in the large Lithang Monastery by PLA troops. The Chinese bombarded the monastery with mortars, and then, unable to persuade the Tibetans to surrender, summoned the air force. The monastery was bombed by twin-jet bomber aircraft that the Chinese had recently received from the Soviet Union. Hundreds of Tibetans within the monastery grounds were killed or wounded; others were killed by the PLA troops who stormed the monastery. Dzachukha Monastery in Golok and several other places were also bombed.

By the end of 1956, all Tibetan areas outside the TAR had been subjected to democratic reforms and all had erupted in revolt. The Chinese did not decrease the pace of reforms in the face of the rebellion, but rather quickened it in order to suppress the rebellion. Democratic reforms were an effective means of eliminating Tibetan leadership, while collectivization increased Chinese control over the Tibetan population. Chinese officials admitted that their reforms had produced a revolt, but claimed that the revolt was not in Tibet but in western Sichuan and had no nationalist significance.

In Kham, rebellion was continuous from 1956, with only a brief lessening due to a liberalization of Chinese policies in early 1957. Tibetans from Kham gathered in Markham, in the Chamdo district, in 1956 and formed the Tibetan Resistance Army.

By the end of 1957, the Chinese had committed eight PLA divisions and at least 150,000 men to the suppression of the revolt in eastern Tibet. Many Khampas and *Amdowas* who had already left their homes to fight the Chinese now began to move toward Lhasa. However, PLA tactics were to confine refugees in the east; therefore, relatively few Tibetans from the east were able to reach Lhasa without being killed or detained. Many of the deaths during the revolt were of Tibetans fleeing from eastern to central Tibet.

Anti–Local Nationalist Campaign

In early 1956, the Dalai Lama was invited to India to attend the Buddha Jayanti, the 2,500th anniversary of the birth of Lord Buddha. The Chinese did not want to allow him to go, but having only recently, in 1954, established relations of "peaceful coexistence" with India, could not prohibit his acceptance of the invitation without international embarrassment. In late 1956, the Dalai Lama, accompanied by the Panchen Lama, began his visit to India. When he met with Indian prime minister Jawaharlal Nehru, the Dalai Lama indicated that he was considering seeking asylum in India because of the hopelessness of the situation in Tibet. Nehru, emphasizing that the Tibetans could not expect help from India, suggested that the Dalai Lama try to resolve his differences with Zhou Enlai, who was due to arrive in Delhi at the end of January.

The Dalai Lama subsequently met with Zhou, who, when informed that reforms were being imposed against the will of the Tibetans, seemed surprised and responded that local Chinese officials should not have introduced reforms without the Tibetans' consent. Zhou promised to convey the Tibetans' complaints to Mao Zedong. After a trip to Europe, Zhou returned to India to meet again with the Dalai Lama. Zhou informed the Dalai Lama that the Chinese government had decided to postpone reforms in Tibet for six years and that they could be postponed for fifty years if necessary. Given Zhou's and Nehru's assurances that China intended to respect Tibetan autonomy, the Dalai Lama was persuaded to return.

The Chinese intention to delay reforms in Tibet was confirmed by Mao in his February 1957 "On Contradictions among the People" speech, in which he promised that Tibet would be exempted from reforms for the period of the next Five-Year Plan and for the subsequent plan as well if the Tibetans themselves were not ready to accept them.[16] Since reforms were to be delayed, some Chinese personnel could be withdrawn from the TAR.

The Chinese leadership apparently took several factors into account in deciding upon a retrenchment. One immediate reason was the need to lure the Dalai Lama back from India and to silence criticism from Tibetan exiles in India or Indian supporters of Tibet. The CCP also feared the spread of the revolt in eastern Tibet to the TAR. Chinese authorities in Lhasa admitted that the decision to postpone reforms in the TAR was made because of the disturbances that the reforms had caused in eastern Tibet. However, they made it clear that the retrenchment was a temporary measure and that Tibetans would eventually have to accept democratic reforms. The Tibetans were also warned that opposition to Chinese rule would continue to be vigorously suppressed. The 1957 retrenchment policy was not a Chinese recognition of the legitimacy of or the need for Tibetan autonomy. Rather, it was simply an attempt to prevent violent revolt and political embarrassment to China.

In his speech, Mao identified one of the contradictions in Chinese society as that between the Han and the minority nationalities. Mao defined this, like the contradiction between the party and the intellectuals, as nonantagonistic, or "within the people," rather than antagonistic, "between the people and their enemies." In other words, he believed that the minority nationalities had fundamentally accepted Chinese rule and their inclusion within the Chinese state. Therefore, as with the intellectuals, he invited criticism to resolve remaining "nonantagonistic" problems. However, the subsequent criticisms from many nationality cadres revealed a fundamental rejection of the legitimacy of Chinese rule over non-Chinese people.

The "Hundred Flowers" liberalization period produced demands from minority nationalities for increased cultural, religious, and political autonomy, for expanded nationality regions, and even for separate nationality-based Communist parties. These demands were credited by the Chinese to the survival of "local nationalism" within the party. This was particularly threatening since it contradicted the ideological and tactical premises of the nationalities policy, which assumed that local nationalism could be defeated by educating minority nationalities' cadres in Marxist-Leninist nationality theory and policy. Education in Marxism-Leninism was intended to reveal the class basis of local nationalism and transfer cadres' loyalty to the Chinese multinational state. Instead, nationality cadres demanded that socialism be built within their own nationalities and cited Marxist-Leninist theory as well as CCP nationalities policy to make their case. These local nationalist phenomena were condemned by the Chinese as a rejection of Chinese culture and Chinese assistance to the nationalities.

The CCP attempted to rectify the troubling criticisms from nationality cadres at a meeting on nationalities policy in August 1957 at Tsingtao, presided over by Zhou and Mao. In a "Report on the Rectification Campaign" delivered at the Tsingtao meeting, Deng Xiaoping, who had been appointed head of the antirightist campaign, stated that some elements, including some of those who had expressed the rightist and reactionary ideology of local nationalism, had been exposed as enemies of the people and had to be repressed. Deng went on to recommend that nationalities should be reminded of the differences between the new society and the old, as well as "the benefits and necessity of national solidarity and unity within the big family of nationalities under the leadership of the Chinese Communist Party." Nationalism should be exposed as a bourgeois ideology "opposed to Marxism-Leninism and Communism." He further recommended that minority nationality schools should stress "class education and education in the Marxist-Leninist position on the nation."[17]

After the Tsingtao conference, a "Socialist Education Movement Opposing Local Nationalism" was launched with the goal of combating local nationalism with education on socialism and patriotism. Because bourgeois nationalism reflected the struggle between socialism and capitalism, some manifestations of local nationalism were characterized as antagonistic contradictions, and local nationalists were accordingly condemned as enemies of the people.[18]

The reason the rise of local nationalism was so threatening to the Chinese state was that it revealed that Marxist-Leninist ideology and the CCP's nationalities policy were not an automatic solution to the national question, as previously thought, but that they had in fact aroused anti-Chinese nationalism among the nationalities. The aim of the party nationalities policy was not to eliminate nationalism but to shift its focus onto the multinational Chinese state. Bourgeois local nationalism was to be transformed into patriotism to the Chinese state, which, by Marxist definition, was not bourgeois or even nationalist because the PRC was a socialist state that had theoretically transcended both the bourgeois stage and nationalism. Local nationalism was condemned by the CCP as contrary to the "inevitable historical merging of nationalities" and the need for unity against foreign imperialism. Local nationalism was infuriating to many Communist cadres, who imagined that their policy was vastly superior in its treatment of minorities compared to that of Chinese governments of the past. Some nationalities had even revealed separatist sentiments and had rejected nationalities' unity and the assistance of the Chinese. The CCP had devoted great efforts to helping the minorities in achieving "democratic reforms" and "socialist transformation," none of which seemed to have been appreciated by the minorities themselves.

Nationality cadres' calls for increased autonomy, including federative status, were rejected with the argument that "historical development" had not provided any conditions for the setting up of federal republics. Demands for increased autonomy, nationality-based Communist parties, or separate national socialist development were rejected because of the impossibility of minority nationalities building socialism without the help of the CCP. Minorities' opposition to Chinese colonization was refuted with similar arguments:

> It must be understood that the question of wanting or not wanting Han cadres and resettlers is, in a large measure, the question of wanting or not wanting socialism and prosperity for the minorities. . . . The opposition to all anti-Chinese tendencies constitutes an important facet of the struggle against local nationalism. In ousting the Chinese, certain people do so under the pretext of the so-called assimilation problem. They describe the efforts exerted by Chinese cadres and people to help the fraternal minorities construct socialism as efforts to "assimilate the minorities." This, of course, is absurd. The gradual fusion of the various nationalities on the basis of equality is the natural law governing social development. . . . We have all along opposed the assimilation of the minorities by force, because that is oppression. But we will never oppose the natural fusion among the nationalities, because this is the progressive trend of historical development.[19]

The phenomenon of local nationalism was accurately identified by the Chinese as a rejection of Chinese culture and Chinese "assistance," and, despite party warnings, it aroused the most chauvinistic and nationalistic reaction among Han cadres. This was apparently true even at the highest level; Mao himself was reportedly offended during the Hundred Flowers by the ingratitude of the minority nationalities. The survival and even exacerbation of anti-Chinese nationalism among minority nationality cadres trained in Marxist-Leninist and CCP nationalities policies exposed the failure of those policies to "solve the national question." The campaign against local nationalism thereafter was effectively unrestrained; many Chinese cadres called for the elimination of the United Front policy, the system of national regional autonomy, the policy of preserving minority nationalities' cultures, and nationalities' freedom of religious belief.

Mao transformed the antirightist campaign that followed the Hundred Flowers into a purge of his enemies both within the CCP and in the society at large. This purge paved the way for the next collectivization campaign, the "Great Leap Forward" of 1958, a campaign that not only furthered China's socialist transformation but, because of the increased political control inherent

in collectivization, also provided another means for the suppression of anti-socialist rightists and local nationalists. The atmosphere of fear already engendered by the antirightist campaign added a new level of coercion to collectivization. Any opposition to collectivization was characterized as rightist, anti-party, and antisocialist.

The Great Leap Forward was designed to collectivize agriculture and to employ the surplus thereby accumulated to industrialize and achieve the transition from socialism to communism. Collectivization and the socialist consciousness that would theoretically follow were presumed capable of producing a "great leap" in agricultural and industrial output; this, of course, was totally contradictory to Marx's fundamental doctrine that economic factors determine consciousness, not the other way around. The Great Leap greatly exacerbated all of the problems in nationality relations already created by the High Tide and the Anti–Local Nationalist campaigns. Nevertheless, Mao's decision not to deny the nationalities the "benefits" of rapid socialist transformation was not altered during the Great Leap Forward. At its height in August 1958, many nationality areas were precipitously communized, without regard to their previous level of "socialist transformation."

The collectivization campaign was also pushed because of the greater degree of party control that collectivization facilitated and, in areas still unsettled by rebellion, as a means of suppression of revolt. Previous restrictions on alteration of traditional minority cultures were loosened during the Great Leap, and nationalities' autonomy was less respected. Because local nationalism had been declared rightist and antisocialist, the preservation of local nationalist cultures and traditions was also denounced as rightist. During the Great Leap, nationalities were pressured to adopt Chinese culture, because Chinese culture was considered equivalent to socialism, and to drop those of their traditions considered to be impediments to socialist development. The CCP declared itself the judge of which aspects of minority nationalities' traditional cultures were innocuous and would be allowed to survive, and which were incompatible with socialism and would therefore be repressed. Religion was declared to be among those nationality customs unfavorable to socialism:

> Since religion is harmful to the socialist construction of the mother country, it will inevitably prove harmful to the progress and development of the minority nationalities. Religion is not a condition for the formation of a nationality, still less is it a condition for the development and advance of a nationality. All national characteristics unfavorable to socialist construction and national progress can and should be reformed.[20]

The Great Leap Forward saw a greater emphasis on class struggle and assimilation in nationality policy, corresponding to the "coming together" element of communist theory on nationality relations at the expense of the "flourishing of nationality culture" aspect of that theory. The CCP justified socialist assimilation as being entirely different from capitalist assimilation. Socialist assimilation was defined as natural and voluntary. As Zhou Enlai said in a speech on nationalities policy in 1958: "Assimilation is a reactionary thing if it means one nation destroying another by force. It is a progressive act if it means natural merger of nations advancing toward prosperity. Assimilation as such has the significance of promoting progress."[21] Assimilation was considered progressive, historically determined, and just, based upon the Marxist doctrine that national identities and national interests were merely misplaced or misconstrued class identity and class interests.

Mao's formula that "the national question is in essence a class question" epitomized this doctrine. This slogan was first formulated by Mao in 1956, and it "began to appear and prevail in the Chinese press in the early 1960s." Its origin is the Marxist-Leninist theory that class interests are more fundamental than nationalism and, specifically, Lenin's class-based definition of *nation*.[22]

In Tibet, where religion remained the primary institutional and ideological obstacle to Chinese socialist ideology, the campaign against religion was intensified. Tibetans of Qinghai and Kham were coerced into denunciations of lamas and religion. Party propaganda claimed that the Tibetan masses had realized the falsity and exploitative nature of religion:

> In this violent class struggle, after a campaign of propaganda and education was deeply carried out and after contrasting the old and new societies, the class consciousness of the vast labouring herdsmen was rapidly promoted. After they perceived the reactionary essence of the feudalistic exploiting class, they were all greatly surprised; and rose up with set teeth to accuse the exploiting class of their heinous crimes; and they voluntarily bound the counterrevolutionary elements and bad elements and handed them over to the government, asking for them to be punished. After stripping off the religious cloak of the counterrevolutionary elements in religious circles, they exposed their fraud; and the masses say: "We shall never permit these man-eating wolves to do evil things while riding on the neck of the people waving religious banners." At the debate meetings, the masses were so excited that they shouted continuously: Long Live Chairman Mao! Long Live the Communist Party! We Are Liberated![23]

The Anti–Local Nationalist campaign and the Great Leap Forward led to an increased pace of democratic reforms and collectivization in eastern Tibet, despite the already open revolt there. Tibetan areas outside the TAR, including pastoral areas, were precipitously communized in August 1958 and were said to have "flown over several ages in the short period of a fortnight, and, singing and dancing, have now reached heaven in one stride, taking them into People's Communes in which are carried the seeds of communism."[24]

Collectivization was undertaken not only despite the revolt but as a means of quelling it. Equivalent to forced detention in a circumscribed area, collectivization was employed to concentrate and control Tibetans and to prevent their contact with the resistance. However, the pursuit of democratic reforms in late 1957 and the initiation of collectivization and communization in 1958 only intensified the unrest in Amdo and Kham.

Tibetan Revolt

The precipitous communization of the summer of 1958 exacerbated the ongoing revolt in Kham and revived it in Amdo. Agricultural areas of Amdo had undergone democratic reforms in 1956, but many nomadic areas did not experience the full impact of Chinese control and reform until the collectivization in 1958.

The policies of the Great Leap Forward transformed the localized revolt in eastern Tibet into a general uprising, which soon spread to the TAR. Tensions continued to mount in the TAR due to the constant influx of refugees from Kham and Amdo carrying tales of Chinese brutality, including the humiliation, arrest, and public execution of lamas and the looting and destruction of monasteries. The 1957 retrenchment policy in the TAR therefore ultimately failed to prevent the spread of the uprising to central Tibet.

By the middle of 1958, despite the efforts of the Lhasa government to dissuade Tibetans from rising in revolt against the Chinese, the rebellion had substantially shifted to central Tibet. The Tibetan resistance, now mostly under the command of the Chushi Gangdruk ("Four Rivers, Six Ranges," a traditional name for Kham), fought a series of running battles with the Chinese over the next nine months, inflicting numerous casualties but always being ultimately overpowered by Chinese superiority in numbers, armament, and mobility. They were also powerless against the Chinese use of aircraft for surveillance and attack.

The situation finally reached a climax with an invitation from the Chinese commander in Lhasa to the Dalai Lama to attend a theater performance in the Chinese military camp on 10 March 1959. The Dalai Lama was instructed to bring none of his attendants or bodyguards, an extraordinary request that led Tibetans to believe that he was to be kidnapped. The Dalai Lama had been invited to attend the Chinese National People's Congress the next month, which he had refused; however, Chinese cadres in Tibet had promised Beijing that he would attend, leading to the suspicion that they hoped to isolate him from his advisers in order to pressure him to attend the NPC or simply to transport him to Beijing against his will.

On 10 March, a crowd of Tibetans surrounded the Norbulingka Palace to prevent the Dalai Lama from leaving to attend the theater. The Dalai Lama announced that he would not attend and, fearing Chinese reprisals against the crowd, requested that the crowd disperse. Instead, they took matters into their own hands, organizing a permanent guard at the Norbulingka and then, in a hastily assembled Mimang Tsongdu convened at the foot of the Potala, declaring Tibet's independence. On 12 March, a rally and assembly of the women of Lhasa demanded the withdrawal of the Chinese from Tibet and the restoration of Tibetan independence. During the following days, most Tibetan government officials declared their support for independence. An official resolution to that effect was passed in a meeting with leaders of the Mimang Tsongdu. The three great Lhasa monasteries, Sera, Drepung, and Ganden, also declared their support for independence.

On the evening of the 17th, the Dalai Lama escaped with the aid of his bodyguard and his closest advisers. The Chinese in Lhasa were unaware of his escape for several days. On 20 March, the Chinese began a bombardment of the Norbulingka and an attack on all the Tibetans' fortified positions in Lhasa. Many thousands were reportedly killed in the process; the streets of Lhasa and the Norbulingka were littered with bodies. Many Tibetans, both active resistance fighters and ordinary villagers, attempted to escape to India, but many were not successful. At Lhuntse Dzong, before crossing the Indian border, the Dalai Lama and his government formally repudiated the Seventeen-Point Agreement and established a temporary government. On 31 March, the Dalai Lama and his party entered India.

The Tibetan Revolt that culminated in Lhasa in March 1959 was only the climax of a process set in motion by the forcible incorporation of Tibet within the Chinese state. The period from the 1951 Seventeen-Point Agreement to the rebellion in 1959 was one of transition for Tibet from a de facto independent state to a part of the People's Republic of China. Many Chinese who were sent to Tibet may have thought that they were truly liberators and would be welcomed as such by Tibetans, but by the end, most knew that their presence was opposed by the majority of Tibetans. Chinese administrators and soldiers in Tibet gradually responded by adopting the typically defensive attitudes of colonialists. While many Chinese in Tibet may have attempted to apply minority nationalities policy conscientiously in the beginning, few did so by the end.

Tibetan nationalism, a previously unfocused or localized ideology among most Tibetans, was aroused by the Chinese invasion of Tibet. However, effective resistance against the Chinese was precluded by the Tibetan government's

earlier acceptance of the terms of the Seventeen-Point Agreement. In addition, the Chinese policies of friendly and respectful treatment of Tibetans in general and the employment of the former ruling class within the United Front were initially very effective. The upper classes were prevented from playing their natural role as leaders of resistance to the Chinese, while the lower classes were cultivated as activists, or, if they attempted to resist, found no support from their traditional leaders. The CCP nationalities policy was effective in creating social divisions and in cultivating collaborators, but was ultimately counterproductive in that it stimulated the very nationalist consciousness it was intended to suppress.

The inevitable upsurge of Tibetan resistance was delayed until the imposition of "democratic reforms" and "socialist transformation," which, for most Tibetans, actually constituted a greater intrusion upon their lives than had the original entry of the Chinese into Tibet. The initiation of "class conflict," which for the Chinese had no nationalist content, was for the Tibetans almost entirely of nationalist significance—a fact that Chinese propaganda was unable to obscure. For most Tibetans, the initiation of democratic reforms produced not an upsurge of class anger against class oppression, but a national uprising against national oppression. The true significance of democratic reforms, as was obvious to all Tibetans, was the replacement of Tibetan leadership and political authority by Chinese colonial rule.

The Chinese reacted to Tibetan opposition and resistance with increasing oppression and brutality. China finally achieved the political integration of Tibet within the Chinese state not by the successful employment of Marxist-Leninist and CCP nationalities theory and policies (except in that deceit was successfully employed), but by a relentless imposition of force and usurpation of political authority in Tibet, which culminated, like it began, in violence. The Tibetan Revolt ultimately refuted China's claim that Tibet constituted an integral part of China or that it was "peacefully liberated."

By 1959, the Chinese were not entirely averse to a final showdown with the Tibetan "government of serf-owners," since they were secure in the knowledge that they had attained a preponderance of force and could not be dislodged from Tibet. The Tibetan Revolt was not without advantage for the Chinese. Mao had previously said that the particular policies applied to Tibet would either be successful in preventing revolt or that "bad elements" would lead a rebellion—but either scenario, he said, "will be favorable to us."[25]

In 1956, Mao had expressed little concern about the possibility that the Dalai Lama might seek exile in India, an attitude that might indicate that Mao considered the Dalai Lama an impediment to Chinese plans for Tibet and would ultimately have to be removed in one way or another. Although the revolt and the exile of the Dalai Lama were an international embarrassment for the Chinese, they were also undoubtedly relieved to finally have a completely free hand in Tibet. However, this does not mean, as has been suggested, that the Chinese purposely allowed the Dalai Lama to escape. In a conversation with Soviet premier Nikita Khrushchev on 3 October 1959, Mao admitted that China was waiting for an opportunity to crush resistance in Tibet: "We could not launch an offensive without a pretext. And this time we had a good excuse and we struck." When Khrushchev charged that letting the Dalai Lama escape was a mistake, Mao said: "We could not keep the Dalai Lama, for the border with India is very extended and he could cross it at any point."[26] In fact, the Dalai Lama did cross at an unusual point, to the east of Bhutan, whereas the usual crossing point is to the west, between Bhutan and Sikkim.

In the final analysis, the Chinese Communist program for Tibet's incorporation differed little from traditional Chinese frontier assimilationist policies. CCP nationalities policy promised to provide the benefits of Chinese socialist culture in exchange for minority nationalities' territories and resources, a bargain calculated to benefit the Chinese, not the people whose territory was incorporated. Modern ideological rationalizations were incapable of disguising this reality. Mao and the Chinese leadership unintentionally exposed their real concerns toward Tibet and other frontier territories by repeatedly expressing the rationale that good treatment of minority nationalities was necessary because their territories and resources were essential for the strategic security and economic development of China. Presumably, once those territories were firmly secured, the rationale for good treatment of minority nationalities would disappear. The 1959 revolt hardened Chinese attitudes toward Tibetans and changed Chinese policy in Tibet from "voluntary" reform to involuntary reform and repression of all resistance.

The Chinese Communists assumed that assimilation, at least within socialist states, was natural and progressive, calling it a "natural merger of nations advancing toward prosperity," a "natural law governing social development," and a "progressive trend of historical development." Both the autonomy promised in the Seventeen-Point Agreement and that of the CCP's national regional autonomy system were considered temporary expedients until Tibetans could be persuaded or coerced into "voluntarily" accepting socialist assimilation. The only permanent autonomy that minorities could expect was in those aspects of their cultures that the Chinese regarded as not being reactionary, opposed to socialism, or conducive to local nationalism. What this meant in practice was that only certain superficial and innocuous aspects of nationality culture, such as singing and dancing, were to be allowed to exist, and even these were to be altered by the substitution of progressive socialist content to replace any reactionary, backward elements. Tibetans could not be allowed any real political autonomy, since it could lead to local nationalism.

The same was the case for economic autonomy, because the CCP insisted on exercising centralized control over the economy.

Notes

1. Dalai Lama, *My Land and My People* (New York: Potala Press, 1983), 93.

2. Mao Zedong, "On the Policies of Our Work in Tibet," in *Selected Works* (Beijing: Foreign Languages Press, 1977), 5:74.

3. Mao Zedong, "Radio Address of Leosha Thuptentarpa to the Religious and Secular Officials of the Tibet Local Government and the Entire Tibetan People," *People's Daily*, 22 November 1952, quoted in *Tibet, 1950–1967*, comp. Ling Nai-Min (Hong Kong: Union Research Institute, 1967), 43.

4. "Statement of the Dalai Lama to the Legal Inquiry Committee at Mussoorie, India," 14 November 1959, in International Commission of Jurists, *Tibet and the Chinese People's Republic: A Report to the International Commission of Jurists by Its Legal Inquiry Committee on Tibet* (Geneva: International Commission of Jurists, 1960), 311.

5. "Tibetan-Inhabited Areas: Demographic Changes," *Beijing Review*, 4 April 1988.

6. The PRC's calculation of the population of what was to become the TAR at that time, derived from a Tibetan government estimate, was only one million (increased to 1.27 million by the "return" to Tibet of the Chamdo district in 1956). China later claimed, in response to the Tibetan government-in-exile's claim that 1.2 million Tibetans had lost their lives due to the Chinese occupation, that this was impossible since there were only one million Tibetans in Tibet.

7. "Text of Agreement on Measures for Peaceful Liberation of Tibet," New China News Agency, 27 May 1951.

8. Chang Chih-I, *The Party and the National Question in China*, trans. George Moseley (Cambridge, MA: MIT Press, 1966), 56.

9. Ibid.

10. Joseph Stalin, *Marxism and the National-Colonial Question* (Moscow: Proletarian Publishers, 1975).

11. Walker Connor, *The National Question in Marxist-Leninist Theory and Strategy* (Princeton, NJ: Princeton University Press, 1984).

12. Zhou Enlai, "Some Questions on Policy towards Nationalities," *Beijing Review*, 3 March 1980 (from an article written in 1958 but not published at that time).

13. Dalai Lama, *My Land*, 133.

14. Chen Yi, "Summary Report of the Central Government Delegation to Tibet," *People's Daily*, 15 September 1956.

15. "Upsurge of Socialism in China's Countryside," *Current Background* [publication of the U.S. Consulate in Hong Kong], no. 388 (February 1956). See also Warren W. Smith Jr., *Tibetan Nation: A History of Tibetan Nationalism and Sino-Tibetan Relations* (Boulder, CO: Westview Press, 1996), 391.

16. Mao Zedong, "On the Correct Handling of Contradictions among the People," in Robert R. Bowie and John K. Fairbank, *Communist China, 1955–1959: Policy Documents and Analysis* (Cambridge, MA: Harvard University Press, 1962), 287.

17. Deng Xiaoping, "Report on the Rectification Campaign," 23 September 1957, in Bowie and Fairbank, *Communist China*, 356.

18. Hsien Fu-min, "Socialist Education Movement Opposing Local Nationalism," March 1958, in Ling, *Tibet*, 271.

19. Wang Feng, "On the Rectification Campaign and Socialist Education among Minorities," New China News Agency, 28 February 1958.

20. "Communists Are Complete Atheists," *Nationalities Unity*, no. 18 (March 1959), in Ling, *Tibet*, 246.

21. Zhou, "Some Questions," 19.

22. "Is the National Question Essentially a Class Question?" *Beijing Review*, 25 August 1980, 17.

23. Liu Tse-hsi, "Herdsmen on the Tsinghai Pastures Advance Bravely with Flying Red Flags," *Nationalities Unity*, no. 11 (6 November 1958), in Ling, *Tibet*, 325.

24. Hsien Chan-ju, "Communization in a Single Stride," *Nationalities Unity*, no. 11 (6 November 1958), in Ling, *Tibet*, 330.

25. Mao, "Our Work in Tibet," 5:74.

26. "Discussion between N. S. Khrushchev and Mao Zedong," Archive of the President of the Russian Federation, *Cold War International History Project: The Cold War in Asia*, http://cwihp.si.edu.

3

Democratic Reforms

T̲HE FLIGHT OF THE D̲ALAI L̲AMA IN M̲ARCH 1959 eliminated the last obstacle to Chinese control in Tibet. The "Tibetan local government" was dissolved by order of the State Council, Zhou Enlai announced on 28 March. The Preparatory Committee for the Tibet Autonomous Region (PCTAR) theoretically became the administration of Tibet, but all actual power was exercised by the People's Liberation Army (PLA) and its Military Control Commissions, which were established in all districts of Tibet except Shigatse, home of the Panchen Lama. The Dalai Lama's position as chairman of the Preparatory Committee was preserved based upon the belief that he was being held under duress in India. In his absence, the Panchen Lama was to be the acting chairman of the committee.

The Chinese claimed that, since the Tibetan government had been dissolved, there was now no longer any need to delay the democratic reforms that the Tibetan serfs had supposedly been demanding. The Chinese emphasized their own patience in implementing reforms. That social reforms would eventually be carried out was said to have been "unequivocally stated in the agreement on measures for the peaceful liberation of Tibet." The CCP claimed that it had "consistently adhered" to the provisions of that agreement and had provided many "fine things, all beneficial to the Tibetan people," such as the United Front and the PCTAR, all initiated only after full consultation with "persons of the upper social strata." Nevertheless, the "clique of reactionaries in Tibet do not want regional autonomy at all. What they are after is the so-called 'independence of Tibet' plotted by the imperialist aggressors for many years." The problem, the Chinese complained, was that some Tibetans had never actually been reconciled to their "peaceful liberation" and had not accepted the socialist road as the "inevitable trend of the development of history and the common desire of the people of all nationalities."[1]

The Chinese maintained that the Tibetans themselves would carry out the democratic reforms, which were the means by which they would finally be liberated from the feudal serf system and become "masters of their own fate." However, the true purpose of democratic reforms was revealed by the fact that repression of the revolt and democratic reforms were carried out simultaneously; in fact, the first priority of democratic reforms was the suppression of rebellion.

The format of reforms was announced at a meeting of the PCTAR in July. Chang Kou-hua, commander of the PLA in Tibet, characterized the rebellion as a bad thing that had changed into a good thing since it allowed the Tibetans to "speed up the period of conducting the democratic reforms so as to march forward on the road of socialism." He announced that the reforms would be carried out in two stages simultaneously: "The first stage will consist of mobilizing the masses, through suppression of the rebellion and the campaign to oppose the rebellion, and the conducting of the 'Three Anti's and Two Reductions' movements. The second stage will be the redistribution of land."[2]

The PCTAR's "Resolution on Carrying Out Democratic Reform in Tibet" reiterated Chinese justifications for dissolving the former Tibetan government and implementing a new political system in Tibet:

> The second Plenary Session of the Preparatory Committee for the Autonomous Region of Tibet fully approves the reports delivered by Panchen Erdeni, Acting Chairman of the Preparatory Committee; Chang Kuo-hua and Ngapo Ngawang-Jigme, Vice-Chairmen of the Preparatory Committee. The session unanimously maintains that the existing social system in Tibet is a reactionary, dark, cruel and barbarous feudal serf system and only by democratic reform can there be emancipation of the people and economic and cultural development in Tibet and thus the building up of the foundations for a prosperous and happy socialist Tibet. The carrying out of democratic reform in Tibet was affirmed in the Agreement on Measures for the Peaceful Liberation of Tibet signed by the Central People's Government and the former Tibetan local government early in 1951. This task could not be realized during the past eight years owing to the many-sided obstruction and sabotage by the former local government and the upper strata reactionary clique in Tibet in an attempt to preserve their feudal rule.
>
> Over the last eight years, the central authorities always adopted an attitude of patient education towards the reactionary clique of the upper strata in Tibet and patiently waited for them to see reason. The reactionary clique, however, not only failed to show any sign of repentance but went to extremes by staging an armed rebellion on March 10, 1959, betraying the motherland and the people and undermining the national unity. The rapid putting down of the armed re-

bellion has brought them shameful defeat and also brought Tibet to a new stage of democratic reform. On the one hand, the dens of the armed rebels have already been destroyed; the reactionary clique of the upper classes has become completely isolated among the people and their traitorous, criminal activities which have brought calamities to the people are bitterly condemned by the people; and the reactionary former Tibetan local government has been dissolved. On the other, the broad masses of the working people are resolutely demanding the carrying out of democratic reform; the patriotic, progressive elements of the upper classes are actively supporting the reform; and local Tibetan cadres have grown up in large numbers. This shows that the conditions are ripe for the realization of democratic reform in Tibet.[3]

The resolution specifies that, in agricultural areas, the lands of the "three kinds of estate holders"—the government, aristocrats, and monasteries, including their agents who took part in the revolt—would be redistributed to the tillers of those lands. For those estate holders who took no part in the revolt, 80 percent of the produce of their lands would go to the tillers, and they could keep 20 percent. The manorial serfs, or "slaves" as the Chinese termed them, were to be liberated. All debts owed by the working people to the three kinds of estate holders were abolished. In pastoral areas, livestock owners who had taken no part in the uprising could keep their animals, while those who had taken part had to give up their animals to other herdsmen. Again, all debts would be forgiven.

The document declared that freedom of religious belief would be protected, as would patriotic and law-abiding temples and monasteries. Historical cultural relics would also be protected. A campaign would be launched in temples and monasteries against rebellion, feudal prerogatives, and exploitation. The policy of buying out would be applied to patriotic and law-abiding temples and monasteries.

Tibetan farmers were gathered for meetings at which land deeds and loan papers were burned. Former serfs were given title to lands—but only temporarily; the same land would soon be confiscated by the state during collectivization. Confiscated personal property was also redistributed. Valuable items became the property of the state; Tibetans report that the Chinese kept the best of everything. The houses of Tibetans who had fled or been arrested were sealed and their contents were carried off. Eventually, all Tibetans except the poorest were required to bring their valuables, including all religious objects, to Chinese offices, where they were confiscated. Many of the people of Lhasa reportedly threw their valuables into the Kyichu River rather than give them up to the Chinese.

Tibetans were told that everything now belonged to "the people," who were to exercise the "people's democratic dictatorship." Tibetans were informed that the Han in Tibet were also "the people" and that Tibetans must support Han "working personnel" who had sacrificed so much for the liberation of Tibet. Furthermore, Tibetans were told that they must help alleviate famine (caused by the Great Leap Forward) in the interior of China. In the words of Thupten Khetsun, who was released from prison in March 1963 and heard the stories of democratic reforms from his family in Lhasa:

> In the Democratic Reform campaign which followed the suppression of the up-rising, not just members of the government, noble houses and monasteries who had participated in the uprising but all those even slightly associated with them had their wealth confiscated, the exceptionally precious riches of many genera-tions, which were stockpiled by the Chinese government's so-called Office of In-dustry and Commerce to be transported back to China. Their furniture, chests, tables, feather pillows, Chinese and antique Tibetan carpets and floor rugs were taken by Chinese government offices for their own use. Superb articles of cloth-ing, the finery once worn by the nobility for state occasions made of old brocades with their own distinguished histories, precious furs, and different grades of broadcloth, and many other exquisite and valuable accoutrements were traded by the Chinese officials among themselves. The three kinds of sacred images (statues, scriptures and stupas) confiscated from the government, nobility and monasteries were stockpiled by the so-called Cultural Relics Preservation Office, and the historic books among them and especially rare, hand-written works were set aside and taken to China, where today they are kept in the so-called Nation-alities Cultural Palace in Beijing. . . . After taking the best of what Tibetans had for themselves, the Chinese government and its officials carried out "Democratic Reform" by distributing useless clothing, worn-out bedding and farm tools and so on among the people, while shaking both sky and earth with propaganda that they were justly re-distributing to the masses the goods which the "three feudal lords" had amassed through their exploitation and oppression of the masses in the past.[4]

Tibetans were divided into "study groups," within which socialist transfor-mation was intended to take place by means of study and mutual criticism. Study groups were employed to propagate the party line from the center and to initiate the myriad political campaigns characteristic of Chinese Commu-nist society. Policies were constantly elaborated or refined and new campaigns initiated, facilitating a continual process of identifying whether individuals were "progressive" or "reactionary." Lack of active participation in the group was considered equivalent to opposition; therefore, even refuge in silence was not available. The requirement within the small groups to inform upon and to criticize others led to conformity to the required political line, at least out-wardly. The study group broke the bonds of trust within traditional groups such as family and peer groups because pressures to reveal any deviation were so intense that even trusted friends and relatives informed on others.

Within study groups, which met after work each day, often until late hours, policies presented via cadres' speeches or newspaper articles were studied and discussed. Personal attitudes were examined by requiring each individual to review his or her life history, especially examining one's background for evidence of having exploited others. These personal histories were then subjected to self-criticism and mutual criticism, with rewards for accusations and punishment for refusing to accuse others. Groups were judged on their ability to create conflict and struggle, upon which transformation was considered to be dependent, a process initiated by activists but in which everyone was required to participate.

Democratic reforms also involved the initiation of class divisions and class struggle. The primary divisions in Tibetan society between the aristocracy and the lower classes were obvious, but differentiations among the lower class were not so apparent. In the absence of other indicators, such as obvious wealth, divisions were made according to percentages of hired labor. The process of class division and class struggle continued by further class divisions within the middle class and through constant campaigns targeting various individuals, institutions, or ideologies. Class conflict, considered essential to socialist transformation, was thus extended to all Tibetans.

> Those identified as reactionaries, exploiters, or opponents of the Chinese regime were subjected to "struggle," or *thamzing*. Thamzing could take place within the study group, or larger meetings could be summoned for more serious or symbolic cases. Thamzing was usually begun by Tibetan activists who accused the subjects of various crimes. The Tibetan audience was required to add their accusations, with the incentive that lack of display of a "revolutionary consciousness" would reveal their own reactionary minds and possibly make them subject to the same process. As one Tibetan relates, the struggle process separated the "reactionary supporters of feudalism" from the "progressive supporters of socialism." "Either you stand for socialism or for feudalism. There is no other way. If you don't participate in thamzing, then you're for feudalism; if you're for socialism then you must pursue criticism until a person confesses. If you're not for socialism then you yourself must have thamzing."[5]

Some Tibetans, especially the young who were easily indoctrinated, the poor who stood to benefit, and the opportunistic of all types, became enthusiastic converts to the Chinese cause. After 1959, political activism in support of the Chinese policies was the most obvious and practically the only route to advancement for Tibetans. Most Tibetans, however, became adept at outward conformity to required political rituals while sublimating and concealing their actual beliefs. Tibetan cadres became particularly adept in the required jargon, often while hiding their true feelings. This produced a situation where not only were Tibetans unable to trust one another but neither could the Chinese trust the loyalty of any Tibetans, even their most ardent collaborators.

As the Chinese Communists Party (CCP) cultivated more Tibetan activists, many from the ranks of the "liberated serfs," it relied less on its United Front policy of cooperation with the former upper class. Therefore, as time went on, more of the upper class were identified as having sympathized with the revolt, as reactionaries or exploiters of the people, or simply as being less than enthusiastic about the new regime. They were then subjected to confiscation of their property, thamzing, and often imprisonment.

Because the religious establishment was identified as one of the "three pillars of feudalism," it was a primary focus of democratic reforms. Most monasteries were assumed to have supported or at least sympathized with the revolt. All monasteries, even those that had not supported the revolt (such as some of those in the Panchen Lama's jurisdiction), had their monk populations drastically reduced by means of forced secularization. Even those large and famous monasteries that continued to exist after the revolt (such as Tashilhunpo, Ganden, Drepung, and Sera) had drastically reduced numbers of monks. Evidence of support for the revolt included any of a monastery's monks supplying the rebels with arms or food, joining the rebels, or fleeing to India after the revolt. Monastic officials and high lamas were often subjected to thamzing by their own monks or local villagers and were sent to prisons or labor camps. Monks were confined in monasteries until their participation in or sympathies with the revolt could be determined. Many, if not most, monks were suspected of disloyalty to the new regime because of their religious affiliation. If nothing else, they were inherently guilty, according to the Chinese definition, of exploitation of the people simply by being monks. Closed monasteries had all of their wealth in religious statues, artworks, and implements confiscated and transported to China. This was justified as a part of the redistribution of wealth of democratic reforms. Religious practice within monasteries and elsewhere was repressed.

American journalist Anna Louise Strong was told in late 1959 that 2,136 monasteries in the Tibet Autonomous Region (TAR) had "joined the revolt," which meant that they would have been subjected to democratic reforms.[6] In his famous 70,000-character petition to the Chinese government in 1962, the Panchen Lama revealed that out of the 2,500 "large, medium and small monasteries" in Tibet—that is, the TAR—before democratic reforms, "only 70 were still functioning, a reduction of more than 97 percent," after the reforms, and that the 110,000 monks and nuns had been reduced by 93 percent to just 7,000.[7] Similar figures were found by a Chinese Academy of Sciences survey in Tibet in the late 1980s. The clerical population of the TAR, estimated in a Chinese census of 1958 at 114,100 (9.5 percent of the total population of the TAR), had dropped to 18,104 (1.4 percent of the population) in 1960. The number of "functioning monasteries and temples" in the TAR dropped from

2,711 in 1958 to 370 in 1960.[8] In Tibetan areas outside the TAR, with a population of Tibetans greater than that within the TAR, the number of monasteries destroyed may be assumed to be comparable.[9]

Dawa Norbu writes that the lamas of Sakya Monastery were accused of "reactionary rebellion to separate Tibet from the Motherland" not because of any direct involvement in the revolt but because they had performed rituals against the "enemies of the faith," the Communist Chinese. The Chinese denied that such rituals had any power to harm them, but nevertheless insisted that the intention to do so, though useless, was a betrayal of the motherland. The remaining lamas and monks were also accused of having allowed the Sakya Lama and some others of Sakya's lamas and aristocrats to escape to India.[10]

Those of the monastic officials, high lamas, and aristocrats who had not escaped were told to report for "study." So naive were they that they reported as ordered, even when some of them might still have been able to flee to India. "Study" turned out to be imprisonment, interrogation, indoctrination, and thamzing, accompanied by starvation rations. The prisoners were told to confess their crimes of exploitation of the people and to inform upon others. To assist them in realizing their crimes of exploitation, they were required to write and rewrite their biographies from an early age of childhood. Since all of the former lamas and aristocrats were found to be guilty of exploitation of the people, they were sent to hard labor in prisons or labor camps.

In Sakya, the houses of those who had escaped were initially sealed, but then they were reopened and their contents redistributed. Petty merchants were required to deposit any cash they had in the new People's Bank, from which, once deposited, it could not be taken out again. The wealth of the richest lamas and aristocrats of Sakya was displayed for the ordinary people to see. The most valuable objects of jewelry and gold and silver were confiscated by the Chinese and later reportedly transported to China. The local people of Sakya received an assortment of the clothes and household implements of those who had fled.

The Chinese themselves kept the best of what was confiscated, leading to discontent among the Tibetans, even among the poor who were supposed to have benefited most from the redistribution. As one expression put it, "The uncles [Chinese] ate all the meat and gave us the bones." To counter this discontent, the Chinese launched a new political campaign with the slogan "A needle is better than a bar of gold," meaning that practical things were more valuable than ornamental things. The Chinese asserted that things made of gold were practically useless and an "imperialist insanity." They said that the precious objects confiscated from the monastery and the aristocracy would be sold and used for the economic development of Tibet.[11]

The remaining Tibetan population of Sakya was subjected to a long process of investigations and interrogations in order to identify exploiters of the people. The worst of those so identified were then subjected to thamzing. Dawa Norbu writes that the charges against the accused would have been dismissed as baseless by any recognized court, but in the People's Court, the accusers were also judge and jury and conviction was therefore automatic. Since the purpose of thamzing was to "imbue the people with proletarian consciousness and disgust for the feudal past, and also to 'de-class' the ex-rulers, it was not thought relevant to check the accuracy of the charges." "Struggle" was defined by Mao as the technique for producing a class catharsis in society, and so thamzing of every imaginable enemy of the regime followed, including any accused of class exploitation, sympathy or association with the revolt, or counterrevolutionary or reactionary sentiments or actions. Even the effigies of those who had escaped to India were subjected to thamzing to help the Sakya Tibetans raise their class consciousness.

Sakya was also subjected to the "Speaking Bitterness" campaign, in which Tibetans were expected to pour out their stories of suffering in the old society. Every misfortune in the past had to be blamed not on the Buddhist concept of *karma* but on the evils of the feudal system. Each family was required to write down its history of suffering in the old society and to recite it in public meetings. Dawa Norbu writes that anyone who did not shed tears and cry aloud was suspect, since the Chinese were thoroughly convinced that, in pre-liberation Tibet, the life of everyone but the feudal lords had been one of continual oppression and suffering. As in the thamzing sessions, if one were exceptionally emotional at these Speaking Bitterness sessions, it could lead to being characterized as revolutionary and progressive, and if insufficiently enthusiastic about participation in the drama, one could be accused by the Chinese or Tibetan cadres of a reactionary attitude. The Sakya Tibetans took advantage of this to turn these sessions into farcical dramas complete with fictional stories, crying, and fainting, all of which the Chinese had to tolerate since this kind of dramatic performance was in accord with their purposes and their expectations.

According to Dawa Norbu, once the people of Sakya were educated about who their former exploiters had been, it was time to split up the common people and divide them into further classes.

> This was the preparation for the ceaseless class struggle in which not only did the poor maliciously criticize the rich but children were forced to criticize their parents and their teachers and friend criticized friend. Our individual characters and identity were to be extinguished in the fire of revolution, and we were to foster, from collective living, new uniform characters whose only object of worship would be an impersonal Motherland, personified by a living deity, Chairman Mao.[12]

Class divisions were made based upon the percentage of hired labor a family employed. If 40 to 50 percent of the family's labor was hired, the family was designated as rich farmers or upper middle class; if 30 to 40 percent hired labor, as lower middle class; and if 30 percent or less, as poor farmers. Only the lowest class was considered to be free of any class exploitation.

The Sakya Tibetans were then organized into mutual aid teams. Chinese and Tibetan cadres demanded that Tibetans sing while they worked to express their joy at being liberated. They were forced to sing even if they didn't feel like it. In addition, the songs had to be sung at the new forced pace at which they were required to work, rather than at the old relaxed pace, and the words were changed to praise the new order rather than the old.

Because of the improvements that were made, particularly in irrigation, and the frenzied pace at which they were required to work, the 1959 harvest was good. But when it was harvested, the Chinese and Tibetan cadres carefully weighed it themselves, allowing Tibetans only a meager ration of 22 pounds of barley per person per month, while taking all the rest in the name of various taxes.[13]

Although nomads were not subjected to the same class divisions, at least at first, they were subjected to the same sort of taxes as the farmers. Animals were confiscated to feed the starving Chinese PLA, and in 1964 the Chinese traded 10,000 sheep confiscated from the nomads for rice from Nepal, all of which was consumed by the Chinese.[14]

The account of a Tibetan monk, Palden Gyatso, from the Gyantse area not too far from Sakya, also illustrates the goals and techniques of democratic reforms.[15] He happened to be in Lhasa at the time of the revolt in 1959 and, along with many other Tibetans, had gone to the Norbulingka. He had been issued an old British rifle to defend Drepung Monastery, where he was visiting, and at one time had been sent to defend the Norbulingka, but otherwise was merely a spectator to the events of the revolt. Palden escaped before Drepung was surrounded by the Chinese and returned to his monastery of Gadong near Gyantse. There he found that no one had even heard of the revolt or the flight of the Dalai Lama to India. His monastery remained peacefully isolated and undisturbed until June 1959, when three Chinese officials came to exchange the old Tibetan money for new Chinese currency. He heard that Gyantse Monastery had been closed and its monks arrested.

Palden thought that his monastery might remain unaffected since it had not participated in or supported the revolt. Gadong was within the domains of the Panchen Lama, who was still on good terms with the Chinese and whose area had been little affected by the revolt. However, in the middle of the summer, he awoke one morning to find the monastery surrounded by PLA troops. All the monks of the small monastery were required to gather in the courtyard, where they were confronted by several Chinese officials. Palden does not say how many monks were there at the time, only that Gadong at one time had had as many as two hundred monks. The senior official addressed the monks and told them that reactionary bandits had betrayed the motherland and kidnapped the Dalai Lama. Gadong Monastery, too, was accused of having "betrayed the unity of the motherland," without specifying in what way except that the monastery had "associated with reactionaries." A list of the monk officials was read out, and these monks were shackled and taken away without any specific charges. Later it was learned that they had been imprisoned. The remaining monks were told that they would have to declare their loyalties, confess their crimes and submit to the will of the masses, and cleanse their minds and learn to identify the real enemies of the people. The monks were then led away at gunpoint and locked in a large room in the monastery.

Over the next month, the monks were subjected to study sessions, at which they were lectured about the "three exploitative classes":

> The word "study" suggests a noble pursuit but in Chinese hands it was demeaned into something quite different. A "study session" involved keeping groups of us in a kind of quarantine and then subjecting us to a barrage of accusation and intimidation. Soldiers patrolled on all sides. . . . I could see that the villagers had been forced into groups out into the fields for study sessions, herded and pinned there like cattle.[16]

The monks were told that the Tibetan people had for centuries lived beneath the weight of three mountains, but had now cast aside these burdens and arrived at a new era in Tibetan history. The exploited classes had overthrown the masters who had lived on their backs, and now sky and earth had changed places.

The monks were bewildered and had no idea what the Chinese official was talking about, so he had to explain that the three classes that had exploited the Tibetan masses were the Tibetan government, the aristocracy, and the monasteries. The monks were still confused, since they didn't know what he meant by "exploited." Their incomprehension was interpreted as obstinacy, and they were told that they had "green brains" and that they should abandon "old thoughts." The monks were told that even within the monastery there were different classes and that they should each declare their class background. They were categorized into three classes: rich monks, middle monks, and poor monks. All monks, they were told, were exploiters, but their crimes varied according to their individual class status. Palden Gyatso writes that the Chinese had expected that, after being confronted with these facts, the monks would spontaneously begin denunciations of the feudal system and one another and arrive at a sudden understanding of the class struggle.

Another monk, Tashi Palden of the Upper Tantric College in Lhasa, who was arrested for participation in the revolt and subjected to forced labor at Nachen Trang, reports a similar process of indoctrination:

> The most favorite question in the beginning was "What is oppression and deception?" It was some time before we discovered the right answer to that question was "The old society." Once everybody had this fact right the next vital question was launched: "How and by whom were you oppressed and deceived in the old society?" A number of people cited examples of oppression and deception. But when the monks' turn came we replied unanimously that we never suffered any oppression or deception because we were earning our living by saying prayers for others and we never had a reason to complain. Our interrogators were very patient. "So you did not suffer in the old society," they noted. "But we are all agreed that the old society was synonymous to oppression and deception. This means that you must have oppressed and deceived others, because it is a fact that everybody who was in the old society has either suffered themselves or has inflicted sufferings on others. So now tell us, one by one, who did you oppress and deceive and how?"[17]

Palden Gyatso relates how at Gadong the Chinese attempted to create divisions between the monks and between the monastery and the outside society. The monks were told that the nearby villagers had denounced the monastery as an exploiter and oppressor of the masses. An elderly monk of a wealthy family was singled out for criticism. His relatively numerous and high-quality belongings were piled in the courtyard for all to see, and he was denounced by the Chinese officials. Sometime later, the local villagers were also brought in to denounce the rich monk and the monastery itself. The villagers marched on the monastery carrying banners in Chinese and Tibetan and chanting "Destroy the three exploiters!" and "Destroy the reactionaries!" The villagers pretended to be shocked at the display of the rich monk's possessions. The monk himself was already under arrest.

The rest of the year was spent in endless meetings and "study sessions."

> There were denunciation meetings, confessional meetings, meetings to criticize reactionaries, meetings to oppose imperialists and even meetings known as "bitter memory" meetings in which we would sit while a "serf" told stories about his suffering at the hands of landlords. We were expected to cry during such meetings.[18]

These meetings ended only in November when, Palden thinks, it was too cold for the Chinese to continue. At the end, those monks who remained in the monastery were lined up and issued a paper with writing in Chinese that none of them understood. They were told that this paper was very important and that they must have it with them at all times. Later, he found that these papers gave each individual's name, age, class status, and political background. Palden was categorized as "son of a rich landlord." He subsequently learned that class status determined everything, including access to education and employment, and that his status meant that he had no future in the new proletarian society. His political background was listed as "not yet investigated." This meant that his loyalty to the new regime was suspect.

Investigations at Gadong continued at the beginning of 1960, led by a new team of more strict Chinese officials after it was determined that the previous team had been too lenient. The new group accused the monks of supporting reactionary bandits and clinging to outdated feudal ways. A particularly ominous development for Palden Gyatso was that they began asking if any of the monks had been in Lhasa at the time of the revolt. They also searched all the monks' rooms and belongings, during which they discovered a photograph of Palden's teacher, Gyen Rigzin Tenpa, who was of Indian origin, in India with Indian political leaders, including Mahatma Gandhi and Jawaharlal Nehru. Gyen had been sent by the Tibetan government to India after World War II as part of a delegation to establish Tibetan relations with India's political leaders prior to Indian independence. However, the Chinese interpreted this as evidence that Gyen was an Indian spy. Gyen had demanded the right of repatriation to India but was arrested by the Chinese. Palden was implicated as his student.

Palden now found himself the subject of intensified interrogation. He was accused of concealing both his presence in Lhasa and his association with an Indian spy. Palden explained that his teacher had no interest in politics and was not a spy, but the Chinese insisted that he was and that Palden must confess to his association with him. He was told of the party's policy of leniency for those who confessed their crimes and severe repression for those who didn't. Palden was later to understand that, for the Chinese Communists, being accused of a crime was the same as being guilty of it; therefore, the only option was to confess, without any regard to whether the charge was true or not. However, he refused to confess to an obvious falsehood and was then beaten and tortured.

Palden was interrogated repeatedly over the next days and weeks, accompanied by repeated beatings, always with the demand that he confess. He still refused to do so. He was required to give his life history. Palden says that almost all the monks, and many outside as well, were repeatedly subjected to this type of investigation. These life histories were written down in Chinese, and then the Chinese cadres compared each person's story with previous versions and with those of others in an attempt to get people to implicate each other or to discover inconsistencies in their accounts. Palden's interrogation went on until the summer of 1960, when he along with several of the monastery's monks who had also been undergoing such interrogations were transferred to another nearby monastery that now functioned as a prison.

At the prison, the interrogations continued. Palden was required to retell his life story, with the Chinese cadres still looking for inconsistencies. He was again told the party's policy of leniency for confession and was required to name all those with whom he had associated in Lhasa. It was then that he realized anyone he named would come under the suspicion of the Chinese. The Chinese were particularly interested in who had organized the demonstrations in Lhasa and with whom they were connected. His interrogator demanded that Palden denounce his teacher as a spy, and when he refused, he was again beaten.

Only later did Palden come to understand the significance of confession for the Chinese Communists. Anyone arrested had to confess, without regard to truth or falsity, because the party had to be shown to be always correct. He realized that confession was not about guilt or innocence but about enforcing the power of the party over the lives of the people. The people had to submit to the power of the CCP, no matter what the party said or did. The Communists often did not even reveal why a person had been arrested. Detainees were simply required to confess their crimes, and if they could think of no crimes they had committed, they were retained and interrogated until they could think of some way in which they had oppressed the people or opposed the party. Tibetans were required to denounce others in order to satisfy the requirement to confess, and in this way a widening circle of people was implicated. For the Chinese, the significance was not the guilt or innocence of these people—all were probably guilty of opposing the Chinese in some way—rather, it was that all should bow to the all-encompassing power of the party.

After several months of investigation, Palden Gyatso was sentenced to seven years in prison for participation in the revolt in Lhasa. He never confessed to the false accusation that his teacher was a spy. Even after his sentencing, the interrogations went on, since in the Chinese system the emphasis was on rejection of the old society and acceptance of the new.

Palden's experience was typical of that of many Tibetans during democratic reforms. It was also typical of virtually every Communist regime worldwide.[19] Communist regimes have been characterized by massive repression of their enemies, whether real or imagined. The existence of the enemies of the revolution, both domestic and foreign, served to justify the extreme repressive measures of Communist society. The opposition and sabotage of the enemy was used to justify violence and terror as tools of repression and as an excuse for all the mistakes and failures of the Communist leaders. Communist administrations commonly resorted to the manufacture of enemies, often from their own ranks, who were then purged in public trials in order to educate the masses. In Tibet, the purge of the Panchen Lama was to serve this purpose.

Usually, Communist governments had no lack of enemies, since the popular support communist ideologues expected was rarely manifested. These regimes tended to blame this lack of the anticipated popular support on the constant regeneration of capitalism and class enemies, but also on foreign enemies, since there was a need to explain domestic opposition to what was supposed to be the perfect political system. Those arrested for political crimes were therefore harangued to name both their domestic collaborators and their foreign instigators. Torture techniques ensured that no one could resist confessing their "crimes" and identifying their conspirators, thus forever expanding the regime's list of enemies. The party and its leaders felt empowered to exercise this degree of totalitarian power because of the belief that their legitimacy derived from the immutable laws of history as discovered by Karl Marx. The creation of the utopian socialist society of the future justified any means necessary to achieve it. The future of mankind took precedence over the fate of individual man; therefore, any means were justified against the enemies of the revolution.

The totalitarian nature of Communist regimes led to the attempt to politicize all aspects of life. Because political meaning was attached to everything, political deviance was defined very broadly, and vast numbers of people were subject to persecution. Loyalty was constantly tested, perhaps because of such regimes' inherent illegitimacy. One of the surest means to demonstrate loyalty was by informing on others. Citizens were under enormous pressure to denounce others, especially if their own loyalty was in question. Because the Communists saw enemies everywhere, preventative measures were taken proactively to repress opponents among groups thought to have even the potential for opposition. In Tibet, as in other countries, the religious community was an obvious target. Communist officials often arrested people on vague suspicion of such potential for opposition, or simply to make an example for others. Interrogation and torture were employed to discover the predictable guilt of those arrested and their accomplices.

Since the reputation of the regime was at stake and Communist regimes, as representatives of the infallible laws of history, could not make mistakes, those arrested had to be proven guilty, by their own confession, with little regard to objective facts. Those arrested in Communist countries found that they were subjected to relentless pressure to confess and that their interrogation and torture would not end until they did so. They were informed of the party's policy of leniency for confession and repression for resistance. Usually, those arrested were not informed of any charges against them. Instead, the interrogator would say that the authorities knew all about the person's crimes but they wanted the criminal to realize his own guilt. Torture was usually employed to accelerate the process. Personal histories had to be written and rewritten until a person realized his crime, and in the process, implicated others. Only after confession was a sentence announced, and even after sentencing, prisoners found themselves subject to education and reformation to repent of their crimes and accept the authority of the Communist Party. This was especially prevalent in China, where thought reform was an essential part of imprisonment.

Communist administrations were characterized by cults of personality, despite the obvious fallibility of the Communist regimes and their leaders. This is perhaps due to the quasi-religious nature of communism, which demands the eradication of true religion, substituting instead worship of the party and its supreme leader. Communist regimes were also characterized by continual tests of loyalty, perhaps because of the fear of enemies but also due to an underlying sense of illegitimacy. Such loyalty tests included individual interrogations and mass rallies, such as the mass thamzings in Tibet, at which the masses were expected to demonstrate their loyalty to the party and condemn its enemies. Such obeisance to the party cult and its leaders served to debase the people and enforce their obedience. All Communists dehumanized their opponents by means of propaganda campaigns against enemies or classes of enemies, but China was distinguished by its public shaming and humiliation of those designated as enemies.

The democratic reforms campaign in Tibet was intended to establish the total dominance of the Communist Party over every aspect of Tibetans' lives. It was also intended to establish China's complete control over Tibet. Tibetans opposed the CCP as much because it was Chinese as because it was Communist. Persecution of Tibetans during the democratic reforms had an undeniably ethnic and nationalist component. Once the Chinese learned that they were regarded not as liberators but as colonialists, they tended to suspect that many, perhaps most, Tibetans were opponents of the new regime. Communist investigation and interrogation methods also inevitably increased the number of suspects because of the requirement that persons prove their loyalty by denouncing others. The Communist need for enemies to blame for failures led to a constant reexamination of loyalty and discovery of new enemies.

Thus, at the end of democratic reforms, only those Tibetans of the lowest-class backgrounds whose records had been declared clean had not been persecuted by the regime. Therefore, not only did democratic reforms not produce a spontaneous democratic revolution by Tibetans in overturning the old society and creating the new, but Tibetans felt newly oppressed by a totalitarian Chinese regime. Most Tibetans were resentful of the political repression of Tibetans by the alien Chinese who had come uninvited to Tibet purportedly to liberate Tibetans from themselves. Palden Gyatso writes that Tibetans referred to the democratic reforms as "the time the Chinese showed their true face."[20] Tibetans also described the democratic reform process as being akin to the Turkic and Mongol torture technique of using a wet leather helmet that crushed the skull as it dried.

When Serfs Stood Up in Tibet

When Serfs Stood Up in Tibet was written by Anna Louise Strong based on her trip to Lhasa in late 1959. Although describing herself as an American journalist, Strong was a proponent of the Chinese Communists from the earliest years, writing her first book about the revolution in China, *China's Millions*, in 1927. This was followed by *One-Fifth of Mankind* in 1939, an account of the CCP's United Front policy with the Kuomintang against the Japanese. In 1949, she wrote *The Chinese Conquer China*, an eyewitness account of Mao Zedong and other Chinese Communist leaders at Yenan. Strong took up permanent residence in the People's Republic of China in 1958 and wrote *Rise of the Chinese People's Communes* in 1959.

After the 1959 revolt in Tibet, Strong wrote *Tibetan Interviews*, the result of interviews with Tibetans in Beijing, which is described as "dealing with the exploitation and misery of the Tibetan people and their aspirations and struggles."[21] In Beijing, she interviewed several Tibetans, including the Panchen Lama, then acting chairman of the PCTAR in the absence of the Dalai Lama; Ngawang Jigme Ngapo; Sherab Gyatso, chairman of the Chinese Buddhist Association; Chang Ching-wu, Beijing's representative in Tibet; a Captain Yang, who had entered Tibet in 1950 and been stationed there ever since; and two "runaway serfs" then at the National Minorities Institute. She also recounts her visit to a traveling exhibition about the revolts that had taken place in eastern Tibet before 1959, in which were displayed weapons air-dropped to the rebels by Chiang Kai-shek and the Americans, as well as instruments of torture allegedly used by the serf-owners against the serfs of eastern Tibet. This exhibition was apparently the first of a series that the Chinese used to justify their liberation of the Tibetans.

Strong began *Tibetan Interviews* with an overview of the Tibetan situation that does not deviate in any way from the Chinese account. In particular, Strong accepted the Chinese Communists' class version of Tibetan history, in which Tibet had always been ruled by China and the only issue of Tibet was the liberation of the Tibetan serfs from the feudal serf system. Strong was adamant that China had not invaded Tibet in 1950, based upon China's contention that the Chamdo region was not part of Tibetan territory at that time.

She accepted that Tibet had willingly entered into the Seventeen-Point Agreement of 1951, after which the PLA entered Tibet; that the autonomy guaranteed to Tibet in that document was sincere; and that Beijing had adhered scrupulously to the terms of the agreement while the Tibetan "local government" did not.

The former serfs Strong interviewed were from the Chamdo area. They had run away from their masters when the PLA entered the area and had been surprised at the good treatment they and other serfs received at the hands of the PLA soldiers. Both had been sent to the Minority Nationalities Institute in Beijing, and now they, along with some fifteen hundred other Tibetans, were to be sent back to Tibet to participate in the reform. These included eleven hundred from the minority nationality school near Xian, four hundred from the Chengdu institute, and 53 from the institute in Beijing.

Strong's interview with Ngapo was taken up with his denunciations of the Dalai Lama's recent statement from his refuge in India. Ngapo maintained that the document was a forgery by the Indians, since the Dalai Lama's condemnation of Chinese policies in Tibet from 1950 to 1959 did not accord with Ngapo's personal experience with the Dalai Lama during that time. He maintained that the Dalai Lama was loyal to China and had not expressed any such opinions. However, Ngapo was speaking under restraint to Strong, as undoubtedly was the Dalai Lama to Ngapo before the revolt. The Dalai Lama knew that Ngapo reported to the Chinese in Lhasa. In her account of the interview with Ngapo, Strong had to explain some inconvenient facts, such as why Ngapo had been sent as governor to Chamdo when, according to the Chinese, Chamdo was not even in Tibet. Ngapo claimed that no Buddhist temples or monasteries had been damaged in the "Tibet area" up to 1959, which pointedly excluded all of eastern Tibet.

Sherab Gyatso, a Tibetan lama from Amdo who had gone over to the Communists, echoed Ngapo's contention that the Dalai Lama's statement made in India was a fake. Sherab was one of those Tibetans, like Bapa Phuntsok Wangyal, who had read Marxist literature on minority nationalities policies and believed in the Communists' policies until reality demonstrated otherwise. Sherab extolled the CCP's donations to the preservation of numerous Buddhist temples in China and Tibet, saying that even the patronage of the famous Indian king Asoka could not compare to that of the CCP. He also told Strong that the Dalai and Panchen Lamas were equals, the difference in status being due only to which was older and therefore the tutor of the other at any time. Unfortunately for Sherab and his belief in the beneficence of the CCP toward Tibetans and the Buddhist religion, he was subsequently persecuted during the Cultural Revolution as a "reactionary" and "local nationalist," resulting in his death.

Strong then describes "Uprisings in Szechuan, Chinghai, and Kansu," an exhibition that was traveling from city to city and was "awakening the Chinese people to what serfdom meant in Tibet." The CCP had blamed the pre-1959 Tibetan revolts in Sichuan, Qinghai, and Gansu on instigation from the Tibetan government in Lhasa, specifically on certain ministers of that government who were accused of having fomented revolt in that area when they returned to Tibet after the National People's Congress (NPC) meetings in Beijing in 1954–1955. A theme of the exhibition was that these revolts were instigated by Lhasa and supported by the Americans and the Chinese nationalists with airdrops of men and weapons. The displays included documents related to the Tibetans' attempts to organize resistance to the Chinese as well as some of the weapons of foreign origin captured by the PLA.

The Uprisings exhibition comprised three rooms, each with a different theme. The first, "Before the Social Reform," was filled with torture instruments supposedly used in monasteries and by feudal lords. There were descriptions of "eighteen types of torture," including methods more imaginary than known from Tibetan history. The worst of the exhibits were the actual skins of people, mostly children, supposedly skinned alive because they were suspected to be some sort of demons. The second room was titled "Armed Rebellion under Cloak of Religion" and included appeals to Tibetans to resist the Chinese for the sake of defending Tibetan religion. Also included were U.S. military items such as parachutes and radio equipment, reputedly dropped to the rebels by planes from Taiwan. The third room, "The Rebellion Suppressed," contained photographs of Tibetans joyously celebrating democratic reforms, accusing former oppressors of their crimes, and demanding the organization of communes. The prosperity of some communes that had already been set up was also displayed.

Strong interviewed a PLA officer, Captain Yang, about the Lhasa revolt. Yang had entered Tibet, or at least the Chamdo area, in 1950, and he asserted that the PLA had not entered Tibet—what China defined as Tibet—until after the signing of the Seventeen-Point Agreement and its approval by the Dalai Lama. He said that the PLA adhered to scrupulous respect for Tibetan customs and that the Tibetan people had welcomed them, especially since they paid for all their supplies and transportation. Yang claimed that most Tibetans, even in Lhasa, were friendly, but that it was obvious that some of the upper-class serf-owners were hostile. It was these people, he said, that fomented the revolt with support from India, Taiwan, and the United States.

Yang emphasized that the PLA had been very restrained in response to the demonstrations that led to the revolt in Lhasa—to the consternation of many Tibetans, he claimed, who wanted the PLA to put down the revolt more quickly. Numerous Tibetans helped the PLA round up rebels after the revolt, Yang said.

The rebels were accused by Yang and other PLA officers Strong interviewed of many atrocities against Tibetans, particularly rape, which alienated them from most Tibetans. Rape is a common charge made by the Chinese against the Tibetan rebels, although this appears to be an organized propaganda theme to counter the rebels' claim to be defenders of Buddhism. Captain Yang portrayed the PLA as being primarily occupied with relief work with poor Tibetans, especially those abused by the rebels, rather than with suppression of the revolt and arrest of those involved.

Strong also interviewed the Panchen Lama, who was in Beijing for the NPC meeting as the acting chairman of the Preparatory Committee. She assumed that his new position meant that he was actually the head of the "local government" in Tibet and that the coming reforms would be implemented under his direction, which was hardly the reality. Strong tried to rationalize the Panchen Lama's new role by claiming that he and the Dalai Lama were actually equals and that the Panchen Lama had often been more prominent in the past due to the failure of several Dalai Lamas to reach maturity. In the interview, the Panchen Lama denied that either he or his territory had ever been under the authority of Lhasa. Strong quoted the Panchen Lama as being confident that religion and monasteries would be protected: "Since the present Chinese government gives religious freedom and even compensates monasteries for losses suffered in the democratic changes, one need not fear."

Strong ends *Tibetan Interviews* with a description of postrevolt events in Lhasa. Writing in Beijing, she describes a supposedly spontaneous rally of twenty thousand Tibetans in Lhasa, "the biggest Lhasa had ever seen," to celebrate the suppression of the uprising. She describes the PCTAR, now "Tibet's local government, its membership 95 percent Tibetan," as being in actual control of the government in Tibet. For these descriptions, Strong relied on the reports of Xinhua and other Chinese sources, which were sending stories from Tibet about the enthusiastic suppression of the revolt; the Tibetan people's assistance to the PLA in rounding up the rebels and the voluntary surrender of others who had been duped by the serf-owners; the PLA's welfare activities for those abused by the rebels, especially the women they had raped; the organization of schools previously repressed by the serf-owners; the sufferings of the now liberated serfs; and the Tibetans' demands for immediate democratic reforms and socialist transformation.

After sufficiently ingratiating herself with the Chinese Communist leaders, particularly with *Tibetan Interviews*, Strong was allowed, despite her advanced age of 74, to join the first group of international journalists, all from Marxist political parties or Communist countries, to travel to Tibet after the revolt. The group of nineteen journalists went to Tibet in August 1959, only five months after the revolt. Strong was accompanied by her own Chinese interpreter and assistant. Upon arrival in Lhasa, the group of Communist journalists was greeted by their Tibetan hosts with the words: "A million serfs have stood up. They are burying the old serfdom and are building a new Tibet. This land frozen for centuries has come to life and its people have taken their destiny in their own hands."[22] This and all the other statements by Tibetans, filtered through their Chinese and Tibetan interpreters, were taken by Strong, and presumably by the other journalists, as the accurate, uncoerced, untutored, and sincere opinion of all Tibetans.

In their first briefing in Lhasa, the journalists were given a litany of propaganda presented as fact: Tibet had been an integral part of China for seven hundred years, as was accepted by all Chinese and by almost all Tibetans. The Dalai and Panchen Lamas were equal in Tibet, and all their titles and positions had come by appointment of the Chinese emperors. Four of the six Tibetan government *kalons*, 70 percent of the 642 noble families, and 2,136 monasteries had joined the revolt. The Tibetan rebels had abused the Tibetan people in a variety of colorful ways and were therefore hated by the people; many Tibetans who wanted to attack the rebels had to be restrained by the Chinese. The PLA was greatly assisted by many Tibetans in repression of the rebellion. The lack of support to the rebels was evidence that the Tibetan Revolt was not about nationalism or religion but was simply the serf-owners' attempt to preserve their feudal privileges. After the revolt, the Tibetan people helped the PLA to round up the remnant rebels, all of whom had abused the people terribly—in contrast to the PLA soldiers, who acted with benevolence and restraint. After the revolt, the PLA and Chinese cadres had been besieged by appeals from the serfs for democratic reforms, and when these were announced, the people of Lhasa sang and danced in the streets. Because the PLA patiently waited before repressing the rebellion until Tibetans could see that the rebels were agents of the landlords, the Tibetan people did not see the revolt as a conflict between China and Tibet but as a struggle of the Tibetan people against feudalism. As Strong wrote, "The people, without conflict of loyalties, could realize how deeply they hated those old torments and how now they could be free."

Throughout her visit to Lhasa, every Tibetan Strong was allowed to meet told her of their sufferings of the past and their unbounded happiness at the prospects for the future. No doubt many of those she met had actually suffered, although even Strong was suspicious that many of the tales seemed to have been repeatedly told and suitably elaborated. Nevertheless, she believed that she had obtained a true picture of reality in Tibet, despite the fact that she met no one who had supported the revolt nor even a single Tibetan who had any complaints about the situation at all. She did not question the truthfulness of any of the Tibetans who told her their stories or the accuracy of the translations of her Chinese and Tibetan interpreters. Perhaps because of her own need to believe that a new reality was being created in Tibet, she made no effort to ascertain if there were any alternatives to the reality being presented to her.

Strong was told that some of those who had participated in the revolt, having "expressed a desire to work for the Tibetan people," were working at the site of the hydroelectric power plant construction project east of Lhasa at Nachen Trang. Although this site was only a few miles outside Lhasa and their group visited a manor site nearby, apparently neither she nor any of the journalists asked to see for themselves how the captured rebels were treated. Strong was told that about a thousand captured rebels were working there, "not even under guard but organizing their own supervision. They got a small sum of pocket money besides their food, and from time to time, a group was released." Strong wrote, "The awakening of human beings from bondage to freedom has happened often before in human society. Usually it has been in bloody uprising at heavy human cost. Seldom has it been done with such careful social engineering as today in Tibet."

Tibetans who were there tell a considerably different story about Nachen Trang: There were tens of thousands of Tibetans working at Nachen Trang, male and female, and it was surrounded by barbed wire fence interspersed with guard towers manned by Chinese soldiers. Tibetan prisoners were tormented by harangues from Chinese officials. The prisoners were told that they had exploited the masses for generation after generation and were guilty of opposing the state and the masses by participating in the uprising. However, in accordance with the correct policy of the party, they would be given the opportunity to become new people through labor reform. They were forced to endure political education after their lengthy workdays. At work, they were made to sing songs like "Socialism Is Great, Socialism Is Good" and to engage in competition between work teams that led to exhaustion, death, and suicide. The work was very dangerous; many prisoners were killed by rockfalls and landslides. Prisoners who failed to meet their quota of a certain number of baskets of rock rubble per day were subjected to thamzing.

What Strong thought was a positive aspect of Nachen Trang, the system of self-supervision by Tibetans, was in fact one of the most oppressive aspects of the Chinese Communist regime, under which Tibetans were made to spy and inform on each other, and each was made responsible for the behavior of others. What Strong imagined was careful social engineering was confirmed by one Tibetan prisoner, but with a different purpose, as a "Chinese plot to break the spirit of the Tibetan people by enslaving them under the pretext of reform through labor."[23]

Strong and the other journalists attended the thamzing of Lhalu, one of the large landowners near Lhasa and the governor of Chamdo until shortly before

the Chinese invasion. The foreigners were told by a Chinese official that
Lhalu's struggle was intended to be a cathartic experience for the Tibetans attending:

> This meeting is not primarily to condemn Lhalu but to teach his former serfs
> that they are now the masters and need not fear their former lord. It is a first step
> towards organizing democratic self-government. The serfs must learn to speak
> out, to expose their injuries, to find the cause of their long misery not in some
> karma from a past incarnation as they were always told, but in the evil system of
> serfdom which must be destroyed.

Lhalu was condemned for a variety of abuses by some of his former serfs,
from which Strong was able to gain some understanding of the feudal system:
"It was clear that, even under serfdom, there were supposed to be limits to exploitation, enforced by custom. It was equally clear that when a master chose
to demand more from the serf than was his due by custom, there was nothing
the serf could do but obey." Strong and the other journalists were exposed to
an endless litany of the serf-owners' abuses that gave the impression that all
serf-owners had been horribly abusive. However, even Strong had some
doubts about the value of the accusations, saying that it was unclear in many
cases if the serfs were directing their accusations against Lhalu or his steward,
that there was no attempt to check the accuracy of the accusations, that some
of the accusations seemed to be dramatized for effect, and that it was possible
that some of those making the accusations may have been hoping for some reward from the Chinese. After Lhalu's struggle, all the serfs' land deeds and debt
papers were burned, as was typical at many such events during democratic reforms.

The group of journalists also visited the Potala Palace, where they were
shown that the PLA had not destroyed anything or looted the Dalai Lama's
treasury after the revolt. They also went to Drepung, where they were told
that, of the previous total of 5,687 monks, there were now only 2,800, the reduction being due to that number having taken part in the revolt and subsequently having fled or been arrested. They were shown an exhibition organized at Drepung, presumably for the education of the remaining monks. The
exhibits consisted of the arms and ammunition that had been discovered at
Drepung; a display of the means by which the monastery had exploited its
serfs; another about freedom of religion, which maintained that most monks
had been involuntarily enrolled in Tibet's monasteries; a demonstration of the
"crimes of the monastery," in which were displayed skull cups and thigh-bone
trumpets that, they were told, had been taken from living victims; and instruments of torture used by the lamas on monks and serfs. An account of a tax-
gathering trip by higher lamas included mass extortion and rape.

At Drepung, the journalists witnessed another thamzing, this time of a "living Buddha," or *tulku*, who was accused of persuading many of Drepung's monks to take part in the uprising. His monk accusers said that he was guilty of sin for persuading others to fight, for forcing lower monks to take up arms against the lawful government, and even for giving them charms that had proven ineffective. He was also accused of having predicted that the PLA would be defeated, which presumably demonstrated his lack of ability to predict the future. Strong was told that the lama being struggled was far from the worst of the lot; others had been guilty of raping monks and women who came to the monastery, and even all of the women of surrounding areas. Young monks were said to have been in special demand by the upper lamas as sexual objects, and fights between lamas and even killings were said to have been common "over the possession of handsome boys." Strong admits that there was "no way of checking such stories, nor did we try to. The mere repetition of such accusations . . . testified to a 'way of life' in Drepung, if not to the precise incidents."

The foreign visitors were given a briefing by Chinese officials of the Religious Affairs Committee that revealed the process by which Tibet's monasteries were emptied during the democratic reforms. The officials said that the PLA did not try to control or reform all monasteries. They had "picked the ten biggest rebel monasteries, put them under control and helped their lower lamas organize. . . . We try to make them examples of what a democratic law-abiding monastery should be." The Chinese officials themselves, as well as the monks, had learned from this process the extent to which the monasteries had exploited the people: "We also learned through this how deeply the Tibetan people hate the monasteries. Drepung has committed so many crimes in the past that there is a wide demand in Tibet to abolish Drepung entirely." This demand had been resisted by the Chinese, who had decided to preserve Drepung and other monasteries as historic monuments, the ultimate fate of which would be decided by the Tibetan people. The Chinese officials were careful to claim that no monasteries had been destroyed and none had been looted of their relics or treasure. They explained that they had not forced any monks to leave the monasteries; on the contrary, they had tried to persuade them to stay, at least temporarily, due to the difficulty of quickly absorbing so many of them into secular society. They said that the monks' desire to leave the monasteries at that time was strong because the reputation of the monasteries was very low due to the extent of the crimes and exploitation that had been revealed.

Strong also visited a harvest festival at a village near Lhasa, which took place at the end of the first phase of democratic reforms, at which land deeds and debt papers were burned. She saw Tibetans parading through the fields with portraits of Mao and Liu Shao-chi, who, she was told, had been chosen by the Tibetans to replace the gods to whom they were used to praying at harvest time. While celebrating the harvest, they sang songs such as this one:

> The Dalai Lama's sun. Shone on the lords.
> Chairman Mao's sun. Shines on the people!
> Now the lords' sun sets. And our sun rises!

Anna Louise Strong left Tibet with the firm conviction that a new era of freedom and prosperity had dawned for the Tibetan people. What Strong saw in Tibet was composed in part of Tibetan reality, no doubt, but also of considerable portions of Chinese propaganda and her own delusions. In all likelihood, some of the Tibetans whose words were interpreted for her had actually suffered abuses as serfs, while others were undoubtedly convinced by Chinese Communist ideology and still others were opportunists who were attracted by the promise of personal rewards. Nevertheless, Strong was readily willing to believe that abuses of serfs by landlords and of monks by lamas were typical rather than aberrant. She was predisposed to find that the new world predicted by socialist doctrine was not only possible but was actually happening in Tibet. Strong was, like the Chinese, willing to portray reality as it should be, rather than as it was. She acknowledged no issue of the legitimacy of Chinese rule over non-Chinese people, believing the Chinese assertion that the result of the revolt in Tibet and democratic reforms was that Tibetans would rule themselves. She accepted without question the Chinese claim that Tibetan feudalism had been a malignant evil from which Tibetans were forever grateful to have been liberated.

The Panchen Lama's 70,000-Character Petition

In May 1962, the Panchen Lama, then acting chairman of the PCTAR, the ostensible government of the TAR, submitted a personal petition to Zhou Enlai, the premier of the PRC, expressing concerns about the results of the suppression of the revolt and the introduction of democratic reforms. The document became known as the Panchen Lama's 70,000-Character Petition because, although written in Tibetan, it was of that length in its Chinese translation. Its full title is "A Report on the Sufferings of the Masses in Tibet and Other Tibetan Regions and Suggestions for Future Work to the Central Authorities through the Respected Premier Zhou." The Panchen Lama's petition was couched in the most respectful language, and it extolled the CCP leaders' correct policies in Tibet. The Panchen Lama wrote that he wished only to point out some mistakes by lower-level cadres that had led to deleterious results for

Tibet and Tibetans. He expressed his confidence that such mistakes would be corrected. In his report, he was careful to praise the doctrines and policies of the CCP and adhere to the party line that class struggle rather than national conflict was the source of the revolt in Tibet. However, he emphasized that Tibetan Buddhism and Tibetan national identity were threatened and the loyalty of Tibetans to the Chinese government was at stake.

The Panchen Lama's petition is the most significant document on the period after the March 1959 revolt and one of the most important documents in modern Tibetan history. It reveals much about Chinese policies in Tibet at that time. For many years, its contents and significance were only rumored, since the actual document was not revealed to the outside world. The text of the Panchen Lama's petition was finally disclosed in 1996, when it was anonymously delivered to the office of the Tibet Information Network in London.

The petition proved to be as significant as rumored. The Panchen Lama was unique in that he was educated in both Marxist and Buddhist ideologies. He, perhaps better than any other Tibetan, understood the ideological goals and actual results of Chinese policies in Tibet. No other Tibetan was able to understand or to describe in such detail the aftermath of the revolt and the implementation of democratic reforms. The period after the revolt was the time when Tibetan life was most radically changed and when the Chinese assumed full control over Tibet and proceeded to radically alter the fundamental nature of Tibetan society. The Chinese themselves regard this period as the most significant in the modern history of Tibet, when Tibetans were finally truly liberated and achieved their own democratic revolution.

The Panchen Lama was not entirely naive in his hope that his petition would be well received. He had previously expressed criticisms to some of the CCP's Nationalities Affairs officials and even directly to Zhou about excesses in the repression of the revolt and the implementation of reforms. He reminded the party leaders that after being informed in 1960 of some mistakes in the work in Tibet, they had sent officials to correct the situation. The CCP had at that time admitted that collectivization had been begun too soon, that some people not guilty of participation in the revolt had been unjustly repressed, and that religion had been too severely suppressed. He wrote that these corrections had allowed the people of Tibet to realize that the errors were those of lower-level cadres and not of the central authorities or the party. He also described his tour of southern China that he took after the 1 October celebrations in 1960, along with some Nationalities Affairs officials, including Li Weihan, the negotiator of the Seventeen-Point Agreement, and Wang Feng of the United Front Work Department. During this tour, the Panchen had reported on the errors and mistakes made in Tibet. Li had encouraged him to make a written report and even to expand his report to include areas outside the TAR. After his return to Beijing, he had made a similar report personally to Zhou and to Mao. His criticisms at that time were well received, and all the officials to whom he spoke promised that corrections would be made in Tibet.

Despite the Panchen Lama's optimism due to the favorable reception of his earlier criticisms, upon his return to Tibet in 1961 he found that his monastery, Tashilhunpo, had been subjected to democratic reforms, during which, "through voluntary withdrawal, under the policy of religious freedom," the monk population had been cut in half, from approximately four thousand monks to 1,980.[24] After this time, the Panchen Lama said that he began to devote himself to the preservation of Tibet's religious heritage. He took measures to repair Lhasa's temples and monasteries and to save their treasures, moving many artifacts from the now nearly depopulated Drepung, Sera, and Ganden monasteries to the Lhasa Jokhang. He also began a series of public religious sermons, attended sometimes by several thousand people, during which he instructed Tibetans to cooperate with the Chinese and accept their assistance, but he emphasized that, as Mao himself had instructed, Tibetans had to develop and govern Tibet themselves. He assured Tibetans that CCP nationalities policy allowed religious freedom and encouraged them to practice their Buddhist faith. He also offered prayers for the health of the Dalai Lama and for his eventual return to Tibet.

In April 1962, the Panchen Lama was again in Beijing for the annual meeting of the NPC, after which a conference on nationalities policies was convened. This turned into a monthlong meeting, during which Tibet policy was the primary topic and in which the CCP heard much criticism about its policy from Tibetan cadres. Despite the meeting having been convened by Li Weihan, approved by Zhou and Mao, and attended by Deng Xiaoping, Zhou, and Zhu De, it turned into a repeat of the Hundred Flowers phenomenon when the party invited criticism only to turn around and punish those who criticized. Like the Hundred Flowers, the nationalities conference itself was characterized by openness, but the repercussions were to come later. On 18 May, while the conference was still in session, the Panchen Lama submitted his petition, which he had been writing for several months.

The petition began by praising the wisdom of the CCP leadership and its correct nationalities and Tibet policies. It also extolled the Chinese revolution and the peaceful liberation of Tibet, obtained under the "radiant illumination of the Party and the Great Thought of Chairman Mao." The Panchen Lama said that, despite the CCP having proceeded "consistently, steadily and carefully with the work in Tibet," having "exercised forbearance, utmost tolerance and patience," and having given "patient instruction and assistance," the reactionaries among the upper class had attempted to "continue their life of exploitation and oppression" and prevent the liberation of the Tibetan serfs and slaves and the elimination of the "cruel, dark and backward feudal serf system." The upper-class reactionaries had launched an armed rebellion to "betray the motherland, betray the revolution, betray the people and betray democracy and socialism." To disguise their real intentions, the upper-class reactionaries had deceived the masses by claiming that the CCP wanted to eradicate Tibetan religion and the Tibetan race. They said that all Tibetans who eat *tsampa* and practice Buddhism should unite to save the Tibetan religion and preserve Tibetan independence. These slogans deceived many Tibetans who joined the rebellion.

The Panchen Lama claimed that when the ordinary people of Tibet were told the truth about the crime of the upper-class reactionaries' rebellion, they supported the PLA in putting down the uprising and demanded the implementation of democratic reforms.

> The broad masses of the Tibetan working people demanded that democratic reform be carried out promptly in Tibet, and that under the leadership of the Party, all the shackles of the feudal system which had bound them should be cut off, in order to realize their urgent desire for freedom.

Because of this urgent demand by the people of Tibet, the Panchen Lama spoke to the NPC meeting in April 1959 about the need for democratic reform. He described a meeting with Mao and Zhou in which he received instructions and promises about how the reform was to be carried out. He had been told that, in addition to the repression of the "most reactionary feudal lords, their associates and counter-revolutionaries," monasteries and temples would also have to undergo democratic reforms "in order to completely get rid of the feudal system, exploitation and oppression, and to eliminate rebellious activity" and that the number of monks had to be "appropriately reduced." Monasteries, temples, and religious believers who were patriotic and obeyed the law would be given protection, under the party's principle of freedom of religious belief, and a certain number of monks would remain in monasteries to carry out religious activities.

The Panchen Lama described how, under the leadership of the party, the democratic reform was supposed to be carried out throughout Tibet:

> Because of the mobilization of the masses, the broad serfs and slaves, who had endured tragedy and suffering . . . awakened and acquired revolutionary fervor and class consciousness. . . . The liberated broad masses of the working people used their own hands to completely overthrow and eliminate the great burden of the system of feudal serfdom and rule by the three types of feudal lords. . . . They broke every shackle of the feudal system from their bodies, stood up and gained complete liberation and became masters of the new society and of the land.

Under the leadership of the Party, each level of government of the working people was established and the people's democratic dictatorship was put into practice, enabling the old Tibet, which was still a feudal serf-owning society, to be
transformed into a new Tibet, a democracy of the people with a glorious future.
This was an extremely grand and glorious cause, and it was a very happy event
in the development of humankind. For Tibet itself it was a turning point between the old and the new, darkness and light, bitterness and happiness, oppression and equality, poverty and prosperity; historically, this began a glorious new
era. Tibet was walking down the road of democracy and socialism like all other
nationalities of the motherland, and the light of prosperity and happiness shone
out in all directions. . . . Therefore, the monastic and secular masses of all strata
in Tibet have feelings of respectful love, support and gratitude towards the CCP
and the great leader Chairman Mao, and will never forget it was they who saved
them from the bitterness of the rule of the feudal serf-owning system and placed
them in the happiness of the people's democracy.

After making this required eulogy to the party's correct policies in Tibet, the
Panchen Lama went on to say that it was understandable that during democratic reforms—which were carried out in conjunction with the suppression
of the rebellion and were a "large-scale, fast moving, fierce, acute and life-and-
death class struggle, which overturned heaven and earth"—it was possible
that some "unavoidable errors and mistakes" might arise. In addition, "some
unnecessary and disadvantageous mistakes were also made during the campaign." The Panchen Lama divided the problems that had arisen during the
suppression of the revolt and the implementation of democratic reforms into
eight sections: "On Suppression of the Rebellion"; "On Democratic Reform";
"On Production in Agriculture and Animal Herding and on the Livelihood of
the People"; "On the United Front"; "On Democratic Centralism"; "On Dictatorship"; "On Religion"; and "On the Tibetan Nationality."

The first section, "On Suppression of the Rebellion," began by declaring
that the policy adopted by the party to subdue the rebellion was "entirely correct, essential, necessary and appropriate." The Panchen Lama approved of the
party's policy of combining "military attack, political winning-over and mo-
bilization of the masses" to suppress the rebellion. He said that the CCP's policy was to distinguish between the leaders of the revolt and those who had
been fooled or forced into following. The specific circumstances of each individual were to be determined, and those found to have been fooled by the revolt's leaders and who later repented their mistakes were to be treated with leniency. In regard to those people, the "Four Don'ts" policy was to be applied:
do not kill, lock up, struggle, or condemn them.

However, he said, this policy had not been followed and many who had "put
down their arms and surrendered, having realized and regretted taking the

wrong road," were "fiercely struggled against, arrested and imprisoned and met with severe attack." The Panchen Lama complained that CCP cadres "adopted vengeful, discriminatory, casual and careless methods." He said that because of these deviations from policy, and also because religion was a target of repression, the party's reputation had been harmed both domestically and abroad, and "the work of political winning-over was not done well enough, which caused the rebellion to be large-scale, to involve many people, to last a long time, to be stubborn in its stance and to rebel to the end."

In the second section, "On Democratic Reform," the Panchen Lama said that the policy to be followed during democratic reforms was that only the most reactionary feudal lords, their associates, reactionary elements, and counterrevolutionaries were supposed to be struggled against and repressed. However, the Panchen Lama complained, no distinctions were being made and all those who had any involvement or even any suspicion of involvement in the revolt had had their property confiscated without compensation and were subjected to thamzing and imprisonment. People who had merely given food or shelter to the rebels were considered supporters of the revolt. Even the Panchen Lama's own relatives, including his parents, had been falsely accused and subjected to thamzing. The Panchen also protested that the confiscation and redistribution of land had been unfair and that land reform had not won the support of the people. Some of the middle-class farmers and herdsmen who should have benefited from the redistribution of lands and herds were also subjected to confiscation of their property and thamzing. In pastoral areas, democratic reforms were supposed to have been conducted at a slower pace than in agricultural areas, but the Panchen said that party activists had "launched a fierce and acute struggle against very many herd owners."

The Panchen Lama wrote that class divisions should have been made carefully by investigation into each person's situation. However, party cadres had not been discriminating about whether punishment was correct or not; the only thing that was important to them was the "scale and quantity of the attack." They had branded village headmen and monastic officials, some of whom had been elected to their positions by ordinary people, as feudal lords. He said that the purpose of thamzing was supposed to be to mobilize the Tibetan people for the exercise of people's democracy, to expose the crimes of the feudal serf system and the serf-owners, and to eliminate the feudal system and create a new democratic and socialist society. However, in practice, people were being blamed for the sins of their class without any individual distinctions. Many people had been falsely accused and unjustly subjected to thamzing. Overzealous activists had resorted to violence as a common method during thamzing. The result was that the people had not been mobilized as willing participants in democratic reform but had become alienated and oppressed.

The Panchen Lama particularly complained about the recruitment and motives of the activists and the methods they used to conduct thamzing, saying that many Tibetan activists had base motives for their political involvement. Many sought economic benefits or political privileges, some were criminals who sought to conceal their crimes, and others sought to settle scores with their personal enemies. These activists were also encouraged with the promise that the more people they identified as exploiters, who thus would have their property confiscated, the more property would be redistributed among the activists themselves. Because of these incentives, many unworthy activists were cultivated. They tended to be arrogant with their newly acquired political power and to be abusive of the ordinary people. Both Chinese and Tibetan activists tended to be impatient and to forcibly subject Tibetans to thamzing without explanation to the people. Because of their impatience, thamzing tended to get violently out of control, and the activists mistakenly regarded violence as a measure of their success.

According to the Panchen Lama, activists had mobilized the poorer people with the promise that they would benefit from the confiscation and redistribution of the property of the wealthy. This was all that many people understood about the purpose of democratic reforms. People were forced to participate in thamzing and to criticize others under the threat that, if they did not, they too would be labeled as reactionaries and be subjected to thamzing themselves. Because people were falsely accused and subjected to thamzing without justification, the Tibetan people had come to regard the democratic reforms not as democracy or popular liberation but as unjust oppression. The Panchen Lama warned that the base motives of many of the activists were apparent to the people, and the injustice of so many innocent people being subjected to thamzing could not be concealed from them.

The Panchen Lama claimed that, during democratic reforms, many people were struggled against even if they had not committed any serious crimes or mistakes. Activists and cadres fabricated accusations against such people without regard to right and wrong, and thus people felt extremely fearful and scared. They experienced suspicion and loss of hope, and some even fled to foreign lands or committed suicide. The Panchen Lama also criticized the practice of "repeated investigations," referring to the process of continually making new class divisions and investigating people's class background and their loyalty to the old or the new government. He further mentioned that the activists seemed to regard all monks and lamas as reactionaries and therefore subjected many of them to thamzing, resulting in a threat to the survival of Tibetan religion, a theme he would return to in a later section of his petition.

In the third section, "On Production in Agriculture and Animal Herding and on the Livelihood of the People," the Panchen Lama said that a "cooperative wind" had affected Tibet when Tibetans were only experiencing the "democratic revolution." Collectivization, in the form of mutual aid teams, was introduced when Tibetans were just beginning to undergo democratic reforms and were unprepared for socialist transformation. Having only recently achieved democratic reforms and acquired their own property, Tibet's former serfs were not enthusiastic about collectivization because they feared that they would lose their newly gained property. Some people did not want to join mutual aid teams but were required to do so, and others who might have joined were not allowed to because of their bad class background. The mutual aid teams were therefore less than successful. At the same time, most private enterprise was restricted. The Panchen repeated this claim in a 1987 speech to the NPC: "In 1959 a large number of Chinese cadres were sent to Tibet. At that time the leftist influence became firmly rooted in Tibet. These cadres immediately introduced the commune system, long before democratic reforms were completed."[25]

The Panchen Lama wrote that in 1959–1961, the years of the Great Leap Forward, harvests in Tibet were good. Nevertheless, because cadres had inflated production figures in order to promote themselves, they were required to deliver a large portion of the Tibetan harvest to the state in the form of a variety of taxes. Tibetans actually suffered food shortages despite the fact that their own harvests were good.

> During the big movement for competition in production [Great Leap], because of a tendency to boast and exaggerate, there were false reports of increased production which were inconsistent with reality. There were those who in order to cover up their own lies took the falsely reported production indicators as the basis, and after the collection of patriotic public grain, apart from some seed grain, grain for everyday consumption, and animal fodder, bought up the majority of the remainder, and tapped past grain reserves [from estates and monasteries]. Because this was done too strictly, difficulties arose in the livelihood of the masses.

The Panchen Lama said that in the southern border areas many people had fled to Nepal and India due to excessive repression of the revolt. In pastoral areas, there had been losses due to the rebellion and the disruptions of democratic reforms. Some herdsmen had slaughtered their livestock rather than give them up. Also, exchange between agricultural and pastoral areas had been cut off, and although the state had distributed grain to the nomads, it had not been enough and the nomads had been forced to slaughter more livestock in order to subsist. Nomads lacked grain, while villagers lacked meat and butter.

Handicraft industries had been restricted, resulting in shortages of necessary items. Subsidiary production in commerce and agriculture had also been restricted by the state emphasis on primary products such as grain, resulting in shortages of other items. Many private traders had been repressed or had fled the country, resulting in disruptions to commerce. Other trade activities had been limited, particularly trade with India and Nepal.

Merchants had been required to report all their assets so that the state could determine what was to be confiscated and what had to be paid in taxes. A few merchants had falsely reported their assets, resulting in the suspicion on the part of cadres that all merchants were trying to cheat the state. The cadres then levied unreasonable taxes on all merchants. Because the merchants were unable to pay these taxes, they were therefore forced out of business, resulting in further disruptions to commerce and distribution.

With the natural system of trade and commerce replaced with a system of state control, there had been disruptions, shortages, and inequality in distribution. Many people suffered shortages simply due to inefficient or irrational state distribution. Some were refused grain rations based on cadres' belief that they were hoarding grain, when they actually had none. As the Panchen Lama said:

> Because at that time there was a shortage of grain, people who lacked grain could not obtain it from elsewhere. Consequently, in some places in Tibet, a situation arose where people starved to death. . . . In the past, although Tibet was a society ruled by dark and savage feudalism, there had never been such a shortage of grain. In particular, because Buddhism was widespread, all people, whether noble or humble, had the good habit of giving help to the poor, and so people could live solely by begging for food. A situation could not have arisen where people starved to death, and we have never heard of a situation where people starved to death.

In the fourth section, "On the United Front," the Panchen Lama again raised the issue of many Tibetans who were unjustly repressed and subjected to thamzing after the revolt and during democratic reforms. United Front policy was that those in the upper class who were "anti-imperialist, patriotic and progressive" should "recognize the crimes of that class." If they did so, they were not to be subjected to public thamzing and confiscation of their property without compensation. However, many of the upper class had been forced to undergo thamzing without regard to whether they had repented their own crimes and the crimes of their class. The Panchen Lama complained that, with a few exceptions of some important people, "many other of our friends encountered great difficulties, fear and anxiety during the democratic reform period." He continued: "Under the preferred method of arbitrary attack, the feudal lords and their agents and some well-off serfs were indiscriminately attacked, with no rational distinction being made between black and white, and those who attacked more fiercely being regarded as heroes." The Panchen Lama said that this nonadherence to the principles of protection, unity, and winning people over had caused many people to become scared, discouraged, and dissatisfied, thus alienating them from the party and even strengthening the forces of opposition.

The fifth section, "On Democratic Centralism," was divided into two parts, one dealing with democracy and the other with centralism (perhaps an acknowledgment of the incompatibility of these two policies). The Panchen Lama noted that Chairman Mao had described the political system of China as centralized, democratic, disciplined, and free.

In the first part, on democracy, the Panchen Lama complained that party cadres did not listen to the concerns of ordinary Tibetans but instead dictated to them and criticized their opinions as evidence of their lack of ideological education, or their "green brains." He emphasized that neither Chinese nor Tibetan cadres should apply policies to Tibet without taking into account and making exceptions for Tibet's special characteristics.[26]

The Panchen Lama said that cadres had not listened to the people but had instead dictated to them and had branded their opinions as reactionary if they differed from party policies. Many Tibetans had been subjected to thamzing just for expressing contrary opinions. Instead of learning to exercise "people's democracy," Tibetans had been taught that only unquestioning conformity to policies dictated from above would be tolerated. Meetings were held at which everyone was in seeming agreement, but this was only because the people were afraid to say anything different or express any opinions or opposition. The Panchen Lama complained that this was not democracy and that the CCP was alienating itself from the people by its dictatorial methods.

In the second part regarding the principle of centralism, the Panchen Lama complained that the principle of centralism did not allow any exercise of autonomy by the Preparatory Committee, which, after the dissolution of the Tibetan government, was supposed to be the highest administrative organ in the TAR. The Panchen Lama said that the PCTAR should "exercise leadership of organizations directly under its control and of all levels of government, allocate work and have proper control of working methods, investigate and report, praise achievements and put right errors and mistakes." However, many governmental organs and prefectural officials "paid insufficient attention to the fact that the Preparatory Committee was their leadership organ." In addition, they had filed reports claiming that there were no problems when this was clearly not the case. The upper-level administration was therefore deceived into thinking that work in Tibet was going entirely smoothly without any problems whatsoever.

In the sixth section of his petition, "Regarding the People's Democratic Dictatorship," the Panchen Lama returned to his complaint that Tibetans had been indiscriminately arrested in large numbers after the revolt and had been imprisoned without any trial or any regard to their innocence or guilt. He reiterated that the repression of the rebellion was supposed to be directed only at the leaders, while all others should have been pardoned and reeducated to support the party's policies. One of the party's principles was that "dictatorship should only be exercised towards rebels who obstinately stick to the wrong course, counterrevolutionaries and the most reactionary of the feudal lords and their agents." However, in Tibet, "many good and innocent were unscrupulously charged with offences, maligned and categorized with criminals; this has astounded people of integrity."

The Panchen Lama said the number of people jailed or subjected to labor reform had "reached a percentage of the total population which has never been surpassed throughout history." In 1987, after his rehabilitation, the Panchen Lama gave a more detailed estimate of the numbers of Tibetans imprisoned after the revolt:

> In my 70,000 character petition I mentioned that about five percent of the population had been imprisoned. According to my information at that time, it was between 10 to 15 percent. But I did not have the courage to state such a huge figure. I would have died under *thamzing* if I had stated the real figure. In Qinghai, for example, there are between one to three or four thousand villages and towns, each having between three to four thousand families with four to five thousand people. From each town and village about 800 to 1,000 people were imprisoned. Out of this at least 300 to 400 people died in prison. This means almost half of the prison population perished. Most of these people were completely innocent.[27]

The Panchen Lama described how public meetings and thamzings were regarded by Tibetans with fear and apprehension. He said that when called to "study meetings," people's "hearts palpitated with terror. . . . People of integrity felt discouraged and disheartened." Others learned "the technique of keeping a considerable distance between what they said and what was in their hearts." One effect of such public assemblies was that there emerged many people who were "good at flattering with deceitful talk and brandishing their willingness to pander to others." This created a situation where "on the surface it appeared that achievements had been made, but underneath it was the complete opposite." Tibetans appeared to have reformed their ideology, but in fact they had only learned to hide their true feelings.

The Panchen Lama complained that many Tibetans had died in prisons or labor camps due to poor treatment. He described how Tibetans were beaten in prison, overworked, underfed, and protected from cold only by thin cotton tents and blankets. Many Tibetans in their fifties and sixties had died due to the heavy physical labor and poor treatment. Many people had been executed in prison for any resistance to reform or any expression of opposition to the Chinese. The Panchen Lama said that this indiscriminate treatment had brought sadness and grief to Tibetans, increased their opposition to the new government, and harmed the image of China.

In the seventh section, "Regarding Religion," the Panchen Lama said that 99 percent of the Tibetan people had great faith, love, and respect for religion. Therefore, this was a crucial matter, and how it was handled was directly related to whether or not the party would be able to obtain the sincere support of the people. The Panchen Lama said that Mao and Zhou had told him that the government would "continue to give the masses, both monastic and secular, freedom of religious belief, but also would protect law-abiding monasteries and believers, and that we could carry out religious activities including teaching, debating, writing as before." At the same time, monasteries would be cleansed of the feudal serf system and the systems of oppression and exploitation that had stained religion and were incompatible with the development of society. Because there were an excessive number of monks who did not participate in material production or human reproduction, there was a need to reduce their number. However, there should remain in the monasteries a certain number of good monks to carry out religious activities.

The Panchen Lama wrote that he himself had made a study of the religious problem and agreed that there were many monks and lamas in monasteries who did not pursue the study of religion and did not follow the religious doctrines. Some of these would voluntarily enter the secular life in order to start a family; others who were unsuited to the religious life should be forced to secularize in order to increase production. Monasteries should undergo democratic reforms; they should be deprived of their estates and serfs and their management should be democratized. For the good monks who were engaged in religion and for the elderly and ill monks who should be allowed to remain in monasteries, the state should provide some support, while the monks should also engage in some productive labor. The Panchen Lama also emphasized that it was of utmost importance that proper protection be given to all those monasteries having historical significance, as well as to all Buddhist images, texts, and shrines.

However, the Panchen Lama said, "when work in religion and the monasteries was actually carried out, there arose many things which should not have happened, and which were inappropriate and unfortunate. This made people feel astonished and lose heart." He admitted that many monasteries and many monks had taken part in the rebellion, but not all of them had. Also, he said, religion itself was not to blame for supporting the rebellion. There should be careful discrimination between those monks who supported the rebellion and those who did not, and whole monasteries should not be condemned for the actions of a few of their monks. But because the monasteries had been labeled as one of the three pillars of feudalism, the entire monastic institution and religion itself were attacked. There were many activists who were infected with the leftist ideology that all religion was bad and who thought that democratic reforms offered the opportunity not to reform religion but to completely eliminate it.

The Panchen Lama said that during democratic reforms, the party's policies on religion had not been followed, and the cadres and activists had instead pursued a policy that the Panchen Lama called "doing away with religion, eradicating Buddhist images, sutras and shrines, and forcing monks and nuns to secularize." Monks and nuns who had refused to renounce their religion were subjected to fierce thamzings and often imprisoned. Almost all others were forced to secularize so that monasteries were virtually depopulated. In some places, monks and nuns had been lined up on opposite sides of a courtyard and forced to select marriage partners from the other group.

In many remote monasteries, the Panchen Lama wrote, there were many extremely holy and otherworldly lamas who had no understanding of the demands of cadres and activists and so resisted reeducation. They had therefore been arrested and imprisoned as reactionaries. In spite of these forcible methods being applied, the cadres and activists had claimed that democratic reform had been carried out and that monks and nuns had voluntarily secularized and attained liberation and freedom of religious belief. As the Panchen Lama said, "This statement does not fit with what is acknowledged as the thinking of more than 90 percent of the Tibetan people including myself."

With regard to Buddhist statues, scriptures, and shrines, the Panchen Lama said that there had been massive destruction: "Innumerable Buddhist images, sutras and shrines have been burnt to the ground, thrown into rivers, demolished or melted. There has been a reckless and frenzied destruction of monasteries and shrines. Many Buddhist statues have been stolen or broken open for their precious contents." Tibetans' religious sentiments had been intentionally insulted by using holy Buddhist scriptures for toilet paper or as an inner lining for shoes. *Mani* stones had been used to construct toilets or for walkways so that Tibetans would have to desecrate them by walking on them. Some of the cadres claimed that all of this had been done voluntarily by Tibetans whose political consciousness had been raised by democratic reforms. However, the Panchen Lama said, "This is sheer nonsense which comes from a complete lack of understanding of the actual situation in Tibet." All of this had been done, he said, "in a situation in which Han nationality cadres provided the idea, Tibetan cadres mobilized the people, and activists with no common sense carry out the destruction."

As to the destruction of monasteries and religion, the Panchen Lama wrote:

> Before democratic reform in Tibet there were over 2,500 large, medium and small monasteries in Tibet [meaning the TAR]. After democratic reforms, only 70 or so monasteries were kept in existence by the government. This was a reduction of more than 97 percent. Because there were no people living in most of the monasteries, there was no one to look after their Great Prayer Halls and other divine halls and the monks' housing. There was great damage and destruction, both by men and otherwise, and they were reduced to the condition of having collapsed or being on the point of collapse. In the whole of Tibet [TAR] in the past there was a total of about 110,000 monks and nuns. Of those, possibly 10,000 fled abroad, leaving about 100,000. After democratic reform was concluded, this number of monks and nuns living in the monasteries was about 7,000 people, which is a reduction of 93 percent.

Of those monks and nuns remaining in the monasteries, the Panchen Lama said that they were "generally of low quality." The high-level religious practitioners and scholars that he had hoped would be allowed to remain in monasteries and continue religious practice and tradition had instead almost all been subjected to thamzing, arrested, and imprisoned. He lamented that "the monasteries have already lost their purpose and significance as religious institutions." The remaining monks and nuns were forced to engage in labor and production to the extent that they had no time for religious activities.

The actual result of democratic reforms was that the religious life in monastic and secular society had been eliminated. People had been forced to take down the prayer flags from their roofs and cease to wear their protective amulets. They had had to hide statues of the Buddha, scriptures, and other religious objects. They could no longer chant Buddhist mantras or turn prayer wheels. Burning juniper incense or making offerings at holy places was no longer possible. The Tibetans could not sponsor Buddhist rituals, even for the dead. As the Panchen Lama said, "The number of religious activities are as scarce as stars in the daytime. The passing on of the knowledge of the three precious gems [*kunchok sum*: the Buddha, the *Dharma*, and the *Sangha* or the religious community] has been abandoned."

The Panchen Lama declared that he spoke truthfully and that 90 percent of Tibetans agreed with him, despite the fact that none but he was willing to speak out due to the pervasive fear of being criticized as reactionaries.

In his eighth and final section, "On the Tibetan Nationality," the Panchen Lama began by describing the CCP's policy of equality for all nationalities and the importance of the unity of nationalities. Although Tibet had been "under the jurisdiction of the motherland for several hundred years," he wrote, Tibetans still "strongly perceive themselves as Tibetan, and only have a weak perception of the motherland." The Panchen Lama said that because the rebellion in Tibet was widespread and because it was antiparty, antirevolutionary, and antimotherland, many Han-nationality cadres had been of the opinion that the Tibetan nationality as a whole should be blamed and repressed.

The Panchen Lama complained that all aspects of Tibetan national identity were being suppressed—in particular, religion, language, and national dress and customs. All aspects of Tibetan dress and national customs that distinguished Tibetans from Chinese were being repressed and eliminated. Because of the resentment of what they regarded as the Tibetans' betrayal of the motherland, Han cadres had denigrated all aspects of Tibetan culture, including Tibetan dress and language. For example, Tibetan cadres had been prohibited from wearing Tibetan dress.

Despite the regulation that all government documents should be in both the Chinese and Tibetan languages, only Chinese was actually used. This meant that Tibet was allowed no autonomy because all business was conducted by Han cadres in Chinese and Tibetan cadres were not even consulted. The Tibetan language had been altered and was being replaced in government and education by Chinese. The Panchen Lama criticized those who said that the Tibetan language was unable to adapt to new terminology. He said that attempts to simplify the written language by making it correspond to the spoken language in each area had damaged it and the nationality by eliminating a common written language for all Tibetans. He warned that language and customs were the identifying characteristics of a nationality and that if those characteristics disappeared, then the nationality itself would disappear or change into another nationality.

The Panchen Lama said that so many Tibetans had been killed during the rebellion or imprisoned during democratic reforms and died in prison that there had been great damage to the Tibetan nationality by a serious reduction in the population: "In regions which have been affected comparatively seriously, on looking at the inhabitants, it can be clearly understood that only women, infants and the elderly are left; those of youth and middle age and knowledgeable people have become fewer." The Panchen Lama said that the situation in Kham and Amdo was even worse than in the TAR, and that conditions were still bad there. There had been so many deaths in Kham and Amdo that the Tibetan nationality and religion were in danger of extinction in those areas. Since these were areas of Tibetan nationality, these conditions affected the Tibetan nationality as a whole.

Although the Panchen Lama was required to refer to only the TAR as Tibet, he said that the degree of success or failure of the work done in any area of Tibetan nationality had an influence the other areas:

So any victories and achievements obtained by brother Tibetan areas are like victories and achievements obtained in Tibet itself. Disasters and losses created by errors and mistakes in the work in brother Tibetan areas are, similarly, like disasters and losses created by errors and mistakes in the work in Tibet itself.

Because of this interrelationship between Tibetan areas, the Panchen Lama said that he thought it appropriate to make some comments about Tibetan areas outside the TAR, based upon his tour of Kham and Amdo in 1961. He wrote that he had been encouraged by some Chinese officials to inspect these areas, and he hoped his comments would not be regarded as interference in the affairs of neighboring provinces.

He wrote that initially he had great difficulty in convincing Tibetans in those areas to voice their true opinions. Once he had gained their confidence, they revealed that the areas of Tibetan nationality outside the TAR had suffered all of the same problems as the TAR but that the problems were "longer in duration, more serious and more leftist than in Tibet." This was because reforms had begun earlier there and with little or no preparation. He said that the problems of nationality and religion in Kham and Amdo had been due to extreme leftist deviation, and that there was absolutely no democratic life in those areas. The cadres had been so dictatorial, he said, that if anyone said anything that even slightly conflicted with the opinions of the cadres, they were immediately labeled as counterrevolutionaries and severely attacked. He said that the Tibetans in Kham and Amdo described to him a life of unbearable suffering.

In Kham and Amdo, according to the Panchen Lama, most people believed that the CCP was intent on destroying the Tibetan religion and nationality. The rebellion was crushed with excessive force, he said, resulting in indescribable disaster and endless suffering to the Tibetan nationality. There should not have been such severe military repression, he insisted. Even Tibetans who gathered together for religious rituals were thought to be rebels and were attacked. The indiscriminate attacks on Tibetan religion and nationality had intensified the rebellion and increased its duration, turning it into a conflict between the Han and Tibetan nationalities.

The Panchen Lama said that most of the men in Kham and Amdo had been killed during the revolt or arrested and imprisoned afterward. The uprising and imprisonment of Tibetans had resulted in a

huge number of abnormal deaths, creating a phenomenon where not all of the prisoners' corpses could be buried. Therefore, hundreds of thousands of parents, wives, children, friends and relatives of those who died of abnormal causes were extremely grieved, their tears welled up, and they wailed and cried bitterly.

This situation occurred everywhere, he said, and was difficult to describe:

> Because rebellions occurred in most of the Tibetan areas, many people were lost in battle. Second, many people were arrested and imprisoned during and after the period of suppression of the rebellion, which caused large numbers of people to die abnormal deaths. Third, for a period, because the life of the masses was poverty-stricken and miserable, many people, principally the young and old, died of starvation or because they were physically so weak they could not resist minor illnesses. Consequently, there has been an evident and severe reduction in the present-day Tibetan population. Needless to say this was not only harmful to the flourishing of our Tibetan nationality, but it was also a great threat to the continued existence of the Tibetan nationality, which was sinking into a condition close to death.

Because so many people had been killed and imprisoned, agricultural and pastoral production had suffered. At the same time, the people's communes were started in Tibetan areas outside the TAR before the proper economic and ideological conditions had been created. Property was collectivized, and some was confiscated by the state, with the result that agricultural and pastoral production was severely damaged. Unrealistic production targets were set, and taxes were collected based upon those targets even though they were not met. Tibetans were left with insufficient food for survival. Communal grain rations had to be supplemented with wheat husks, grasses, tree leaves, and roots. Even this was in limited supply and could not satisfy hunger:

> Because the anguish of such severe hunger had never been experienced in Tibetan history and was such that people could not imagine it even in their dreams, the masses could not resist this kind of cruel torment, and their condition declined daily. Therefore, in some places, colds and other such minor infectious diseases caused a percentage of people to die easily. In some places, many people directly starved to death because the food ran out; therefore, in some places, there was the phenomenon of whole families dying out. The mortality rate was critical. Those abnormal deaths were all caused by the lack of food, and in fact they all should be counted as having starved to death.

The Panchen Lama declared that the numbers of monasteries and monks in Kham and Amdo had been reduced by 99 percent. The most learned lamas had been attacked, and now the only remaining monks were political activists unworthy of the religion. Monasteries had ceased to exist, religious culture was disappearing, and "the future of religion has in reality been destroyed; therefore, in fact religion has no future."

By way of conclusion to his report, the Panchen Lama wrote that the main cause of Tibetans' suffering was the revolt itself. Many Tibetans had revolted because they were deceived by the use of slogans in regard to religion and nationality; however, the Panchen Lama also blamed the revolt on the misapplication and abuse of CCP nationalities policy by cadres in Tibetan areas. He complained that many Han cadres were unfamiliar with conditions in Tibetan areas and that they tended to regard themselves as superior to Tibetans. Tibetan cadres, on the other hand, tended to be enthusiastic but barely educated in basic knowledge or in the party's nationalities policy.

The Panchen Lama said that he had written his report in the spirit of "benefiting and enhancing the reputation, esteem, glory and prestige of our patron, the CCP, the great Chairman Mao and the motherland" and in the spirit of the saying "Uncomfortable words are found in the mouths of those who love you." He said that his concerns could be summarized as being about three problems: religious freedom, the repression of the rebellion, and the fate of the Tibetan nationality and the livelihood of the Tibetan people.

With regard to freedom of religion, the Panchen said that the party needed to counteract the opinion among many both at home and abroad that the CCP wanted to destroy religion and would not permit religious belief. Tibetans must be allowed to believe in religion and to practice their religion. They must be allowed to join monasteries, and the monasteries must be permitted to maintain Buddhist rituals and scholarship. The democratic management committees in the remaining monasteries must be composed of genuine monks who want to preserve religion, not activists who want to destroy it. He asked for the patronage of the state in support of the monks and monasteries.[28]

With regard to the repression of the rebellion, he wrote that it was inevitable that the revolt and its suppression would arouse animosities between nationalities. But Tibetans—even those not guilty of supporting the revolt—felt that their nationality and their religion were being attacked because of the revolt; therefore, "doubts, panic, anxiety, fear and great hatred arose in the minds of many Tibetan people of all strata." These feelings "harmed the affection" between nationalities, which could not be repaired by a few words. Instead, there must be a rebuilding of what was destroyed, compensation for those who suffered, true equality of nationalities in the great family of the motherland, and assurance that Tibetans "would not be changed into another nationality." Tibetans needed to be convinced that the mistakes made in Tibet were the errors of lower-level cadres and not of the CCP and its leaders if Tibetans were to regain their loyalty to the party.

With regard to the livelihood of the people, the Panchen wrote that work should proceed cautiously and that requisitions from the masses should take their burdens into consideration. He also asked that the lives of Tibetans in areas outside the TAR, who were "sinking into a miserable plight," be considered, in order to prevent people from leading such "poor, bitter and indescribable lives" and to ensure that "nobody dies of starvation." If this was done and there were a good harvest, then the ideological basis would be created in those areas for Tibetans to "advance in the direction of the revolution."

The Panchen Lama proclaimed that he wrote his petition on behalf of the Tibetan people, all of whom shared his concerns. He declared his loyalty to the party and to its leaders, who he said had helped him to achieve a "certain revolutionary viewpoint." He asserted that he had "done a little work" for the party and the revolution and had never done any harm. He felt that his report was "another good and significant thing which I have done in my history." He asked that the leaders to whom his report was addressed "exercise magnanimity and a holy and pure spirit" when examining it.

> If only the CCP Tibet Work Committee knows about errors and mistakes in the work in Tibet and, no matter whether they are serious or not, carries out both the special characteristics of the CCP [to make self-criticisms] and the CCP's wise and good work style with sufficient courage and makes prompt and clear reports to the central authorities, without hiding or concealing anything and to the letter, then this will enable the central authorities to see the victories and achievements in the work in Tibet and to be acquainted with the errors and mistakes.

Despite his hope that his criticisms might be well received, they reportedly aroused the resentment of the senior Chinese cadres responsible for Tibet, who began to plot against him. Temporarily, however, under the leadership of Zhou, the CCP formulated new policies for its work in Tibet in the light of the Panchen's criticisms. These included revival of the United Front policy of cooperation with the former upper-class people who were loyal to the party, more respect for freedom of religion, more discrimination regarding who should be accused of having supported the revolt, and more care in the selection of cadres and activists.

These policies were never implemented, however, because Mao regained control of the CCP after having been relegated to a background role after the disasters of the Great Leap Forward. Mao reacted far differently to the Panchen's criticisms than Zhou had. Mao described the petition as a "poisoned arrow aimed at the heart of the Party by reactionary feudal overlords" and criticized the Panchen Lama personally, reportedly saying that he was not destined to be a leader of the Tibetan nationality.

Mao and other CCP leaders were reluctant to believe that conditions in Tibet were as bad as the Panchen Lama claimed, especially since he was the only one voicing such complaints. They preferred to think that his complaints merely reflected the discontent of the former upper class at having lost their status and privileges.

In response to the Panchen Lama's criticisms, Chinese officials in Tibet mounted a propaganda campaign to discredit him. In late 1962, Chinese officials demanded that he denounce the Dalai Lama, which he refused to do. After this, his public appearances and political role were diminished, although he retained his official position.

In August 1964, in conjunction with the "new leftist wind" implemented by Mao known as the Socialist Education Movement, the Panchen Lama was denounced as a "rock on the road to socialism," deprived of his position as head of the PCTAR, and subjected to seventeen days of thamzing. He was accused of being a "reactionary enemy of the State" and a secret supporter of the Dalai Lama. During his thamzing, the Panchen Lama was accused of many preposterous crimes, including "attempted restoration of serfdom," murder, planning to launch a guerrilla war against the state, illicitly cohabiting with women, "criticizing and opposing China in a 70,000 character document," "declaring open support for the Dalai Lama and misleading the masses," and "theft and plunder of images and other property from monasteries."[29] Meetings were held all over Tibet to denounce the Panchen Lama to Tibetans, who wondered how someone so loyal to the Chinese until then could now be such a traitor.[30]

In December, he was taken to Beijing, where he lived under house arrest until the beginning of the Cultural Revolution, when he received another thamzing at the Minority Nationalities Institute. In 1968, the Panchen Lama was imprisoned, where he was to remain for nine years and eight months until his release in October 1977. He was not allowed to return to Lhasa until July 1982.

In 1987, the Panchen Lama revealed that he had been accused in 1964 of "turning against the motherland" and "trying to start a secessionist rebellion." He said that Mao had warned him: "Even if the whole of the Tibetan population is armed, it will only make over 3 million people. We are not scared of this." The Panchen Lama said, "On hearing this, I felt very sad and realized how it is to be without freedom."[31]

What the Panchen Lama's petition revealed was that the CCP was repressing all Tibetan opposition to Chinese rule with little regard to the niceties of nationality autonomy policies. The Panchen repeatedly complained about the indiscriminate repression of Tibetans for the slightest expression of opposition or even the *suspicion* of opposition. An unjustifiable number of Tibetans had been killed during the uprising or later in prisons and labor camps. Because the religious establishment was identified as one of the three pillars of feudalism, it was attacked without regard to the promise of religious freedom. Monasteries almost without exception were deprived of their lands, their monks forcibly secularized and their material possessions confiscated as part of the redistribution of wealth of democratic reforms. Religious practice was repressed, and Tibet's religious culture was practically eradicated. Most of the former aristocracy were purged due to their class status, and the United Front policy was essentially abandoned. Despite Tibet's good harvests during the years of the Great Leap, exactions by the state had resulted in widespread famine, especially in Tibetan areas outside the TAR. The people's democracy that was supposed to be created by democratic reforms had instead produced tyranny, fear, conformity, and despair. China's repression of all aspects of Tibetan culture and national identity led the Panchen Lama to fear for the survival of the Tibetan nationality. His frequent mention of the danger of Tibetans being "changed into another nationality" reveals the assimilationist pressures experienced by Tibetans after the revolt and during democratic reforms.

The Panchen Lama submitted his petition in the belief that the party would correct its mistakes in Tibet to adhere to its own policies about nationalities autonomy and religious freedom. He also imagined that the CCP valued the loyalty of Tibetans and particularly that of the Panchen himself. He may have thought himself immune from purge since he was the only remaining Tibetan in the Chinese administration who commanded any traditional respect among Tibetans.[32]

The Panchen Lama's complaints show that the revolt was of an undeniably nationalist character and that the party was carrying out the suppression of Tibetan resistance in an equally nationalist manner. The Panchen Lama found himself in an impossible position in trying to follow the party line on the non-nationalist character of the revolt when the CCP was using the suppression of the revolt and the subsequent democratic reforms to eliminate all Tibetan opposition to Chinese rule. Despite their doctrine that nationality issues were really disguised class issues, the Chinese in Tibet reacted to the Tibetan Revolt as treason against China and branded all Tibetan opposition as anti-Chinese.

It is clear that the Panchen Lama was having difficulty understanding the necessity for the repression of religious leaders and the religious establishment that he saw taking place all around him. He obviously believed that the party was sincere in its policy on freedom of religion and did not fully comprehend the incompatibility of Marxism and religion.

The Panchen Lama was lured into expressing his criticisms not only by his idealistic belief in CCP nationalities doctrine but also by the intricacies of party politics at the time. At first, his criticisms received a favorable response from the most liberal of the party's leaders, including Li Weihan, Deng Xiaoping, and Zhou Enlai. These leaders were in actual command of the CCP in 1960 and 1961, after Mao had been forced to allow them to repair the results of his Great Leap. However, once Mao regained control, he reverted to his own leftist inclinations, one of which in regard to nationalities policies was that the national issue was in essence a class issue. What this meant was that the upper classes of any nationality would use nationalism to preserve their own status and privileges. Nationalism then, according to a strict Marxist reading, had no real meaning, and national identity, including minority nationality identity, had no value and no reason to be protected or preserved. In pursuit of a class-based revolution, nationalism of all types had to be eliminated—although in Tibet, the Chinese were much less tolerant of Tibetan nationalism than of Chinese (Han) nationalism.

The CCP imagined that, because it was a revolutionary party, it was free of nationalism itself, even in its pursuit of the liberation of non-Chinese peoples such as the Tibetans. All of the Chinese Communists believed in an ultimately assimilationist solution to the minority national question; the only debate was over the rate of assimilation. The most liberal favored a gradual policy of respect for nationalities' cultures and autonomy until they voluntarily and inevitably chose assimilation themselves. The most leftist and revolutionary found it hard to tolerate the United Front policy and preferred a more coercive assimilation. The latter group prevailed in the CCP's policies in Tibet after the revolt, as it had after the Hundred Flowers debate and as it would in every instance in the future when minorities demanded the autonomy they had been promised.

The purge of the Panchen Lama signified that the Chinese Communists did not even feel the need for a figurehead leader representing Tibet's previous political system. His removal marks the end of China's respect for Tibetan autonomy based on the Seventeen-Point Agreement. Now that China had total control in Tibet, there was no longer any need for any cooperation with the representatives of the previous system or even any pretense of cooperation. The United Front policy fundamentally conflicted with the doctrine that the former upper class were enemies of the revolution and enemies of the people. It also conflicted with the need to eliminate nationality leadership in favor of Chinese control. The Chinese were able to dispense with the upper-class United Front collaborators because they had by now cultivated many lower-class collaborators and activists.

The disregard for the role of the Panchen Lama was all the more obvious because his purge was not necessary. His petition could have remained a party secret, as the text actually did for the next thirty-four years. However, so offended was Mao at the Panchen's criticisms and so little did the CCP see any remaining need for a figurehead in Tibet, that the party preferred to make an example of him. This also served the party's need for constant lessons to Tibetans about the perils of opposition to Chinese rule, even by the highest official of the supposedly autonomous administration of Tibet.

The purge of the Panchen Lama and the abrogation of the type of autonomy promised in the Seventeen-Point Agreement also set the stage for the subsequent Cultural Revolution, when there was not even a thought given to Tibet's supposed autonomy. Even before his purge, the Panchen Lama revealed that there was no autonomy in Tibet. He complained that the PCTAR, of which he was the head, was not really in charge of administration. Instead, the Chinese were administering Tibet through their own party organizations and the PLA. As was the case in all of the PRC, an atmosphere of conformity was pervasive, due to past purges of critics of Mao's campaigns. No one, with the exception of the Panchen Lama, dared to report to Beijing any problems in the administration of Tibet. Beijing therefore tended to think that anyone expressing any complaints about conditions in Tibet must be an opponent of the new regime.

Serf

The film *Serf*, made by a PLA film company in 1963, tells what is purported to be a typical story of a Tibetan serf and his—as well as all Tibetan serfs'—liberation by the Chinese People's Liberation Army.[33] It is set in the period just before the 1959 revolt, after which, according to the Chinese version of Tibetan history, the Tibetan serfs achieved their final liberation. The film is in black and white, with Tibetan actors who appear to be speaking Tibetan, but all the sound appears to have been recorded in the studio and the dialogue is dubbed in Chinese. Tibetans who were in Tibet at the time say there was also a Tibetan version, which all schoolchildren were required to see. Several said that the audience typically kept quiet during the showing of the film out of fear of expressing incorrect attitudes.

According to several Tibetans, *Serf* was enormously significant for Chinese audiences in the formation of their opinions about Tibet and the Chinese role there. It was shown all over China and Tibet and was reportedly very popular. This film was perhaps the most significant source, in some cases the only source, for many Chinese in forming their impressions about Tibet. Even many Tibetans, especially those of a young age, were influenced by this film in their opinions about the reality of traditional Tibet.

In the Chinese version of the film, the only two named actors are Chamba, the mute serf, and Lenga, the blacksmith's daughter. These are Chinese transliterations of the Tibetan names Jampa and Namgang, which we will use in preference to the Chinese mispronunciations.

Serf begins with a written foreword:

This is a blood and tears story of serfdom. It is an account of the life story and enslavement of thousands of Tibetans. The Tibetan minority group has one of the longest historical traditions out of all our ethnic brothers in China's big family. In past history, the common people of this great region spent their whole lives shackled and carrying heavy loads. In 1951, after the Peaceful Liberation, the Chinese Government had compassion for the Tibetan aristocracy and tried to reeducate them. But some of them still tried to control all the other Tibetans. They started an uprising against the Chinese government in 1959. As the uprising grew larger and larger, the Chinese Government offered the common people a new chance at life through democracy.

The film begins with a scene of serfs, male and female, carrying heavy loads up a hill toward what appears to be a feudal estate, while other serfs are seen wearing heavy wooden punishment stocks. They are all ragged, dirty, struggling with their loads, and very obviously oppressed by their labor. They are carrying bags of grain that are apparently their taxes to the estate. A well-dressed official records their loads and makes an ink mark on each serf's cheek. The serfs wear expressions of barely contained rage at their oppression. One woman collapses under the weight of her load and falls down a long flight of stone stairs.

The same exhausted serf who fell is shown later in her dirt hovel with a new child, Jampa, whom she tells to remember that he was born as a human being, the proof of which is that a birth tax was paid to the lord by the grandmother. The grandmother, looking suitably threadbare and subservient, is shown paying the tax to an official, who looks appropriately wealthy and arrogant. She asks that the father of the child be allowed to see the child's face one time.

The next scene shows female serfs, young and old, carding, spinning, and weaving wool for the feudal lord. In contrast, the children of the lord are shown as well-dressed, happy, and playing. The children are greeted at the entrance to the manor by a steward, who then notices a male serf, ignored by the lord's children, at the foot of the steps leading to the manor, chained and bleeding, obviously having been whipped. The steward pokes the man with his foot and tells him he can go ahead and die, because his wife has had a baby boy. The lord approaches, looks at the serf, declares him dead, and curses him for being brave enough to oppose him. He shouts at the dead serf that he was lucky that his tongue was not cut out. He tells his steward to demand from the dead serf's wife that she pay back taxes for three generations as well as a death tax. If she cannot pay, then she is to replace her dead husband's labor with her own by symbolically returning a whip that is delivered to her by the steward. Obviously the point here is that the serfs had to pay taxes for everything from birth to death.

There follows a long emotional scene in which the wife, with tears in her eyes, is forced to leave her child in the care of the grandmother and go to serve the lord. She picks up the whip and shuffles from her hovel (all serfs are shown shuffling about almost on the point of collapse and with downtrodden expressions) up a long path to the manor, where she sees her husband's dead body. She collapses on the body but is dragged away to a dungeon and placed in leg shackles along with several other serfs. Another female serf in the dungeon puts her hands on the mother's head and thinks she's dead, saying, "Buddha, she's gone to heaven. *Om mani padme hum, Om mani padme hum.*" This is the last we see of Jampa's mother.

Next the grandmother is shown tending to the baby Jampa, saying, "Don't cry! You need to grow up fast," as she spins her prayer wheel. The film then fast-forwards several years to a time when Jampa, still with his grandmother, appears as a young boy. He offers to carry a water jug for a young girl, Namgang. Namgang asks Jampa if he is going to the monastery and, if so, if he will pray for her to the White Tara, who looks so beautiful and whose compassion must be very great because she has so many eyes and therefore must be able to see everything. Jampa promises to pray to Tara on behalf of Namgang.

The grandmother, Namgang, and Jampa then encounter an old blacksmith, who we later learn is Namgang's father, working near a Buddhist *chorten* at the entrance to the monastery. The grandmother inquires if the blacksmith is now back, to which he replies, "Yes, and now I have chains." The grandmother says, "Om mani padme hum," and advises him to not run away again. He replies, "I won't. Wherever you run to, it is still the same." The blacksmith's son says that when he grows up he will run away, but when his father asks where he will go, the boy replies that he doesn't know.

Grandmother tells Jampa not to eat food from the blacksmith. The smith tells Jampa that since birth the blacksmith's bones are black. Whoever comes into contact with outcasts like the blacksmiths will have bad karma. Then the grandmother tells the blacksmith that it shouldn't be so, that hunger should know no such distinctions. Namgang asks her father if their bones are really black. The father says that they aren't, but that others have painted them so.

As he finishes, a group of nobles approaches, several on horses, led by the lord who has killed Jampa's father and enslaved his mother (it is not obvious whether Jampa is aware of these facts, but the grandmother surely is). The lord's son, presumably not having his own horse, is being carried on the back of a serf, whom he beats with a whip. The blacksmith's family has to bow as the nobles pass. Jampa and his grandmother also have to get out of the roadway and bow. However, Jampa does not bow fully, perhaps showing the dawning of an antifeudal consciousness.

Next we see the feudal lord and his son, dressed in fine silks, greeting a young lama on the roof of a monastery. "Greetings, Enlightened One," says the nobleman, to which the lama replies, "Greetings, Uncle, Cousin." The lord, who constantly strokes his evil-looking goatee, says, "Enlightened One, your prayers are very powerful." The young lama laughs. As the lama and the lord survey the monastery's lands, the lama says, "This Spring we had much rain, so our grain crop was enough to fill two casks and five full storage rooms. Our lands are bountiful and broad." "We have held these lands for many generations," the lord replies. They laugh again as they observe some serfs delivering more grain up a long flight of stone stairs. The young lama is portrayed as being as evil as the lord, though without the silks and goatee. They are obviously related, and the point is that the aristocracy appoints the lamas, both of whom are feudal lords and oppress the serfs.

We now see Jampa and his grandmother enter the monastery. The grandmother prostrates herself, but the hungry Jampa eats some of the butter intended as an offering for the butter lamps. This scene reflects an aspect of Tibetan culture that was most irritating to the Chinese: Tibetans wasting their good butter on offerings to nonexistent gods. The grandmother catches Jampa eating the butter and stops him, saying, "Jampa! This is for the butter lamp for Buddha. To eat this is a sin."

They then enter the monastery behind a line of serfs, including children, bringing water for the monks. As they circle the altars, the grandmother pours butter into each large butter lamp. Jampa, meanwhile, has entered the shrine room of the White Tara, where he remembers his promise to Namgang to pray for her. As Jampa prays for Namgang, he remembers her words about how Tara must be so compassionate because she has so many eyes. As he prays, Jampa is distracted by the *torma* offerings, made of sculpted *tsampa* (roasted barley flour). His hunger gets the best of him; he looks around to see if anyone is watching, then reaches for one of the torma, knocking over a butter lamp in the process. Finally, he reaches a torma, takes a bite of it, and conceals the rest in his robe.

Just then, Jampa turns and is surprised by a very large and very stern monk, perhaps a *dob dob*, one of the "fighting monks" who were a part of every monastery, who grabs him and drags him outside. On the entrance steps, in front of several other monks, the monk accuses Jampa, "He blew out the butter lamp! He stole the consecrated tsampa offering to eat as food! Cut out his tongue! Cut off his hands!" Jampa's grandmother rushes up and falls at the monk's feet, crying, "Cut out my tongue! Cut off my hands! It's my fault!" The monk's reply is to kick her down the steep stone steps. (The scene appears to have been filmed at one of the large *lhakhangs* or assembly halls at Drepung.)

The lama and the lord approach, and the lord says, "Oh, this is my slave. My management has not been strict enough. I will bring him back to the village for punishment." The lama, looking very pious, declares, "When one sins without intent, it is not truly a sin. Even the smallest living creature is worthy of compassion. There are many people suffering in the world, and Buddha's compassion is very great." A crowd of serfs has gathered and, as Jampa is tossed down the steps, they beg, "Let him go. Let him go." The lama glances toward the skies and says, "He stole the offering from Buddha and his offense is against Buddha." To Jampa, he adds, "Heaven will punish you. Heaven will punish you, by making you mute. You must atone for your sin." As the lama and several monks (who appear to be reluctantly playing a role in this film) reenter the monastery, one monk tells Jampa and his grandmother, "Quickly, go home."

Back at their serf hovel, the grandmother prays over Jampa and burns incense. She says that she will go to the monastery to obtain a protection amulet for him and asks Namgang to look after him while she goes to the monastery. The grandmother obtains an amulet at the monastery and then departs with the typical serf shuffle. But as she staggers back across a shallow stream, she falls in and drowns (in about six inches of water, deep enough to cover only half her face), still holding the amulet in her hand.

Jampa has meanwhile been fetched by the lord's steward, who laughs and calls to the nobleman's son, "Young Master, Young Master, I found you a pony!" While the lord's daughter is pushed in a swing, the steward says to Jampa, "Neigh like a horse and call him Master. Call him Master and neigh like a horse." The son, who appears about the same age as Jampa, approaches and commands him, "Get down! Get down!" The steward pushes Jampa to the ground, and the lord's son mounts him like a horse, grabbing his hair and whipping him as Jampa moves around. The lord's wife approaches but ignores Jampa. Apparently none of the aristocratic family, laughing all the while, find anything wrong with Jampa's humiliation. Namgang observes this scene from concealment with tears in her eyes.

In the next scene, Jampa has run away and approaches a cliff, from which it appears he contemplates jumping. Then Namgang finds him and asks what he is doing. But Jampa does not reply. Namgang cries, "Why won't you talk? Are you really mute?" "They made me neigh like a horse!" Jampa replies. "They made me call him Master! I won't speak! I won't ever speak!" Jampa bites his tongue, drawing blood. From this point on, Jampa is mute.

The flowing river signifies the passage of time, apparently about ten years. Jampa is now seen as a grown man, still mute. He is in a pasture as Namgang approaches. She says that she had wanted to see Jampa the day before because she had something to tell him. We then see the scene that she is describing. A rather well-dressed Tibetan man stops at the blacksmith's and asks for a drink of water. The smith's son asks the traveler if he will drink the unclean water of an outcast. The traveler withdraws from his satchel a cup that bears the inscription "People's Liberation Army" in Chinese characters and declares that whatever water is put into that cup will be clean. While the man drinks the water, the smith's son says that no army can be good. But the man replies that he has traveled all over Tibet and even to China and has never before seen an army like this. The PLA, he says, is the kind of army that breaks your chains, pointing to the son's chains, and adds that it is not far away! The smith's son looks at his own chains and then at the traveler hopefully. The man says that everyplace this army has passed, people tell the same story.

Namgang conveys to Jampa the good news brought by the traveler to all the Tibetan serfs and slaves:

> There's a red sun rising in the East. There's a giant Buddha standing in the sun. He can see everything. He has seen the highest place in the world and he has also seen the people who suffer there so terribly! Buddha's hand is pointing. The Army of the Bodhisattvas has crossed many mountains and many rivers and has come to alleviate the suffering of the people. Every one of the Bodhisattva soldiers wears a hat on his head with a red star!

The next scene is at the monastery, where a wise-looking old monk is telling the lama about a recent trip he has made to Lhasa and about his impressions of the PLA:

> The sun shines on top of the Snow Mountains. Tibet could be peacefully liberated. The central government is supporting us. Look, these are the 17 agreements [as he hands the text of the Seventeen-Point Agreement to the lama]. We must follow these, and work everything out through discussions with each other. I've seen it. When I was a child I heard about the Communist Party. This time, in Lhasa, I saw them for myself. This is a very virtuous army. The Communist Party itself is not Buddhist, yet when they are building their roads and they see *mani* stones they don't step over them; they walk around them.

The old monk says that before returning to his own monastery, he wanted to see the lama because he feared that the lama would listen to the wrong people. He says that he has seen much trouble and much killing and foreign countries trying to attack but that now China is gathering together and growing stronger and wealthier. But, he says, there are still a lot of bad people in the aristocracy who imagine that they can defeat the Liberation Army. This, he insists, cannot be done! All the while the lama listens to the monk, he appears uncomfortable, and his agreement with what the monk is saying appears insincere.

Next we see the lama performing a ritual seated on a throne before rows of monks. The ceremony, which appears to be for expelling demons, takes place before what appears to be a temporary screen outside a lhakhang that can be seen in the background. During the ritual, the lama plunges a *dorjee* (ritual dagger) into each of the five points of a torma in the shape of a star. At the climax of the ceremony, the lama, with great deliberation, plunges the dorjee into the center of the star, which obviously represents the PLA. The symbolism is apparently that the lama wishes to expel the Chinese army from Tibet.

In the lama's quarters, the son of the lord, now grown, gazes at a photograph of his father, who is presumably deceased. The son, now the new lord, angrily tears up the text of the Seventeen-Point Agreement and throws it to the floor. The lama reminds him that their lands have been in their hands for centuries and says that he doesn't want any peaceful liberation of their lands and serfs. The lama admits that everywhere the Liberation Army has been, they have respected the monasteries; they have brought a peaceful life for everyone and everyone has praised them. (Even the reactionaries cannot deny that the PLA has behaved admirably.) He tells the lord to go visit the army as the monastery's representative and to try to make trouble: "No matter whether one eats tsampa or rice! Make trouble between the Tibetans and this non-Buddhist army!"

We next see the smith's son excitedly telling Jampa that he has seen the army approaching! The PLA soldiers approach in single file and with dramatic music while the smith's son, whose legs are still chained together, observes them. As he runs alongside a stream, he stumbles and catches the attention of two of the soldiers. Two fresh-faced and obviously benevolent soldiers, the first Chinese to appear in the film, rush to help him. They observe his chains and exchange shocked glances with each other and meaningful looks of sympathy with the smith. One soldier grasps the chains with an intensity that indicates his intention to free the Tibetans from such slavery.

Meanwhile, Jampa is called by the steward to get the lord's horse ready because the nobleman is going to see the army the next day. We see the lord having his hair fixed by two female servants while a third brushes his boots. He mounts his horse by stepping on Jampa's back. Jampa then leads the horse to the river, where they cross on a yakskin coracle, leaving the horse behind. On the far side, Jampa has to carry the lord on his back. We see the barefoot Jampa struggling over the sharp stones on the bank of the river carrying the lord. Going up the bank, Jampa stumbles and falls, dropping his master, who proceeds to kick him and call him a stupid animal. His kicking is halted by the approach of the PLA soldiers. The lord suddenly finds that he can walk for himself as he greets the soldiers, one of whom, of course, rushes to assist Jampa.

Jampa is next shown being treated by several attractive and attentive female PLA nurses. As he awakens, he sees the red star on one of the nurses' uniforms and, remaining mute, remembers the words of Namgang: "The Army of the Bodhisattvas has crossed many mountains and many rivers and has come to alleviate the suffering of the people. Every one of the Bodhisattva's soldiers wears on his hat a red star." The steward comes to summon Jampa, and the nurses have no choice but to return him. As they assist him outside, there is a horse waiting with some PLA soldiers. Assuming that he is supposed to assist one of the soldiers in mounting the horse, Jampa drops to his knees. All the soldiers are horrified, and one of them raises Jampa up with a soulful look in his eyes. Jampa is given the reins and assisted onto the horse's back. As he departs, led by another soldier, the nurses and soldiers wave good-bye.

The feudal lord's revenge is swift. In the next scene, we see Jampa being led by a rope tied to the horse of the lord's steward. The steward says, "I will cleanse you of these unwholesome tendencies," and then spurs his horse, dragging Jampa along the ground behind him. This is observed by the blacksmith's son, whose rage has apparently reached its limits. We see the smith's son, still dragging his chains, attacking the steward, throwing him from his horse and pummeling him on the ground, after which he frees Jampa. After this, the scene shifts to the blacksmith's hovel at night. The smith's son is attempting to break his chains, while Jampa lies on the ground. Jampa arises and, seeing what the smith's son is trying to accomplish, exchanges long expressive looks with him and then offers to help break the chains. As Jampa prepares to wield a large hammer, the smith's son shouts, "Break them! Smash them! Smash the chains that have bound my family for generations! Smash them! Smash them!" As the chains shatter, the two exchange another soulful look and embrace.

The smith's son tells Jampa to go quickly to find his sister, Namgang. "She will understand when she sees the chains. Let's leave from here and join the Liberation Army!" Next we see Jampa on a horse behind Namgang. They encounter some of the lord's men, who chase them to the edge of a cliff. Here they are surrounded, and Namgang cries, "Jampa! Let's die together. Buddha won't blame us." The two then proceed to ride the horse over the cliff into the river below. Both survive the fall. Namgang is picked up by a passing coracle, but Jampa is captured by the lord's men at the edge of the river. He is then seen displayed in a public place in a wooden cage for all to see. The crowd is heard to murmur: "Poor boy! He's been fighting against the Masters, poor boy."

Next we see the wise old monk asking the lord, "What are you doing? The Communist Party's Liberation Army—" He is interrupted by the lord: "I'm doing this to him according to the rules of my family, which have been followed for many generations. I didn't skin him alive. I have not yet lit the butter lamp for his death. I think this punishment is far too lenient for him. The Liberation Army comes along and suddenly everyone forgets the rules and traditions of their origins." The old monk looks to the lama, who is present but silently refuses to intervene. The monk says to himself, "I'm getting old. I can see the whole world becoming peaceful. But some people are still trying to damage this progress toward peace. I will go back to my sacred monastery." To this the lama agrees, saying to him, "Old Master, you should take a rest. I will sort out this problem." The wise old monk replies, "Buddha says every life is equal. Every life is equal, no?"

After the monk has left, the feudal lord reacts with disgust: "Ptooey! Speed to your death, old man!" The lama says, "One bird has flown away. The rest of the birds may follow. The slave's disobedience must be punished as an example to the others." The lord agrees: "Animals don't speak. He doesn't speak. There is no difference between them. There is no reason for him to be alive." "You should punish him," the lama says, "but not too severely. Times are different now. The support of the people rests on the edge of a knife. We are on one side and on the other side . . . it is unclear which side the people will choose. I'll take him in, by God's will, to regain the people's hearts."

In the next scene, we see the lama on the steps of the monastery surrounded by monks. Below are the people and between, lying on the steps, is Jampa. The lama makes a speech: "In the ocean of suffering there are many people who show ingratitude for the kindnesses Buddha bestows upon them. Yet, Buddha still has compassion for these thankless souls, who must cleanse their ingratitude through a life of prayer." The crown murmurs, "Buddha, Buddha, Bless you, long life, Lama." Jampa is then allowed to become a monk.

An old monk is seen in front of a huge clay statue under construction. He tells Jampa, now with his head shaved and dressed in monk's robes, "This is the lama's favor. He asked me to keep you as my student. You don't blame me for being old and poor, so I don't blame you for being mute. No matter whether you have a good or bad life in this lifetime, you should still pray and hope to have good fortune in the next life. So, if you help me to build the statue, all our sins will be washed away." In contrast to the wise old monk who welcomes the Liberation Army, this one seems not to question the feudal system. Jampa mutely applies clay to the statue.

Next we see a scene of road construction, with numerous laborers, both Tibetans and PLA soldiers. A truck is arriving on the completed portion of the road, and dynamite explosions occur in the distance. A Chinese soldier, whom we have seen before at the hospital where Jampa was treated, arrives on the truck. He approaches two Tibetans who are working as blacksmiths, one of whom is the blacksmith's son, now apparently having joined the Liberation Army. The son, now wearing a cap with the red star, offers the Chinese officer a drink of water, but with the warning, "If you drink from the blacksmith's cup you will have bad luck." The officer just laughs and drinks some more.

In the next scene, a blackboard is shown, with words in Tibetan and Chinese: *Tractor, Tashi, Barley, Jampa.* A group of young Tibetan boys and girls is reciting the words and learning both Chinese and Tibetan scripts. One of the students is Namgang, who, when she hears the name Jampa, is reminded of her friend the mute Jampa. She runs away from the lesson into a barley field, where she is apparently overcome with her memories of him.

Jampa is seen in the monastery with the words of Namgang echoing in his head: "The Army of the Bodhisattvas has crossed many mountains and many rivers and has come to alleviate the suffering of the people. Every one of the Bodhisattva soldiers wears a hat with a red star." Jampa also remembers the kindly face of the Chinese officer as he raised him from the ground and placed him on the horse.

The old monk with whom Jampa is supposed to be working approaches and asks him if he is still thinking unwholesome thoughts. He says that the lama has told him that the deities will punish him if he continues doing so. The old monk then resumes gilding the immense Buddha statue. As he sits within the outstretched palm of the Buddha, applying the last of the gold paint, the monk rubs his eyes and then is unable to see. He cries out to Jampa that he is blind. (Perhaps he has been blinded by the mercury traditionally used to make gold paint in Tibet.) The old monk, still not questioning what he has been taught, says, "My sins are wiped clean! The statue of the Buddha is finished!" Then we see the large statue being consecrated in a ceremony presided over by the lama. Holy texts, precious jewels, and auspicious items are put into the statue through an opening the size of a door in the front. The statue appears to be at least thirty feet high, on a pedestal of another twenty feet. The monks have to climb a ladder just to reach the door at the base of the statue into which the precious objects are placed.

As this scene fades, we hear the sound of a Morse Code–type message being received by radio. The lord, the lama (smoking a cigarette), and other Tibetans huddle around the radio in a darkened room. Then the sound of an approaching airplane is heard, and the lord and lama look expectantly toward the sky. An airplane of an American type (a C-119, which was not the type actually used) is seen dropping supplies by parachute. The parachutes land almost directly on the monastery, and several Tibetans, who appear to be both servants of the lord and monks, go to fetch what has landed. They retrieve military-style rifles, which they bring into the monastery and hide inside the base of the large Buddha statue.

Jampa observes this activity from hiding, but he is discovered by the lama. However, the lama realizes that Jampa cannot reveal what he has seen: "You are a mute; you can't tell anyone what you have seen. You should keep the temple clean and take care of the statue that you built." Then we hear the sound of rifle practice as the old blind monk enters the monastery and calls for Jampa. He says that he hears strange sounds and pleads, "Tell Buddha to let me die." Jampa is there, but does not reveal himself to the blind monk. "Jampa!" the monk calls. "You're not here? Buddha, please help my student. I can't see. But I still know that his sins are not yet cleansed." Jampa still doesn't answer and appears unconvinced by the old monk.

Meanwhile the lama and several Tibetans are back at the radio sending a message. One Tibetan arrives and tells the lama, "If the Tibetan Army's cavalry doesn't come soon we can't defeat the Liberation Army." The lama asks about General Wei Jiaojing (perhaps this refers to Gompo Tashi Andrutsang, the leader of the Tibetan resistance), but is told that they have all fled. The lama explains that they can't get through on the radio to Lhasa, that the Tibetan government is finished. He says they are trying to send a message to their outside allies.

The lama is informed that he has a visitor, the wise old monk who is opposed to resistance against the PLA. The lama leaves the radio room to greet the old monk. "Old Master, why have you come here at this time?" The monk tells him, "Many bad people are destroying all the monasteries. General Wei Jiaojing has been raping nuns! They burn the sacred books. They even take the gold from the Buddha statues! The Communist Liberation Army has been in Tibet for 8 years [1951–1959] and has done us no wrong. These people [the Tibetan rebels] have gone against all of our teachings. They are not students of Buddha."

Next we see the lama with the feudal lord. The lord moans, "It's over! Everything is over!" The lama disagrees: "It's not over. It's not over. Not yet! Leave all the guns for me. Get out now and take all the rebels with you. Anyone who might make trouble. Everyone here believes that I support the Liberation Army. Don't you see, that old monk, who can't die soon enough, came here to seek refuge with me! When you go abroad, tell our friends that in Tibet there are still good students of Buddha like myself."

Soon both Chinese and Tibetan PLA soldiers and cadres, male and female, are being welcomed to the monastery by the lama. As the lama receives a *katak* (silk scarf) from each, he is surprised when he recognizes one as the son of the blacksmith, now a clean-shaven PLA soldier. The lama makes a distasteful face, but is forced to treat the smith's son with at least superficial respect. The lama says to him, "You are from here. Welcome back to your hometown." They then all enter the monastery.

The blacksmith's son is next seen in an office that appears to have formerly been a shrine room of a house or the monastery. Now, a portrait of Mao decorates the wall. The smith's son is on the phone. He is now apparently a local official and is receiving a call about the lama. There seems to be some question about the lama's real loyalties. The smith's son says that the lama is a good person, but he is told that some Tibetan officials will be sent to the town to investigate. As the two Tibetan officials approach the town on horseback, we see that one is Namgang. As they enter the monastery, Namgang recognizes her brother, who appears to be conducting a meeting about the lama. They embrace. The blind old monk hears their voices and asks who it is. Namgang answers, "Old Master. It's Namgang." The blind old monk tells her that the lama is a good person because he saved Jampa. Namgang is happy to hear that Jampa has survived, but then the old monk says that the evil lord has taken him away.

Tibetan resistance forces are seen fleeing toward the Indian border. Among them are men with guns as well as monks. The evil lord is also there, being led on a horse by Jampa. The rebels are shouting, "Hurry up! Quick, quick! We are close to the border! Hurry up! Hurry up! The Liberation Army is coming!" The PLA is seen leaving in pursuit, sent off by Tibetans with kataks.

The resistance fighters approach the border, their baggage being carried by serfs, whom they kick and threaten with guns to make them hurry. As machine-gun fire is heard, the rebels panic, and the serfs drop their loads and run away. Jampa is unable to flee, however, because the lord holds a pistol on him. He forces Jampa to carry him on his back up what looks like a steep snowfield (actually, this appears to have been filmed at the well-known sand dunes on the side of a mountain to the south of Lhasa).

Jampa has finally had enough. He dumps the lord and struggles with him as they roll down the slope. A PLA soldier, the same soldier who once helped Jampa recover from the lord's abuse, runs to Jampa's assistance, but he is shot in the chest by the lord. Though gravely wounded, the soldier is still able to kill the lord with his rifle. Jampa kicks the lord's body down the slope and then returns to the PLA soldier. The soldier is mortally wounded, but he revives sufficiently to look with typical PLA benevolence toward the now liberated serf, Jampa. The soldier withdraws a katak from his shirt that is stained with his own blood. As Jampa stares in amazement at the bloodstained katak, the PLA soldier dies.

Jampa covers the soldier's face with the katak, and we hear a song, dramatically sung by a chorus, that expresses the thoughts of the still-mute Jampa: "Oh Snow Mountains! Oh pines! You are greater than Snow Mountains and pines. You are greater than Snow Mountains and pines. Oh, Liberation Army! I presented you with a katak of white cloud. And you gave it back to me painted with blood! Oh, Liberation Army brothers! Oh Liberation Army brothers!"

Jampa runs back the way he came, eventually reaching the monastery. He goes to the Buddha statue, climbs up onto the base, and breaks open the door in the base of the statue. He throws down the rifles hidden inside. The lama sees Jampa doing this and hides behind a pillar. As Jampa approaches the door of the monastery with some of the rifles, the lama stabs him in the back and Jampa falls to the ground. The lama unceremoniously tears down a *thanka* (scroll painting) and some kataks and dips them in the burning butter lamps. He uses these to set fire to tapestries and wall hangings. Soon the monastery is aflame. As the monastery burns, flaming objects fall, one hitting the prone Jampa, who moves, revealing that he is still alive.

Many people run up to the monastery, yelling, "The temple is burning! The temple is burning!" The lama is led away by a soldier, who takes him to Namgang and her fellow cadre and tells them that the lama was running away. The lama denies this, claiming that the soldier burned the temple, that the soldiers are trying to destroy his religion, and that he was not running away. The lama calls out to the people, "Everyone listen! The army and the blacksmith are trying to kill me." But Namgang says that this is not true, that the lama is at fault and is trying to shift the blame to others for his own crimes.

The blind old monk is still confused as to what is happening, while another old Tibetan murmurs that the lama must be good because he is a lama. The lama looks around uneasily to see whom the crowd will believe. As he does so, Jampa comes stumbling out of the monastery door with several rifles in his arms. The lama looks alarmed as Jampa, still mute, staggers toward him, throws the weapons at his feet, and points an accusing finger at him. The lama looks downcast, knowing that he has been exposed, as Jampa collapses.

In the next and final scene, we see Jampa in bed being tended by Namgang. A portrait of Chairman Mao is on the wall. Outside the window, we hear a large crowd shouting, "Long live the Liberation Army!" (This appears to be actual footage of one of the "spontaneous" rallies that the Chinese organized in Shigatse on 30 March 1959 and in Lhasa on 31 March.)

Namgang asks Jampa if he has heard what the crowd is shouting. She tells him, with tears in her eyes, "Everything is changed! All the repressed have started to speak! Jampa, it's me, Namgang! The Namgang who was freed from her chains. [Namgang was never seen in chains in the film.] Our life has also changed. We are liberated! We will never again have to be under the feet of the master. We never again have to work like a cow or a horse. Jampa, speak!"

Jampa raises his head and says, "I'll speak! I'll speak! I have a lot of things to say! I will speak!" Jampa, perhaps finding that he need say only one thing, slowly turns his gaze to the portrait of Mao and cries out dramatically, "Chairman Mao!"

Mao's name is the last word of dialogue in the film, and practically the only word ever said by the film's main character, Jampa. The film ends as Jampa's face fades into scenes of Tibetan streams, forests, and mountains. As the orchestra plays, a woman's voice sings: "Even the highest mountain, Himalaya, has a top. Even Yalong [Yangtze], the longest river, has a source. The Tibetan people's suffering, however great, has an end. The Liberation Army came and the suffering turned to sweetness. The suffering turned to sweetness."

According to the credits, *Serf* was finished in December 1963. Most Tibetans report seeing it between 1964 and the late 1960s. It was shown in many villages, and all schoolchildren were required to see it. Many Tibetans who were young at that time say that they were led by the film to believe that things in old Tibet had been as bad as portrayed. A lot of Tibetans have very strong memories of the film. It is not known if Chinese schoolchildren were also required to see the film or if it was simply shown in theaters. However, as anyone knows who has lived in China, films of all types were one of the most popular forms of entertainment. Tibetans say that their typical encounters with Chinese indicate that the film played a large role in forming the image of Tibet in the minds of many Chinese. If this is so, it does much to explain the common Chinese opinion about Tibet.

All of the major themes of Chinese propaganda about Tibet are covered in the film: The serfs were exploited and repressed without compassion. There was nothing but labor and oppression and suffering in their lives. All Tibetans were serfs except the lords, their agents, and the lamas and monks. The feudal lords and lamas were evil without limit and totally without compassion in their treatment of the serfs. The serfs longed for liberation, and the lords and lamas did everything in their power to prevent it, including conspiring with foreign imperialists. The People's Liberation Army is portrayed as entirely benevolent, regarded by Tibetans as an army of *bodhisattvas* (enlightened beings who have given up their reward in paradise in order to return to Earth to help others). There is absolutely no political issue of Tibetans versus Chinese, only a social issue of serfs versus feudal exploiters. Only the feudal lords and lamas are depicted as being opposed to the PLA.

The movie portrays scenes of unimaginable, unrelenting suffering of the serfs. There appears to be no relief from and no alternative to serfdom. Several attempts are made in the film to make the point that the serfs are treated as little more than animals, particularly by having serfs carry the lord's son and the lord himself on their backs. Even worse off than the serfs are outcasts such as blacksmiths, who are characterized as slaves and can be chained for attempted escape. The only lama in the film is depicted as selfish, duplicitous, traitorous, and deceitful. He uses religion only to exploit the people. Much is made of the connection, even a family connection, between the nobleman and the lama, and thus between the aristocracy and religion in Tibet. The lamas are also feudal lords. Monks are seen as sometimes pious, but deceived. One old monk is wise, but he therefore naturally opposes feudalism and supports the Liberation Army.

The PLA soldiers are portrayed as so obviously benevolent that they might well be taken for bodhisattvas. Perhaps as an acknowledgment that they don't speak the same language, communication between the soldiers and the serfs is primarily by means of soulful, meaningful looks. There are otherwise no ethnic or national differences, illustrating that there are no political issues involved in the presence of the PLA in Tibet. By contrast, the lord and the lama are depicted as traitors because they are in collusion with foreign (American) imperialists. Because they have no popular support, their only hope to preserve their status is by means of arms air-dropped by the imperialists. Preservation of their personal status is their only goal; their interests have nothing to do with those of the serfs and, therefore, of the majority of Tibetans.

In contrast to the faultless behavior of the PLA soldiers, the Tibetan rebels are accused of destroying monasteries, looting them of their gold, burning sacred books, and raping nuns. As they flee toward the Indian border, the rebels and the feudal lords are seen forcing serfs to carry their possessions, perhaps illustrating the Chinese contention that many Tibetans, the Dalai Lama included, fled to India only because they were forced to go or were deceived. The liberated serfs are shown cheering the Liberation Army as it leaves to round up the last of the rebels. The lama remains behind, intending to oppose the liberation while pretending to support it. This may be intended to indicate that the lack of loyalty of many lamas and monks was discovered only after the revolt. After the uprising, the liberated Tibetan serfs are shown as being in charge, with no evidence of any Chinese control or even supervision. Those Tibetan serfs, especially old people and monks, who were duped by the religious and feudal ideology of Tibet, have come to oppose the feudal system and the rebellion and to support the PLA and the new government.

The simplistic propaganda of the film is reflected in the opinions about Tibet of many Chinese people. The theme of this propaganda is that Tibet was an unrelenting Hell on Earth for the serfs, who were the majority of the population and were repressed by a tiny minority of rapacious landlords and lamas. The serfs were liberated by the heroic and benevolent PLA, and Tibetans, with a few exceptions, are eternally grateful to the PLA and the Chinese government for their liberation.

This typical Chinese opinion about Tibet, derived from Chinese propaganda such as this film, has become more than an opinion or even an ideology and is now essentially a Chinese mythology about Tibet. Since this mythology is intimately connected to the anti-imperialist ideology of the Chinese Communists, most Chinese are greatly offended by any challenge to this version of history. Even those who have abandoned Marxist ideology still cling to the anti-imperialist ideology regarding Tibet. To abandon this ideology would mean that they were not the liberators of the Tibetans from feudalism and foreign imperialism, but instead were imperialists themselves.

Tibetans point out that there is another aspect of the Chinese attitude about Tibetans that is both confirmed and perpetuated by the film. The image of Jampa as a dirty, ignorant, mute, and almost animal-like being reflects a typical Chinese image of Tibetans. The film also portrays Tibetan society as having been brutalized by the feudal lords. Many Chinese tend to fear Tibetans for their supposedly wild and barbaric nature, and they think that the Tibetans can be civilized only by contact with Chinese culture. One Tibetan states that he found that the image of Jampa from the film was so pervasive in China that mothers would discipline their children by threatening to summon Jampa. Thus the image of Jampa is less an object of sympathy than a source of fear and revulsion.

> What is therefore most significant about this film is not simply that it propagates a negative construction of pre-liberation Tibet, but that this particular construction draws on longstanding stereotypes of Tibetans in the Chinese imagination: Tibetans as savage and backward. On one level, this stereotype provides the cultural logic for colonization. In the evolutionary framework of Chinese historiography, Tibetans and other so-called national minorities lag far behind and must therefore be civilized by the more advanced "Han" people. On another level, this negative stereotype reinforces the power of racialized hatred and creates the possibility of racial discrimination in every realm of social, political and economic life.[34]

The film *Serf* depicts the Chinese mythology about Tibet, and it did much to implant that mythology firmly in the minds of many Chinese people. It also contradicts one aspect of typical Tibetan conviction. It is something of an article of faith among Tibetans, or at least exiled Tibetans and their international supporters, that the Chinese really know the truth about Tibet (as the Tibetans see it) but just can't admit it. This common basis of truth is thought to provide the ground upon which a dialogue and a resolution can begin. Despite this Tibetan belief, everything that the Chinese do or say about Tibet, from official propaganda to the privately expressed opinions of Chinese individuals, reveals that there is no common basis of truth. Most Chinese do not believe that Tibet ever was or should be independent, that Chinese motives in Tibet were imperialistic, or that the Chinese who went to Tibet treated Tibetans badly. Instead, many, probably most, Chinese retain opinions about Tibet that are more like those in *Serf*. The Chinese have their own deeply held myths about Tibet that they hold with as much faith as Tibetans believe their own.

Confiscated for the Benefit of the People

It is fairly well known that most of Tibet's many Buddhist monasteries and temples were destroyed during the Cultural Revolution (1966–1976). Less well known is the fact that all but a few monasteries were already empty shells by the beginning of the Cultural Revolution. Not only had all the lamas, monks, and nuns departed for India or a secular life, or to prisons and labor camps, but the monasteries had already been looted of all their valuables. The physical destruction of Tibet's monasteries and religious monuments that took place during the Cultural Revolution was a part of the chaos of that time and was done primarily by Tibetans, even if the instigation and coercion was by the Chinese. However, the earlier looting of the monasteries was planned and systematic and was done entirely by the Chinese army and state.

The Panchen Lama wrote in 1962 that only seventy of the previous 2,500 or so monasteries in the TAR had been spared destruction during democratic reforms. Since there were a comparable number of monasteries in Tibetan areas outside the TAR, the total number of monasteries in all Tibetan areas closed during democratic reforms may be estimated to have been at least four thousand.[35] This number includes monasteries and temples of all sizes, ranging from the huge ones with thousands of monks to village *gompas* with no permanent monks in residence at all.

Tibet's monasteries dotted the landscape, not only in every village but often in some of the most remote places, in accordance with the Buddhist ideal of seeking refuge from the worldly life. They were a defining characteristic of the Tibetan landscape and of Tibetan culture. They were also the repositories of much of Tibet's material and cultural wealth. Much of the material wealth of individuals, as well, apart from land and dwellings, was concentrated in religious objects kept in private household shrines. Almost every household had such a shrine with at least a few offering bowls and perhaps a thanka or small metal sculpture. The private shrines of the aristocracy were often much more elaborate, with many thankas and sometimes valuable statues or other religious objects. The wealth of monasteries also varied; a poor village monastery might have only the basics in terms of wall paintings and clay statues, while the famous monasteries had many shrines and thousands of thankas, statues, precious jewels, and other religious items.

The central lhakhang of the typical Tibetan monastery featured a central statue of clay or bronze, ranging from a few feet in height to truly colossal in size. Usually there were subsidiary statues of other deities on either side. These were accompanied by offering bowls and butter lamps, often of large size. The lhakhang would be festooned with thankas and silk brocades. A large monastery might have many such lhakhangs, while the smallest would have only one. A monastery such as Sakya was said to have had 108 lhakhangs (though this might be an exaggeration, since 108 is an auspicious number in Tibetan Buddhist tradition). The monastery would be in possession of the other religious implements necessary for rituals, such as small ritual daggers (*dorje*) and bells, horns and trumpets, cymbals and drums. There would also be other metallic objects such as the enormous copper kettles used for making butter tea. Many monks would have private shrines in their residences, sometimes with many valuable objects, in the case of lamas and tulkus and monks from wealthy families.

Presumably, most of the contents of monasteries closed during democratic reforms were removed at that time or in a gradual process continuing up to and even during the Cultural Revolution. Perhaps the most common scenario was that the most valuable items, such as precious jewels and statues of gold and silver, were removed first, during democratic reforms, and the items of lesser value, such as statues and religious articles of brass, bronze, and copper, were removed between that time and the beginning of the Cultural Revolution. It is logical to assume that most of the valuable items of monasteries were confiscated during the democratic reforms since the ideology of that campaign was the redistribution of wealth. Tibetans were told that they had been exploited by the monasteries and that now the wealth of the monasteries would be redistributed to all the people. By "all the people," the Chinese meant all Chinese people, not just the Tibetans. The Chinese Communist Party claimed to represent all the people, and therefore it felt justified in confiscating Tibet's wealth for its own purposes.

The Panchen Lama indicated that the democratic reform campaign in regard to religion degenerated into repression of religion, secularization of monks, and destruction of monasteries:

> In relation to formal democratic reform in the monasteries, the existing policies were the "Three Anti's," and in order that these could be perfected the "Three Settling Accounts" were implemented. But during specific implementation, the first task was opposing religion under the so-called "eliminate superstition" slogan; the second task was destroying statues of the Buddha, Buddhist scriptures and stupas; the third task was making monks and nuns return to secular life by any means possible. These were taken as the principal tasks and the "Three Anti's" and the "Three Settling Accounts" became the tools and strategies for realizing these three tasks.[36]

He observed that there had been "massive destruction and elimination" of Buddhist images, sutras, and shrines and that many statues had been stolen or broken open for their precious contents.

As for the eradication of Buddhist statues, Buddhist scriptures and Buddhist stupas, basically speaking, apart from the very small number of monasteries including the four great monasteries [Sera, Drepung, Ganden, and Tashilhunpo] which were protected, in Tibet's other monasteries and in the villages, small towns and towns in the broad agricultural and animal herding areas, some of our Han cadres produced a plan, our Tibetan cadres mobilized, and some people among the activists who did not understand reason played the part of executioners of the plan. They usurped the name of the masses and put on the face of the masses, and stirred up a great flood of waves to eliminate statues of the Buddha, Buddhist scriptures and stupas; they burned countless statues of the Buddha, Buddhist scriptures and stupas, threw them into water, threw them onto the ground, broke them and melted them. They recklessly carried out wild and hasty destruction of monasteries, Buddhist halls, *mani* walls and stupas, and stole many ornaments from statues of the Buddha and precious things from the Buddhist stupas. Because government purchasing bodies were not careful in making distinctions when purchasing non-ferrous metals, they purchased many statues of the Buddha, stupas and offering vessels made of non-ferrous metals and showed an attitude of encouraging the destruction of these things. As a result, some villages and monasteries looked not only as if they were not the result of men's deliberate actions, but rather they looked as if they had been accidentally destroyed by bombardment and a war had just ended, and they were unbearable to look at. . . . It is difficult to imagine and describe Tibet's Buddhist statues, scriptures and stupas being destroyed like this, but some people still say that "the broad masses of the working people have become conscious, and so they have been destroyed."[37]

The Panchen Lama's description of the process of the Chinese government agencies "purchasing" Tibetan metals reveals much about the rationale of China's destruction of Tibet's collected wealth. The collection, by purchasing or other means, by Chinese government agencies of Tibetan metallic objects was apparently regarded as justified by democratic reforms, during which such wealth was to be redistributed, and by a sense that such objects of religious worship and superstition were no longer of any use anyhow. The government agencies that collected these metal objects, such as the cynically misnamed Cultural Relics Preservation Office, purchased them from other government organizations, like the PLA and the Public Security Police, that had confiscated them from monasteries and individuals. These metallic objects would later be trucked to central distribution places in Gansu, Qinghai, and Sichuan, from which they were again purchased by foundries that melted them down. This was "purchasing" only in the accounting sense between different agencies of the Chinese government. Many religious objects were hidden by Tibetans and reappeared in the art markets in Kathmandu or in Tibet many years later. Some also fell into the hands of Chinese officials in Tibet, who showed their artistic appreciation, according to an often-repeated story, by making lamps out of Buddhist statues.

Many Tibetans report seeing convoys of PLA trucks headed to China with the contents of Tibetan monasteries. Ama Adhe, a Tibetan woman imprisoned in eastern Tibet near the traditional border with China, reports having seen convoy after convoy of trucks loaded with Tibetan Buddhist statues headed to China. She remembers that, in the beginning, the trucks contained small, precious statues of gold and silver. Later, the larger and less valuable statues were cut up and transported to China to be melted for the metal.[38] Similar stories were recorded by the International Commission of Jurists in its 1960 report,[39] and by the Tibetan government-in-exile in a 1976 report.[40] In *Red Star over Tibet*, Dawa Norbu, too, reported similar tales.[41] At the same time, according to the Panchen Lama, the Chinese were promising that the religious establishment would be preserved and that the state, under its policy of freedom of religion, would protect patriotic and law-abiding lamaseries and cultural relics in the monasteries.

Chomphel Sonam, a monk official of the Tibetan government who escaped to India in 1963, described the destruction of monasteries and desecration of religious articles:

> The monastic libraries containing thousands of volumes of scriptures have been turned into Chinese assembly halls and storerooms. All the gold and silver images and other valuables from monasteries and hermitages have been taken away to China. Objects made out of other metals have been melted down and used in the manufacture of arms and ammunition; clay images have been thrown into cesspools; the scriptures are either burnt or mixed with manure or used as wrappers in Chinese shops. The particularly thick papers are used as padding between the soles of the shoes. The woodblocks and wooden boards used as covers for the scriptures (which are engraved with sacred images and writings) now form parts of chairs and floor planks. Many large wall scrolls with sacred figures wrought in brocades were cut into pieces and distributed among the poor (who still consider them sacred). All religious costumes have been altered for use by the cultural troupes. It is also heard that a large number of very old religious articles were given to Russia in payment of debts.[42]

According to Tibetan accounts, the most valuable precious stones, gold statues and other golden articles, and the best paintings disappeared. Only the Chinese officials involved know what happened to the most valuable articles. There is a persistent rumor among Tibetans that China paid off its debt to the Soviet Union at the time at least partly in confiscated Tibetan gold and artworks. Some of the finest statues and paintings later showed up in international art collections. However, many of the statues made of gold and silver were melted down for their metal content without regard to their artistic value. The same was true of the thousands of thankas, many of which were reportedly burned. One Tibetan scholar has commented that the Chinese, unlike the Nazis who often appreciated the artworks they stole from the Jews, did not even appreciate or value Tibetan artworks.[43]

Statues and religious utensils of brass, bronze, and copper were almost invariably melted down for their metal content. In 1982, a team of Tibetans led by Rinbur Tulku was allowed to try to recover Tibetan artworks still in China. In particular, they hoped to recover the upper half of the Sakyamuni Buddha statue brought to Tibet by a Nepalese princess, known as the Ramoche Jowo because it had been kept in the Ramoche Temple in Lhasa. That temple had been badly damaged during the revolt, and the statue was cut in half and its contents removed at the beginning of the Cultural Revolution. The lower half had been found in Tibet, but the upper half was thought to have been taken to China. The team went to Chengdu in Sichuan, where they found no one willing to respond to their requests, so they went on to Beijing. In Beijing, they were told that some Tibetan artifacts had been recovered from a foundry, the Precious Metal Smelting Foundry, in 1973 during a brief period of slightly liberalized policies. In a warehouse, they found twenty-six tons of "statues and offering vessels," as well as "nearly a thousand burnished copper statues with gold tracery."[44] One of the large statues they recognized as the upper half of the Sakyamuni Buddha. This statue, along with the twenty-six tons of statues and religious objects from this site and six tons from another—in all, 13,537 statues in various states of damage—were recovered and returned to Tibet. Almost all the statues made of gold or silver had disappeared.

Although thousands of statues were recovered, many more statues and religious implements of brass or copper had been melted. Rinbur was told by one of the Chinese workers in Beijing who had recovered the statues from a foundry in 1973 that they had found around fifty tons of damaged Tibetan artifacts and had managed to salvage twenty-six tons of "serviceable items and pieces." This was the remnant of some six hundred tons of Tibetan statues and vessels of "gilt copper, bronze, burnished copper and brass" that the foundry had acquired and, after removing all gold gilding, had "melted down load by load and used in the production of goods for the state or public consumption."[45] Later, they heard that the foundry had acquired another thirty tons of Tibetan artifacts, from which they were able to salvage six tons. This Chinese worker told Rinbur that Tibetan artifacts were taken from Tibet to Liuyuan (in northwestern Gansu, near Dunhuang, on the railroad from Gansu to Xinjiang, the closest railhead to Tibet at that time) and then on to foundries in Taiyuan (Shanxi), Beijing, Shanghai, and Tianjin. He estimated that other foundries had melted comparable amounts to the one near Beijing.

Upon their return to Chengdu, Rinbur was able to recover another five tons of artifacts from a foundry in Sichuan, mostly so damaged that nothing could be salvaged. Another ton from Taiyuan (Shanxi) and two tons from another foundry at Man Shan in Sichuan was salvaged. Most Tibetan artifacts left in Sichuan had already been smelted.

While Rinbur had gone to Sichuan and Beijing, another Tibetan team had gone to Qinghai, where artifacts from central Tibet were also reportedly taken. The leader of that group, Gatar Tulku, found several warehouses at Huang Yuan, just west of Sining, some of which were still full of statues and some showing signs of having held great quantities of metal objects. One warehouse was empty except that the floor was still covered with Tibetan coins. This team also returned several tons of statues to Tibet. Gatar Tulku relates that he had in his possession a list of all the warehouses in China that had stored Tibetan artifacts, the total tonnage they had received, and the foundries to which the articles had been sent for melting. He regrets that he was required to return the list to Chinese officials and was unable to retain a copy. He also met in Chengdu with Rinbur, and together they went to a nunnery where they found about a hundred baskets each containing dozens of small and valuable Tibetan statues carefully packed and ready for shipment to some undisclosed location. They were unable to recover these statues because they had been "bought" by the current owner and had already been sold to a buyer.[46]

What this information reveals is that the confiscation of Tibetan art and metal works was systematic and was organized by the Chinese government. Those from central Tibet were taken to warehouses at Liuyuan in Gansu and Huang Yuan in Qinghai. Presumably, artifacts from Amdo were also taken to Huang Yuan and perhaps other locations. Items from the areas of Kham that were part of Sichuan were taken to Chengdu or some other location in Sichuan. The trucks that were observed by Ama Adhe were taking Tibetan monastic articles from Kham to Sichuan. From each of the primary warehouses, the artifacts were sold to foundries that melted them down for their metal content. These foundries were state-owned enterprises, and the metal was designated by the government for other purposes. Given that Rinbur Tulku recovered more than thirteen thousand statues and religious articles in various conditions—32 tons out of the 630 tons acquired by the foundry near Beijing—and that several other foundries were rumored to have smelted comparable amounts, the magnitude of the Chinese looting of Tibet's wealth can be imagined. One can see from these figures that the total number of statues and religious articles taken from Tibetan monasteries was many hundreds of thousands. This, of course, does not include any of the most precious statues of gold and silver, most of which simply disappeared, or the thousands of priceless thankas, some of which later appeared on the international art market but most of which were reportedly destroyed.

The recovered Jowo statue was repaired at the Jokhang in Lhasa and re-placed in the restored Ramoche in a ceremony in 1985. Rinbur and his team distributed the other recovered statues and religious vessels and implements to the undestroyed monasteries of Tibet "in accordance with their actual situation." The large monasteries of Drepung, Sera, Sakya, and Tashilhunpo, which had preserved some of their treasures intact, did not receive any of the recovered statues. Rinbur writes that they were sent to the most important monasteries of each sect and in each area, presumably as these monasteries were being restored:

> Destroyed monasteries which had been centers of the various sects, that is, Gan-den (Gelukpa), Mindroling (Nyingmapa), Tsurpu (Kagyupa) and Menri (Bonpo), and those which had been the most important in their prefectures, like Chamdo Gonpa and Nakchu Shapten Gonpa, . . . each received a large Buddha statue, 125 other statues according to their choice and predilection, 20 stupas, 20 sets of vajras and bells, 12 sets of cymbals, and offering vessels and copperware as appropriate. Then a large number of "medium monasteries" like Reting, Nenying, Riwoche, Taklung, etc., each received a medium-size Buddha statue, 75 other statues according to choice and predilection, 8 stupas, 12 sets of vajras and bells, 8 pairs of cymbals, and offering vessels and copperware as appropriate. Smaller monasteries like Ani Tsamkhung (nunnery in Lhasa) each received a Buddha statue, 35 other statues, stupas, bells, vessels etc which were divided up and stored in the largest assembly hall. Then statues, stupas, etc., were distrib-uted to many temples like Ramoche, Trandruk, and Yumbu Lakhar, according to their individual circumstances.[47]

The destruction of Tibet's monasteries and other cultural and religious monuments and the confiscation of the wealth of the monasteries and indi-viduals was not the final liberation of the serfs and the redistribution of wealth purported as the purpose of democratic reforms, but rather a disen-franchisement of the Tibetan state, nation, and people. During democratic re-forms in interior China in the early 1950s, landlords were dispossessed of their lands and property and were subjected to "struggle," often leading to death or imprisonment. In Tibet, it was not simply a social and economic class but the entire Tibetan nation that was dispossessed and repressed. The most distin-guishing characteristics of Tibetan culture and national identity were attacked and destroyed. The "three pillars of feudalism" that were subjected to demo-cratic reforms in Tibet were also the pillars of Tibet's social and political cul-ture.

The destruction of Tibet's monasteries is often mistakenly attributed to the later Cultural Revolution and excused as an aberration in the history of the CCP or as having been suffered not only by Tibetans but by all the Chinese people. However, the repression of the Tibetan upper class and the looting and destruction of Tibetan monasteries was not an aberration. Rather, it was a planned and systematically executed transfer of power and redistribution of wealth, not from the former upper class to the liberated serfs, but from the Tibetan people to the Chinese. The Chinese state used the confiscated wealth for its own purposes in the name of "all the people." The destruction of the Tibetan state, the purge of its ruling class, and the destruction of the most visible aspects of Tibetan culture and national identity were pursued not for the benefit of the Tibetan people but to secure Chinese control by destroying the culture and the national identity of Tibet.

Notes

1. "Put Down the Rebellion in Tibet Thoroughly!" *Peking Review*, 7 April 1959, 7.

2. "Chang Kuo-hua's Speech at the 2nd Plenary Session of Preparatory Committee for Tibet Autonomous Region," New China News Agency, 2 July 1959.

3. "Second Plenary Session of Preparatory Committee of Tibet Autonomous Region Adopts Resolution on Implementation of Democratic Reform," New China News Agency, 20 July 1959.

4. Thupten Khetsun, *A Testament of Suffering: Memories of Life in Lhasa under Chinese Rule*, recently published as Tubten Khetsun, *Memories of Life under Chinese Rule* (New York: Columbia University Press, 2007).

5. Abu Chonga, personal interview, Dharamsala, 1990.

6. Anna Louise Strong, *When Serfs Stood Up in Tibet* (Beijing: New World Press, 1960).

7. Panchen Lama, *A Poisoned Arrow: The Secret Report of the 10th Panchen Lama* (London: Tibet Information Network, 1997).

8. Jing Jun, "Socioeconomic Changes and Riots in Lhasa," 1990, citing Zhang Yianlu, *Population Change in Tibet* (Beijing: Tibetan Studies Publishing House of China, 1989), 28. Jing was a member of a Chinese Academy of Science census team sent to Tibet in the late 1980s.

9. The actual number of pre-1959 monasteries and shrines in Tibetan areas outside the TAR, according to autonomous district statistics collected by two Norwegian researchers, was 1,886 (992 in autonomous districts of Sichuan, 722 in Qinghai, 218 in Gansu, and 24 in Yunnan). Almost all of these were destroyed. The Panchen Lama wrote in his petition that the numbers of monasteries and monks in Kham and Amdo had been reduced by 99 percent. See Ashild Kolas and Monika P. Thowsen, *On the Margins of Tibet: Cultural Survival on the Sino-Tibetan Frontier* (Seattle: University of Washington Press, 2005), 191–208.

10. Dawa Norbu, *Tibet: The Road Ahead* (London: Rider, 1998).

11. Ibid., 203.

12. Ibid., 189.

13. Ibid., 213.

14. Ibid., 205.

15. Palden Gyatso, *The Autobiography of a Tibetan Monk* (New York: Grove Press, 1997), 199.

16. Palden Gyatso, *Tibetan Monk*, 59.

17. "Statement of Tashi Palden," in *Tibet under Chinese Communist Rule: A Compilation of Refugee Statements, 1958–1975* (Dharamsala: Information and Publicity Office of His Holiness the Dalai Lama, 1976), 39.

18. Palden Gyatso, *Tibetan Monk*, 63.

19. Paul Hollander, *From the Gulag to the Killing Fields: Personal Accounts of Political Violence and Repression in Communist States* (Wilmington, DE: Intercollegiate Studies Institute Books, 2006).

20. Palden Gyatso, *Tibetan Monk*, 63.

21. All otherwise unattributed quotes in this section are from Anna Louise Strong, *Tibetan Interviews* (Peking: New World Press, 1959).

22. All otherwise unattributed quotes in this section are from Strong, *When Serfs Stood Up*.

23. Thupten Khetsun, *Testament of Suffering*.

24. All otherwise unattributed quotes in this section are from Panchen Lama, *Poisoned Arrow*.

25. "The Panchen Lama Speaks: Text of the Panchen Lama's Address to the TAR Standing Committee Meeting of the National People's Congress Held in Peking on 28 March 1987" (Dharamsala: Department of Information and International Relations, Central Tibetan Administration of His Holiness the Dalai Lama, 1991).

26. "Special characteristics" was, and still is, a code phrase for Tibet's cultural characteristics that differ from those of China and that justify Tibetan autonomy.

27. "Panchen Lama Speaks."

28. This last request appears to reflect the Panchen Lama's hope that the Chinese Communist government would play a role in Tibet somewhat within the tradition of imperial patronage for Tibetan Buddhism.

29. Kunsang Paljor, *Tibet, the Undying Flame* (Dharamsala: Information Office of His Holiness the Dalai Lama, 1977), 29. The basis for the last charge was apparently the Panchen Lama's attempts to save some of the treasures of Ganden, Sera, and Drepung monasteries by moving them to the Jokhang.

30. Palden Gyatso, *Tibetan Monk*, 105.

31. "Panchen Lama Speaks."

32. The Panchen Lama assured two British socialist journalists in late 1962, after the opposition to him was already gathering, that he was actually in charge of the government in Tibet: "As a cadre of the People's Republic of China, I am performing my duties in accordance with the policies of the Chinese Communist Party and the Central People's Government. There is no question of any misunderstanding between me and them." Stuart Gelder and Roma Gelder, *The Timely Rain: Travels in New Tibet* (London: Hutchinson, 1962), 61.

33. Thanks to Robbie Barnett for providing a DVD of the film and the English translation of the script. All otherwise unattributed quotes in this section are from this script.

34. Tseten Wangchuk, quoted in *Jampa: The Story of Racism in Tibet* (Washington, DC: International Campaign for Tibet, 2001).

35. Kolas and Thowsen, *On the Margins of Tibet*, 191–208.

36. Panchen Lama, *Poisoned Arrow*, 49. The "Three Settling Accounts" applied specifically to monasteries. The accounts being settled were those of political persecution, of oppression between different ranks, and of economic exploitation.

37. Ibid., 50.

38. Ama Adhe, personal interview, Dharamsala, 1990.

39. "Statements Made by Tibetan Refugees," in International Commission of Jurists, *Tibet and the Chinese People's Republic: A Report to the International Commission of Jurists by Its Legal Inquiry Committee on Tibet* (Geneva: International Commission of Jurists, 1960), 221.

40. *Tibet under Chinese Communist Rule: A Compilation of Refugee Statements, 1958–1975* (Dharamsala: Information and Publicity Office of His Holiness the Dalai Lama, 1976), 58, 62, 80, 87, 94, 105.

41. Dawa Norbu, *Red Star over Tibet* (New York: Envoy Press, 1987), 199.

42. "Statement of Chomphel Sonam," in *Tibet under Chinese Communist Rule*, 87.

43. Jamyang Norbu, personal communication, 2006.

44. Rinbur Tulku, *The Search for Jowo Mikyoe Dorje* (Dharamsala: Office of Information and International Relations, 1988).

45. Ibid.

46. Gatar Tulku (Tenzing Norbu), personal communication, Washington, DC, 2006.

47. Rinbur Tulku, unpublished autobiography, translated by Matthew Aketser.

Jampa's mother carrying grain taxes to the lord's manor. Source: *Serf, a 1964 film put out by the Chinese government.*

Jampa's mother, exhausted, about to fall backward down the steep steps. Source: *Serf.*

The feudal lord observing the prostrate body of Jampa's father.
Source: Serf.

Jampa's mother, about to be sent to the lord's prison, hands the infant Jampa to his grandmother. Source: Serf.

The lord's son being carried on the back of a serf to visit the monastery. Source: Serf.

The lama and the lord survey their domains. Source: Serf.

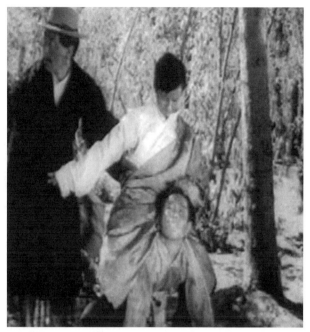

The lord's son riding Jampa like a pony. Source: Serf.

The traveler tells the blacksmith and his daughter about the People's Liberation Army. Source: Serf.

The blacksmith's son, in chains, listens to the traveler. Source: Serf.

Two PLA soldiers examine the blacksmith's son's chains. Source: Serf.

Jampa carries the feudal lord from the boat to the PLA camp.
Source: Serf.

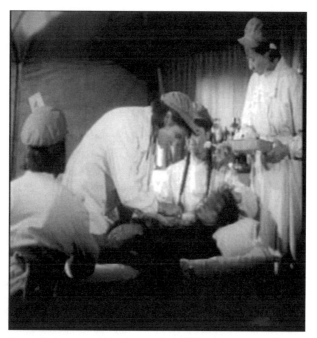

Jampa being treated by benevolent Chinese nurses at the PLA
camp. Source: Serf.

Jampa, being offered a horse by the PLA officer, thinks he is supposed to offer his back for the officer to mount the horse, as he was required to do for the feudal lord. Source: Serf.

Jampa places the bloody katak *on the neck of the dying PLA soldier.* Source: Serf.

Tibetans celebrate their liberation. This is apparently actual film of the Chinese-organized rally in Lhasa after the 1959 revolt. Source: Serf.

Demo Rinpoche and his wife in all their finery being paraded through the streets of Lhasa during the Cultural Revolution.

Panchen Lama, standing, center, and Rinbur Tulku, to his left, with the recovered Jowo statue. 1982. Photo courtesy of Rinbur Tulku.

Panchen Lama, left, and Rinbur Tulku with the restored Jowo statue. 1982. Photo courtesy of Rinbur Tulku.

A serf carries his master up a steep trail. The original caption reads: "Hate flashes from the eyes of the serf as he carries his master up the cliff." Source: Wrath of the Serfs: A Group of Life-Sized Clay Sculptures. *Peking: Foreign Languages Press, 1976. These clay sculptures appeared in an exhibition of the same name.*

"Bartering a child serf for a donkey." The child is seen being dragged away by a monk, making the point that children were forced to join monasteries, perhaps to be used for the lamas' deviant sexual purposes. Source: Wrath of the Serfs.

"Ferocious lords of the manor." The lord and the lama are partners in the trade of the boy for a donkey, making the point, as in the Serf film, of the collusion between feudal lords and lamas. Source: Wrath of the Serfs.

"A woman serf carrying water on her back watches with bitter hatred." Source: Wrath of the Serfs.

"The Man-eating Religious Authority." A mother protests the sacrifice of her son as an offering in the construction of a monastic building. Source: Wrath of the Serfs.

A rapacious monk forces the boy into a box to be buried alive. The original caption reads: *"They are the executioners of the boy and many other serfs like him in their effort to suppress the serfs' revolts and prolong the barbarous rule of the feudal serf system."* Source: Wrath of the Serfs.

Execution of a woman leader of a serf uprising, one of many, according to the Chinese. She is tied to a stake, supposedly preparatory to having her heart gouged out. The original caption reads: "She points an accusing finger at her enemies." Source: Wrath of the Serfs.

"The Serfs' Struggle for Liberation." The original caption reads: "Like angry ocean waves or an erupting volcano, the serfs' rebellions shake the entire Tibetan Plateau." A girl serf paints a red star on the rock in her own blood. Source: Wrath of the Serfs.

Detail of the serfs' final liberation. The original caption reads: "Taking up arms, the million serfs assail the evil estate-holders' manors and the lamasaries, strike at the feudal serf system." Source: Wrath of the Serfs.

A liberated serf smashes his chains. The original caption reads: "Fury flashes in his eyes and hatred pounds in his heart. This courageous serf rises to bury the criminal feudal serf system. Standing erect and with head high, he smashes his fetters and will destroy this dark hell on earth." Source: Wrath of the Serfs.

Chinese dancers in Tibetan costumes welcoming Hu Jintao to the United States. Washington, DC, January 2006. Source: *Photo by Karen Bleier. Reprinted by permission of Getty Images.*

4

Cultural Revolution

BY 1965, THE PART OF TIBET DESIGNATED as the future Tibet Autonomous Region (TAR) was declared ready for national regional autonomous status. This status had already been granted to every other national minority region, including Tibetan districts in Qinghai, Gansu, Sichuan, and Yunnan. The requirements for this status were the successful completion of democratic reforms and the cultivation of a sufficiently large number of local nationality cadres, who were to exercise a theoretically autonomous administration. The process of establishment of the TAR was initiated by elections to people's congresses at the local *hsien* (county) level. Elections at the local level were organized by the Preparatory Committee of the Tibet Autonomous Region (PCTAR) Election Committee, which consisted of "representatives of the Chinese Communist Party and the people's organizations and other patriots."[1] The Election Committee chose lower-level committees, which in turn chose appropriate local candidates (one for each position). The format of choosing candidates was described by Radio Peking: "Before the elections, candidates were compared by the people during discussions, ensuring that only those noted for their firm stands, their obedience to the party and their determination to follow the road to socialism would be elected."[2]

These candidates were then unanimously approved by the people and thus "elected." Those chosen at the county level thereupon elected representatives to the district level. The process of local elections in Tibet continued until all seventy counties of the TAR had finally organized people's congresses. These then chose a total of 301 delegates (226 Tibetan, 59 Han, and 16 of other nationalities) to the regional people's congress, which convened on 1 September

1965 to formally establish the Tibet Autonomous Region. Although the establishment of the TAR was accompanied by much fanfare and propaganda about its significance in the achievement of Tibetan self-rule, it had little meaning for Tibetans since all political authority remained firmly in the hands of the Chinese Communist Party's (CCP) Tibet Regional Committee and the People's Liberation Army's (PLA) Tibet Military Region Command, virtually all of whose members were Han Chinese.

The creation of the TAR in September 1965 marked less the achievement of Tibetan autonomy than the establishment of the permanent system of Chinese control in Tibet, accompanied by acceleration of the pace of ideological indoctrination, collectivization, and assimilation. The Chinese central government representative to the ceremonies marking the establishment of the TAR, Hsieh Fu-chih, was a member of the leftist Maoist clique; his visit to Lhasa was accompanied by an increase of the pace of collectivization and a renewed emphasis on class struggle. Hsieh called for "class education, socialist education and education in patriotism, with class struggle as the central theme," and recited Mao Zedong's leftist slogan "The national question is essentially a class question." As Hsieh said, "The history of Tibet's liberation, and of the 15 years since, is one of sharp class struggle. . . . The armed struggle that quelled the rebellion in Tibet was in essence a class war fought by the million serfs against the extremely reactionary serf-owning class."[3] Hsieh's words presaged the subsequent Cultural Revolution, during which Tibet's recently granted autonomy was respected in neither theory nor practice.

If the Democratic Reforms campaign in Tibet began the process of abrogation of Tibetan autonomy and the repression and assimilation of Tibetan culture, then the Cultural Revolution intensified and radicalized that process. Whereas democratic reforms had been primarily aimed at the repression of Tibetan resistance, the campaigns of the Cultural Revolution attempted a cultural and political transformation of Tibetan society. Democratic reforms had eliminated all autonomous Tibetan institutions; during the Cultural Revolution, the right to autonomy was scarcely acknowledged, and Tibetans came under intense and inescapable assimilationist pressures. The most fundamental identifying characteristics of Tibetan culture, including language, religion, and traditions, were defined as intolerably feudal and were subjected to severe repression. Even Tibetan history was redefined in accordance with the Chinese beliefs that Tibet had been a savage, feudal, and barbaric Hell on Earth and had always been a part of China. Although all of China was subjected to the campaigns of the Cultural Revolution—particularly the campaign against the "four olds"—almost all aspects of Tibetan culture were defined as remnants of feudalism and therefore targeted for eradication. The Cultural Revolution thus had a culturally destructive effect in Tibet not comparable to its effect in Chinese areas.

In January 1965, Mao called for a cultural revolution to combat bureaucratism and restore collectivism and the collectivist spirit. Mao employed his usual technique of trying to create the new by destroying the old, rather than building the new on the foundation of the old. This method, Mao said, was like "writing on a clean slate." In May 1966, he invited students, designated as Red Guards, to attack party bureaucrats, especially those suspected of resisting Maoist policies. Mao directed the Red Guards to destroy the "four olds": old society, old culture, old tradition, and old habits. The cultures and traditions of minorities epitomized the four olds and were thus a particular target. Red Guard groups from Beijing arrived in Tibet as early as the beginning of July 1966. Red Guards sent to Tibet were composed of Chinese students, mostly from Beijing, and Tibetan students from the various minority nationality institutes, led by Chinese instructors.

The Cultural Revolution was officially launched in Tibet on 25 August 1966 when Red Guards attacked the Lhasa Jokhang. Religious objects from Sera, Drepung, and Ganden, previously stored in the Jokhang on the Panchen Lama's orders, were removed and trucked to China. Many wall paintings and scriptures were destroyed on the spot. The Ramoche, Norbulingka, and other Lhasa monasteries and shrines were also attacked; in each case, Chinese and Tibetan Red Guards were led by Chinese cadres. Tibetan Red Guards were encouraged by the Chinese to carry out the actual destruction. Tibetans report that Chinese residents in Lhasa joined in the vandalism and looting.

By mid-September, Lhasa had been transformed. Every doorway, house, or wall in Lhasa had a portrait of Chairman Mao. Lhasa's streets were renamed with new revolutionary Chinese names. Prayer flags were removed from roofs and replaced by the Chinese flag. Former aristocrats and high lamas were paraded through the streets dressed in all their finery and were required to confess their crimes. Tibetans were required to study the "little red book," *Quotations from Chairman Mao*, 28,000 copies of which had been distributed. "Mao's thought" was accredited with mystical powers, supposedly capable of transforming individual and social consciousness. Minority nationalities' backward cultures were regarded as an obstacle to the propagation of Mao's thought.

Every aspect of Tibetan culture came under attack during the Cultural Revolution. The most distinguishing characteristics of Tibetan culture, especially Tibetan religion, were targeted for systematic repression. Most monasteries and shrines, already empty and looted, were physically destroyed. Tibetan Red Guards—or often, all villagers in a particular area—were coerced by Chinese and Tibetan cadres to destroy religious monuments, after the Chinese had removed all remaining portable valuables from the temples and monasteries. Tibetans report that Chinese in Lhasa and other towns were allowed to retain Tibetan religious relics looted from temples and monasteries such as paintings, carpets, and statues. Unmovable religious artifacts such as wall paintings were defaced, and large clay statues smashed. Buddhist scriptures were burned or used by the Chinese to line the innersoles of their shoes or for toilet paper; wood printing blocks were turned into floorboards or furniture or other objects degrading to religious sentiments.

Tibetans were required to dismantle temples and monasteries for their timber and stone, which was then used to construct Chinese offices, housing, or PLA barracks. Other religious monuments, such as small roadside shrines, *chortens*, *mani* stones, or *mani* walls were all destroyed. Mani stones were often employed in walkways or flooring, so that Tibetans would have to desecrate their religion by walking upon them, or were used to construct public toilets. Private religious shrines were also desecrated; Tibetans were required to surrender all personal religious objects of value to the Chinese authorities. Virtually all physical evidence of Tibet's previously pervasive Buddhist culture was eradicated within a few months at the end of 1966 by the Red Guards' rampage, although the seemingly chaotic destruction was obviously planned and systematically carried out.

Tibetans were required to dress like Chinese, cut their long hair short in the Chinese style, sing songs in praise of Mao in Chinese, and replace traditional Tibetan religious holidays and secular festivals with Chinese revolutionary holidays and ceremonies. All aspects of the colorful Tibetan artistic sense in personal and household decoration were replaced with Chinese proletarian green or blue. Tibetans had to paint over their decorative woodwork and painted window borders in dull colors. Even the large brass and copper cooking pots, utensils, and water containers in Tibetan households were confiscated on the pretext that they represented the old society. Tibetan language, characterized by the Chinese as archaic in relation to the so-called advanced Chinese language, was also attacked. The Chinese attempted a radical amalgamation of the Tibetan language with Chinese by adding Chinese vocabulary, intended to produce a "Sino-Tibetan Friendship Language." *Thamzing* was often employed against those identified as reactionary, indifferent, or merely nonparticipatory. Suicide, an anathema to Tibetans as Buddhists, was an often reported response, especially to the trauma of thamzing.

During the Cultural Revolution, Red Guards were ordered by Mao to not only destroy the four olds but also to "bombard the headquarters," that is, to criticize those in the party bureaucracy who were "taking the capitalist road," a euphemism for anyone less leftist than the Maoists. This set the stage for factional fighting within the party, as well as between Red Guards created by the Maoists and rival groups set up by the party bureaucracy. In Tibet, Chinese officials came under criticism from the Red Guards for treating Tibet as if it were their own fiefdom and for defending Tibet's "special characteristics," in particular the "problems of nationalities, religion and the united front." The Red Guards accused the party bureaucracy of using the excuse of Tibet's special characteristics to restrict the Cultural Revolution. They argued that Mao's thought should be the uniform thought within all the territory of China without regard to any special characteristics of any particular region. *Special characteristics* is the code term for the cultural traditions of minorities that justify their right to autonomy. What the Red Guards were criticizing was the very concept of minority autonomy. Of all the minority nationalities within the People's Republic of China (PRC), Tibet had the most special characteristics due to its history as an independent country.

In Tibet, the Red Guards were divided into two factions, the original student Red Guards from the interior, known as *Gyenlok*, and a rival group set up by the Chinese administration in Lhasa known as *Namdrel*, which attempted to divert criticism away from the party bureaucracy to more traditional targets such as class enemies and intellectuals. Conflict between the two groups reflected the struggle between leftists and rightists within the CCP.

Although Tibetans participated in the Cultural Revolution in Tibet, they did so primarily as tools of Chinese Red Guard leaders. Tibetan Red Guards were put in the forefront in the attacks on all manifestations of the four olds in Tibet, but Tibetans apparently had little to do with the ideological battles between factions. The attack on the four olds was virtually all that many Tibetans comprehended about the Cultural Revolution.

By August 1967, factional violence had created such chaos in the Chinese interior that Mao had to order the PLA to assume control. Conflicts between rival Red Guard groups thereafter began to turn more violent in Lhasa, as was the case all over China, since by now the PLA was also split by factionalism and had provided arms to various Red Guard factions. In Tibet, the factional fighting gradually took on a nationalist content as the two Red Guard factions polarized along ethnic lines until the Gyenlok faction was predominantly Tibetan and the Namdrel was mostly Chinese.

For many Tibetans, participation in the Cultural Revolution increased their nationalist awareness. Solidarity among Tibetans increased because of their common experience of Chinese repression. The attack on all aspects of Tibetan culture at this time produced an inevitable nationalist reaction in many Tibetans. Tibetans took the opportunity provided by the Cultural Revolution campaigns to criticize Chinese and Tibetan Red Guards and party members. The chaos and relatively permissive atmosphere of the Cultural Revolution allowed Tibetans to pursue nationalist goals, first by criticism and later, as the level of violence increased, by more violent means. As the factional conflict increased in violence, Tibetans began to attack Chinese cadres on the pretext of factional disputes or Mao's call to "bombard the headquarters."

In 1968, the Chinese revived the communization campaign. This, along with compulsory grain requisitions by the PLA, resulted in food shortages and further Tibetan discontent. In addition, Tibetans report that war hysteria was prevalent among the Chinese, who were convinced that a third world war would soon break out on the Indian border. The PLA therefore requisitioned and stored food, refusing to release food supplies to Tibetans. By late 1968, food shortages and the chaos of the Cultural Revolution had led to revolt in rural areas, beginning in the Nyemo area to the west of Lhasa. Revolt eventually spread to twenty of the seventy counties of the TAR, from Nyemo, Phenpo, and Nagchu near Lhasa, to Biru, Shotalhosum, and Markham in the eastern TAR. The revolt in Nyemo was led by a nun, Nyemo Ani. It became known among Tibetans as the Nyemo Revolt or the "Second Tibetan Revolt." The Chinese referred to the revolt as the "Second Reactionary Revolt."

The Nyemo Revolt had undeniably nationalistic characteristics. Several Tibetans report that the rebellion almost became an independence movement. It involved the rural and nomadic population of a large part of central Tibet. The revolt assumed such a magnitude by late 1969 that PLA units of the Northwestern Military District had to be called in to reinforce units in Tibet. The uprising was finally put down with great brutality; many of its leaders, including Nyemo Ani, were publicly executed in Lhasa.

At about the same time as the Nyemo Revolt in 1969–1970, the Chinese launched an "antirightist rectification campaign," which, in Tibet, was aimed at Tibetan cadres and the Tibetan students who had been sent back to Tibet before the Cultural Revolution or those recruited as Red Guards within Tibet. A youth independence movement was also exposed, and nine members were publicly executed. The most violent period of the Cultural Revolution in the Chinese interior lasted for two years, from mid-1966 to mid-1968. However, in Tibet, the violence lasted much longer. The PLA did not establish control in some Tibetan areas until the spring of 1970.

During the Cultural Revolution, the Chinese abandoned any pretense of respect for Tibetan autonomy; in fact, Chinese and Tibetan cadres were criticized for even suggesting that Tibet's special characteristics meant that it should be treated any differently than any other part of China. The special characteristics of all the PRC minorities not only were not respected but also were a direct target of the campaign against the four olds. Tibet came under relentless assimilationist pressures, despite the fact that Tibetans had been granted theoretical autonomy by the establishment of the Tibet Autonomous Region in 1965, less than a year before the beginning of the Cultural Revolution. While Tibetans of the TAR had supposedly achieved self-government under the PRC's system of national regional autonomy, the reality was that *autonomy* was a word that could not be spoken without inviting repression. The discrepancy between theory and reality reached near totality during the late 1960s, but has been an enduring characteristic of Chinese policies in Tibet.

Rinbur Tulku on the Cultural Revolution in Lhasa

In his autobiography, Rinbur Tulku describes his experiences during the beginning of the Cultural Revolution in Lhasa and the looting and destruction of cultural relics, including the statue of the Jowo that he recovered from China in 1982.[4] Rinbur begins his account in typically Tibetan Buddhist style by recounting a dream he had that the Jowo statue in the Lhasa Jokhang had fallen over on its side. This he considered a bad omen. He consulted a friend, Demo Rinpoche, who said he had also seen some bad omens. Soon the two rinpoches heard rumors that a new campaign called the Cultural Revolution would begin and that the Jokhang would be desecrated by students called Red Guards. He and Demo Rinpoche decided to go to the Jokhang for a last visit, and while there they removed a few irreplaceable religious objects. The next day, Rinbur attended a mandatory reeducation meeting at which a Tibetan-speaking Chinese official announced that the Cultural Revolution had begun and the time had come to destroy the four olds. He said that they would be given a signal to go to the Jokhang to destroy all its sacred objects. They were told that all the paraphernalia of superstition would be destroyed and a totally new Tibet would take the place of the old. They were also informed that if they did not participate in the destruction, it would be taken as evidence that they had failed to abandon old thinking and accept new ideas under the supervision of the revolutionary masses.

The next day, Rinbur and Demo were required to gather together religious scriptures at the Buddhist Association, some three hundred volumes of which were then burned in the courtyard. In looking in the direction of the nearby Jokhang, they saw people taking down the religious symbols from the roof. They saw that religious texts from the Jokhang were also being burned.

> All the books in temples like the Tsuklakhang [Jokhang] and Ramoche and in all the monasteries in Lhasa like Meru, Shide, Gyume, Tsemoling and Kundeling were burned, except for those few which some people managed to hide. Thus thousands of volumes accumulated at great cost over many generations and now very rare were surrendered at the orders of the Chinese officials in each section of the city and for a few days after the clouds of smoke in the sky over Lhasa blotted out the sun.

Rinbur found that houses had also been searched, and all sacred images and religious objects taken away. Many such objects were put into trunks and closed with an official seal. The day after, the two rinpoches and most of the remaining upper-class people of Lhasa were summoned to a meeting by the United Front (to which many of them belonged). They were told that, due to the Cultural Revolution having begun, they would have to discontinue all their other duties and engage in thought reform and reform through labor under the supervision of the revolutionary masses.

The next day, Rinbur's room was searched by Red Guards, who put all his valuables and religious objects in a trunk, sealed it, and then burned all his books. Rinbur writes about the impact upon Lhasa of the beginning of the Cultural Revolution:

> During that period, all the signs of Tibet's ancient traditions, such as rooftop flag-poles, cotton window awnings, black-painted frames around windows and doors, long hair and jewelry were declared "old customs" and removed. The names of important places and people's names were changed; for instance, the main court-yard of the Tsuklakhang temple was renamed "New Courtyard," the public teaching area outside the temple was renamed "New Square," and the summer palace became the "People's Park," and many Tibetans were given Chinese names like "Shangtsi" and "Utung." Ordinary people were ordered by one threatening announcement after another that they themselves had to destroy whatever sacred objects they had in their houses and were not permitted to keep any such thing and that they had to surrender whatever precious items they owned such as gold, silver or copper to the Chinese state bank. Thus most people had no choice but to cast what had previously been the objects of their devotion into the river, and reluctantly hand over their own jewelry to the Chinese bank.

In his account, Rinbur reveals what happened to the sacred objects contained in the Lhasa Jokhang (Tsuklakhang):

> Concerning what I heard about the destruction of sacred images in the Tsuklakhang, Ramoche and former monasteries: on the night before the destruction of the old and blessed images in the two Lhasa temples which Tibetans cherish more than their own lives [Jokhang and Ramoche], the Chinese officials assembled all the caretakers in the Ewam hall [of the Jokhang] and ordered them to remain there that night and not to go elsewhere. Then, at around midnight, several larger and smaller vehicles, possibly from the Chinese Government's "Cultural Relics" office, drew up at the southern entrance to the Tsuklakhang. A large number of soldiers and people who looked like officials gathered at the southern entrance. By dawn, they had collected all the gold and silver crowns, earrings and necklaces ornamenting Jowo Rinpoche and all the other statues on all three floors of the temple, as well as the offering vessels placed before them such as gold butter lamps and silver water bowls, and all the other valuable items assembled there, filled the larger vehicles to the brim, and carried them off. The same thing is reported to have occurred at Ramoche.

Then, on the orders of chief secretary Chen and other evil Chinese leaders of the Regional Party Committee, the senior-most office of the Tibet-based administration, government offices, schools and local administrative offices ordered their members to go and participate in the destruction of sacred objects at the Tsuklakhang. Thus some of those who went did so reluctantly. In the provincial bank (for example), at first all employees, both Chinese and Tibetan, were instructed to go, but later those with evil intentions ordered that all Tibetans were to attend without fail, but that Chinese were not allowed. This supposedly happened in several government departments. I heard that chairman Wang Chimei gave instructions for the statues of king Songtsen and princess Konjo [Wencheng], the Jowo, and others that had come from China to be spared, but I cannot say if this is true. Anyway, under strict orders from the Chinese leaders, a group of people had no choice but to join the desecration.

That day, apart from the statues in the central chapel, Jowo Rinpoche, Mindro Sungjon, Buddha Vairocana, the Bodhisattvas and guardians, the statues of the Buddhist emperors in the "chapel of aspiration," and the statue of king Songtsen in the middle floor chapel, all of the thousands of sacred images on all three floors of the temple, and principally the Mahakarunaka "self-manifest in five aspects" made by king Songtsen as the first Buddhist statue in Tibet, were destroyed, and their capacity to liberate beings brought to an end.

Also that day, in the Ramoche Tsuklakhang, the extraordinarily holy representative image known as Jowo Mikyo Dorje blessed by the Buddha himself with a history of more than 2500 years was desecrated by a few people possessed by the gods of desire and acting under pressure from the Chinese leaders. They employed blacksmiths to drive chisels into the statue's waist on either side of its cupped hands and pound them with hammers until it was broken into two halves, and the filling of powdered jewels and gold dust was scattered to the four winds. The lower half remained for many years in a Chinese government warehouse [in Lhasa], while the upper half went that same year along with most of Tibet's other precious statues to factories in China, and it remained in China for many years. How the two [halves of the] Jowo were reunited will be described in due course [this is the story told by Rinbur about his recovery of the upper half of the statue in Beijing in 1982, related in chapter 3]. But that day, the thousands of ancient sacred images on all three floors of the Ramoche temple ceased to benefit beings. The mural paintings were scraped off the walls with stones, and it was used thereafter as the meeting hall for the North Lhasa neighborhood committee.

At the same time, all of the sacred images in temples such as (Ramoche) Tsepak Lhakhang, Shitro Lhakhang, Jebumgang, and the four Rigsum Lhakhangs, and in monasteries such as Meru, Shide, Gyume and so on were also destroyed. We also heard about the sacred objects and images of the protectors in oracle temples such as Karmasha, Meru Nyingpa, Darpoling, and Trade Khangsar being destroyed. So it was that at that time all the holy objects of worship and propitiation in Lhasa ceased to exist, and people were oppressed by unbearable sorrow.

The statues from those temples and monasteries which were made of gold, silver, precious metal alloys, gilt or burnished copper, brass and suchlike, as well as offering utensils made of these materials, were all confiscated by the state and stored in the warehouse of the "Cultural Relics Bureau." Clay statues were thrown out in the street and their priceless contents scattered in the mud, and other heinous misdeeds were committed. Until then, a few monasteries like Sera, Drepung and Tashilhunpo [in Shigatse] had been spared out of necessity, but at that time most of them were stripped bare.

Events similar to those just described in the Lhasa area took place all over Tibet in those days, and the utterly irreplaceable losses and unbearable physical and mental tortures inflicted on the Tibetan people at that time may be understood in the light of these words by (Fourth Panchen Lama) Je Losang Chogyen: "Some meet their fate with the terror of a deer wounded by the hunter. Others are like an invited guest ambushed while crossing a fearsome desert. Some commit rash and wicked deeds out of a deluded desire for happiness. And experience the fruition of their actions in a flood of tears."

Rinbur Tulku's account reveals the typical process of the looting and desecration of Tibet's temples, monasteries, and household shrines. Even at the beginning of the supposedly chaotic Cultural Revolution, the process was deliberately organized and controlled by the Chinese authorities. Before the "revolutionary masses" were allowed to vent their animosity against the exploitative Buddhist religion and the religious establishment, all shrines were emptied of their valuable contents by Chinese officials and soldiers. All implements made of precious metals and all ornamentations of precious jewels were removed before any more random destruction was allowed. In Lhasa, it appears that all such valuables were stored at the Cultural Relics Bureau and then eventually trucked to China. The artistically most valuable statues and *thankas* (scroll paintings) disappeared, either destroyed, retained by the Chinese state or corrupt officials, or sold on the international art market. Many tons of less valuable metals were melted in several foundries in the Chinese interior and used for utilitarian purposes as described by Rinbur Tulku in his account of the recovery of the Ramoche Jowo statue in chapter 3. Rinbur also reveals the coercion that the Tibetan "revolutionary masses" came under from Chinese cadres to participate in the destruction of their own cultural relics.

Contrary to the version of events often promoted by the Chinese themselves that the process of destruction of Tibet's monasteries began with the Lhasa Jokhang and was confined to the period of the Cultural Revolution, the sacking of the Jokhang actually came near the end of a process that had begun during the Democratic Reforms campaign, which had begun in the summer of 1959 in the TAR and earlier in Tibetan areas outside the TAR. By the beginning of the Cultural Revolution, only the Potala, the Jokhang, and a few of the most important of Tibet's temples and monasteries had escaped the process of looting, desecration, and physical destruction. Such was the volume of religious art in Tibet that the process of looting and destruction of Tibet's cultural and artistic heritage took almost ten years, beginning during the democratic reforms and continuing during the Cultural Revolution until only some ten major monasteries were left standing.

While Chinese sources often try to blame the destruction of Tibet's cultural heritage on the "Gang of Four" and the chaos of the Cultural Revolution, emphasizing that Tibetans themselves participated in the destruction and that it occurred not only in Tibet but all over China, nowhere do Chinese accounts admit the systematic looting of the wealth of Tibet that began long before the Cultural Revolution, during the democratic reforms that immediately followed the 1959 revolt. The destruction of Tibetan cultural monuments and artifacts was an immediate aspect of Chinese policies that began as soon as China gained complete political control over Tibet.

Wrath of the Serfs

In 1965, in conjunction with the ceremonies inaugurating the Tibet Autonomous Region, a Museum of the Tibetan Revolution was opened in Lhasa. The museum, at the southeast corner of the Shol area below the Potala, was reportedly completed in record time by a team of Tibetan workers.[5] Present for the opening were some fifty crippled "liberated serfs" who told their stories of abuse under the feudal serf system to the assembled delegates and visitors.[6] Among the exhibits was the skeleton of a young boy, supposedly one of four who had been entombed beneath each corner of a manor house during its construction. Another boy told the story of how, as late as 1959, he had escaped a similar fate. He said he was supposed to have been entombed in the base of a Buddhist shrine that had collapsed and was to be rebuilt.[7]

The Museum of the Tibetan Revolution contained "hall after hall" of exhibits, including "piles of bones of serfs, slaves and poor monks found on the grounds of the feudal estates and the lamaseries, with clear marks of death by violence, including fractured limbs and shattered skulls." In one showcase were ten thighbone trumpets, "each made from the thighbone of a 16-year-old virgin." Another case contained "15 mounted, mummified human hands for ritual use as well as cups made of skulls, drums of two skulls fixed together and rosaries each of whose 108 beads came from a separate skull." A document on display, with the seal of the Dalai Lama, ordered the delivery of "human heads, blood, meat, fat, entrails, right hands, children's skins, widows' menstrual blood and stones that had been used to crack human heads, . . . for the strengthening of the holy rule." There were also the "severed penises of young men, . . . wrapped in special paper and preserved for use in worship." Displays showed religious decrees prescribing death for witches and devils. There was also the "charred, shriveled corpse of a woman who, because she had borne triplets, was declared a witch and burned alive." The corpse of this woman had supposedly been dressed up in silk robes and a crown and installed among the images in a Buddhist temple.[8]

One exhibit at the museum was about serf revolts and resistance in old Tibet. Such unrest was said to have been constant, although few examples were provided. The exhibit mentions a "wave of slave revolts in the ninth century" that was supposedly a great landmark in Tibet's early history. It was said to have played a decisive role in destroying the old slave-based Tibetan monarchy and clearing the way for the succeeding feudal mode of production. This is obviously an attempt to make Tibetan history fit the Marxist theory of class-based social development, and the "slaves" are depicted as the makers of this history due to their hatred of the slave system. The slave revolts were said to have caused the downfall of the Tibetan Empire and the subsequent rise of the power of religion and the creation of the feudal serf system. The remainder of the serf revolts mentioned are all in the early twentieth century and were supposedly in preparation for the downfall of the feudal system. The instances mentioned are all of a local nature and were caused by individual abuses by estate owners. Serf resistance was said to have increased in the 1950s, culminating in the 1959 revolt and democratic reforms. The long centuries of serf resistance to feudalism were said to have reached their climax in the serfs' active support for the crushing of the reactionary rebellion and their mass participation in the democratic reforms.[9]

In one display was an inventory of the Dalai Lama's private treasure, not counting the portion with which he had escaped. It tallied 110,328 ounces of gold, five million yuan in silver, 20,331 jewels, and 14,675 garments. The total value was given as 98 million yuan ($41 million). Apparently not mentioned was the fact that all this treasure had been confiscated by the Chinese government. According to the display, the Dalai Lama received an annual income from his personal estates of 500,000 kilograms (550 tons) of grain, 30,000 kilograms (33 tons) of butter, 175 bolts of woolen cloth, and 275 animals. The estates owned by the Dalai Lama and his family were enumerated as 27 manors, 30 pastures, 6,170 serfs, and 102 house slaves.[10]

Also in the museum was a letter from Reginald Fox, one of the private British radio operators in Tibet, to the commander of the Tibetan Army, written in January 1950 (when the PLA began to enter Tibetan areas of Kham and Amdo but long before the invasion of Chamdo in October 1950) urging resistance to the PLA in order to mobilize world opinion so that the Americans might provide military assistance, perhaps even by air.[11] There was also an exhibit of the "names, photos and paraphernalia" of the CIA-trained Tibetans who had been parachuted into Tibet in the late 1950s and were captured or killed by the PLA.[12]

Israel Epstein reports that there were similar museums at Sera Monastery, including clay statuary "done by former poor lama craftsmen in Sera monastery, recording past struggles there,"[13] and museums at some of the former manorial houses, such as that of the Phala family near Gyantse and, when communes were established, at commune centers. One such was the "Class Struggle Exhibition" at Khaesum commune in Lhoka, formerly the Surkhang estate, which included clay statuary. Anna Louise Strong visited a similar museum at Drepung in 1959. Epstein also visited the "old Nangtzesha courthouse prison and torture chamber," which had "striking figure groups portraying the brutalities of which it was once the scene in real life." He adds that "many local history exhibits we saw in 1976 had their own sculptural displays." One in particular at the "Zangchin temple near the Nyama Commune was remarkable for its rough strength and immediacy of impact."[14]

In 1975, the Museum of the Tibetan Revolution in Lhasa opened its newest and ultimately most famous exhibit, a series of 106 clay sculptures with the title "Wrath of the Serfs," "complete with decor, lighting, oral explanations and taped music to produce the optimum artistic effects."[15] An illustrated book about the sculptures was produced in 1976 (English-language version) with the title *Wrath of the Serfs: A Group of Life-Size Clay Sculptures*. The book was also produced in Chinese- and Tibetan-language versions and probably other languages as well. The "Wrath of the Serfs" sculptures in Lhasa were required viewing for all Tibetan schoolchildren in the 1970s, and the book of photographs was a major item in China's propaganda about Tibet during that same period.

The sculptures were created during a revived campaign to contrast current conditions with the supposed horrors of the past, similar to the "Remembering Bitterness" campaign of the early 1960s. Since conditions during that period were hardly good, the past was attacked with lurid descriptions of the "hell on earth" that Tibet had supposedly been before the Chinese liberation. Pre-1950 Tibetan society was described as "the most reactionary, dark, cruel and barbarous feudal serf system." Tibet's "million emancipated serfs," who had suffered oppression and exploitation under the feudal serf system, now cherished "boundless love for Chairman Mao, the Communist Party and socialism" and were determined to take the socialist road and never to permit the revival of the serf system. All the resources of Chinese propaganda were devoted to the demonization of preliberation Tibetan society. Individuals who had suffered oppression in the past were collected and, their stories suitably elaborated, required to recite their accounts for Tibetans and foreign visitors.

The "Wrath of the Serfs" exhibit became a required stop on the itinerary of foreign visitors, who were told that the exhibition invoked Tibetans' memories of the "reactionary, dark, ruthless and savage hell on earth" that was old Tibet and made them determined "to educate their posterity never to forget the damnable dark days in old Tibet and to always remember the kindness and concern of Chairman Mao and the Communist Party, and to follow the Communist Party in carrying on the revolution from generation to generation."[16] Tibetans describe the sculptures as so impressively lifelike that they found it hard to resist the appeal of such propaganda.

The book of photographs of the exhibition begins with a quote: "Where there is oppression there is resistance." The million Tibetan serfs (presumably only including the TAR) were said never to have ceased resisting the feudal serf system: "In less than half a century before Tibet's liberation the serfs rose in large-scale revolt more than a hundred times. Wave upon wave they advanced in unyielding struggle for their emancipation, hitting hard at the reactionary rule of the serf-owners." The long years of the extremely reactionary dictatorship of the serf-owner class were said to have kept Tibet "poverty-stricken and backward, stagnant and in utter decadence."

Wrath of the Serfs begins with photos of evidence of the evils of the serf system. One photo shows several horns or trumpets fashioned from the arms and thighbones of young female serfs. These were said to be relics of atrocities by old Tibet's reactionary rulers headed by the Dalai Lama. Another photo is of several drinking bowls made from skulls. According to the caption, the bowls, covered with elaborately worked silver on the outside, are bowls from the household of the Dalai Lama made from the skulls of murdered serfs.

In fact, there is no evidence that young girls were ever sacrificed for the sake of making thighbone trumpets. The reason for using the bones of young girls has to do with the *dakini* tradition of Tibetan Buddhism and the use of reminders of the constant reality of death in meditation rituals. The making of skull bowls is prevalent in much of Inner Asia and derives from Turkic and Mongol culture. The habit was to make a bowl of the skull of some deceased notable, or sometimes a notable enemy, whose psychic influence one wished to imbibe. The practice was usually considered a compliment to the one whose skull was used, even if a defeated enemy, and such bowls were treasured items.

Another photo is of two human skins said to have been stripped from live serfs. Such practices were alleged to have been indulged in at will by the serf-owners. Another photo shows two detached hands and forearms that were said to have been chopped off by lamas during a religious ceremony and two small double-sided prayer drums that were reportedly made of serf victims' skulls and skins. Prayer drums were indeed made of skulls in Tibet, as well as in other Himalayan and Inner Asian regions, but for reasons that involved the role of death in religious practice, not the lamas' exploitation of serfs. Similarly, human skins, not from live victims, were used in rituals intended to remind of the reality of death.

The introduction to the photos of the clay sculptures says that they were produced by art students from the College of Fine Arts in Beijing in cooperation with art workers in Tibet, "with the aim of sharply exposing the evils of the old Tibet and warmly acclaiming the serfs' heroic and brave struggles." There were 106 life-size figures of men and women, with four reliefs and many murals as background. The work was said to have taken 18 months, during which the sculptors traveled more than 5,000 kilometers inside Tibet for the purpose of study and investigation. They reportedly listened to the angry condemnation of past sufferings by a hundred liberated serfs, asked for suggestions from former poor and lower-middle peasants and herdsmen, and improved their work on this basis. This experience was said to have strengthened their determination to be faithful spokesmen for the liberated serfs of Tibet. They studied Chairman Mao's "Talks at the Yenan Forum on Literature and Art" and "made good use of the experience gained in creating the revolutionary model operas." (These were the operas created by Mao's wife.) The artists attempted to insinuate the sculptures with "their own strong class feeling, combining revolutionary realism with revolutionary romanticism." The sculptures "thus reveal the multifarious crimes of the feudal serf system and . . . enthusiastically eulogize the courageous struggle and strongly voiced eagerness for liberation of the million serfs."

The sculptures were arranged in four parts depicting the feudal manor, the lamasery, the former local government, and the serfs' struggle for liberation. Part 1 is titled "The Feudal Manor—Hell on Earth." The introduction to this section says:

> Under the feudal serf system the masses of the serfs were mercilessly exploited and oppressed by the serf-owning class. The feudal lords exacted unpaid hard labor from the serfs, who were bought and sold, used as mortgages or bartered at their owners' will. The life of the serfs was worse than that of draught animals as they struggled to live on from generation to generation.

The first manor scene is "The Plight of *Ula* Conscripted Labor." *Ula* is a Mongolian word meaning the same as the French word *corvée*, or conscripted transport. Ula was instituted in Tibet during the Mongol Empire and the Mongol Yuan dynasty (1250–1368 in Tibet, 1274–1368 in China). It began as a postal service by means of which the Mongols sent messages throughout their empire. As such, it was a major part of the Mongol administrative system. Sometimes messages were sent by couriers, who had the right to demand lodging, food, and transport from the villages through which they passed. Other times, messages had to be passed by villagers themselves. The system was inherited by later Tibetan and Chinese authorities and corrupted by a proliferation of both those who could demand such services and the services they could demand. It became abusive, in that anyone authorized by the government could demand transport services, not only for themselves but also for their baggage and even trade goods. Manchu *ambans* in Tibet were some of the worst abusers of the privilege, often using it to demonstrate their authority. The Chinese Communists have demonized this practice as a particularly Tibetan evil, but in essence it was an essential government administrative service, one that in another context is used by the Chinese Communists to demonstrate the Mongol Yuan's administrative authority over Tibet to which the Chinese now claim to be the heirs.

Feudal lords and monasteries had the right to demand transport from their serfs, but this was not the same as government ula. Nevertheless, in this sculpture, a feudal lord is seen abusing his serfs for what is described as ula service. The lord is seen being carried on the back of a serf up a trail that ascends the face of a cliff. The Chinese make much of the supposedly common practice of nobles being carried by their serfs. However, it is hard to imagine this being more comfortable for the lord than simply walking (or riding horseback). The serf groans under the lord's weight. The caption reads: "In bitter wind and snow conscripted serfs trudge up a cliff on *ula* service. One carries his hated master up a steep mountain path; others stagger under heavy loads of butter, barley and rice which they are forced to transport for their master." A close-up of the serf and his master shows a servant of the lord protecting the lord with a rifle and an umbrella. This is captioned: "Hate flashes from the eyes of the serf as he carries his master up the cliff."

Another servant whips the other serf men, women, and children as they trudge up the mountain. A young female serf is shown hanging off a rock in the cliff face in near exhaustion: "A young woman serf, exhausted and starved, clutches a rock to keep from falling under the heavy load of barley." An old woman is shown bent under a crushing load of grain as she tries to catch a little snow to moisten her mouth: "She can only swallow her tears." An old man has collapsed under his load as other serfs try to help him and the overseer raises his whip to drive him onward. One serf tries to protect the old man and we see a close-up of his angry and determined face.

In the second manor scene, "Unpaid Hard Labor," we see an overseer with a whip forcing a man and woman serf to labor while the woman's baby lies on the bare ground crying with hunger. The introductory caption reads:

> Every inch of the feudal lords' land was drenched with the blood and sweat of the serfs; every grain the serfs reaped was steeped in their bitterness. A new mother

is driven by an overseer's whip to pull a plough while her babe wails in the field. Huge crows swoop overhead, and one eyes the child from a bare branch, threatening it. Beside the young mother is a man serf in iron shackles. He tried once to escape and so also works under the overseer's whip.

The overseer regards the serfs with undisguised contempt and without compassion. The serfs appear ragged, exhausted, and staggering, as usual, but also with the usual simmering rage at the serf system.

The third scene is "Bartering a Child Serf for a Donkey." This implausible story was presumably told to the Chinese students by some former serf. The child is seen being dragged away by a monk, making the point that child monks were usually forced to join monasteries. Perhaps this youth is to be used for the lamas' deviant sexual purposes. A donkey is seen being given to the lord in exchange. The lord is accompanied by a lama, who appears to be the nobleman's partner in the trade. Both appear wholly evil and totally without compassion. The child's grandfather, emaciated and with his eyes gouged out for some prior offense, tries to rescue the child. Two more serfs watch the scene with bitter hatred in their eyes.

The last manor scene is "Inhuman Existence." Its caption explains:

> Three generations huddle in a dismal tumbledown cowshed. The mother grinds peas day and night for the master. Her famished child reaches out with his bowl for food. But where can this exhausted mother get food for him? The wicked master's grinder breaks the serfs' bones and drains their blood but it can never destroy their vengeance born of blood and tears.

The woman is so exhausted that her head almost touches the millstone as she grinds. The tiny child cries tiny clay tears. The grandmother looks almost drained of life as she cards the lord's wool.

Part 2 of *Wrath of the Serfs* is "The Lamasery—Wicked Den for Devouring Serfs." The introductory caption for this part reads:

> The lamasery was a spiritual pillar of the serf-owning class's reactionary rule. The serf-owners used religious authority to lull and persecute the laboring people. Lamaseries had their arbitrary rules and regulations, instruments of torture and prisons. Many serfs were subjected to such unthinkable punishments as chopping off hands, feet or noses, gouging out eyes, pulling out tendons or skinning alive.

The first scene, "Extorting Debts from Serfs," has the introductory caption:

> Dark clouds gather and wolves howl as a destitute herder is to be dragged to death by a horse for debt. From birth he has been saddled with a legacy from his grandfather of huge debts to the lamasery. Never having eaten a decent meal,

every day of his life has been spent in herding cattle and sheep, carrying water and cutting firewood for his lamasery, only to suffer this agonizing end.

In the left foreground is a Buddhist stupa or *chorten.* In the background is a mural painting of a vast Tibetan landscape. The monastery's steward is shown dragging the serf with his horse. "The evil steward's prayer beads do not efface the canine look in his eyes as, with his account book, he fattens on the flesh of the poor herders and serfs." The serf herder is on the ground with his hands tied to a rope that is about to be used to drag him: "The unyielding herder. The torment may claim the skin from his body but it can never quench the flames of his towering hatred. 'We'll have blood for blood from you wolves one day!' he vows."

The next scene, "The Man-Eating Religious Authority," begins with the caption:

> In a dim inner hall a cassocked lama shoves a little boy into a box to be buried alive. In the name of building a temple, the boy is to be placed under a corner-stone of the hall as sacrificial offering. The mother hears her child's screams, rushes up and cries out. She is followed by an old carpenter and other serfs.

Presumably the Chinese art students heard some stories of this sort of ritual. Such ceremonies were in fact practiced in many of the cultures of India, the Himalaya, and Inner Asia, but only in the distant past. Such stories are not common for Tibet at any recent time. Perhaps this is an example of the students' stated intention to "combine revolutionary realism with revolutionary romanticism."

On the left, a monk with a fierce expression is shown shoving the screaming boy into a box. Two lamas stand between the boy and a group of serfs who are observing the scene. "A 'living Buddha' chants piously, reading his beads. He is guarded by a lama holding an iron staff. They are the executioners of the boy and many other serfs like him in their efforts to suppress the serfs' revolts and prolong the barbarous serf system." The boy's mother is distraught and is comforted by the carpenter. Other serfs viewing the scene wear expressions of anger. "They will one day avenge the child's death," the caption assures us. Another caption reads: "A poor herder wants to batter down the man-eating lamasery with his pole."

The third scene, "Connivance and Brutality," begins with the caption:

> The bones of serf victims lie beneath the high lamasery walls; daggers and rifles are concealed in religious robes. Those "living Buddhas" slaughtered innocent serfs like cattle, used their flesh, blood, bones and hearts as sacrificial objects. To crush the serfs' revolts and maintain their reactionary rule, the serf-owners used the lamaseries for conniving with foreign imperialists and selling out China's territories in exchange for arms and ammunition.

On the left, two monks carry boxes of arms from a hiding place. They are supervised by three figures: "A 'living Buddha,' a reactionary local government official and a foreign imperialist direct the unloading of ammunition from a foreign country." The "foreign imperialist" wears Tibetan-style robes, perhaps as a disguise. His country of origin is therefore not distinguishable, but he has a long nose so is presumably meant to be an American.

On the right, a serf is seen in chains being restrained by two monks. One of the monks has a knife in his hand. The caption explains that he is "a serf sentenced to have both hands and feet hacked off by the 'living Buddha' for defying the religious authority of the lamasery and refusing to carry out the master's traitorous intrigue." This scene, like similar scenes in the film *Serf*, reiterates one of the main themes of Chinese propaganda about Tibet: that the lamas and lords traitorously conspired with foreign imperialists to preserve the feudal serf system and to deny the serfs their liberation. Their schemes are opposed by all of the serfs without exception. The lamas and nobility are traitors to China because they oppose the serfs' liberation at the hands of the PLA.

The third part, "The *Kasha*—Reactionary Local Government," begins:

> The *Kasha*, the former local government of Tibet, was the means by which the feudal serf-owner class maintained its reactionary rule. It kept a large reactionary armed force, laid down its own "rules and regulations," inflicted cruel and inhuman punishments and set up prisons to repress the serfs. Under the sanguinary rule of the *kasha* countless serfs died, their families ruined. But none of the serf-owners' atrocities could make the serfs bow their heads, and the serf-owners' dream of preserving the feudal serf system was quite in vain.

Tibet's governing council of ministers, the Kashag, forms one leg of the triangle that the Chinese term the "three pillars of feudal serfdom." By the "sanguinary" rule of the Kashag, the Chinese propagandists probably meant that they were cruel and bloodthirsty. The "large reactionary armed force" was the Tibetan Army, which was, of course, quite legitimate given Tibet's independent status before 1951. Similarly, the "rules and regulations" of the Kashag were the legitimate laws of the Tibetan government. This is an example of the Chinese attempts to delegitimize all the institutions of independent Tibet in order to legitimate the institutions set up by the Chinese state.

The introductory caption to the first scene, "Struggle at the Site of Execution," reads:

> Under a gloomy, leaden sky, a bound woman serf stands heroic before the Potala Palace. Arrested for leading a serf uprising that destroyed estate-holders' manors, an act that shook the rule of the serf-owner class, she has been sentenced to death by having her heart gouged out. Fearless nonetheless, she turns to point an accusing finger at her executioners. The angry masses rush to the site in protest.

On the left are seen a "local government" official, a feudal lord, and a lama, representing the three pillars of feudalism. Between them and the condemned woman is a servant holding a knife and a male prisoner in a wooden cage. The man in the cage is shown in close-up: "A blacksmith locked in a wooden cage seethes with fury at the sight of the man-eating beasts." A close-up of the condemned woman has the caption: "The brave woman denounces the lamasery, nobles and *kasha* for their crimes." Several ragged but resolute serf men, women, and children are seen rushing toward the woman but being restrained by another servant. Nevertheless, "The woman serf's denunciation and the indignant roar of the serfs strike fear into the bloodsuckers in religious robes." Another close-up shows two serfs handcuffed together "glaring in fury at the enemy."

Epstein writes that this scene depicts a 1918 revolt in a nomadic area of northern Tibet, now in Qinghai, that paid feudal tribute directly to the Lhasa government. The woman leader of the serf revolt was Hor Lhamo, who led a delegation representing 150 nomadic families to complain to the local governor about excessive feudal taxes. When the complaint was rejected, Hor Lhamo led an attack against the local ruler. The ruler was killed, and 45 Tibetan Army soldiers were disarmed. A military force was sent, presumably from Lhasa, to subdue the revolt. Hor Lhamo was executed, but the news of the revolt was said to have put heart into the serfs' resistance.[17] An unintended result of this story is to provide evidence that an area now outside the TAR had at that time paid taxes to Lhasa, that Tibetan Army troops were stationed there, and an uprising there was put down by the Tibetan Army.

Public executions using extremely cruel methods are actually a characteristic of Chinese, not Tibetan, culture. One example is execution by the "slicing process," by which a victim's flesh is slowly sliced away until he dies of loss of blood. This type of execution is known in Tibet only from the Qing dynasty, when some Tibetan rebels were executed in this way by order of the Manchu emperor. It is, of course, never mentioned in Chinese propaganda that all punishments involving physical torture or dismemberment were prohibited by the Thirteenth Dalai Lama in 1898 and appeared again in Tibetan history only rarely, particularly in two well-known cases of high political offenses after the Thirteenth Dalai Lama's death. By describing some of the serfs as "glaring in fury at the enemy," the Chinese propagandists meant to establish that the enemy of Tibetans is found within their own society and is a class enemy. There is no issue of any enmity between Chinese and Tibetans.

The second scene, "Exile," begins with the caption: "Under the cruel oppression of the *kasha* many serfs not killed outright were sent into exile. And see how they were sent!" A half-dead serf is shown on the back of an ox led by one of the servants of the feudal lords. He has a wooden *cangue* around his neck. "This serf has been flogged to within an inch of his life, bamboo splints have been inserted under every fingernail and he lies across an ox backwards. Thus he is sent into exile, his motherless daughter trudging along beside him." Another servant is shown kicking a serf who has fallen. The serf wears both a wooden cangue and hand and leg irons. Other bedraggled serf men, women, and children are shown being forced into exile. A close-up shows one woman with a baby on her back. "With her baby born in prison on her back, a woman serf drags herself forward into exile in heavy chains. Through tears she stares into the distance, uttering: 'Where is the end of this long and dark road?'"

This scene takes implausibility to a new level. A major theme of Chinese propaganda is that the serfs' lives were worth nothing, that serf-owners could kill serfs with impunity. But if a serf's life was so worthless, why go to the trouble of forcing them into exile? Why not just kill them on the spot? Why were any serfs so important that they needed to be driven into exile? The truth was that some individual Tibetans were exiled in India, but they tended to be political opponents of those in power in Lhasa. Others went to India for pilgrimage but rarely remained there. Those few Tibetans who settled in India were usually of the upper class. There is nothing in Tibetan history about serfs being exiled. Perhaps this scene is meant to counter the historical fact that many Tibetans were forced into exile not by feudalism but by Chinese repression of the Tibetan Revolt. Also, it must be mentioned that bamboo under the fingernails is a well-known Chinese torture technique experienced by some Tibetans, particularly in eastern Tibet, who were tortured by Chinese warlords.

Part 4 of *Wrath of the Serfs* is "The Serfs' Struggle for Liberation." The introductory caption declares:

> The crueler the oppression, the more violent the revolt. The million serfs could no longer endure the brutal oppression and persecution by the three estate-holders and they rose in one heroic struggle after another, which battered the feudal serf-owners' reactionary rule. "We want our freedom! We want liberation!" shout the million serfs who long for their deliverer, Chairman Mao Tsetung, and the Communist Party.

There is only one, very elaborate, scene in this part, titled "Arise, All Slaves!" Its description reads: "Like angry ocean waves or an erupting volcano, the serfs' rebellions shake the entire Tibetan Plateau. Smash the thousand-year-old yoke! Burn down the man-eating prisons! The million serfs struggle heroically for their final emancipation." Serfs are shown breaking out of prison cells in what appears to be a monastery, now aflame. An escaped serf is shown in close-up: "Fury flashes in his eyes and hatred pounds in his heart. This courageous serf rises to bury the criminal feudal serf system. Standing erect and with head held high, he smashes his fetters and will destroy this dark hell on earth."

Other serfs are shown escaping from prison, smashing their chains, and beating and killing the lords, lamas, and officials who have oppressed them. One serf beats a nobleman with his chains. A close-up of the prison cells has this caption: "A young serf carries an old man out of his prison cell. An infant is rescued from the scorpion pit, which is littered with the bleached bones of serfs." Escaped serfs are shown taking up arms. "Arise all slaves! Holding high the torch of struggle the serfs break through the centuries of darkness and emerge into the light of day. Taking up arms the million serfs assail the estate-holders' manors and the lamaseries, strike at the feudal serf system." One young girl serf is shown on a rock face tracing an outline on the rock. "We want our freedom! We want liberation! This girl serf traces a red star in blood to express her longing for the serfs' deliverer, Chairman Mao, and the Communist Party!" And with this rousing call for liberation, the exhibition, and the book, ends.

The "Wrath of the Serfs" exhibition and the accompanying book may have been somewhat less influential than the film *Serf* in forming opinions about Tibet in the minds of Chinese and even Tibetan people. Nevertheless, it is equally illustrative of what the Chinese want to and need to believe about Tibet. It reflects the political and artistic influence of the Cultural Revolution, as is evident in the introductory remarks that the art students attempted to insinuate into the sculptures "their own strong class feeling, combining revolutionary realism with revolutionary romanticism." They were also said to have "made good use of the experience gained in creating the revolutionary model operas." The exhibition was thus more propagandistic in many ways than *Serf* was. This is particularly evident in the tenuousness of many of the supposedly historical events depicted, in the supposedly unceasing and violent resistance of the serfs to the feudal system, and in the eulogies to Chairman Mao.

Wrath of the Serfs also betrays a Chinese attempt to reverse the facts of the Tibetan Revolt and to absolve themselves of being the oppressors of Tibetans, as was then being charged by the Dalai Lama and other Tibetans in exile. Thus the serfs have to be seen as being in constant revolt against the feudal lords, never against the Chinese. And this revolt has to be seen as spontaneous, rather than as instigated by the Chinese. The feudal serf system must be depicted as brutal without limit, and the serf lords, lamas, and officials as totally without compassion. There can only be black and white in China's portrayal of Tibet, no shades of gray. Any ambiguity about the nature of Tibet's former social system might allow political issues to emerge. The Tibetan feudal lords and the system thus have to be depicted as evil to the core, without any mitigating factors such as compassionate or even benign treatment of serfs. The serfs' lives have to be depicted as an unremitting Hell on Earth, without any escape or relief.

Much of this has to do with the psychological need of the Chinese people to see themselves as the liberators rather than the oppressors of the Tibetan people. Many Chinese, including the art students who went to Tibet and were supposed to have researched the actual reality of Tibet, had a deep psychological need to believe that Tibetan society had been as horrible as imaginable. China's propagandists had a need to create a social fantasy about Tibet that would obscure the political reality, while the artists had to see themselves as revolutionary heroes benevolently devoting themselves to revealing the sufferings of Tibetans.

The exhibition and book also betray China's attempt to obscure the results of its liberation of Tibet. The Dalai Lama and eighty thousand other Tibetans who escaped to India with tales of Chinese repression and brutality were difficult for the Chinese to refute. Therefore, the escapees had to be depicted as either feudal lords and their retainers or those duped by them. Since they were accused of having carried out the abuses of the serf system, the Chinese hoped that their accounts would be suspect. China's goal was to show that, while there had indeed been a revolt in Tibet, it was against the feudal system, not against Chinese control over Tibet. To this end, the Chinese put out propaganda discrediting the accounts of the exiles, organized counterdemonstrations after the revolt, and depicted the evils of the feudal system and the serfs' revolt against it in multimedia propaganda.

Among the Chinese people, such propaganda was quite effective, and it even reportedly had some effect among young Tibetans who had no experience of the old society. Older Tibetans were often restrained in talking to their children about the past, due to a pervasive atmosphere of repression and the constant presence of informers, who might even include one's own children. However, the older Tibetans knew that the old society had borne little resemblance to the Chinese depictions. They also knew that many of their relatives had been killed or exiled or remained in prisons and labor camps. Thus Chinese propaganda about the prisons of the old society, replete with scorpions, must have been particularly galling, especially given the existence at that time of Chinese prisons in Tibet holding thousands of times more prisoners than could have been held in the prisons of old Tibet.

Tibetan schoolchildren report that their visits to the "Wrath of the Serfs" museum were usually accompanied by a visit to the nearby Potala Prison and the Nangtsesha Prison on the Barkor. The Potala Prison had been something of a dungeon, and it was festooned by tales of the scorpions always present; but it was relatively tiny, capable of holding only a few people at the most. The Nangtsesha Prison, also a museum, had only nine cells. In contrast, the Chinese maintained large prisons in Lhasa and other towns, labor camps in Kongpo, and more labor camps and prisons holding thousands in Kham and Amdo. In addition, there were prisons in every town, many of which were larger than the largest prison in old Tibet. One wonders, when the Chinese authors wrote, "Where there is oppression there is resistance," if they had any doubts about their own propaganda or were at all uneasy about the potential for another Tibetan revolt.

The "Wrath of the Serfs" exhibit disappeared sometime after the initiation of the post-Maoist liberalization in Tibet in 1979. The Museum of the Tibetan Revolution itself disappeared during the reconstruction of the Potala Square that took place at the time of the twentieth anniversary of the founding of the TAR in 1985. The type of propaganda of the museum and the exhibits were presumably out of keeping with the policies of the liberalization period.

Nevertheless, in a demonstration of the fundamental role that the demonization of old Tibet plays in the Chinese attempt to legitimize its rule there, the sculptures have been the subject of renewed interest by Chinese propagandists. A Tibetan writer, Woeser, the daughter of a Han Chinese PLA officer and a Tibetan mother, wrote in January 2006 that the book of photos of the exhibit had been republished.[18] Woeser writes that she was surprised, when she walked into the Tibetan People's Press bookstore in Lhasa in 2005, to see copies of *Wrath of the Serfs*, which she remembered from twenty years earlier. Imagining that these must be old copies, she was amazed to see that it had in fact been republished.

According to Woeser, the new introduction reads:

> This year is the 40th anniversary of the founding of the Tibet Autonomous Region. Looking back at the past and forward into the future, we keep firmly in mind that Tibet's journey from darkness toward light, from backwardness toward progress, from autocracy toward democracy, from poverty toward wealth, and from being closed toward being open, has history education significance as well as practical significance. To this end, the Tibetan People's Press is once again arranging and publishing this book and presenting it to everyone. April, 2005.

She also reports a rumor that "a certain important official from Beijing, when on an official visit to Tibet, gave instructions to revive the Wrath of the Serfs sculpture, and that certain cultural officials in Tibet are now doing their utmost to spur on the recreation of Wrath of the Serfs in clay."

Woeser writes:

> For a long time, people's recollection of "old Tibet" has been molded by numerous types of artistic work done by literary and art workers under the Party's leadership, such as the movie *Serfs*, the novel *Survivors*, and the song "Liberated Serfs

Sing," and also including the sculpture Wrath of the Serfs. From beginning to end they are entirely the teachings of the great leader Chairman Mao.

The essence of these teachings, she says, is that nationality issues are really class issues. The issue of Tibet is not between China and Tibet but between the two major classes in Tibet: the oppressed serfs and the oppressor serf-owners. The serf-owners are the "three major feudal lords"—the Kashag government, the monasteries, and the nobility—who were depicted as without human compassion:

> There were four "mosts" in the definition given to the "three major feudal lords" by the Party, which were "most reactionary, most dark, most cruel, and most savage." In these works of art, the images of the "three major feudal lords" are all cut from this cloth; there are none who are not inhuman scoundrels. Since their humanity has been extinguished, none of these "three major feudal lords" are live people; they are abbreviated, demonized symbols. There were only two objectives in this: the first was to awaken a consciousness of hatred among the broad "emancipated serfs." . . . The second objective was to call forth a consciousness of gratitude among the broad "emancipated serfs." To express it using a song popular at the time, it was "don't forget the Communist Party when you are emancipated."

Woeser writes that there were

> 106 life-sized "serfs" and "three major feudal lords" rendered in various horrible or malicious, demonic aspects, along with accompanying music and commentary. . . . Visitors came in a continuous stream, because it was a political duty to do so. The Tibetan people had to accept this kind of "historical education."

She says that the party insisted upon saying that old Tibet was a "living Hell" and that this was effective for someone who, like her, was

> born in the 1960s, did not live in the "old Tibet" and must rely entirely on the likes of *Wrath of the Serfs* to mold our recollections of the "old Tibet." I clearly remember when, at not yet ten years of age, I saw each of those sculpted people in an illustrated magazine. I was filled with a feeling of righteous anger, and was eager to "grab the whip and lash the enemy!"

Although *Wrath of the Serfs* was a product of the Cultural Revolution, which even the CCP had acknowledged as "ten years of disaster," Woeser writes, the republication of the book of photographs was being presented in 2005 to the Tibetan people as a gift, much as it had been thirty years before on the tenth anniversary of the TAR's founding. She says that Cultural Revolution memorabilia was enjoying a revival in China but that there was always an aspect of commercialism and irony involved. Not so with the *Wrath of the Serfs*, which was once again being presented in all seriousness. She writes:

> But this pictorial is not the same at all, because it is a gift, just like its original version was a gift 30 years ago. No matter whether it is the 10th anniversary of the founding of the Tibet Autonomous Region, or the 40th anniversary, the gift is always *Wrath of the Serfs*.

She says that viewing the book took her mind back to that time, "putting me in a language realm colored by red ideology." She wondered whether people with a long memory of history would find the recollection absurd or if those with a shorter memory would be persuaded. She recalls that the original exhibit had a sensational effect in Lhasa, with descriptions such as:

> Many people's breasts were filled with hatred, and they made tearful denunciations: seeing the sculpture; we think of loved ones who were persecuted to death by the three major feudal lords in the old society, and we utterly hate the feudal serf system; we utterly hate Liu Shaoqi, Lin Biao, Confucius, and the Dalai Lama.

Woeser finds that, in describing the themes of the exhibition, she now finds them laughable:

> Thirty years later, the brave words of that time have been reduced to "boasting"; thirty years later, the vehement passion of that time has been reduced to a laughingstock; thirty years later, the untrue words of that time have been exposed; thirty years later, the political mythology of that time has been mocked. This being the case, how can such a spoiled dish be returned to the pot thirty years later and be served up again as a gift?

She observes that the photos in *Wrath of the Serfs* are black and white, just as Tibet has been treated in a black-and-white manner. Tibetans are divided into two categories, either serfs or serf-owners, and Tibetan history is similarly divided into "Old Tibet" and "New Tibet," dated not from "liberation" in 1951 but from the revolt and democratic reforms in 1959. She writes that Tibetans living in this transformative period are also divided into old and new, the old unwanted, the new required. Much effort is required to transform, repackage, and even change the ethics of an old people into a new people:

> For many years, the Party's literary and art workers have, in this dramatized way, revised Tibet, re-painted Tibet, re-sung Tibet, re-danced Tibet, re-filmed Tibet, re-sculpted Tibet. *Wrath of the Serfs* completed the Party's literary and art workers' process of entirely re-imagining Tibet through an extremely dramatized process. Actual history was changed in this image colored by red ideology. The

memories of generations of Tibetans were changed by this image colored by red ideology. I cannot help but admire those literary and art workers who revised our memories in the heat of fervent idealism. I admire even more how, forgetting themselves, they exploded in a creative passion under the power of Mao Zedong's spiritual atomic bomb. It is like they said when discussing what they experienced during the work: "We mixed the clay with our bare feet in early winter, used ovens of sun-dried brick to bake it, and bent the steel rebar ourselves. We used 35 tons of clay for the statues. We carried on continually for several months; there were no Sundays. Was this a hardship? No! To be able to implement Chairman Mao's revolutionary line in literature and art was the greatest good fortune! To struggle for the consolidation of the dictatorship of the proletariat was the greatest good fortune!"

Writing that much of the narrative in *Wrath of the Serfs* "defies everyday logic and historical reality," Woeser says that many of the scenes are inaccurate and overdramatized, which is unfortunate, but that "the insistence on taking artistic work as irrefutable fact can only demonstrate that this exercise is nothing more than an arbitrary tactic of those in power. Regrettably, this is the Party's fine tradition, which to this day is still being developed and enhanced in Tibet."

Woeser wonders if the "Wrath of the Serfs" sculptures will really be recreated. When they were taken away from the Museum of the Tibetan Revolution in 1979, long before the museum itself was destroyed, they disappeared without a trace, as if they had become an embarrassment. Now, however, the book had been republished, and some officials are calling for the sculptures or something similar to be revived.

In 2004, China announced that it would reopen the renovated old Tibetan Nangtsesha Prison as a museum. It had also been used as a museum during the 1970s, but was closed when the liberalization began in the 1980s. The Nangtsesha Prison, located on the north side of the Barkor in Lhasa, was originally built by the Fifth Dalai Lama in the mid-seventeenth century as Lhasa city government headquarters; only later was it turned into a prison. The museum was to provide displays illustrating the tortures and sufferings of the prisoners who were held in Nangtsesha. The announcement said that in order to present the cruel history of old Tibet to visitors from home and abroad, the museum would display the accounts of some of those imprisoned there as well as instruments of torture, photos, and documents. Furthermore, the museum was also intended to have sculptures featuring prisoners suffering from various kinds of tortures.

The new Nangtsesha Museum, the republication of *Wrath of the Serfs*, and perhaps the re-creation of similar displays were apparently intended to revive some of the prominent themes of traditional Chinese propaganda about

Tibet. Many Chinese still believe that old Tibet was a Hell on Earth and that Tibetans were liberated from their sufferings by the CCP. This theme has continued in Chinese publications about Tibet, but it has not recently appeared in any more graphic form. Even the Tibet Museum, opened during the 1990s, refrained from any displays about the supposed horrors of old Tibet. The revival of such graphic displays represents a reversion to the type of Chinese propaganda about Tibet that was prevalent before 1979. This reversion to a type of propaganda that has failed in the past, but which many Chinese seem to fervently believe, may represent a degree of desperation on the part of the Chinese. Many seem genuinely perplexed and wonder why the world cannot accept China's liberating and civilizing role in Tibet.

Tibet Transformed

Tibet Transformed, by Israel Epstein, is by far the most lengthy (550 pages), authoritative (although biased), and informative account in English of the period of Tibet's history from 1950 to 1980, when few other than sympathetic socialist journalists had access. Epstein's book about Tibet, published in 1983, is the result of three trips there, in 1955, 1965, and 1976, in each case as a member of a group of socialist journalists.

Epstein was born in 1915 in a part of Lithuania that had been annexed by Poland. His parents were Lithuanian Jewish socialists who had been active in the failed Russian revolution of 1905. His parents, as members of the Jewish Bund, were at first enthusiastic about the 1917 Russian Revolution, but the Bund soon fell out of favor and the family found themselves exiled to China. Epstein thus grew up in China, educated in English in foreign schools and influenced by his parents' socialism, the Japanese invasion of China, and his sympathy for the Chinese Communist Party.

Epstein began his journalistic career before World War II, reporting from the Chinese Communists' headquarters at Yenan. In 1944, he left China for the United States "to help the Western world understand the Chinese Revolution"; then with the success of the Communist revolution in China he returned in 1951 "to live and work in the new China."[19] He joined *China Reconstructs*, an English-language pictorial periodical meant to promote the Chinese revolution to the Western world. He became a citizen of China, a status that landed him in prison during the Cultural Revolution. Eventually, he became the editor of *China Reconstructs*, a position he held almost until his death in 2005. Epstein was, like Anna Louise Strong, a lifelong Communist, but as a citizen of China and the editor of *China Reconstructs*, he was also a professional propagandist.

Epstein's first visit to Tibet, in 1955, was a fifteen-day trip by road from Chengdu in Sichuan. His visit in 1965 was by air as one of more than two thousand delegates and visitors invited to Lhasa for the founding ceremonies of the Tibet Autonomous Region. His third visit, in 1976, coincided with the death of Mao and the end of the Cultural Revolution. He says that his account of Tibet is "self-told" by the Tibetans themselves, "based on hundreds of on-the-spot interviews, recorded in thousands of pages of notes."[20]

Tibet Transformed suffers from being published so late, in 1983, seven years after his last visit and long after the communes that he extolled as so successful had been abandoned. Epstein makes a rather awkward attempt to retain his conclusions of the previous visits while explaining how de-communization had produced greater prosperity than communization and how liberalization had resulted in a revival of Tibetan culture that he had proclaimed to be already vibrant due to the CCP's policy on nationality autonomy. Thus he declares that socialism has triumphed in Tibet and all the policies of the past were correct, but that the abandonment of the communes, which were the primary achievement of socialism, was also correct. He maintains that Tibetans were happy and prosperous before, but that they were even more happy and prosperous once the policies that had made them so joyful in the past were abandoned.

Epstein writes in his foreword that he hopes the reader will find his account "a true reflection of the essential nature and historically-determined direction of the great and basic process of change that has occurred, and is continuing, in Tibet."[21] This sentence sums up Epstein's dilemma. All of what has happened has to be historically determined, according to Marxist doctrine, as a natural social evolution having everything to do with class conflict and nothing to do with any conflicts between China and Tibet. This historically determined doctrine also has to explain the twists and turns in Chinese policies in Tibet, including the Cultural Revolution and the eventual abandonment of the supposedly correct policies of the past. Epstein rationalizes that "despite all zigzags, there has been tremendous advance." He declares that the peaceful liberation, the defeat of the serf-owner revolt, and the achievement of democratic reforms were all profoundly emancipatory for the majority of Tibetans who enthusiastically embarked upon the socialist path. The fundamental basis of those achievements, he says, is that Tibet is an organic part of multinational China, within which Tibet has its own distinct characteristics. However, he notes, the conclusion from Tibet's particularities is not in favor of separatism, because separatism has always been linked with plots by imperialists to weaken and partition China.

There were errors in the revolution in China, Epstein admits, some of them specific to the minority nationalities, including Tibetans. The primary error, in his estimation, was in deviating from Mao's doctrine that the contradictions between nationalities were nonantagonistic. Because of these errors, "some of the fundamental achievements made in Tibet were accompanied by shortcomings needing correction." He maintains that nationality autonomy was not sufficiently developed in Tibet: "Two specificities had been ignored— that of the minority regions as distinct from the majority (Han) regions of China, and that of Tibet even among minority regions (its rather special history, its relative homogeneity, mixture of religious and national elements, and so on)." Other minority regions were more affected than Tibet, he says, "under the influence of the gang of four." He admits that "ultra-Left" errors had been quite serious in the cultural field, but he claims that the CCP was therefore (in 1980–1982) concentrating on cultural preservation and development.

Epstein writes that the inauguration of the TAR in 1965 marked the beginning of the socialist revolution in Tibet, following on the success of the democratic revolution after the 1959 revolt. These—the democratic and socialist revolutions—were the stages of the inevitable course of history as predicted by Marxist doctrine. They were an "irreversible change" in a Tibet that had made a leap from medieval serf society to socialism in the short span of twenty years. This was a rebirth that the "old local rulers" could never have envisioned. These rulers were unable to prevent this "mass-powered social leap," which the CCP sparked but whose fuel was "the bitterness stored through centuries of oppression in the breasts of Tibet's serfs and slaves." By their resort to "reactionary violence," the serf-owners had assured that the change would come through "revolutionary counter-violence and mass action." Epstein quotes Mao to this effect: "If the reactionaries of Tibet should dare to launch a general rebellion, then the working people there will win liberation all the faster." In regard to strategy, "every major stage was initiated or directly approved by Mao Zedong with Zhou Enlai guiding the actual work from the center."

According to Epstein, the CCP had been magnanimous to the former serf-owners: "The victorious working people in Tibet and throughout China are willing to forgo historical scores with the serf owners, whether for their centuries of past oppression or for their foreign-backed resort to arms against the revolution." This magnanimity included the Panchen Lama who, "pressed by the same class interests and forces as the Dalai Lama before him, was drawn into opposing the reforms," but who had "resumed public life in 1978, speaking in praise of the basic changes that had occurred in Tibet and calling on self-exiled upper-strata figures to return and see for themselves." The Dalai Lama could also be included, if he would accept the principles of the Seventeen-Point Agreement with regard to the unity of China's peoples and nonobstruction of essential reform. However, "the unity of the multinational socialist country, with nationalities enjoying autonomy within this framework, is not subject to bargaining."

The bulk of *Tibet Transformed* is composed of his accounts of visits to various sites and interviews with former serfs he met in each place. His interviews over a twenty-year period reflect the progress of socialist construction in Tibet. Those from 1955 are characterized by the tension between the desire of the serfs for liberation and the resistance of the "local Tibetan government." He describes a Tibet ripe for the socialist revolution, but prevented from achieving it by the restrictions of the Seventeen-Point Agreement. Han Chinese cadres are presented as chafing at the restrictions but nevertheless scrupulously respecting the provisions of the agreement. The interviews of 1965 are mostly about the defeat of the rebellion, the success of democratic reforms, and the establishment of the TAR. His 1976 interviews discuss life in the communes and the prosperity achieved by communization. In particular, having already achieved democratic reforms by their own efforts and the first stage of socialism in the mutual-aid teams, the liberated Tibetan serfs were said to have been anxious to achieve full communization in order to avoid a reversion to capitalism and a revival of class exploitation.

Epstein's interviews mostly describe the suffering of the serfs and slaves under the former feudal system and their incomparably better life after liberation, democratic reforms, and socialist transformation. He denounces old Tibetan society for its "unspeakable medieval squalor." The old ruling class, the aristocracy, and the monastic authorities are described as invariably brutal, vying to outdo each other in "cold-blooded and inventive cruelty." The primary theme of all his accounts is the natural, inevitable, historically determined character of the revolution in Tibet, achieved by the Tibetan people themselves, with some benevolent assistance by the people of all nationalities in China. His interviews are so extensive that they cannot be dismissed out of hand; he undoubtedly encountered many Tibetans with legitimate grievances about the past and many whose lives were better under the Chinese regime. However, his discussions were exclusively with such enthusiastic spokespersons—all chosen for him by Chinese and Tibetan officials—whom he accepts as enjoying a freedom of speech that others have said was entirely lacking during the times of his visits, especially the latter two visits in 1965 and 1976.

He mentions the presence in 1965, at the inauguration of the TAR, of some fifty crippled former serfs who told their stories of abuse under the feudal serf system to the assembled delegates and visitors, and he says that they were "only a tiny fraction of the whole." Despite Epstein's belief that there were many more crippled serfs than those he saw, such Tibetans were cultivated by the Chinese to tell their stories as a semiprofessional career. Those who had suffered the most under the old system were prompted to "speak bitterness" against both the system itself and individuals who practiced oppression and exploitation. The atmosphere of these sessions, stimulated by Han comrades and Tibetan activists, was highly charged emotionally. The best performers at these sessions—the ones whose sufferings were the worst or who were best able to elaborate their accounts, and especially those who were able to show physical mutilation—were promoted to semiprofessional status as raconteurs of the evils of the old society. The best fifty or so of them were taken around to tell their tales at virtually every school, town, or commune in Tibet. Their accounts became highly stylized and theatrical as they literally lived on the dramatic rendition of their past sufferings.

Epstein's interviewees therefore cannot be assumed to be typical nor can it be assumed that they spoke without practice or coercion. Their accounts undoubtedly reflect some of the reality of traditional Tibet, but not the totality or even the primary characteristics of old Tibet. Similarly, his interviews cannot be presumed to reflect the reality of Tibet under Chinese rule.

Epstein begins his historical background with a bit of obscurantism:

> Looking back, and forward, many Hans and Tibetans today do not measure their relations by just when, in what ancient dynasty, their unity began or was formalized. Rather, they see as the common meaning of their overall and particular histories, all China's nationalities contributing, from the earliest times to the formation and stability of the historically formed multinational entity.

He invariably refers to the Tibetan polity as "local," as in "Dalai Lama's local government," "Lhasa's local army," "feudal local government," "serf owner local regime," and so forth. China by contrast is invariably referred to as "multinational": "historically formed multinational entity," "multinational socialist country," "socialist multinational family," "multinational polity," and so on. In all, the Tibetan government is termed "local" thirty-six times, and "multinational" is used in reference to China seventeen times. No opportunity is missed, whenever speaking of China, to say "including Tibet," and Tibet is always referred to as being "within the larger unity" of China. Should anyone doubt that the final word has been spoken on Tibet's status, "historically determined direction," "irrevocable change," and "tide of history" are applied to characterize China's incorporation of Tibet.

Epstein repeats the Chinese argument that Tibet was "peacefully liberated" because the PLA did not invade Tibet:

> From October 1950 until July 1951, the PLA did not advance from the Qamdo area into the areas traditionally under Lhasa's control. . . . Only after Lhasa's ratification [of the Seventeen-Point Agreement] did the PLA resume its march. It entered Tibet peacefully and in accord with the Agreement's provisions. There was no fighting within Tibet.

He gives many glowing accounts of the virtually angelic behavior of the PLA as it entered Tibet, saying that Tibetans called it "Buddha's Army." Mao had instructed the PLA to maintain the most respectful attitudes during the "peaceful liberation" of Tibet, and Epstein implies that this attitude was a permanent and consistent part of the party's policy toward minority nationalities—that is, that this kind of behavior continued after the PLA became well entrenched in Tibet and even during and after the revolt. He also praises the Chinese practice of paying fair wages for labor, especially for road construction work, and fair prices for all purchases. Indeed, Tibetans describe this period as a "rain of Chinese silver dollars."

Epstein quotes Mao's statement about how the PLA should bide its time in Tibet and gather strength, particularly in regard to feeding itself. Mao predicted that the United Front policy would cultivate enough upper-class collaborators, while the reform policy would gain the support of the lower classes, in which case the Tibetan people would "draw closer to us."[22] Epstein says that this shows Mao's "patience and faith in the Tibetan people." He echoes the Chinese contention that it was the Tibetan serf-owners who violated the Seventeen-Point Agreement and brought on the revolt:

> Ultimately, the work-style of the army, which exercised no compulsion for reform, proved to be a factor that led the people to demand reform. The serf owners who would not consult when they could no longer dictate, but instead rose in rebellion, tried to kill the people's hope by armed compulsion. It was they who destroyed the Agreement by taking arms against the PLA. Then, and only then, did the PLA act as the people's own force of compulsion, remove the obstacles to reform and help to carry it out.

Epstein denies that China practiced a divide-and-rule policy in Tibet. Instead, he says, the United Front accepted anyone who was anti-imperialist, who was patriotic to the multinational People's Republic of China, and who supported the Seventeen-Point Agreement. He contends that the CCP had not even tried to make divisions between the classes in Tibet because the United Front accepted even serf-owners if they were patriotic. The United Front had also done all it could to "mediate and reconcile the historic estrangements between the Dalai and Panchen groups and between the authorities in Lhasa and Qamdo." Epstein also denies that China in any way exploited Tibet:

> Different indeed from any colonial or semi-colonial path is the road of Tibet within socialist China. As we have seen from facts and figures, Tibet is massively assisted, and in no way exploited by the majority nationality. Economic errors were made, involving waste of labor and funds, which was true in other areas of China as well, but nothing was taken away from the Region and its people for the material benefit of anywhere else.

In fact, Epstein asserts, Tibet's religious establishment lost only its political power; otherwise, the monasteries "continued to exist, retaining the buildings used for worship and residence." Internally, however, they underwent "revolutionary democratization," by means of which they achieved, for the first time, true religious freedom, for in Tibet, "freedom of religion meant freedom to get out of compulsory confinement in monastic institutions." The government provided subsidies for the upkeep of monasteries, including the preservation of their relics, and for those monks who were old or unable to work. "Thus, not only was there freedom of belief, but monks and laity were assured the continuance and upkeep of places of worship." This was written in 1965, when most of Tibet's monasteries had already been looted and many destroyed. The rest were destroyed during the Cultural Revolution, which Epstein surely must have been aware of by 1976, or at least by 1982 when his book went to press.

Epstein admits that the Jokhang, the Ramoche, and other religious monuments in Lhasa had been damaged during the revolt, but he blames this exclusively on their being used as strongholds by the rebels. Furthermore, he says that all such damage had since been repaired by the government. Outside Lhasa, Ganden Monastery had been destroyed, he admits, but he wrongly credits this to the Cultural Revolution and to Tibetan Red Guards.

In 1976, Epstein found only three hundred monks at Drepung, which he notes was still receiving visitors, but not all of those came to pray; some, he says, came for "class education or as sightseers." Epstein also visited Tashilhunpo in Shigatse, where he was told that during democratic reforms the monastery's monk population fell from 4,000 to 1,980 "through voluntary withdrawals under the policy of religious freedom." In a postscript written in 1979, Epstein says that monasteries in Lhasa were open for worship or for the "historically-minded and the curious."

Epstein does not mourn the loss of Tibetan religious culture; instead, he lauds the development of a new socialist culture. He cites the development of the press and radio, language, theater, and film, all devoted to the propagation of socialism. Printing presses were one of the first items brought to Tibet over the newly completed roads in 1955. These were devoted to the printing of Tibet's first newspaper, the *Tibet Daily*. Epstein says that the progressive nature of this newspaper was revealed by the fact that it was a target of the Tibetan rebels during the 1959 revolt. He also mentions as a positive development the wired radio network in Tibet. This radio, in Chinese and Tibetan, originated in Beijing and Lhasa and was broadcast over loudspeakers in public places and even in private households. Epstein notes that the number of loudspeakers was limited by the Tibetan government before 1959, but that by 1965 there were loudspeakers everywhere and many hours of programming. In fact, these broadcasts did as much to change the character of Tibetan life as any of China's reforms and improvements. The broadcasts from the ubiquitous loudspeakers were loud, irritating, and inescapable, made worse by the poor quality of the loudspeakers, and of course they were exclusively devoted to Chinese propaganda. To outside observers, these loudspeakers, still present in 1982, were a symbol of the harshening and regimentation of Tibetan life under Chinese rule.

Tibet Transformed cites the development of book publishing "with new content," including Marxist works and the works of Mao. The Tibetan language was simplified to better reflect the common language and to incorporate Chinese terms. Song and dance groups were organized, also with "new content." These groups were modeled on the PLA propaganda groups that had facilitated the army's entry into Tibet. The film *Serf* was produced as a stage drama, as was *Heroic City*, about Tibetans' resistance to the British invasion at Gyantse in 1904, and *Blood Accusation*, about feudal oppression and its final revolutionary overthrow. These song, dance, and drama groups were mobile and traveled all over Tibet giving performances and distributing Mao's works and other propaganda. Films were also shown by mobile projection units, often outdoors using the whitewashed sides of buildings or white cotton sheets. Most popular, Epstein says, was *Serf*.

By 1965, according to Epstein, there were permanent theaters in every Tibetan city and town, as well as 121 mobile projection teams. By his third trip in 1976, there were eleven professional stage troupes, fifteen hundred amateur troupes, and 429 film projection teams. Many Chinese operas had been translated and performed in Tibetan, and traditional Tibetan operas had been altered to incorporate new socialist content. Epstein admits that this went too far during the Cultural Revolution, when "Jiang Qing and her cohorts denied the national character of the arts of the national minorities," but he says that in 1979 many Tibetan cultural and artistic works that had been repressed by the Gang of Four reappeared; their repression had been due to "anomalies" of the past and would not recur.

Epstein is most informative about the progress, and success, of democratic reforms and socialist transformation. He describes the process of democratic reforms and the formation of mutual-aid teams, the first stage of collectivization:

> First came a preliminary campaign known as the "three againsts" (against the rebellion, personal servitude and corvee labor) and "two reductions" (of rent and interest). Then the serfs and slaves divided their former masters' estates. Still later they united into mutual-aid teams to raise production for themselves and all Tibet. Steadily, the Communist Party was built from their ranks and the new state power of the oppressed set up in every village. It was in these campaigns, aided materially and morally by the people of all China, that Tibetan cadres were

trained, and the masses won their understanding of what had happened in the past and what had to be done in the future.

Although Epstein describes the process of further collectivization as deliberate, democratic, and voluntary, his informants told him that most agricultural areas went directly from mutual aid to communes from 1967 to 1969, during the height of the Cultural Revolution:

> In Tibet, as distinct from most other parts of China, there was generally no intervening stage—of agricultural cooperatives—between the mutual-aid team and the commune. There the transition from individual to semi-socialist and then fully socialist ownership took place within the commune form.

He thus reveals the key to understanding the actual process of communization in Tibet. Communes were formed for political reasons at the time of the political reorganization that took place during the creation of the TAR and during the height of the chaos of the Cultural Revolution. Communes facilitated Chinese control over all aspects of Tibetans' lives and their agricultural production.

The transition from the most basic level of collectivization to its ultimate stage, at least in administrative form, is presented as having been voluntarily decided by the Tibetans themselves. Epstein says that Chinese cadres attending the 1965 inauguration of the TAR were petitioned by Tibetans for the immediate establishment of communes. He describes the process as being led by the poorest, who had the most to gain by the most radical redistribution of wealth. He says that the poor referred bitterly to mutual-aid teams as "mutual aid without mutual benefit" and were the most eager for communes. This was said to be due to the contradiction, inherent in mutual aid, between individual economy and collective labor. Those who had more property and wealth, even if only slightly more, were reluctant to give it up to the collective. At each stage of collectivization, there was always the danger of a polarization of property and wealth and the restoration of capitalism. The only way to prevent this, from the point of view of the poorest, was to achieve full communization as quickly as possible.

This choice was reportedly made naturally because of the superior performance of the communes, which were assisted by state aid, including the provision of machinery, fertilizers, and agricultural advice. Epstein provides many pages of statistics to prove the amazing success of the several communes he visited in 1976, although this makes it even more difficult for him to explain how the ultimate dissolution of the communes resulted in even greater prosperity and was not an abandonment of the communist ideal. He writes that "subsequent reviews and re-examinations were to reveal many errors along the ultra-Left line, some common to the whole of China, some of a local character." It had been wrong to prohibit all individual production as capitalist. Some communization policies had been transferred from other areas of China without considering Tibet's particular conditions. Some class divisions had been too severe, particularly classifying some former serfs as rich peasants. Some aspects of Tibetan customs had wrongly been condemned as backward. Epstein admits that the curtailment of constitutionally guaranteed religious freedom had occurred under the influence of the Gang of Four. Nevertheless, he says, despite these problems, Tibetans would never revert to the past, separatism would inevitably fail, and unity would prevail as the natural tide of history.

In 2005, the year of his death, Israel Epstein's autobiography, *My China Eye: Memoirs of a Jew and a Journalist*, was published. In it, he describes his life in China, including his imprisonment during the Cultural Revolution. At the beginning of the Cultural Revolution in 1966, Epstein and his wife Elsie joined a Red Guard unit composed of foreigners working in China. The unit was called the Bethune-Yan'an Rebel Regiment of Mao Zedong Thought, after Norman Bethune, a famous Canadian doctor who worked in China. The Red Guard unit had been proposed by some foreigners in China who wanted the opportunity to participate in the great cultural and political event of the Cultural Revolution. They, like all Chinese Red Guards, pledged their loyalty to Mao. They also insisted that they and their children be treated not as foreigners and no differently than ordinary Chinese. The group obtained the endorsement of Mao and eventually Epstein became its leader. He gave speeches to many Red Guard units in 1966 and 1967, believing them all to be equally devoted to Mao and the revolution and disbelieving in the possibility of the factionalism that ultimately occurred.

Epstein was greatly surprised when, in 1968, foreigners began to become victims of Chinese xenophobia. Like many others, Epstein himself was accused of being a spy for some unspecified foreign government. His many years of work at *China Reconstructs* were characterized as a foreign plot to dominate China's voice to the outside world.[23]

Epstein and his wife were imprisoned, separately, at Qincheng Prison near Beijing. At first, he could not understand how he—a man who had devoted his life to China's revolution, who was personally known to China's leaders as the editor of one of its foremost official publications, who had followed every turn in Chinese politics "right up to campaigns against 'revisionism' culminating in the Cultural Revolution in which I unquestioningly marched calling for the downfall of Liu Shaoqi and Deng Xiaoping"—could be accused of disloyalty. Even his leadership of the foreigners' Red Guard group had not protected him. He even questioned the historical propensity of Communist regimes to dissolve into factionalism and to persecute many of those who had earlier been revolutionary heroes. He thought: "Was it true that the class struggle by its objective laws, independent of human will and even perhaps of self-knowledge, turned friends into enemies as well as foes into friends?" However, like others so imprisoned by Communist regimes, he soon decided that he could never abandon the socialist revolution to which he had devoted his life and that he would accept whatever fate the revolution had for him.

For the next five years, Epstein had no contact with any human being except his interrogators. He was never physically abused but heard sounds of abuse of prisoners in nearby cells. He was questioned repeatedly and instructed that he must confess his crimes. When he asked what crimes he was accused of, he was told that he himself knew and that he must examine his life and his thoughts to know what crimes against the revolution he had committed. This was typical of Communist interrogation techniques, intended to force confessions of real or imaginary crimes. Only when completely subservient to the party's discipline could one begin to be reformed. Also typical was the requirement to reexamine one's life from an early age. Epstein eventually wrote 1,500 pages of self-criticism of his life and yet was repeatedly condemned for failure to realize and confess his real crimes.

Eventually, upon his release, his interrogators confessed that they also did not know what his crimes were supposed to have been, but were told to pretend that they knew. He was released, along with his wife and many other foreigners, shortly after U.S. president Richard Nixon came to China, which Epstein thinks not coincidental. Nixon's visit had been prepared by Edgar Snow, who was told by Mao in 1970 that Nixon was welcome, and Snow had mentioned to Mao that he did not understand why so many foreigners sympathetic to the Chinese revolution were then imprisoned.[24]

After his release, Epstein rationalized that the interrogation techniques to which he and his wife had been subjected may have been unjust when applied to them, but were necessary to expose those who were actually guilty of harming the socialist cause. Soon, their previous enthusiasm for the revolution returned. Both returned to work at *China Reconstructs*, Israel Epstein remaining active until his death in 2005. He remained a Marxist convinced of the ultimate success of socialism. He recognized many of China's mistakes but continued to believe that the revolution had many more positive achievements than negative. Epstein bemoaned the mistake of the violent repression at Tiananmen Square in June 1989 but suspected a CIA hand in exacerbating the crisis. In the end, he proclaimed satisfaction with his life as a proponent of the socialist cause.

In his autobiography, Epstein renounces none of his previous conclusions about China's role in Tibet. Having updated his Tibet experience with another visit in 1985, he still thought Tibet's transformation the most dramatic in

China: "A leap over a thousand years from theocracy, serfdom, and slavery to the building of Socialism."[25] A chapter on Tibet in his autobiography does little more than reaffirm and update the successes he had previously claimed for Chinese policies in Tibet. He continues to laud China's selfless assistance to Tibet and to deny any exploitation. He continues to maintain that it was the "serf-owning local regime" that had torn up the Seventeen-Point Agreement by launching a revolt. In retrospect, he analyzes the policy of the CCP in Tibet:

> The policy of the Chinese Communist Party, as conceived and practiced by Mao Zedong and Zhou Enlai, was to give the feudal elite leeway until, as was inevitable, the most hardcore elite elements would expose itself to an increasingly aware majority of the commonality through overt rebellion. And when that happened, to strike down the old social order with the help of the oppressed majority.

Epstein extols the three generations of the new Tibetan social order: those who had joined the Long March in the mid-1930s, those who had become cadres in the 1950s, and those who had joined the revolution after the revolt. These Tibetans were, he said, "impressive examples of the abilities and human dignity latent in the ranks of the formerly downtrodden." He mentions the high positions achieved by many of those he had interviewed in previous years, without any acknowledgment that many Tibetans considered them little more than Chinese puppets without any real authority. He acknowledges no repression or destruction of Tibetan culture, during the Cultural Revolution or any other time. Instead, he says, "Preserved and developed were the best cultural achievements of Tibet's warm, brave talented and hard-working people over the centuries—in architecture, medicine, arts and crafts, beautiful and vigorous songs, dances operas and dramas, and literature."

He again admits to

> errors affecting the whole of China as well as specific ones relating to minority nationalities—the Tibetans among them. . . . In the case of national minority regions, such Leftist actions sometimes even confused mere dissimilarities between ethnic groups with basic class antagonisms. Methods and tactics suited only to the Han areas were sometimes unduly copied.

Nevertheless, he declares, "All these defects, from the 1980s on, were noted and being corrected." If there was any retreat, he says, it was not toward Tibet's old society, but to the policies of the early postrebellion and postreform periods, which he again claims that Tibetans remember as the "golden age" of democratic and socialist advance. And, he repeats, none of the mistakes of the past had anything to do with colonial or class exploitation: "Very significant funds were put into the region and no profits taken out."

Epstein dismisses the anti-Chinese demonstrations of the 1980s as having been instigated, as usual, from outside. He bemoans the international respect and praise for the Dalai Lama, without any mention of his serf-owning past. His conclusion about Tibet's fate is that Tibet is "an organic part of a multi-ethnic China, its woe and weal linked to those of its other areas and peoples. Within this larger entity, Tibet has distinctive features—historical, social, linguistic and cultural." However, "secession is not a rational conclusion from these peculiarities." "Overall, the Tibetans are better off within the family of China's peoples than they would be with an 'independence,' which would not be real at all, but merely make them a satellite."

Epstein's stubborn refusal to admit any but the most superficial faults in Chinese policy in Tibet reflects not only his slavish adherence to every incomprehensible twist and turn in Chinese politics but also his inability to admit that the socialism to which he devoted his life was not the inevitable course of history. However, his refusal to acknowledge any Tibetan right to independence or national self-determination has more to do with an adopted Chinese chauvinism than with socialism.

That he may indeed have had some doubts about China's role in Tibet is indicated by a website message in response to an online article about Epstein's death in 2005. The writer, who preferred to remain anonymous, claimed to be related to Epstein and said that Epstein had realized he had been wrong about Tibet.[26] The fact that he never admitted it publicly is a testimony to his life-long devotion to the socialist cause and his willingness to propagandize that cause even when contrary to the truth.

On the front cover of *Tibet Transformed* is a photo of the Potala, which appears strangely unfamiliar until one realizes that the photo negative has been reversed. It is perhaps symbolic that neither Epstein, who claimed to be so familiar with Tibet, nor his editors at New World Press noticed this error. Perhaps this is what he and the Chinese meant by "Tibet Transformed."

Notes

1. "Electoral Regulations for Tibet Made Public," New China News Agency, 30 March 1963, in *Tibet, 1950–1967*, comp. Ling Nai-Min (Hong Kong: Union Research Institute, 1967), 503.

2. Radio Peking, August 1965, as quoted by the U.S. ambassador to the United Nations at the United Nations General Assembly, 17 December 1965 (A/PV/1401), in *General Assembly Official Records, Twentieth Session* (New York: United Nations, 1967), 11.

3. "Great Revolutionary Changes in Tibet," *Peking Review*, 10 September 1965, in Ling, *Tibet, 1950–1967* (Hong Kong: Union Research Institute, 1967), 468.

4. Rinbur Tulku's biography was published in Tibetan in Dharamsala in 1989. It has been translated but not yet published in its entirety by Matthew Akseter. However, several excerpts, including Rinbur's experiences in the Cultural Revolution, were published in Andre Alexander, *The Temples of Lhasa: Tibetan Buddhist Architecture from the 7th to the 21st Centuries* (Chicago: Serindia, 2006). All otherwise unattributed quotes in this section are from this work.

5. Israel Epstein, *Tibet Transformed* (Beijing: New World Press, 1983), 33.

6. Ibid., 137.

7. Ibid., 140.

8. Ibid., 138.

9. Ibid., 481.

10. Ibid., 412.

11. Ibid., 214.

12. Ibid., 225.

13. Ibid., 61.

14. Ibid., 384.

15. *Wrath of the Serfs: A Group of Life-Size Sculptures* (Beijing: New World Press, 1976). All otherwise unattributed quotes in the middle of this section are from this work.

16. "Wrath of the Serfs—A Tableau of Sculptures," *Peking Review*, 19 September 1975.

17. Epstein, *Tibet Transformed*, 482.

18. Woeser, "Regarding the Re-Published Cultural Revolution Pictorial, *Wrath of the Serfs*," unpublished article in Chinese, translated by Radio Free Asia, January 2006. All otherwise unattributed quotes in the remainder of this section are from this work. Efforts to secure a copy of the republished *Wrath of the Serfs* went unrewarded until Woeser sent me the copy she had purchased in the Lhasa bookstore. Others who searched for the book in late 2006 and 2007 reported it unavailable in bookstores in Lhasa. Perhaps Woeser's criticisms had embarrassed Chinese officials and they decided to remove the book from circulation.

19. Israel Epstein, *My China Eye: Memoirs of a Jew and a Journalist* (San Francisco: Long River Press, 2005), 11.

20. Ibid., 271.

21. All otherwise unattributed quotes in this section are from Epstein, *Tibet Transformed*.

22. Mao Zedong, "On the Policies of Our Work in Tibet," *Selected Works* (Beijing: Foreign Languages Press, 1977), 5:74.

23. Epstein, *My China Eye*, 288–98.

24. Ibid., 299–319.

25. All otherwise unattributed quotes in this section are from Epstein, *My China Eye*.

26. Anonymous response to Warren W. Smith, "The Life and Death of Israel Epstein," TimesofTibet.com, July 2005.

5

Autonomy or Assimilation

A FTER THE DEATH OF MAO, the fall of the Gang of Four, and the ascendancy of Deng Xiaoping to China's leadership role, a more pragmatic policy was adopted with regard to many issues, Tibet among them. The visit of Hu Yaobang to Tibet in 1980 revealed to Chinese leaders that the situation there was not as stable as they had imagined. Hu initiated several reform measures, some of which, like the dissolution of communes, were common to all of China, but also others that were specific to Tibet. These involved some of the autonomous rights that China had promised to Tibet in the Seventeen-Point Agreement and the National Regional Autonomy system but had never allowed in practice. Although the number of Chinese cadres was planned to be reduced, reportedly by 85 percent, the remaining Chinese in Tibet would maintain ultimate political control, but Tibetans would be allowed more cultural and religious freedom.

The liberalized economic and cultural policies in Tibet after 1980 produced a dramatic revival of Tibetan religion and culture. This was a surprise to the Chinese, who thought they had convinced Tibetans of the superstitious and counterrevolutionary nature of Tibetan Buddhism. Even more surprising to the Chinese, who thought they had eradicated all Tibetan thoughts of separatism, was a revival of Tibetan nationalism centered in the rebuilt and repopulated monasteries. The revival of Tibetan religion and nationalism culminated in several demonstrations and riots in Lhasa in 1987–1989, after which the Chinese essentially abandoned the experiment of allowing any real Tibetan autonomy.

Despite Chinese attempts to control the effects of the liberalization policy, the resurgence of Tibetan culture and nationalism was an inevitable result of the liberalization of previously very repressive Chinese policies in Tibet. The unexpected results of the post-Maoist liberalization led the Chinese Communist Party (CCP) to reappraise its policies. Recognizing that the policy of allowing the unsupervised revival of religion had led to a resurgence of Tibetan nationalism, the CCP moved to restrict the reconstruction of monasteries, the number of monks being initiated, and religious instruction by monks. The party also attempted to control monasteries from within by instituting "democratic management committees." The CCP attempted to confine the religious revival to individual expressions of faith and the most superficial aspects of religious practice. Dialogue with the Dalai Lama was essentially abandoned, although the Chinese continued to maintain that they were willing to negotiate if he would give up the "idea of independence."

In 1984, the CCP adopted a new economic policy intended to integrate the Tibetan economy into that of interior China, further making Tibet an integral and inseparable part of China. A significant aspect of that policy was the abandonment of Hu Yaobang's commitment to allow Tibetan autonomy by restricting the number of Han Chinese in Tibet.

The decision to rely on economic development and to allow Chinese cadres, workers, and entrepreneurs into Tibet to pursue that development was a turning point in post-Maoist Chinese policy in Tibet. The influx of Chinese, especially the private entrepreneurs, who took Tibetans' jobs and business and showed no signs of leaving, increased the discontent of Tibetans, who were well aware that a primary component of the post-Maoist reform policy had been the promise to reduce the number of Chinese in Tibet. In 1987, Deng Xiaoping declared that development in Tibet should not be hindered by "judging the success of our Tibet policy based upon a limitation of the numbers of Han in Tibet."[1] The essence of Deng's Tibet policy was that the CCP would no longer restrict the number of Han in Tibet because they were necessary for Tibet's development. Deng's statement opened the doors to unrestrained Chinese colonization in Tibet.

The death of the tenth Panchen Lama in January 1989 removed the most important Tibetan proponent for Tibetan autonomy. He had been a spokesman for Tibetans and for the pragmatic faction within the CCP on Tibet policy. The Panchen Lama was opposed by hard-liners, especially Chinese cadres and some Tibetans who favored a continuation of strict CCP control in Tibet. His demise reduced the influence of the pragmatic faction and increased the strength of the hard-liners. The hard-liners were further strengthened by the demonstrations and riots in Tibet from November 1987 to March 1989, after which the Tibet Autonomous Region (TAR) was placed under military law for a year, and by the Tiananmen Square demonstrations and ensuing crackdown of June 1989. After these events, there was little tolerance for any sort of liberalism within the CCP nor any policy in favor of autonomy in Tibet. The hard-line faction that predominated in Chinese politics after 1989 reportedly blamed the disturbances in Tibet, and the revival of Tibet as an international issue, on the liberalization policy of the 1980s. Similarly, they blamed the 1959 Tibetan Revolt on the retrenchment policy of 1957. Chinese hard-liners—and it may be assumed the majority of Chinese policy makers—apparently learned the lesson that whenever China allows a modicum of autonomy in Tibet, Tibetan nationalism rapidly coalesces into anti-Chinese resistance.

Normally, the Panchen Lama's reincarnation should have been found in three years, but the political implications involved delayed the process until 1995. A Tashilhunpo selection committee was allowed to search by the traditional Tibetan methods, provided they found the incarnation within the People's Republic of China (PRC). They did so, discovering a child in Nagchukha, but they secretly conveyed the news to the Dalai Lama and requested his approval. The Dalai Lama announced his recognition of the Panchen Lama's reincarnation in April 1995, setting off furious denunciations from the Chinese, who claimed that the Dalai Lama was violating historical precedent by recognizing the incarnation when that right lay exclusively with the Chinese government. Nevertheless, the Dalai Lama's choice for the Panchen Lama's reincarnation was not immediately rejected; the Chinese simply maintained that the choice was theirs to make.

For some time, until November, it seemed that an amicable solution might be worked out. The Chinese had been embarrassed by the Dalai Lama's preemptive recognition, but this did not necessarily mean that they had to reject his choice. They could easily have ignored his selection as inconclusive while proclaiming their choice of the same child as authoritative and official. In this way, they could have had a Panchen Lama recognized by the Tibetan people. However, the Chinese government ultimately rejected the Dalai Lama's and the Tashilhunpo authorities' choice, a child already widely accepted by Tibetans as the legitimate reincarnation, in favor of a child of their own choice whose acceptance would have to be forced upon the Tibetan people. The Chinese chose another boy as Panchen Lama and, after a drawing of lots from the golden urn, installed him in a ceremony in Lhasa (in secret in the middle of the night). The Dalai Lama's choice, Gendhun Choekyi Nyima, and his family were retained and disappeared.

The Chinese had apparently been willing to allow the Dalai Lama some role in the selection process in order to legitimate the candidate, but only so long as he requested the Chinese government's final approval. His failure to do so was considered a challenge to the government's final authority in the matter and, therefore, a challenge to the legitimacy of Chinese authority over Tibet.

Tibetan reincarnation politics were traditionally the means by which China had in the past exerted its pretensions to authority over Tibet. In 1793, the Qing had instituted the system of choosing lots from a golden urn as a means to establish Qing authority over the selection of the Dalai and Panchen Lamas. China's claim to sovereignty over Tibet rested upon its authority to appoint officials or, in the Tibetan context, to recognize incarnations; therefore, the Chinese government could accept no challenge to that authority. The rejection of the Dalai Lama's choice for Panchen Lama demonstrated that the Chinese cared less for Tibetans' sentiments than for what they perceived as China's unity and national security. They were willing to impose an unpopular choice for Panchen Lama on the Tibetan people in order to reject the Dalai Lama's influence in Tibetan affairs. China's uncompromising policy in regard to the Panchen Lama's reincarnation indicated that it had no intention of making any compromises with the Dalai Lama.

For China, the issue was more political than religious; it was a question of the unification of the motherland and of Tibet's subordination to the Chinese central government. The Chinese claimed the authority to recognize the reincarnation of the Panchen Lama "according to the Chinese constitution"—a document not known to have anything to say about reincarnation. The Dalai Lama's unilateral action in recognizing the Panchen Lama's reincarnation was condemned as "going against Buddhist doctrine," "infringing upon state sovereignty," and "splitting the motherland through religious means." He was condemned for ignoring historical conventions and religious rites, a reference to the drawing of lots from the golden urn, a procedure that the Chinese claimed was equivalent to "religious commandments." The Dalai Lama's role in the process was condemned as "no longer a religious issue, but a political plot of the splittists."

Arjia Rinpoche of Labrang Tashikyil Monastery in Gansu described the initiation ceremony in Lhasa as exceedingly tense. Chinese soldiers lined the road all the way from the airport to Lhasa, a distance of fifty miles. The Tibetan attendees were awakened in the middle of the night for the actual ceremony, which was held at 3 a.m. without previous announcement. Again, People's Liberation Army (PLA) soldiers lined the road, shoulder to shoulder, on the route to the Jokhang.[2]

In 1992, Chen Kuiyuan, the hard-line CCP secretary in Tibet, declared Tibet's "special characteristics" insufficient reason why policies in Tibet should differ from those in any Chinese province.[3] The particular issue to which Chen was responding was Chinese migration to Tibet. His statement indicated that Tibet's special characteristics would not be allowed to restrict

Han migration. Chen also renewed restrictions on other aspects of Tibet's culture, including language and religion.

In July 1994, the CCP summoned its "Third National Work Forum on Tibet" in Beijing. The primary themes of the forum were "stability and development," as is evident in the title of the final document, "Decision to Accelerate Development and Maintain Stability in Tibet." The expected "cultural" implications of development were indicated by remarks at the forum by Jiang Zemin:

> While paying attention to promoting Tibet's fine traditional culture, it is also necessary to absorb the fine cultures of other nationalities in order to integrate the fine traditional culture with the fruits of modern culture. This will facilitate the development of socialist new culture in Tibet.[4]

The influx of even more Chinese into Tibet was justified as necessary for Tibet's development.

The Third Forum determined that the cause of instability in Tibet was the "Dalai Clique's splittist activities." It maintained that the Dalai clique, in collusion with the "hostile forces of western countries," hoped to split China and establish Tibetan independence. In particular, the Dalai Lama was suspected of using religion and reincarnation politics in order to gain influence within monasteries in Tibet. China's competition with the Dalai Lama was characterized as an "antagonistic contradiction with the enemy," a Maoist category that does not allow for compromise. Although the CCP remained officially open to a return of the Dalai Lama, the language of the Third Work Forum made it apparent that the party was not serious about a dialogue with him. The primary task in Tibet was defined as the struggle against splittism and opposing the Dalai clique. Since monks and nuns had been at the forefront of protests in Tibet, the Third Work Forum decided to place firm restrictions on religion, the rebuilding of monasteries, and the numbers of monks and nuns.[5]

After the Third Tibet Work Forum and the Panchen Lama affair, the Chinese initiated a campaign to eradicate the Dalai Lama's influence in religion as well as politics inside Tibet. The subsequent Patriotic Education Campaign in Tibetan monasteries and nunneries was an attempt to transform Tibetan nationalism into patriotism toward China and to eradicate Tibetans' loyalty to the Dalai Lama. Monks and nuns were subjected to lengthy indoctrination sessions and were required to denounce the Dalai Lama and Tibetan independence, pledge loyalty to China, and recognize the Chinese choice of Panchen Lama. Photographs of the Dalai Lama were no longer permitted. Democratic management committees supervised by outside officials were instituted in every monastery and nunnery. Nevertheless, many monks and nuns refused to denounce the Dalai Lama and were forced to leave their monasteries, some escaping to India.

The CCP's Fourth Tibet Work Forum, held in July 2001, confirmed the policy of economic development in Tibet, accompanied by repression of political dissent, cultivation of loyal Tibetan cadres, restriction of autonomy, and fostering of Chinese colonization. In his address to the forum, Jiang Zemin pointed out that the primary tasks in Tibet were still to promote stability and development. The primary source of instability was said to be the Dalai Lama and his separatist activities.[6]

Since 1989, China has instituted a policy in Tibet of restrictions on all aspects of Tibetan cultural and political autonomy that have nationalist implications, which effectively means almost all aspects of autonomy. This has been combined with continuous repression of opposition, patriotic education campaigns, and economic development that buys the compliance of some Tibetans but also supports Chinese colonization. The Third and Fourth Tibet Work Forums, along with the Great Western Development Plan, indicate China's policy to resolve the Tibet and Xinjiang issues by means of economic development and the consequent influx of Han Chinese. The completion of the railroad to Lhasa in 2006, along with the appointment of a new party secretary, Zhang Qingli, whose previous role was as head of the Chinese agency in Xinjiang responsible for Han colonization, the Production and Construction Corps, was further indication that China was committed to an economic development and colonization policy in Tibet.

Patriotic Education Campaign

The Patriotic Education Campaign was instituted in all of China in 1996 as a part of the CCP's attempt to arouse Chinese patriotism after Tiananmen and to equate that patriotism with support for the party. In Tibet, the purpose of the campaign was to transform Tibetan national identity into Chinese identity, to eradicate Tibetans' loyalty to the Dalai Lama, and to cultivate Tibetan loyalty to China instead. The significance of China's Patriotic Education Campaign in Tibetan monasteries and nunneries, and later in secular society as well, is that it reveals exactly what the Chinese want Tibetans to believe about their own history, about Tibet's relationship with China, about the supposed evils of Tibetan independence and the Dalai Lama's splittism, and about the supposed inevitability and advantage of Tibet's union with China. The success or failure of this campaign is equivalent to the success or failure of China's efforts to transform Tibetan national identity and loyalty to the Dalai Lama into Chinese national identity and loyalty to China.

After the Panchen Lama reincarnation controversy, the Chinese began an intense anti–Dalai Lama campaign within Tibet. Shortly thereafter, in 1996, the Chinese instituted the Patriotic Education Campaign in monasteries and nunneries. The Patriotic Education Campaign was initiated in monasteries because the monasteries and nunneries were identified as the centers of the revival of Tibetan nationalism. It was begun by sending teams of CCP cadres to spend three months or more in monasteries. These work teams instructed monks and nuns in the Chinese version of Tibetan history, forced them to denounce the Dalai Lama, and required them to adhere to Chinese government regulations and restrictions on religion.

Monks and nuns were required to study four books during compulsory study sessions. At the end, they were tested on the contents of these books and made to memorize the required answers about Tibet's history as a part of China, the Dalai Lama's splittist activities, China's legal system, and Chinese regulations on religious practice. Those who resisted this indoctrination or who failed the tests were subjected to punishments such as expulsion or even imprisonment. Many monks were expelled during this process, either because they refused to denounce the Dalai Lama or because they failed to adhere to Chinese regulations on religion, such as that no one below the age of eighteen could become a monk or nun.

The first of the four indoctrination books that Tibetan monks and nuns were forced to study is about the history of Tibet. The second attempts to turn Tibetans against the Dalai Lama by accusing him of supporting Tibetan independence. The other two books are about the Chinese legal system, regulations on the practice of religion, the restrictions imposed upon monasteries, and justifications for the Patriotic Education Campaign.

The title of the first section of the first indoctrination book is "Tibet and China Coexisted in Friendship from Ancient Times." It maintains that relations between Tibet and Tang China were amicable, citing two marriage alliances, and claims that in the Sino-Tibetan treaty of 822, the Chinese and Tibetans agreed to "unite their territories as one." However, the fact is that relations between China and Tibet during this period were characterized by Sino-Tibetan hostility rather than amicability. In the treaty of 822, the "union" of Tibet and China was clearly in the sense of a union only in agreement. The treaty speaks of China and Tibet each guarding the borders of their separate territories.

The second section is "How Tibet Came to Be Part of China." China claims that Tibet formally became an integral part of China in the thirteenth century during the Yuan dynasty, when Tibet as well as China were both part of the Mongol Yuan Empire. The third and fourth sections attempt to demonstrate Chinese authority in Tibet by citing how the Yuan appointed officials in Tibet and instituted census, taxation, and postal systems.

The next two sections are titled "How the Ming Dynasty Exercised Effective Control of Tibetan Areas" and "How the Ming Dynasty Gave Edicts to the Big

Lamas of the Various Sects of Tibet." China claims that the Chinese Ming dynasty continued to exercise the authority established by the Mongol Yuan. In fact, the Ming had no real interest in Tibet beyond Tibet's role in Ming relations with the Mongols, who still posed a threat to the Ming. Once the Mongol threat passed, the Ming were no longer concerned with Tibet and did little to substantiate their claim to authority there.

The next section is "The Relationship between the Qing Emperor and the Dalai Lama Is Like a Master and His Servant." The Dalai Lama's title is said to have become official only by means of Qing recognition of the Fifth Dalai Lama in 1650. However, the Dalai Lama's title derived from the Third Dalai Lama's meeting with the Mongol Altan Khan in 1579. The title derived its legitimacy from the Tibetan and Mongol peoples, not from recognition by China.

Further sections of the book are about how the Qing expelled the Zungar Mongols and the Gurkhas and established a new administrative system that confirmed Qing authority over Tibet, a part of which was the golden urn ceremony for confirming the selection of the Dalai Lama and Panchen Lama. The book claims that the Chinese central government of the Qing dynasty had the authority to recognize the reincarnation of the Dalai Lama and other high lama reincarnations and to preside over the enthronement ceremonies. The Tibetan understanding and actual practice, however, was to choose their own reincarnations by their own methods and then inform the Manchu emperor. The golden urn ceremony was sometimes held—to confirm an already chosen reincarnation—when there was a strong Manchu *amban* who insisted, but more often it was altogether neglected.

The first indoctrination book addresses the beginning of the twentieth century with a section titled "The KMT Government Exercised Control over Tibet as Before." The book says that the Kuomintang (KMT) declared Tibetans one of the "five races" of China, citing this as further proof that Tibet was a part of China. It claims that the existence of the Mongolian and Tibetan Affairs Commission, established by the KMT in 1928, proves that China had control over Tibet. The indoctrination book admits that the KMT had little or no actual authority in Tibet, but claims that China still "owned" Tibet.

Despite the admitted lack of KMT authority in Tibet, the book nevertheless maintains that China approved the choice of the Reting Regent when the Thirteenth Dalai Lama died in 1933 and that a Chinese official officiated over the installation of the Fourteenth Dalai Lama in 1938. Chinese approval of the choice of the Fourteenth Dalai Lama is said to demonstrate Chinese authority over Tibet. As the indoctrination book says, "If the Chinese government did not give its permission the 14th Dalai Lama could not have been recognized. It is clear from this that Tibet was a part of China." However, the invitation to the KMT to send an official to attend the Fourteenth Dalai Lama's recognition ceremony did not in any way imply a Tibetan request for approval of the reincarnation or that the Chinese official would preside over the ceremony. In fact, the Chinese official attended the ceremony as a guest, after which he deceived his own government by claiming that he had presided.

The last two sections of the first indoctrination book are entitled "How So-called Tibetan Independence Came About" and "The Complete Defeat of the Invading Forces of the Imperialists Is the Watershed in Time Since When the People of China No Longer Have to Suffer Oppression from Others." The theme of these sections is that the very idea of Tibetan independence is the creation of foreign imperialists, the previous history of brotherly relations between Tibetans and Chinese proves that Tibet has been a part of China throughout its history, and it is only because of British imperialism in Tibet that Tibetans ever got the idea of independence. According to this logic, both the Tibetan declaration of independence by the Thirteenth Dalai Lama in 1912 and Tibet's attempt to negotiate its independence at the Simla Conference in 1914 were creations of the British imperialists. Further attempts by the Tibetans up to 1950 to demonstrate their independence were all plots by the imperialists, whether British or American. The Patriotic Education Campaign indoctrination book maintains that Tibetans wanted only union with China and that liberation by and union with China meant freedom, while independence under the domination of the imperialists would have meant slavery.

The book goes on to say that it was the duty of the Chinese people to liberate the Tibetans from the foreign imperialists and that this was the wish as well of the Tibetan people, who welcomed the PLA when it entered Tibet. The Tibetan Army's resistance at Chamdo was supposedly directed by British and American imperialists. The Seventeen-Point Agreement for the Peaceful Liberation of Tibet ended the imperialists' schemes to detach Tibet from China. The book describes the Seventeen-Point Agreement as an example of voluntary cooperation between brother nationalities. After the PLA entered central Tibet, Tibetans were truly liberated. Since then, Tibetans have enjoyed wealth and happiness courtesy of the Chinese people's government. Without the leadership of the Chinese government and the communist system, Tibetans would not have been able to free themselves from feudalism and imperialism.

China's Patriotic Education Campaign in Tibet attempts to convince Tibetans that they are really Chinese, that they are lucky to have been liberated by China, and that they have no reason to desire freedom from Chinese control. China's argument about the idea of Tibetan independence being the invention of foreign imperialists denies any legitimacy to Tibetans' desires to be free from Chinese control.

The second Patriotic Education Campaign book is about the Dalai Lama's splittist activities, the feudal nature of old Tibet, the inevitability of Tibet's union with China, and the necessity of preserving that unity so that Tibet might develop and prosper. It attempts to convince Tibetans to regard Tibetan independence as the Chinese regard it—as an unmitigated evil—while seeing union with China as natural, necessary, inevitable, and irreversible. This book has four sections. The first is about how the Dalai Lama clique instigated the 1959 revolt and has promoted splittist activities from exile since that time. The second is on the evils of the old society in Tibet before liberation. The third is on the inevitability of the defeat of the splittist forces. The fourth is on the antisplittist struggle within Tibet and the necessity of Tibet's union with China.

The introduction of the second book reiterates the theme that China is a unitary nation of many nationalities that have voluntarily united in a spirit of friendliness and cooperation to create a big family of the motherland. Tibet, like the other minority nationality territories, is an inseparable part of China. Nevertheless, the book says, the Dalai Lama, with the support of Western hostile forces, declared the independence of Tibet and opposed the integrity of the motherland and the unity of nationalities. It is necessary to understand and to oppose the Dalai Lama's counterrevolutionary separatist activities in order to preserve the integrity of the motherland and the unity of nationalities and to promote stability and economic development.

The first section of the second indoctrination book is on the 1959 revolt. Although many progressive Tibetans favored the reforms that were specified in the Seventeen-Point Agreement, some reactionaries opposed them and plotted to sabotage the agreement. In 1952, some of these Tibetan leaders formed the illegal Mimang Tsongdu and demanded that the PLA leave Tibet. Tibetans in eastern Tibetan areas, outside the TAR, resisted reforms in 1955, and in 1956 they organized an armed revolt. Tibetan government officials refused to suppress the revolt because they thought they could successfully oppose the Chinese government. The Tibetan Revolt also received foreign support from the American CIA, which trained Tibetans abroad and parachuted them back into Tibet along with arms and ammunition. In March 1959, reactionary elements in Lhasa started rumors that the Chinese were planning to kidnap the Dalai Lama and take him to Beijing. They organized a demonstration outside the Norbulingka to prevent the Dalai Lama from leaving. They formed another Mimang Tsongdu that repudiated the Seventeen-Point Agreement, declared Tibetan independence, and called on Tibetans to revolt against the Chinese. They abducted the Dalai Lama and began an attack against the PLA troops in Lhasa. The rebellion was quickly put down by the PLA with the help of patriotic Tibetans who opposed the revolt.

Although the Dalai Lama is said to have been kidnapped by the rebels, he is blamed for setting up a Tibetan government-in-exile. He is denounced for establishing Tibetan resistance forces in Nepal, promulgating a Tibetan constitution in exile, opening representative offices in several countries, and publishing books and magazines advocating Tibetan independence. "Taking refuge in the hands of Western enemy forces they spread lies and propaganda about the so-called Independence of Tibet throughout the world, which led to lowering the Motherland's image in the world." The book says that the Dalai Lama's government-in-exile could not survive and could not continue its separatist activities without the support of foreign anti-China forces. These anti-China forces attempt to use the issue of human rights to interfere in China's internal affairs and to internationalize the Tibet issue. The Dalai Lama is accused of violating his vows as a monk to not tell lies, such as that Tibet is under foreign domination, that a million Tibetans were killed, that Tibetans have no human rights, and that China is colonizing Tibet, all of which harm the international image of China.

Since the opening of Tibet in 1979, the Dalai Lama is accused of sending agents into Tibet to cause sabotage and resistance. He and the Tibetan government-in-exile are accused of attempting to exploit the religious revival in Tibet for political purposes, of seeking to gain control of monasteries, and of attempting to control the selection of *tulkus*, in particular the reincarnation of the Panchen Lama. The Dalai Lama is accused of using the reincarnation of the Panchen Lama as a means of challenging the authority of the Chinese government and the Communist Party over religious issues in Tibet. He is further denounced as the chief of the splittist Tibetan independence movement, a tool of Western anti-China forces, the source of all disturbances in Tibet, and the biggest obstacle to the normal practice of Buddhism in Tibet. In conclusion, this section warns monasteries that if they oppose the CCP and the Chinese government by supporting the Dalai Lama, they risk losing their permission to exist as religious institutions.

The title of the following section is "The Tibetan People Will Never Bring Back the Dead Unity of Religion and State System." Contrary to the claims of Tibetan separatists, old Tibet was not at all peaceful and harmonious; rather, it was a barbaric, dark, oppressive, and feudal serf system. The sufferings of the serfs were worse than those of animals. Tibetan society remained backward because no progress was possible under the feudal serf system. Serfowners and their agents were only 5 percent of the population, all the rest of whom they oppressed. Monks and nuns were also part of the exploitative system because they contributed nothing to production.

The title of the third section of the second indoctrination book is "There Is Nothing but Defeat in Store for the Splittist Activities of the Dalai Clique." There are five subsections whose self-explanatory themes are: "To split the motherland is against the objective law of historical development"; "The Dalai's disguise as a religious leader can never deceive the Tibetan people and

the people of the world who love peace and want to see the truth prevail";
"Whoever betrays the interests of the motherland and the people and be-
comes a tool of the international forces opposed to China will never come to
a good end"; "As it is against the Chinese nation's interests for the Dalai to betray the nation and split the motherland the whole of the Chinese people, including the Tibetan people, will resolutely oppose him"; and "The new socialist relationship of the nationalities is firm and irrevocable."

The title of the final section of the book is "Launching an Anti-splittist
Struggle with Pointed Spears in Order to Continue the Defense of the Unity
of the Motherland and the Friendship and Solidarity of the Nationalities." The
themes of its four subsections are: "The Tibet Autonomous Region could have
a brilliant future if it follows the socialist path within the great family of China
under the leadership of the Chinese Communist Party"; "By recognizing the
reactionary nature of the Dalai clique clearly, they must be opposed with
pointed spears"; "With resolute determination, infiltration must be prevented
completely and dealt a severe blow"; and "The management and control of the
monks and nuns in the monasteries must be strengthened in accordance with
the provisions of the law."

The theme of this section is that Tibetans can be the masters of their own
lives and homes only by following the socialist path under the leadership of
the CCP. Tibetans had no control over their own lives or futures under the
feudal serf system of old Tibet, but liberation and democratic reforms under
the Chinese made Tibetans the owners of Tibet. Since then, Tibet has gone
from a stagnant feudal society to a society with transportation facilities, elec-
tricity, industry, telecommunications, education, health care, and a modern
economy. All of this development would have been impossible without Tibet
being a part of China and receiving the help of all China's fraternal nationalities. China has never taken a single penny from Tibet; on the contrary, it has
spent more than 25 billion yuan on Tibet's development. In order to raise the
standard of Tibet's culture, health, science, and technology, China has sent
thousands of experts there. Under the current open door and market economy policies, Tibet is a scene of economic development, political stability,
unity of nationalities, social progress, and a happy and contented people.

The second indoctrination book maintains that, in contrast to this picture
of stability and unity, the Dalai Lama continues to try to sabotage the Tibetan
people's happy life in order to restore feudal serfdom and split Tibet from
China. Therefore, to preserve Tibet's stability and unity, all Tibetans must reject the Dalai Lama's influence. China has been benevolent toward the Dalai
Lama, offering to allow him to return if he would give up the idea of Tibetan
independence. Instead, he has chosen to rely on Western anti-Chinese forces
in an attempt to split Tibet from China. All Tibetans must oppose the Dalai

Lama's splittist activities. Similarly, all monasteries must reject the Dalai Lama's influence and accept the leadership and supervision of the CCP.

The third Patriotic Education Campaign book is about China's legal system and how it applies to Tibetan religious institutions and the activities of monks and nuns. Its title is "A Brief Explanation of the Propagation of Knowledge about the Legal System." There are subsections on the need for education about China's legal system; the necessity that the monasteries obey the law; the Chinese constitution; the criminal code; laws on public demonstrations, security measures, and punishments; policies on religious activities; policies on the religious activities of foreigners resident in the PRC; State Council regulations on controlling religious activities; and regulations on the registration of places where religious activities are conducted. The book emphasizes that the campaign to educate monks and nuns about the laws of the PRC is meant to reflect the party and government's concern for them. China allows freedom of religion; therefore, study of the legal system simply informs monks and nuns about their rights.

The first section explains that China's laws disallow any opposition to the four fundamental principles as decreed by Deng Xiaoping: socialism, democratic dictatorship, Communist Party rule, and Marxist-Leninist-Maoist political ideology. Any talk or activities in contradiction to these four basic principles are illegal. Illegal gatherings intended to cause disturbances, plotting rebellion, demonstrations without permission, opposition to the government, and any attempts to split the motherland or gain independence by destroying the unity of nationalities are crimes against the people. Opposing the Communist Party and the socialist system is a punishable offense. Tibetan monks and nuns are instructed to make themselves aware of these laws and to restrict their speech and behavior in accordance. They are told that they must be self-supporting, respect the regulations, abide by the law, love their country and their religion, and be good monks and nuns as well as good citizens.

The next section, titled "The Law Must Be Implemented in the Monasteries," begins by saying that the Patriotic Education Campaign has raised the awareness of the law among Tibetans and has contributed to safeguarding the unity of the motherland, strengthening the solidarity of nationalities, and stepping up the struggle to control the splittists. Because of this campaign, the splittists have been isolated and the number of instances of illegal disturbances has been reduced. Nevertheless, the education about the legal system still has not deeply penetrated the monasteries. This has allowed the splittists to use the monasteries as bases for their activities. Some monasteries have actually come under the influence of the splittists and are centers for opposing the people's political authority. They have become a political base for the Dalai clique to infiltrate Tibet and propagate splittist activities. Because these activities undermine the social discipline and prevailing atmosphere of stability and unity, they must be vigilantly opposed.

Monks and nuns were informed that the purposes of the Patriotic Education Campaign were to pursue the struggle against the splittists, defend the unity of the motherland, strengthen the solidarity of nationalities, and promote peace, stability, and social progress. They were required to learn about the legal system in order to obey the laws and to know their rights under the laws. They were particularly to learn about the laws on security, on public gatherings and demonstrations, and on the management of monasteries. Monks and nuns have no special rights or privileges. They have the right to religious freedom, but religion and religious laws must be subordinate to state laws. They are not allowed to use religion to oppose the interests of the nation or society or to undermine the unity of nationalities. Monks and nuns should love religion, but they must also love the country and oppose the splittists. It is the duty of all citizens, including monks and nuns, to safeguard the unity of the motherland and the solidarity of nationalities.

This section concludes by blaming the Dalai Lama for colluding with foreign reactionary countries to split Tibet from China. His splittist activities are said to be the root cause for instability in Tibet. Monks and nuns are therefore required to renounce their loyalty to him. The Dalai Lama has betrayed the motherland and is therefore no longer the rightful leader of Tibetan Buddhism. Loyalty to Buddhism is separable from loyalty to the Dalai Lama. Monks and nuns are warned that they must obey the law and renounce splittist activities or they will be expelled from their monasteries. Monasteries are also warned that they must be patriotic or they will be closed.

A final section is about the Chinese constitution, which is the basic and highest law of the country. Theoretically, no one, not even the CCP, can contradict the provisions of the constitution. Provisions in the constitution declare that all Chinese have the rights to vote, to run for elections, and of speech, publication, assembly, and demonstration. However, no citizen is allowed to harm the interests of the nation or society. All citizens are required to support and protect the unity of the motherland. National minorities have the right to exercise regional autonomy, which represents China's wish to guarantee and respect the rights of minority nationalities to internal autonomy and to ensure common progress and prosperity for all based upon equality and unity of nationalities. All autonomous regions are declared to be inseparable parts of China. Nationalities are said to be equal; they have all voluntarily united within the Chinese state and have decided that they are inseparable from one another and from the majority nationality, the Han Chinese. They are all required to preserve the unity and friendship of all the nationalities of China.

The fourth Patriotic Education Campaign indoctrination book is "A Summary Explanation of the Policy on Religion." This book has sections entitled "The Fundamental Position of the Party and the State on Religion," "Religious Activities Must Be Carried Out in Accordance with the Constitution," "Rules and Regulations for the Monks and Nuns Must Be Carried Out to Enforce Discipline," and "Members of the Religious Community Must Unite with Non-believers in the Struggle to Develop a Socialist System with Chinese Characteristics."

The fundamental policy on religion in China is that religion must adapt to socialist society and religious believers must obey the law, support stability and unity, and oppose separatism. No one is allowed to use religion to interfere with the administration of the state, the law, or education. Children cannot become monks or nuns before age eighteen. Some monasteries are allowed to exist in order to serve the needs of religious believers, but only those approved by the government. People are not allowed to build or restore monasteries or other religious places at their own initiative with their own funds; this is meant to control the revival of Buddhism in Tibet and the number of monks and nuns. No one is allowed to propagate religion outside the confines of approved religious establishments. Besides their religious studies, monks and nuns must study modern subjects, including patriotism and socialism.

Hostile foreign forces, including the Dalai Lama and Tibetans in exile, are not allowed to control or influence religious organizations or religious affairs. All Tibetans must be vigilant in opposing the infiltration of foreign splittist forces under a religious guise. Before 1959, central Tibet had 110,000 monks. Afterward, this number fell to less than 10,000, a reduction that is said to have been achieved in consultation with Tibetan leaders in order to contribute to Tibetan production. In the past, it is said, lamas oppressed not only the Tibetan serfs but also the lower classes of monks and nuns. They also imposed their religious ideology upon the people. Now, however, all Tibetans are united in their love for the Chinese motherland and their faith in socialism and the CCP. They understand that the CCP is their liberator and that only the pursuit of socialism under the leadership of the party can bring them happiness. The conclusion says that religion must adapt to socialism, and there is no conflict in doing so because there is no conflict between love for religion and love for socialism and (Chinese) patriotism.

As the Patriotic Education Campaign book says, rules and regulations are necessary for the proper functioning and protection of monasteries and nunneries.

> Since 1987, some monks and nuns of certain monasteries have frequently caused and participated in social disturbances by ignoring the country's constitution

and laws and by violating religious commandments and rules. They became the vanguard of separatist forces and co-operated with internal and external separatist activities. They had a bad impact on our region's construction of a modern society and the daily life of the people. They sabotaged our region's stability and solidarity.

It goes on to say that the Tibetan people themselves requested that the political activities of monks and nuns be restricted. Limitations are necessary in order to ensure social stability and to reassure the public. The argument is made that it is necessary to restrict religion in order to ensure freedom of religion. If religion were unrestricted, it might undermine the interests of society.

The summary of China's rules and regulations on religion says that all religious establishments and believers must obey the laws, are not allowed to use religion to interfere with the government administration or education, and should accept the leadership of the party and government and support the socialist system. The number of religious institutions in Tibet is said to be adequate, and no more are allowed to be established without government permission. All monasteries must be governed by democratic management committees composed of religious personnel who are politically reliable, patriotic, and law-abiding.

After having completed their study of the four Patriotic Education Campaign indoctrination books, Tibetan monks and nuns were tested on their contents. Only by passing the test were they allowed to remain in the monasteries and nunneries. Those who passed were issued either a red pass, which allowed them to remain officially in the monastery, or a blue pass, which was temporary and conditional upon good behavior for a one-year period. If those given blue passes kept out of trouble for one year, they might be issued red passes. Whether or not individual monks or nuns were allowed to stay in their monasteries also depended upon their age, the quota set by the Chinese government, the political reliability of themselves and their families, and the availability of a teacher or supervisor. The teacher or supervisor was also responsible for the monk or nun being patriotic and devoted to religion.

The number and order of questions on the examination varied from region to region and from monastery to monastery, but they always covered the main themes of the Patriotic Education Campaign. The first question was about the reasons for the campaign. The required answer was that it was necessary for the unification of the motherland, political stability, solidarity between nationalities, and the struggle against separatists.

The next question was about the character of the Dalai Lama, the answer to which effectively required monks and nuns to denounce him. In response, Tibetans were required to repeat the characterizations of the Dalai Lama as the head of the splittist clique that is plotting the independence of Tibet, a faithful tool of international powers that oppose China, the main source of social unrest in Tibet, and the biggest obstacle to the establishment of a normal order in Tibetan Buddhism.

Another question was about China's policy toward the Dalai Lama. The correct answer was that the Dalai Lama could return to China if he would acknowledge that Tibet is an inalienable part of China, give up the idea of Tibetan independence, and abandon all splittist activities. Monks and nuns were then asked about what separatist activities the Dalai Lama engaged in. The correct answer was that he instigated the revolt in 1959, he set up a government-in-exile, he sought Western support to promote the idea of Tibetan independence, and he attempted to infiltrate his ideas and his agents into Tibet in order to promote splittism. A further question asked about the nature of the struggle with the Dalai Lama. The correct answer was that it is not an issue of religion or autonomy, but only about the unity of the motherland. It is a class struggle between classes in Tibetan society, not a national struggle between Tibetans and Chinese.

These questions reveal that a primary theme of China's Patriotic Education Campaign in Tibet was to oppose the Dalai Lama's influence and to force Tibetan monks and nuns to denounce him. It was intended to repress monks' and nuns' opposition to Chinese rule and to transform their loyalty from the Dalai Lama and their religion into patriotism to China and obedience to China's laws. China's Patriotic Education Campaign attempted to portray China's policy on religion as rational, liberal, and beneficial to religion and religious practitioners. However, China's religious policy in Tibet is intended to control religion and religious influence on society; to reduce the influence of monasteries and nunneries in the revival of Tibetan religion, culture, and nationalism; to restrict the role of monks and nuns in politics; and to restrict the role of religion in the education of Tibetans and in their national culture and national identity.

The CCP claimed considerable success in its Patriotic Education Campaign in Tibetan monasteries and nunneries. The campaign was said to have won understanding from and support of lamas and laymen alike. Monks and nuns were taken on organized visits to see how much Tibet has developed economically. They were presented with evidence about the close relationship between Tibet and the motherland. Many monks and nuns were said to have lacked knowledge about the reality and history of Tibet. But after their education, they had realized that the Dalai Lama is not their spokesman or their religious leader but the head of the clique that seeks to split China and hinder the normal functioning of Tibetan Buddhism. The administration of monasteries was said to have been improved by the establishment of democratic management committees. Discipline of monks and nuns had improved. Construction of new monasteries without permission and recognition of tulkus without approval had been stopped. All of these rules and regulations were said to be for the benefit of monks and nuns so that they could abide by the laws and so that they could use the law to protect their personal and religious rights.

The Patriotic Education Campaign has continued off and on in Tibet, not only in monasteries but among the general population as well, from the mid-1990s to the present. There was a significant revival of the campaign in 2005. According to a report by the Tibetan Center for Human Rights and Democracy (TCHRD) in Dharamsala, in April 2005, officials from the Lhasa Religious Bureau began to conduct a three-month-long campaign at Sera Monastery, near Lhasa. The monks were issued six different pamphlets to study, and four education sessions per week were conducted. The pamphlets were titled "Handbook on Crushing the Separatists," "Handbook of Contemporary Policies," "Handbook of Policies on Religion," "Handbook on Law," "Handbook on Ethics for the Masses," and "Handbook of History of Tibet." The monks were subjected to random questions regarding the texts, and an examination was conducted at the end of the campaign in July 2005 to test their knowledge regarding the handbooks and their allegiance to the state. TCHRD said that it had documented expulsions of 11,383 clergy between January 1996 and August 2004 under the Patriotic Education Campaign.[7]

China's State Council White Papers on Tibet

Between 1991 and 2006, China published forty-nine State Council White Papers, the highest-level official publications of the Chinese government. Of these, six are on Tibet—the most on any single subject except human rights, which is the topic of seven papers, all of which also address minority rights issues, including Tibet. Another two papers are on the National Regional Autonomy system, now translated as Regional Ethnic Autonomy, both of which concentrate on Tibet.

The themes of the White Papers on Tibet are that Tibet has always been a part of China; that there is no political issue of Tibet, only the social issue of Tibet's peaceful liberation from the dark, savage, and cruel feudal serf system, for which Tibetans are eternally grateful to the CCP; and that China has unselfishly helped Tibet develop economically without taking anything at all from Tibet. The White Papers reveal that they are a response to criticisms from the "Dalai Clique and Hostile Western Forces" by their numerous denunciations of the Dalai Lama's separatist activities.

The first White Paper on Tibet, "Tibet—Its Ownership and Human Rights Situation,"[8] published in 1992, was only the third White Paper published by the PRC (the first, on human rights, came in 1991). The sections of this paper are "Ownership of Tibet," "Origins of So-called 'Tibetan Independence,'" "The Dalai Clique's Separatist Activities and the Central Government's Policy," "Feudal Serfdom in Old Tibet," "The People Gain Personal Freedom," "The People Enjoy Political Rights," "Economic Development and Improvement of Living Standards," "Freedom of Religious Belief," Development of Education and Culture," "People's Health and Demographic Growth," "Protection of Living Environment," and "Special State Aid for Tibet's Development."

That the first White Paper was intended to counter adverse international opinion on the Tibet issue is obvious from the preface:

> Once regarded as a mysterious region, Tibet has long thrown off its veil to reveal itself to the world. She is now experiencing earth-shaking changes in a shift from medieval extreme backwardness to modernization. However, the world still knows very little about real developments in this region. So those who once committed or attempted aggression against her yell at the top of their voices that Tibet is being invaded; others who once deprived the people of this region of all personal freedom shout that the human rights of the people there are being infringed. Rumors, distortion, suspicion, misunderstanding, all combine to form a layer of mist to envelop this region. In order to know the situation there, it is imperative to look at the facts.

The White Paper begins by establishing China's "ownership" of Tibet:

> By the Tang Dynasty (618–907), the Tibetans and Hans had, through marriage between royal families and meetings leading to alliances, cemented political and kinship ties of unity and political friendship and formed close economic and cultural relations, laying a solid foundation for the ultimate founding of a unified nation. . . . In the mid-13th century, Tibet was officially incorporated into the territory of China's Yuan Dynasty. Since then, although China experienced several dynastic changes, Tibet has remained under the jurisdiction of the central government of China.

In substantiating the claim that Chinese rule over Tibet was continuous after the thirteenth century, the White Paper puts an interesting twist on the question of Ming authority over Tibet by claiming that the third Ming emperor, Chengzu (r. 1403–1424), did not desire to rule Tibet directly because he "saw the advantage of combined Buddhist religious and political power in Tibet and rivalry between sects occupying different areas." The White Paper was equally creative in refuting the Tibetan claim to de facto independence during the Republican and Nationalist periods. It cites the rules and regulations promulgated by the Republic of China to deal with Tibet, including unilateral declarations that Tibet formed a part of the Republic, the "five races" policy, the Bureau of Mongolian and Tibetan Affairs, and Chinese representatives appointed to handle administrative affairs in Tibet, without mentioning that none of these measures was ever put into effect because China had no control over Tibet at the time. In addition, the central government is said to have supervised and approved the selection and installation of the Fourteenth Dalai Lama. The White Paper notes that Tibetan representatives participated in the Chinese National Assembly in 1946. In 1950, it says, after peacefully liberating the "provinces bordering on Tibet," including Xikang, from the rule of the KMT, "in light of the history and reality of Tibet, the central people's government decided to do the same for Tibet."

The White Paper claims that the liberation of Tibet and the Seventeen-Point Agreement "enjoyed the approval and support" of the Tibetan people and the Dalai Lama. The revolt in Tibet is blamed exclusively on the "reactionary clique of the upper social strata" supported by "foreign anti-China forces." The Dalai Lama was said to have been against the rebellion, but he was spirited away under duress. Only after reaching India, where he was surrounded by "foreign anti-China forces and separatists," did he "renounce the patriotic stand which he once expressed," and repudiate the Seventeen-Point Agreement. Only then did he claim that Tibet had ever been independent. In fact, the White Paper says, "There was no such word as 'independence' in the Tibetan vocabulary at the beginning of the 20th century."

The White Paper's solution to the dispute with the Dalai Lama is for him to "renounce separatism and return to the stance of patriotism and unity." There can be no discussion about Tibetan "independence, semi-independence or disguised independence" (as the Chinese characterized the Strasbourg formula). "The central government will make not the slightest concession on the fundamental issue of maintaining the motherland's unification." China was said to be willing to hold talks with the Dalai Lama at any time, "so long as the Dalai Lama can give up his divisive stand and admit that Tibet is an inalienable part of China." The Dalai Lama must "stop activities to split the motherland and change his position for 'Tibetan independence.' All matters except 'Tibetan independence' can be discussed."

The White Paper attacks the "Dalai clique and international anti-China forces" for their championing of human rights in Tibet when it was they who were responsible for the "dark, savage and cruel feudal serfdom" from which China had liberated Tibet. It went on to extol the virtues of the Democratic Reform Campaign:

> After the quelling of the armed rebellion in 1959, the central people's government, in compliance with the wishes of the Tibetan people, conducted the Democratic Reform in Tibet and abolished the extremely decadent and dark feudal

serfdom. The million serfs and slaves were emancipated. . . . The Democratic Reform in 1959 put an end to the political system of combining religious with political rule and introduced the new political system of people's democracy. Under the Constitution of the People's Republic of China, the Tibetan people, like the people of various nationalities throughout the country, have become masters of the country and enjoy full political rights provided for by the law.

The White Paper admits that there were abuses of religious freedom during the Cultural Revolution, but maintains that China's policy on religious freedom has since been restored and measures taken to repair the damages of the past:

> The government has exerted every effort to locate those Buddhist statues, instruments used in Buddhist services and other religious articles that got lost during the "cultural revolution" and distributed them to the various monasteries and temples, to the welcome of monks and lay people.

According to the White Paper, Tibet has experienced great economic development with the assistance of the Chinese government. All aspects of traditional Tibetan culture, including language, religion, literature, art, drama, music, education, and scholarship have been protected and furthered. It denies any validity to the claim of Tibetans in exile that many Tibetans have died due to Chinese repression:

> On the question of the size of the Tibetan population, the Dalai clique has spread many rumors. The most sensational was that more than 1.2 million people were killed after the peaceful liberation of Tibet. In 1953, the Tibetan local government under the Dalai Lama reported the population stood at 1 million people. If 1.2 million inhabitants had been massacred, it would have been a case of genocide and certainly the population in Tibet could not have increased to the present 2 million. . . . Another lie is the claim that a large number of Hans have migrated to Tibet, turning the ethnic Tibetans into a minority.

What the White Paper does not say is that its figure of 1 million Tibetans was only for the TAR. And even this figure was simply an estimate by the Tibetan government in 1953 and did not include the 274,000 (according to a Chinese census) in the Chamdo area. The White Paper admits that the total number of Tibetans in China according to the first national census in 1953 was 2.77 million. Therefore, there were at least 2.77 million Tibetans, not 1 million, a figure that makes the claim of 1.2 million killed more feasible.

The Chinese White Paper maintains that the human rights issue was a subterfuge by separatist forces "to realize their dream of dismembering China, seizing Tibet and finally subverting socialist China."

The Dalai clique and international anti-China forces, who flaunt the banner of "champions of human rights," do not denounce the dark, savage and cruel feudal serfdom at all, under which the Tibetan people were deprived of all human rights by the serf-owners. But they continue to tell lies even after lies they told previously have been exploded, alleging that the Tibetan people, who have become masters of the country, have lost their human rights. . . . Here lies the essence of the issue of so-called human rights in Tibet. No plot to split China will ever succeed. The close relations between the Tibetan people and other ethnic groups in China have lasted for several thousand years. And Tibet has been unified with other provinces and autonomous regions to make up a unitary country for seven centuries. In such a long period of time, Tibet's relations with other provinces and autonomous regions have become closer and closer, and there has never been separation. . . . Unity spells common prosperity, and separation would mean peril to both parties. The long-lasting unification of Tibet with other parts of China is the inevitable outcome of a long history. So the Han people and other ethnic groups absolutely will not accept separation of Tibet from China, nor will the Tibetan people themselves.

The Tibetan government-in-exile responded to the Chinese White Paper with a position paper of its own entitled "Tibet: Proving Truth from Facts."[9] The Tibetan exiles characterized China's historical claims to Tibet as imperialist, as revealed by China's use of the term *ownership* in the title of the White Paper. They maintained that, no matter how much China had been able to dominate Tibet in the past, Tibet at no time had become an integral part of China. Tibet retained, in the past and even until the present time, all the characteristics of a nation and therefore was deserving of the right of self-determination. The Seventeen-Point Agreement was characterized as an unequal treaty of the type that the Chinese themselves frequently condemned as having been imposed upon China by foreign imperialists in the past.

The second Chinese White Paper on Tibet, "New Progress in Human Rights in the Tibet Autonomous Region" (1998), has four sections: "Ethnic Regional Autonomy System and the People's Political Rights," "Economic Development and the People's Rights to Existence and Development," "The People Enjoy the Rights to Education, Culture and Health Protection," and "The Right to Freedom of Religious Belief."[10] Beginning with this White Paper, *minzu*, which had previously been translated as "nationality," was translated as "ethnic," and the previous translation of the title of the PRC system of nationality autonomy, National Regional Autonomy, became Regional Ethnic Autonomy. This appears to be an intentional downgrading, at least for a foreign audience, of the status of Tibet and the other minority nationalities to which the system applies, from nations, or "nationalities" in Chinese Communist parlance, to ethnic groups. This may be regarded as an attempt to deny any of China's nationalities the right of self-determination granted to nations (or "peoples" as specified in the Universal Declaration of Human Rights and the International Covenants on Human Rights) in international law.

The theme of this second White Paper is to reiterate the claim that Tibet's human rights situation was continually advancing due to social and economic progress and development:

> The Democratic Reform carried out in Tibet in 1959 ended the history of a feudal serf system which merged religion with politics, and gave the more than one million serfs and slaves the right to be their own masters. Following the Democratic Reform, Tibet entered a new era of social development and progress in human rights. . . . In recent years, thanks to the care and support of the Central Government, the unstinted assistance from other parts of China and the efforts of the people of all ethnic groups in Tibet, the Region's economic and social development has been remarkably speeded up, thus further promoting the development of the cause of human rights there.

The White Paper says that Tibetans enjoy "the political rights of the people of all ethnic groups in Tibet to participate in administration of state and local affairs on an equal basis, especially the Tibetan people's autonomous right to independently administer local and ethnic affairs."

> As the organs of self-government, the Tibet Autonomous Regional People's Congress and the Regional People's Government exercise the power of autonomy according to law. In accordance with the Chinese Constitution and the Law on Ethnic Regional Autonomy, all areas entitled to ethnic regional autonomy enjoy the extensive rights of autonomy, involving legislation, the use of local spoken and written languages, the administration of personnel, the economy, finance, education and culture, the management and development of natural resources, and other aspects.

Between 1965 and 1992, more than sixty local laws and regulations were worked out with regard to Tibetan language use, the environment, regional administrative issues, and traditional festivals and holidays.

The chairmen of the TAR have all been Tibetans since its creation, the White Paper notes—without mentioning that the chairman of the CCP in Tibet, which exercises all real power, has never been a Tibetan—and more than 90 percent of officials at all levels in the TAR have been Tibetan or other minorities (all such officials have a Han subordinate who exercises all real authority). The paper lists numerous economic development projects, all undertaken with the assistance of the central government, and many preferential economic policies that benefit Tibetans. There are statistics about how much assistance China has provided to Tibet, how much the Tibetan economy has improved, and how many motorbikes and TV sets Tibetans now own. This is contrasted with the situation in old Tibet where the wealth was controlled by a few and most Tibetans were living as poverty-stricken serfs and beggars.

China has also improved Tibetans' medical care, which has resulted in an increase in the Tibetan population, unlike in old Tibet, which supposedly suffered from population stagnation due to the feudal and monastic systems. As proof, the White Paper observes that during the Qing dynasty, a 1734–1736 survey revealed a Tibetan population of 941,200. The population in 1953 was still only 1 million, which is said to mean that the Tibetan population was stagnant. In contrast, the White Paper says that from 1953 to 1993 the population increased to 2.3 million, which refutes the lie emanating from the "Dalai Lama and some Western sources" that there had been a genocide in Tibet under Chinese rule and illuminates "the human rights situations in the new and old Tibet."

What the White Paper does not mention is that the 1734 census covered all of Tibet, not just what became the TAR, and it only estimated the number of households and then multiplied that by a nominal seven members per household. The 1953 number of one million, on the other hand, was for only the TAR (excluding Chamdo) and was also an estimation. The Chinese census in 1953 of all Tibetans in the PRC, which incorporated the one million estimate, was 2.77 million; using that figure, from 1734 to 1953 the population had increased from less than one million to almost three million, not stagnated as the White Paper claims. The increase of the Tibetan population in the TAR to 2.3 million in 1993 does not refute the claim that there was a genocide in Tibet, because the 1953 number was only an estimate, most Tibetan deaths due to the Chinese occupation were in eastern Tibet outside the TAR, and a natural population increase should have produced a greater number than 2.3 million by 1993.[11]

The second White Paper maintains that "the Chinese Government respects and protects its citizens' right to freedom of religious belief in accordance with the law," adding that "since the peaceful liberation of Tibet the Chinese Government has accorded consistent respect and protection to the Tibetan people's right to freedom of religious belief." It says that the Chinese government promised in the Seventeen-Point Agreement to protect Tibetan monasteries and religious sites and that the most significant sites were indeed put under state protection, without mentioning that it was *only* these few sites that survived democratic reforms and the Cultural Revolution. The paper lists all the support the Chinese state has given to the restoration of religious sites, though it fails to explain why they needed to be restored. Similarly, it lists the religious texts that have been republished with state support without mentioning the almost total eradication of all such texts during the Cultural Revolution.

The conclusion reveals that this White Paper, like the one before, is directed at the negative image of China's role in Tibet created by the Dalai Lama and Tibetan exiles:

A host of facts show clearly that human rights in Tibet are making unceasing progress. The Central Government and the local governments at all levels in the Tibet Autonomous Region have made great efforts to safeguard and promote the progress of human rights in Tibet. The situation as regards human rights in old Tibet bears no comparison with the situation in Tibet today. The fact that human rights in Tibet have improved is beyond all dispute. All people, Chinese and foreign, who have been to Tibet and are acquainted with Tibet's history will draw such a fair conclusion. The Dalai Lama vilifies the present human rights situation in Tibet. But, ironically, under his rule in old Tibet human rights were wantonly trampled on in wide areas—a crime stemming from the dark, savage and cruel system of merging politics with religion and the feudal serfdom. Making no mention whatsoever of the situation where trampling the people's basic human rights was commonplace in old Tibet, the exiled Dalai Lama has tried by every means to cover it up and vilify and attack the development and progress in new Tibet. He also fabricates sensational lies to befuddle world opinion. One of the fundamental commandments of Buddhism forbids the spreading of falsehoods. The Dalai Lama's wanton fabrication of lies and his violation and trampling of this commandment serve only to expose him in all his true colors: He is waving the banner of religion to conduct activities aimed at splitting the motherland.

China's third White Paper on Tibet, "The Development of Tibetan Culture," was published in 2000.[12] Sections of this paper are entitled "The Spoken and Written Tibetan Language Is Widely Studied and Used, and Being Developed," "Cultural Records and Ancient Books and Records Are Well-Preserved and Utilized," "Folk Customs and Freedom of Religious Belief Are Respected and Protected," "Culture and Art Are Being Inherited and Developed in an All-Round Way," "Tibetan Studies Are Flourishing, and Tibetan Medicine and Pharmacology Have Taken On a New Lease of Life," "Popular Education Makes a Historic Leap," and "The News and Publishing, Broadcasting, Film and Television Industries Are Developing Rapidly." While not failing to condemn traditional Tibetan culture for its feudal inequality, this paper is more respectful of Tibetan culture and even acknowledges some of its non-Chinese antecedents. The emphasis is on the preservation and development of Tibetan culture under Chinese rule, with the encouragement and assistance of the Chinese government. Unsurprisingly, nothing is said about the repression and destruction of Tibetan culture during the democratic reforms and the Cultural Revolution.

Despite claiming that China has preserved, protected, and promoted the Tibetan language and that "the spoken and written Tibetan language is universally used," the White Paper fails to mention that Chinese is used almost universally in all government business in Tibet and that even Tibet University has discontinued instruction in Tibetan in all classes except those specifically about Tibetan culture. The paper declares, "Since the Democratic Reform, the Central People's Government has attached great importance to the protection of cultural relics in Tibet," yet this is precisely when the destruction of Tibetan culture began. Those few historical sites that survived the Cultural Revolution are mentioned by name, without any mention of how many were destroyed. China's assistance in the renovation of those surviving Tibetan historical sites is emphasized, as is archaeological research, most of which has been devoted to proving that ancient Tibetan culture is related to Chinese culture.

The White Paper says that the "state respects and safeguards the rights of the Tibetans and other ethnic groups in Tibet to live their lives and conduct social activities in accordance with their traditional customs, and their freedoms to engage in normal religious activities and major religious and folk festival celebrations." It describes all reforms of Tibetan culture as voluntarily undertaken by the Tibetan people:

> As society progresses, some decayed, backward old customs despising laboring people that bear a strong tinge of the feudal serf system have been abandoned, which reflects the Tibetans' pursuit of modern civilization and a healthy life as well as the continuous development of Tibetan culture in the new era.

The paper extols the flourishing of Tibetan literature and art that supposedly took place after the democratic reform with the assistance of fraternal nationalities:

> After the peaceful liberation of Tibet, a group of literary and art workers from different ethnic groups went into the thick of life in Tibet to explore and inherit the fine aspects of the local literature and art tradition. They created a lot of poems, novels, songs, dances, fine art works, films and photos, introducing new literary and artistic ideas. . . . Particularly after the Democratic Reform in 1959, a number of excellent literary and art works emerged in Tibet and, to a certain degree, influenced people both at home and abroad. These works include the songs "On the Golden Hill of Beijing" and "Liberated Serfs Sing," the song with actions "Strolling Around the New Town," the song and dance combination "Washing Clothes," the dance epic with music "Emancipated Serfs Turn Toward the Sun," the drama "Princess Wen Cheng" and the movie "Serf."

The development of publishing, newspapers, radio, films, and television is also commended. The White Paper justifies all changes in Tibetan culture as being due to the liberated serfs developing their own culture while abandoning the culture of the former serf-owners. Some "fine aspects" of traditional

Tibetan culture have supposedly been carefully preserved and carried forward, the "liberated serfs" having presumably chosen which aspects were "fine" and "progressive" and should be preserved, and which were feudal and should be discarded. In fact, however, it was the Chinese who chose which aspects of Tibetan culture should be preserved and which repressed. Chinese political expediency dictated those aspects of Tibetan culture that had to be discarded because of their nationalist and separatist content. Even the most liberal of the Chinese Communists ultimately found that only the most superficial aspects of Tibetan culture, such as song and dance, could be allowed—and even these had to be significantly altered in content.

In sum, what has happened to Tibetan culture is justified as voluntary and natural and as in no way an intentional destruction of Tibetan culture by the Chinese state:

> It deserves careful reflection that, although Tibetan culture is developing continuously, the Dalai Lama clique is clamoring all over the world that "Tibetan culture has become extinct," and, on this pretext, is whipping up anti-China opinions with the backing of international antagonist forces. From the 40-odd years of history following the Democratic Reform in Tibet it can be clearly perceived that what the Dalai clique is aiming at is nothing but hampering the real development of Tibetan culture.
>
> With the elimination of feudal serfdom, the cultural characteristics under the old system, in which Tibetan culture was monopolized by a few serf-owners, was bound to become "extinct," and so was the old cultural autocracy marked by theocracy and the domination of the entire spectrum of socio-political life by religion, which was an inevitable outcome of both the historical and cultural development in Tibet. Because without such "extinction," it would be impossible to emancipate and develop Tibetan society and culture, the ordinary Tibetan people would be unable to obtain the right of mastering and sharing the fruits of Tibet's cultural development, and it would be impossible for them to enjoy real freedom, for their religious beliefs would not be regarded as personal affairs. However, such "extinction" was fatal to the Dalai Lama clique, the chief representatives of feudal serfdom, for it meant the extinction of their cultural rule. Therefore, it is not surprising at all that they clamor about the "extinction of traditional Tibetan culture."

China's fourth White Paper on Tibet was 2001's "Tibet's March toward Modernization."[13] The subsections are "The Rapid Social Development in Tibet," "Tibet's Modernization Achievements," and "The Historical Inevitability of Tibet's Modernization." Published on the fiftieth anniversary of Tibet's peaceful liberation, it was devoted to the goal of "clearing up various misunderstandings on the 'Tibet issue' in the international community and promoting overall understanding of the past and present situations in Tibet."

The theme of this paper is that Tibet's history under Chinese rule, from the peaceful liberation, democratic reforms, and socialist construction to reform and opening up, has followed the inevitable historical laws of social development and modernization: "The development in the past 50 years has demonstrated the historical inevitability of Tibet's march toward modernization, and revealed the objective law of Tibet's modernization." In other words, Tibet's recent history was not determined by China—certainly not by any Chinese invasion or "annexation" of Tibet or by any reforms involuntarily imposed upon Tibetans—but was instead an inevitable and predetermined course of history.

This White Paper, as a retrospective of the fifty years since Tibet's peaceful liberation, returns to the fundamental justifications for Chinese rule over Tibet. These are all social in nature and are based on a comparison between Tibet's backward and stagnant feudal serf system and the progress and modernization achieved after reforms were undertaken by the Tibetan people themselves with the assistance of the CCP. Tibet's modernization, China maintains, is inseparable from Tibet's peaceful liberation and could not have taken place under the previous regime of feudal serfdom:

> Over a long period of time, between the Dalai Lama clique and international hostile forces on the one hand and the Chinese Government and people on the other, there have been struggles on the "Tibet issue," with the former trying to split Tibet from the rest of China and halt its modernization, and the latter trying to maintain the unity of the country and promote Tibet's modernization. . . . After Tibet's peaceful liberation, the Dalai Lama clique, regardless of the patient forbearance of the Central Government and the strong demand of the Tibetan people, spared no efforts to try to check the Democratic Reform and modernization drive, and, with the support of international hostile forces, stirred up an armed rebellion for the purpose of splitting the motherland. When the rebellion had failed and the Dalai Lama clique fled abroad, it even did not scruple to collude with the international anti-China forces to constantly whip up world opinion, wantonly conduct activities aimed at splitting China, slander Tibet's achievements in economic construction and social progress, and by every means hinder and sabotage the modernization of Tibetan society.

The White Paper maintains that Tibet's "peaceful liberation opened the way for Tibet to march toward modernization." It claims that "the fine aspects of traditional Tibetan culture have been explored, protected and developed," and "Tibet's characteristics and traditions have been respected and carried on in a scientific way." "The Tibetan people's freedom of religious belief and their traditional customs and habits have been respected and protected," the paper insists, and "since the 1980s the state has allocated more than 300 million Yuan and a large amount of gold, silver and other materials for the maintenance and protection of the monasteries in Tibet." Furthermore, "the Tibetan people's freedom to study, use and develop their own spoken and written language is fully protected."

> To sum up, the development history of Tibet in the past five decades since its peaceful liberation has been one of proceeding from darkness to brightness, from backwardness to progress, from poverty to prosperity and from isolation to openness, and of the region marching toward modernization as a part of the big family of China.

The fifth White Paper on Tibet, "Ecological Improvement and Environmental Protection in Tibet,"[14] was published in 2003. Section titles are "Progress of the Ecological Improvement and Environmental Protection Work in Tibet," "Ecological Improvement and Biodiversity Protection," "Ecological Improvement and Environmental Protection amid Economic Development," "Building an Ecology-Friendly Railway Line—The Qinghai-Tibet Railway," and "The Strategic Choice for Sustainable Development."

As was the case with previous policy statements, it was meant to counter criticism from the Dalai Lama and other international sources:

> The Dalai clique and the international anti-China forces shut their eyes to the progress in the ecological improvement and environmental protection work in Tibet. They have spread rumors all over the world that the Chinese government is "destroying Tibet's ecological environment," "plundering Tibet's natural resources" and "depriving the Tibetan people of their right to subsistence," and so on and so forth, in order to mislead world public opinion and deface the image of China. Camouflaging themselves with pretensions of concern about eco-environmental protection in Tibet, they want really nothing but to hamper the social progress and modernization of Tibet and to prepare public opinion for their political aim of restoring the backward feudal serfdom in Tibet and splitting the Chinese nation.

The paper relates that the Chinese government sent a research team to the Tibetan Plateau in the early 1950s to "unveil the mysteries of the Qinghai-Tibet Plateau and promote Tibet's social progress and development" and to "explore and assess land, forest, pastureland, water conservancy and mineral resources in Tibet." In fact, this research expedition may be more accurately described as China's initial exploration of a heretofore unknown territory in an effort to confirm the long-held belief that Tibet was a storehouse of mineral resources now in the hands of China. China's environmental White Paper on Tibet is composed of a long list of China's scientific surveys, environmental protection policies and projects, and state support for environmental protection in Tibet. It asserts a generally benevolent regard for Tibet's environment and natural resources.

China claims to have introduced a rational plan for the use of grasslands for the first time in Tibet's history (despite an ancient history of ecologically sustainable nomadic pastoralism in Tibet). China's "rational" plan involves settlement of nomads and partitioning of grazing lands, which contradicts the rationally evolved nomadic system of rotation of grazing according to season and arrangement between nomadic tribes. China claims that the grasslands are overgrazed due to a population increase after liberation, when in fact it was caused by a policy of increasing herd sizes beyond the carrying capacity of the environment (against the advice of the nomads). China's resettlement of nomads is more for reasons of political control than rational land management and has resulted in overuse of areas where herders and their animals are settled.

Similarly, the White Paper claims that a strict limitation on forest exploitation is in effect, without mentioning that it was put into effect only in 2003 after floods in the Yangtze River Valley were caused by the heavy deforestation of areas of eastern Tibet that form the headwaters of the Yangtze. Much is made about China's reforestation plans in Tibet, without acknowledging the deforestation that made reforestation necessary. The ecologically sensitive plans for the Qinghai-Tibet railway are extolled, while its actual justifications and purposes are only vaguely hinted at:

> Building the Qinghai-Tibet Railway has been the long-cherished wish of people of all ethnic groups in Tibet. It is not only essential for strengthening links between Tibet and the hinterland, accelerating the economic and social development of Tibet and improving the local people's material and cultural well-being, but is also of great significance for enhancing ethnic unity and common prosperity.

The political purposes of the railway—"strengthening links between Tibet and the hinterland" and "enhancing ethnic unity"—are in fact paramount, while its economic purposes are obscured. The railway will finally allow China to fully exploit many of Tibet's mineral resources that have only been superficially exploited until this time due to logistical difficulties and costs.

Significantly, China's environmental White Paper on Tibet makes absolutely no mention of mining for mineral resources. Given that the exploitation of mineral resources is one of China's main reasons for annexing Tibet, one of the most environmentally damaging activities, and one of the primary purposes of the railway, this is a significant omission. Despite the claim that the railway is intended to increase the prosperity of people in Tibet, the natural resource exploitation facilitated by the railway will not do so since, according to Chinese law, Tibet's resources are not owned by the Tibetan people or the TAR but by the Chinese state. Tibetans do not participate in any decisions about natural resource exploitation or in any of the economic benefits of the exploitation of "their" natural resources.

China's latest White Paper on Tibet, "Regional Ethnic Autonomy in Tibet," was published in 2004.[15] Its subsections are "The Establishment and Development of Regional Ethnic Autonomy in Tibet," "The Tibetan People Enjoy Full Political Right of Autonomy," "The Tibetan People Have Full Decision-making Power in Economic and Social Development," "The Tibetan People Have the Freedom to Inherit and Develop Their Traditional Culture and to Practice Their Religious Belief," and "Regional Ethnic Autonomy Is the Fundamental Guarantee for Tibetan People as Masters of Their Own Affairs."

This Chinese White Paper is the first one to focus specifically on the system of autonomy in Tibet. Previous White Papers, like the present one, have maintained that Tibetans enjoyed full autonomous and human rights due to the national regional autonomy system This sixth paper seems to justify the change in nomenclature from "National Regional Autonomy" to "Regional Ethnic Autonomy," which had been employed since the 1992 White Paper, by declaring that the Han are 90 percent of the population, while "the populations of the other 55 ethnic groups, including the Tibetan people, are relatively small, and such ethnic groups are customarily called ethnic minorities," not national minorities or nationalities. This, like all previous White Papers, is intended to counter international "misperceptions" about the Tibet issue:

> To recall the four glorious decades of regional ethnic autonomy in Tibet, and to give an overview of the Tibetan people's dramatic endeavors to exercise their rights as their own masters and create a better life under regional ethnic autonomy is beneficial not only to summing up experiences and creating a new situation for regional ethnic autonomy in Tibet, but also to clarifying rights and wrongs, and increasing understanding of China's ethnic policy and the truth about Tibet among the international community.

This White Paper also provides a rationalization for China's role in Tibetan history that credits all progressive developments to Chinese administration and blames indirect rule for failure to achieve ethnic or social equality. In other words, Tibetans could achieve equality among themselves and be "masters of their own affairs" only under Chinese rule.

> After Tibet became part of the territory of China in the 13th century, the central governments of the Yuan, Ming and Qing dynasties and the Republic of China, while assuming the responsibility of approving the local administrative organs, and deciding and directly handling important affairs concerning Tibet, maintained, by and large, the region's original local social setup and ruling body, widely appointed upper-strata ecclesiastic and secular members to manage local

affairs, and gave the Tibetan local government and officials extensive decision-making power. This played a historically positive role in safeguarding the unification of the country, but as the feudal autocratic rulers in various periods exercised an ethnic policy marked by ethnic discrimination and oppression, keeping the original social system and maintaining the power of the local ruling class for their administration of Tibet, they did not solve, nor could they possibly solve, the issue of ethnic equality and that of enabling the local people to become masters of their own affairs.

This latest Chinese White Paper on Tibet is distinguished by its uncompromising position on recent Tibetan history, acknowledging only unbroken progress in social reform, economic development, and human rights since Tibet's liberation in 1951. Unlike previous Chinese propaganda documents on Tibet, this version does not mention any mistakes in Chinese policy in Tibet, even during the Cultural Revolution.

> Since regional ethnic autonomy was implemented in 1965 in Tibet, the Tibetan people, in the capacity of masters of the nation and under the leadership of the Central Government, have actively participated in administration of the state and local affairs, fully exercised the rights of self-government bestowed by the Constitution and law, engaged in Tibet's modernization drive, enabled Tibetan society to develop by leaps and bounds, profoundly changed the old situation of poverty and backwardness in Tibet, and greatly enhanced the level of their own material, cultural and political life.

It continues:

> Regional ethnic autonomy means, under the unified leadership of the state, regional autonomy is exercised and organs of self-government are established in areas where various ethnic minorities live in compact communities, so that the people of ethnic minorities are their own masters exercising the right of self-government to administer local affairs and the internal affairs of their own ethnic groups.

The paper emphasizes the regional rather than the ethnic nature of the system by pointing out that in the TAR there are other ethnic groups besides Tibetans, including Han, Hui, Moinba, Lhoba, Naxi, Nu, Drung, and others.

The White Paper declares that "the Tibetan people enjoy full political right of autonomy," "the Tibetan people have full decision-making power in economic and social development," "the Tibetan people have the freedom to inherit and develop their traditional culture and to practice their religious belief," and "regional ethnic autonomy is the fundamental guarantee for Tibetan people as masters of their own affairs." It asserts that the current system of autonomy is appropriate and successful, and it envisages no need to alter or change the system. The paper goes on to reiterate the Chinese contention that Tibet's current situation is the natural and inevitable result of the development of human society:

> Historical facts indicate that the institution of regional ethnic autonomy in Tibet was the natural result of social progress in Tibet, and that it accords with the fundamental interests of the Tibetan people and the inexorable law of development of human society. To advance from a feudal, autocratic medieval society to a modern, democratic society is the inevitable law of development of human society from ignorance and backwardness to civilization and progress. It is the irresistible historical trend of modernization of all the countries and regions in modern times. . . . After the founding of the People's Republic of China, the Central Government brought peaceful liberation to Tibet, and instituted the Democratic Reform and regional ethnic autonomy there, completing the task of the anti-imperialist and anti-feudal national democratic revolution. As a result, Tibet broke away from the control of imperialism, leapfrogged several forms of society, and entered socialist society. Tibet saw the completion of the greatest and most profound social transformation in its history, and in its social development achieved a historic leap never before seen. This is in line with the law of development of human society and the progressive trend of the times. It also reflects the requirements of social progress in Tibet and the fundamental wish of the Tibetan people.

Renewed Propaganda Campaign

In 1993, the External Propaganda Committee of the PRC Propaganda Department held its third annual meeting in Beijing to coordinate China's international propaganda on Tibet. Three of the eight prepared speeches at that meeting, as well as a speech by a Tibetan official, Tenzing, at a subsequent meeting in Lhasa to convey the decisions of the Beijing meeting, were subsequently revealed to the outside world.[16] The meeting was attended by officials of the Chinese Government Propaganda Department and the State Council Information Office, the New China News Agency (Xinhua), and officials from the TAR and autonomous districts of Sichuan, Qinghai, Yunnan, and Gansu.

The first speech was by Zeng Jianhui, vice minister of the Propaganda Department of the CCP Central Committee. Zeng began by citing recent successes, beginning with the publication of China's first White Paper on Tibet, which, he said, even in Western countries was described as reasonable and accurate. He said that the External Propaganda Committee had confronted the Dalai clique at the United Nations Human Rights Commission with eight pamphlets in English and French on the history, human rights situation, and social development in Tibet. More than two thousand copies of propaganda materials had been distributed at the UN Environmental Conference in Brazil, which the Dalai Lama attended. A video was made of conditions in Tibetan prisons and presented to a UNESCO conference in Paris.

Zeng said that because of recent successes in creating stability in Tibet and promoting China's version of Tibetan reality by means of external propaganda, the Dalai clique had changed its strategy. Previously it had tried to stir up trouble in Tibet, but recently the Dalai Lama had begun to talk about negotiations and increased autonomy. This strategy was dismissed as "an attempt to further seek the independence of Tibet." To counter this, he recommended that the External Propaganda Committee produce "multi-level and different forms of vivid and lively propaganda regarding sovereignty and human rights." He added:

> We should organize experts and scholars to write articles and books and use historical facts to declare righteously to the world that Tibet is an inseparable part of Chinese territory. . . . We should use facts to present the human rights situation of Tibet and its progress and to demonstrate that the majority of Tibetan masses support the leadership of the Communist Party, support the socialist system and support the People's Government.

Zeng said that the external propaganda work on Tibet involved not only the External Propaganda Committee, but also the State Council Information Office, Xinhua, the United Front Department, the State Nationalities Commission, relevant provinces and regions, and Chinese embassies and consulates abroad. Since 1991, all these bodies had coordinated their work against the Dalai clique. He suggested that China's embassies and consulates, as well as delegations attending events abroad, should report back on the anti-China activities of the Dalai clique. The departments concerned with external propaganda should then develop materials to be distributed by China's organizations and news agencies abroad. Zeng recommended that they "infiltrate our propaganda into the mainstream life of the West." China should continue to send Tibetan scholars and singing and dancing troupes abroad to lecture and perform, and embassies and consulates should counter the activities of the Dalai clique with speeches, picture exhibitions, and other forms of propaganda. He suggested that foreign journalists should be invited to visit Tibet: "By arranging foreign journalists and other people to go and visit Tibet we should be able to use foreign forces to carry our external propaganda and gradually change their mind about us through what they have seen with their own eyes." Finally, he recommended cultural exchanges as having the potential to be "very infiltrating and influential."

The author of the next speech was not identified but was apparently someone speaking on behalf of the Central Committee of the CCP. This person said that there were more and more people in the world who knew the real situation in Tibet but that the "distorted propaganda and attacks of the Dalai Clique and international enemy forces still enjoy a large market in the world." This speaker recommended more propaganda on the theme of the "two rights: sovereign rights and human rights."

> We should continue to use historical comparison and the facts about the dark, barbaric and cruel serf system of old Tibet to expose the hypocritical features of the Dalai Clique. . . . We should publicize the social stability, market prosperity, national unity, freedom of religion and belief, the development of culture and the full guarantee of the fundamental democratic rights of the people in Tibet. We should present facts such as the social economic development and the progress in human rights situation in Tibet to demonstrate that the majority of Tibetan people support the leadership of the Communist party, support the socialist system and support the Government, and that they are steadfast in opposing all forms of splitting and sabotage activities.

The Central Committee representative then listed the recent accomplishments of propaganda organs, mentioning that *Beijing Review* did a series of articles on the White Paper. Several books had been published on the late Panchen Lama and Tashilhunpo, on different regions of Tibet, on the Potala, on Tibetan Buddhism, on arts and crafts, and on historical studies, including *Selected Files from Archives on the Historic Relationship between Tibet and the Central Government since the Yuan Dynasty*, *Study on the Tibetan Local Governments since the Yuan Dynasty*, and *Study on the Formation of the Society of Feudal Serf System of Tibet*. In the field of cultural exchanges, the Tibet Singing and Dancing Troupe would perform in Hong Kong and the Tibetan Shigatse Performing Arts Troupe in Nepal. The China International Book Trading Company would hold an exhibition of books on Tibet in Nepal. An exhibition of Tibetan cultural relics would be shown in Argentina and Chile. There was also an exhibition of cultural relics and an exchange of religious activities with Taiwan. The External Cultural Exchange Association of Tibet was to send delegations to Nepal, India, the United States, Canada, Great Britain, and France and had already sent delegations of scholars to India, Italy, and Britain.

The last document was a speech by Comrade Tenzin, deputy secretary of the TAR Party Committee, at the TAR Regional Conference on External Propaganda Work, held in Lhasa. Tenzin began by citing the achievements of the past year, including the publication of the first White Paper on Tibet. Tenzin said that ten experts had contributed to the report and ten editorials had been written about it. The TAR had entertained six groups of journalists, seventy-five in all, from China and abroad. The journalists from Hong Kong had published more than a hundred articles that had presented the situation in Tibet "in a relatively objective way."

Tenzin repeated much of what had transpired at the conference in Beijing, including the contention that more people in the world knew the truth about Tibet due to their efforts, but that the Dalai clique still had an audience in the world. International sympathy for the Dalai Lama's point of view was credited exclusively to anti-China motives: "International enemy forces do not want to see a strong China." These anti-China forces used human rights and the "so-called Tibet Question" to hinder China's reform and development. Their ultimate goal was to separate Tibet from China. Although the Dalai clique had adjusted its strategy in favor of dialogue and autonomy, "they have not changed their position of insisting on the independence of Tibet and the splitting of our country." The Dalai clique had become even more deceitful, which had "exposed their obstinate and scheming reactionary nature." The Dalai clique "uses negotiation as a smoke screen, anxiously trying to gain some progress in their favor when the old generation of our revolutionaries is still alive and to deceive the international public opinion as well." The reference to the "old revolutionaries" is apparently about the Tibetans who collaborated with the Chinese but who knew many of those Tibetans who went into exile and might have some sympathy with them.

Tenzin also laid out China's conditions for negotiations with the Dalai Lama, which were that there was nothing to negotiate except the terms of his and other exiles' return to the motherland.

> The nature of negotiation is that it is an internal affair of China, which is between the Central Government and an exiled religious leader, the purpose of which is to solve the problem of his repatriation and that of the people who follow him. The solution of the Tibet problem should not be the same as that of Taiwan. The future of Tibet is national regional autonomy and the realization of socialism.

These conditions deny that there is any political issue of Tibet about which to negotiate, including a status of "one country, two systems," like that offered to Taiwan. The Chinese maintain that the status of Tibet has been permanently decided as an autonomous region of China under the national regional autonomy system and Tibet's path is not the Dalai Lama's "Middle Way," but the path of socialism.

The struggle with the Dalai clique and the international enemy forces had to be carried out through propaganda and public opinion, Tenzin emphasized: "External propaganda work on the question of Tibet has bearing not only on the progress and development of Tibet, but also the image of China as a whole in the world." The Dalai clique was accused of fabricating rumors to mislead the public, but its propaganda was said to be vulnerable to the reality of Tibet: "Truth and justice are in our hands. . . . The current human rights situation in Tibet is our strong point. We should feel justified and righteous."

With regard to external propaganda plans, Tenzin reiterated the list of items from the Beijing conference. He also mentioned the opening of "two more external propaganda tourist spots." Presumably this refers to such projects as the Splendid China theme park in Florida, which displayed miniatures of many Chinese architectural sites, including the Potala in Lhasa and many other minority nationality sites, along with propaganda about the happy lives of the people in China. (Opened in 1993, Splendid China closed in 2003 due to controversy and lack of attendance.) Tenzin mentioned some of the propaganda materials that he said should be produced in Tibet, including "high quality external propaganda material and goods characteristic of Tibet, including music and video, books, magazines, maps, tourist guides, notebooks, pins and expensive gifts wrapped in gift boxes." He also revealed that there was some degree of pressure from the External Propaganda Subcommittee of the Party Committee of the TAR to produce such items. Every department in the TAR government was required to produce one item suitable for external propaganda, and an examination and competition would be held to reward departments and individuals who had done outstanding work in regard to external propaganda.

In June 2000, the Central Government Propaganda Department and the State Council Information Office held a conference of propaganda officials and Chinese Tibetologists. This conference further confirmed the use of academic Tibetology in propaganda work. Zhao Qizheng, the minister in charge of the Information Office of the State Council, gave a speech with the title "Tibet-Related External Propaganda and Tibetology Work in the New Era."[17] He described the aim of the conference as "to make our Tibetology work more effective for external propaganda on Tibet." He added that this was the first meeting intended to discuss ways of "improving Tibetology work from the point of view of external publicity" and "improving our external publicity on Tibet from the perspective of Tibetology." Zhao described external publicity on Tibet as an "important element of our country's external propaganda. It is also a very important element of our struggle against the Dalai clique and hostile western forces." Zhao characterized the "so-called Tibet issue" as a strategy of anti-Chinese Western countries, in collusion with the Dalai Lama, with the goal of weakening and splitting China.

The so-called issue of Tibet is the main pretext for western countries, including the United States, to westernize and split our country. Western countries, including the United States, want to topple our country and further the cause of their own social and value systems and national interests. In order to achieve this, they will never stop using the Tibet issue to westernize and split our country and weaken our power. The Dalai clique has never changed its splittist nature; it has never stopped its activities to split our country. Therefore, our struggle against the Dalai clique and hostile western forces is long-drawn, serious and complicated.

Zhao explained that the struggle with the Dalai clique had taken a new turn with the intervention of NATO countries, led by the United States, into the affairs of Yugoslavia under the doctrine of "humanitarian interventionism." This, he said, had led to an increase by the Western countries in the exploitation of the Tibet issue, as manifested in the promotion by these countries of dialogue between China and the Dalai Lama. He characterized the "clamor for dialogue" as a part of the Dalai clique's strategy to internationalize the Tibet issue.

Complaining that the Dalai Lama was pursuing his splittist activities under the guise of international visits, Zhao said that the Dalai Lama attended international conferences and gave spiritual teachings as a means of advertising Tibetan independence. The Dalai Lama contacted international human rights experts and UN officials with the aim of getting the Tibet issue before the UN Human Rights Commission. Zhao complained that international leaders competed with each other to give the Dalai Lama more status, to enhance his image, and make him an international figure. The Dalai clique had become ever more open in its splittist campaign against China, including sponsoring demonstrations against Chinese leaders during all their international travels.

Zhao also said that the Dalai clique had attempted to create solidarity with other anti-China and splittist forces, such as the China democracy movement, Falun Gong, and the Xinjiang and Taiwan independence movements. In this way, "the Dalai clique tries to create a united anti-China force." A meeting of Tibet Support Groups had been held in an attempt to create an international network of Tibet supporters. The Dalai clique had protested against Chinese development projects in Tibet and "has intensified the splittist campaign of Tibetan independence movement." Zhao said that the Dalai clique had recently changed its strategy to become more beguiling than ever before:

> During public gatherings, the Dalai portrays himself as a humble spiritual teacher and pretends to be seeking dialogues and autonomy. He lays pretence to non-violence and makes utmost efforts not to mix politics in his talks. He speaks on religion, ethics, culture, democracy, freedom and human rights. In tune with the international trend for resolving conflicts through dialogues and discussions, the Dalai clique clamors everywhere for dialogues and puts public opinion pressure on our country. Since western countries recognize Tibet as an inalienable part of China, the Dalai states that he has given up independence in favor of au-

tonomy. In this way, he mobilizes the public opinion in favor of joint intervention and pressure for dialogues. Waving the banner of democracy and human rights, the Dalai publicizes that he does not want to revive Tibet's old social system. Instead, he expresses the need to have democracy in Tibet. By using democracy and human rights to gain western favor, the Dalai tries his best to westernize and split our country. The Dalai says all kinds of things in the name of religion and culture. He accuses our country of destroying the religion and culture of Tibet; he claims that he is seeking autonomy to protect Tibetan culture and religious freedom.

Zhao said that China was at somewhat of a disadvantage in regard to the international propaganda struggle about Tibet because "the world media is monopolized by westerners," and "the Dalai clique's long deceptive propaganda, having taken a lead, has a good standing in the world public opinion." They have used modern media facilities, he said, to carry out "massive propaganda in a number of imaginative ways. . . . As a result of this, lies advocated and spread by them are considered as reliable facts on the issue of Tibet."

"The eastern and western views on human rights are different," Zhao noted. "Our value system is different from that of the west. Our historical development, religion, and level of economic development are also different from theirs. This makes our thinking different." He admitted that this disadvantage would be difficult to overcome: "In a short time, it is difficult to reverse the present situation where the enemy's fortune on the international arena is running high and ours low."

Nevertheless, Zhao insisted that China had several considerable advantages. Reflecting the importance of the Tibet issue, President Jiang Zemin himself had given systematic guidance on the struggle against the Dalai Lama and on external propaganda on Tibet. China's greatest advantage was that no country in the world could deny the fact that Tibet is part of China. Therefore, "ours is a just struggle against the splittists while the Dalai clique's splittist campaign is unjust and has few friends." Tibet was under the effective control of the Chinese Central Government: "We have implemented the Party's benevolent nationality religious policy in Tibet and made its people rich. The progress and development of Tibet is apparent to all." "We have the truth and others' support on our side. Therefore, we need not fear any ideology or argument." China's political security, economic development, social progress, nationality unity, and ever-increasing international prestige were also very favorable conditions. In contrast, the Dalai Lama was nearing his end and the Tibetan exiles' internal differences were becoming more acute. "Therefore, we have the time on our side." China also had considerable experience in the field of external propaganda on Tibet, many well-trained Tibetologists, and unity in the struggle under the leadership of the central government.

In a review of China's propaganda on Tibet to date, Zhao said that it had improved and become more effective: "Our external propaganda against the Dalai clique and hostile western forces has continued to make improvements over the past decade. With the passage of time, our propaganda has become more effective, and the target and goal clearer." He revealed that since 1991 the Central Government External Propaganda Department had organized a series of annual meetings to review, plan, and organize external propaganda work on Tibet. A special group to carry out foreign propaganda had been formed, and it had succeeded in "protecting our national interests and improving our image." "Relentless efforts" had been made over the past decade to publicize Tibet's progress and development. The Dalai Lama's crimes had been exposed and his claims had been refuted.

According to Zhao, China had published more than five hundred news reports and made nearly a hundred films and television programs "exposing the Dalai Lama's crimes," which were distributed in more than a hundred regions. In excess of two million copies of more than sixty types of Tibet-related information material had been distributed. Twenty-three groups of artists had been sent to give performances in more than eighty cities in forty countries. Different types of exhibitions were held in some fifty countries, including France, Italy, India, and Australia. Four hundred foreign delegations, consisting of more than two thousand journalists, government officials, and other dignitaries, had been invited to visit Tibet.

> These programs were very effective in making the international community understand the true situation of Tibet, in clearing up the concerned foreign dignitaries' misunderstanding on Tibet, in challenging the Dalai clique and hostile western forces' rumors, and in undermining the influence of hostile international elements.

However, Zhao cautioned, more must be done, because "our voice in the international arena is still modest." One recent innovation was to create websites on the issue. Another new strategy was to employ academic Tibetology to promote China's propaganda on Tibet:

> We should maximize the use of our 50 Tibetology centers and 1,000 Tibetologists to carry out external propaganda work on Tibet. Under appropriate banners of non-governmental organization, they should form a national force of Tibetologists and participate in Tibet-related activities of international non-governmental organizations. Our Tibet specialists should make well-planned visits to foreign countries. Similarly, foreign Tibetologists should be invited to our country for conferences on Tibet. In this way, we should promote cultural exchange, discussion, cooperation, and friendship with foreigners. We should enhance our influence on international Tibetologists. By means of cul-

tural exchange, we should enhance our influence on western community and its opinion. By means of culture, we should promote effective struggle for favorable public opinion regarding our work in Tibet. . . .

The external propaganda on Tibet issue is a very complicated matter. The Dalai clique and hostile western forces have a history of several decades of anti-China activities and propaganda. As well as having complete experience and expertise, they command an army of specialists in this field. They have also developed a complete network of cooperation between nations, between organizations, between parliaments and governments, between governments and peoples, between grassroots level organizations, between media and governments, between non-governmental organizations and media, etc. In this way, they launch their campaigns under various guises and through different methods. In the struggle for public opinion on the issue of Tibet, our adversary is an organized international anti-China force. . . .

The Dalai clique and hostile western forces use deception to create anti-China public opinion; they distort the facts. More importantly, they have created a culture of false arguments. If we want to separate truth and myth about Tibet and conduct an effective propaganda on our works in Tibet, we have to develop an intellectual argument on issues of nationality, religion, human rights and culture. . . . As well as explaining Tibet's history and present situation, the argument should drive home the benevolence of our policies in Tibet, and refute the disinformation of the Dalai clique and hostile western forces. The argument should prove that Tibet is an inalienable part of China, that the democratic reform was absolutely necessary, that the present autonomous arrangement for Tibet is the best and most effective way to protect the equality of nationalities and to guarantee the right of autonomy to the Tibetan people, and that the atheist Communist Party of China gives religious freedom.

Zhao said that China's external propaganda on Tibet would be effective, "as we are confident that truth is on our side." China's Tibetologists had worked hard, he said, and had made "tremendous contribution to the unity of the Motherland and nationalities, to the preservation of Tibetan culture and tradition, and to the success of our external propaganda for public opinion on Tibet." However, there was still "little research to build an intellectual argument to carry out our external propaganda." He acknowledged that not all Tibetology research need concentrate on external propaganda work; however, "a section of Tibetologists should make considerable efforts to build an intellectual argument to meet the needs of our external struggle on Tibet issue." How could China's Tibetologists participate in international conferences on Tibet, Zhao said, if they did not address the current situation in Tibet and challenge the lies promoted by the Dalai clique and hostile western forces? Chinese Tibetologists should develop their own arguments to defend China's position on Tibet "built on the foundation of Marxist views on nationality, religion, culture and human rights."

Zhao said that international Tibetan studies had grown in recent years, but unfortunately,

> the majority of western Tibetology institutes and Tibet-related organizations have connections with western government and the Dalai clique. Even if they do not have direct connections, they still have deep influence on western perspective and the Dalai clique. Their research on Tibet is politically biased and fraught with many mistaken views. A section of them serve western anti-China forces and the Dalai clique. Under the pretext of research work on Tibet, they malevolently distort Tibet's history and the Central Government's policy in Tibet.

Therefore, he said, China's Tibetologists should "publish books and articles that are geared to meet the confrontational needs of our struggle against the Dalai clique and hostile western forces." Zhao said that the Propaganda Department would finance such research and publications. It would also arrange visits by foreign Tibetologists to Tibet and would organize Tibetology conferences in China. Zhao ended his speech by saying, "In short, we should make every effort to convert the Tibetology institutes and specialists into an effective army of our external propaganda for public opinion on Tibet."

Zhao's speech revealed much about Chinese attitudes, or at least those of the Propaganda Department, about the "Tibet issue." They believed that the issue was entirely fabricated by the "Dalai clique and hostile western forces" to oppose China, to weaken China and to separate Tibet from China. There was no acknowledgment of any fault on the part of China with regard to its role in Tibet or its Tibet policy. China's policies in Tibet were characterized as benevolent, and their results as having achieved development and prosperity for the Tibetans. This fact, they imagined, "is apparent to all." China's policies in Tibet being flawless, therefore, there was no "issue" of Tibet and no reason to discuss it with the Dalai Lama or anyone else. The Dalai Lama's and Western countries' campaign for dialogue was rejected as nothing more than an attempt to create a role for the Dalai Lama and foreign countries in Tibet's politics, to westernize China, to internationalize the Tibet issue, and to separate Tibet from China. Even the Dalai Lama's call for autonomy in Tibet was regarded as duplicitous, since Tibet already had autonomy under the CCP's national regional autonomy system. The promotion of democracy and human rights was similarly dismissed as part of the campaign to westernize and split China.

In May 2006, Xinhua published an article about the China Research Center for Tibetan Studies in Beijing. The center's research in Tibetan studies was said to be

> of extremely important significance to inheriting and carrying forward the outstanding Tibetan culture, promoting reform and opening up, economic devel-

opment, and social stability in Tibet and other areas inhabited by Tibetans, resisting the plot of the Western hostile forces to westernize and disintegrate our country, and safeguarding ethnic solidarity and the reunification of the motherland."

A Chinese official explained that the purpose of the center was to "adhere to the correct direction of the research work of Tibetan studies," "defend the reunification of the country, safeguard ethnic solidarity, and maintain the development and stability of the areas inhabited by Tibetans," and "establish and train a contingent of high-quality researchers in Tibetan studies and work hard to train a group of Marxist Tibetologists having an influence at home and abroad."[18]

Some results of China's policy to invite foreign journalists to Tibet were revealed in 2003 and 2004, when groups of foreign journalists were given tours of Tibet. Most of the first group of forty-three journalists were based in Beijing and represented a variety of international media. They were subjected to the usual propaganda in Lhasa and in other places they visited in Tibet such as Shigatse, Gyantse, and Tsetang. However, they also enjoyed an unusual degree of freedom in their reporting. Despite Chinese expectations that they would be impressed with economic development in Tibet, many wrote articles highly critical of Chinese policies in Tibet.

The journalists in general did not fail to see the economic development that had taken place in Tibet, but they also could not miss the fact that it had primarily benefited Chinese migrants rather than the Tibetans themselves. In fact, the most predominant theme of the articles was Chinese migration to Tibet, stimulated by Chinese government economic development policies and Chinese domination of the Tibetan economy. Another dominant theme, since the journalists visited Shigatse and Tashilhunpo, was Tibetans' rejection of the Chinese Panchen Lama. Other themes included the railroad being built into Tibet and how it would only increase Chinese migration to Tibet, Chinese tourism in Tibet, and prostitution.

Many of the journalists observed that Tibetans were still loyal to the Dalai Lama despite China's perpetual anti–Dalai Lama propaganda campaign. They knew about the Patriotic Education Campaign to which monks and nuns were subjected. The reporters noticed the ugly buildings that were crowding out the Tibetan character in every Tibetan town and city. They also observed the rampant prostitution in Tibetan cities and identified it as an accompaniment of Chinese colonialism in Tibet. Although they were occasionally able to speak with Tibetans without supervision by officials, they found that Tibetans did not feel they could speak freely. In Shigatse, the journalists visited Tashilhunpo, where they could tell that the monks were reluctant to speak and would not talk about the dispute over the selection of the Panchen Lama. One writer said that the reincarnation dispute had caused a deep unease and shame to hang over the monastery that "seems to have had its heart torn out."[19]

In general, most of the journalists were well informed about the reality of Tibet before they arrived there, so they were not fooled by Chinese propaganda. They were treated to a warning from Jampa Phuntsok against the Dalai Lama meeting with American president George W. Bush during the Dalai Lama's 2003 visit to the United States, saying that such a meeting would not be beneficial to an improvement in relations between the Dalai Lama and the Chinese government.[20] Jampa Phuntsok's warning leads to the speculation that the curtailment of the Dalai Lama's international activities was what the Chinese hoped to achieve by offering the possibility of dialogue with the Dalai Lama's representatives.

The next year, another group of foreign journalists visited Tibet with similar results. This group noticed the complete lack of images of the Dalai Lama during their tour. Some of them reported that they were asked by many Tibetans if they had pictures of the Dalai Lama, even pictures of him in books that Tibetans could see if only briefly. The journalists were impressed with the intense desire expressed by Tibetans to see images of the Dalai Lama. A Chinese official, Wu Jilie, deputy chairman of the TAR government, denied that there was any official ban on the display of photos or images of the Dalai Lama, asserting that the lack of photos and other images of him was the voluntary choice of the Tibetan people themselves. Wu maintained that Tibetans chose not to revere the Dalai Lama because he had aroused the distrust and resolute opposition of the vast majority of the Tibetan people. According to Wu, this mistrust derived from the fact that the Dalai Lama had launched a subversive revolt in 1959 and had again created riots in 1987. The Tibetan people did not place their trust in such a political exile who had long harmed the country and religion. Besides this unconvincing claim about the unpopularity of the Dalai Lama, the Chinese official further stretched credulity by claiming that many of the Chinese troops were in Tibet just to protect wildlife.[21]

This second group of journalists was also exposed to a new type of propaganda in Tibet, although a type long known to Communist propaganda elsewhere. They were taken to a village called Gongzhong in Chinese in a nomadic area some eight hours by road from Lhasa. After five days of meeting with officials in Lhasa and being given statistics about the development of Tibet while meeting few ordinary Tibetans, the journalists were hopeful that they would see something of what Tibet was really like. However, they found that the village seemed too perfect to be real. The first suspicious thing that the foreigners observed upon arriving at the village was a paved parking lot for tourist buses such as theirs. A small pristine stream flowed through the village, and all the grass looked perfect and untrammeled. All of the houses looked like they were taken from picture books, and none looked lived in. Wood piles were perfectly stacked. Prayer wheels were evident but looked new and unused. No actual work or even ordinary life seemed to take place in the village; instead, Tibetans dressed in their best clothes were observed practicing traditional Tibetan dances. The journalists were unable to find any ordinary villagers to interview. Instead, they were allowed to talk only to local Tibetan officials. When questioned about the unreality of the place, Chinese officials admitted that the village perhaps represented the future rather than the current situation in Tibet. One ethnic Chinese journalist from Hong Kong commented that the village was the Chinese idea of what a Tibetan village should be like.

The "typical" Tibetan village was so obviously fake that many of the writers complained about the obvious attempt to deceive them. The journalists had expected that they would be used for China's propaganda purposes, but they had thought that the picture presented to them would be reasonably authentic; otherwise, it would not be believable and China's propaganda purpose would not be achieved. However, they found that Chinese officials expected them to accept an entirely contrived and unreal portrayal of Tibetan life. China's propaganda about life in Tibet therefore failed, and many of the journalists reported instead on the Chinese attempt to deceive them.[22]

Another project of China's international propaganda campaign entailed holding large Tibetan cultural festivals in foreign countries. Xinhua announced a festival to be held in Austria in October 2006 and said that this would be the sixth large exhibition of Tibetan culture held abroad since 2001.[23] One such festival, a "China Tibetan Culture Week," was held in September 2002 in Toronto. The organizers of that show were the China International Culture Association, the Foreign Cultural Exchange Association of Tibet Autonomous Region, and the National Congress of Chinese Canadians, an alliance of some eighteen Chinese-Canadian associations from Toronto, Vancouver, and Ottawa. The China Tibetan Culture Week was intended "to expose Canadians to the history, diversity and development of Tibet, highlighting traditional and modern Tibetan art, language, dance, theater and spirituality." The festival included ten song and dance performances, five exhibitions of *thankas* and photographs, and two films, *Red River Valley* and *Song of Tibet*. Also scheduled was a presentation by four Tibetan academics. The organizers passed out a large amount of Chinese propaganda about Tibet, including print publications and a CD-ROM.

The Chinese organizers of the event said that Toronto was chosen as the site for the festival because it is a very multinational and multicultural city, home to people from some 160 countries who speak more than a hundred languages. The local organizers explained that, through this festival, they hoped to reach out to Canadians and show them that today's Tibet is an amazing place of beauty, music, dance, song, and art. They added that they hoped to give Canadians a chance to see the people and traditions of Tibet so that they might form their own opinions about the reality of Tibet today.

The organizing committee in China for the Tibetan festival revealed its true nature, however. The honorary director of the festival was Zhao Qizheng, minister of the Information Office of the State Council, the head of the External Propaganda Committee on Tibet. Other Chinese and Tibetan officials involved were from the China International Culture Association and the Foreign Cultural Exchange Association of the TAR.

The messages from the Chinese and Chinese-Canadians presented the festival as entirely a cultural exchange with no political implications whatsoever. The messages from the Canadian officials reveal some confusion as to the nature of the event, though, with several welcoming the "Tibet Cultural Splendor" festival and others welcoming the "Song and Dance Ensemble of the TAR" for what they seem to have understood to be a one-day performance. The Canadian officials welcoming the festival seemed to have been unaware of the weeklong nature of the event, the arts exhibits, the film showings, the academic lectures, and the distribution of propaganda materials. They had apparently responded to the requests of the Chinese-Canadian community to hold this event and did not imagine that it was essentially a propaganda exercise by the Chinese government. Many were subsequently surprised at the controversy the festival aroused.

Unfortunately for the Chinese organizers of the exhibition, who had chosen Toronto partly because of its multiculturalism, Toronto was the home of a very politically active community of some 1,500 Tibetans. They protested the plan to hold the festival, arousing a controversy that surprised the Canadian officials who had approved and welcomed the event. The festival thus got much unwanted negative publicity even before it began. The Toronto Tibetans demonstrated at every event of the festival.

All visitors to the festival received a large shopping-style bag, printed with colorful Tibetan scenes, containing several gifts and propaganda items. Included were a brochure; a CD-ROM, *China's Tibet*, in a fancy box printed with scenes of the Potala and with a velvet-lined interior; a large glossy book, *Social History of Tibet, China—Documented and Illustrated*; a smaller book of mostly economic data about Tibet called *China's Tibet: Facts and Figures*; a small book on Tibetan history, *History Testifies*; a travel guide to western China, including Tibet, Qinghai, and Xinjiang; a tourist map of Tibet; and several pamphlets on various Tibetan subjects, including "Feudal Serf System in Tibet" and "Did Tibet Become an Independent Country after the Revolution of 1911?"

The academic dialogue, the "Tibetologist and Living Buddhas Exchange Delegation," was supposed to be held at a university, but the university refused to hold it after the Chinese organizers would not allow anyone but their own scholars to participate. The event was finally held as a closed meeting of mostly Chinese where four Tibetan academics presented China's version of Tibet's history.

The result of the Chinese propaganda show in Toronto was that the Chinese sponsors were challenged everywhere by the local Tibetan community. Several negative articles about the nature of the event and about China's role in Tibet appeared in local newspapers. The Tibetans' demonstrations were covered by local TV stations, and several Tibetans were interviewed. The event was ultimately so poorly received that it had to be limited to an audience of the local Chinese community and a few invited friends. The public at large was excluded due to Chinese fears of demonstrations and protests. China's Propaganda Department ultimately succeeded in calling attention to the political issue of Tibet, but the resulting publicity did more to promote the "Dalai Clique's" propaganda than that of the PRC.

Notes

1. Deng Xiaoping, "Speeding Up Tibet's Development on the Basis of Equality among Various Nationalities," quoted in "Tibet Article Urges 'Correct' Nationalities Views," *Tibet Daily*, 4 July 1994, in Foreign Broadcast Information Service, FBIS-CHI-94-137, 18 July 1994, 77. The origin of Deng's article was actually a few remarks made by him in defense of China's Tibet policy to former U.S. president Jimmy Carter during Carter's visit to China in 1987. In reply to a question about China's population transfer to Tibet, Deng said that it was "inappropriate to judge China's nationalities policies and the Tibet issue against the number of Han people in Tibet. . . . The key criteria should be what benefits will rapidly accrue to the people of Tibet and how Tibet should be made to develop rapidly and stand at the forefront of China's 'Four Modernizations.'" Deng's remarks were later expanded into what was purported to be a "guiding document" on Tibet policy.

2. Arjia Rinpoche, personal communication, Washington, DC, 2004.

3. *Cutting Off the Serpent's Head: Tightening Control in Tibet, 1994–1995* (New York: Tibet Information Network, Human Rights Watch/Asia, 1996), 20.

4. "Third National Work Conference on Tibet 20–23 July," New China News Agency, 26 July 1994.

5. *Cutting Off the Serpent's Head*, 155.

6. *News Review: Reports from Tibet, 2001* (London: Tibet Information Network), 11.

7. "China Recommences 'Patriotic Education' Campaign in Tibet's Monastic Institutions," in *Human Rights Update* [publication of Tibetan Center for Human Rights and Democracy] (September 2005).

8. "Tibet: Its Ownership and Human Rights Situation" (Beijing: Information Office of the State Council of the People's Republic of China, 1992).

9. "Tibet: Proving Truth from Facts" (Dharamsala: Department of Information and International Relations, Central Tibetan Administration, 1993), 3.

10. "New Progress in Human Rights in the Tibet Autonomous Region" (Beijing: Information Office of the State Council of the People's Republic of China, 1998).

11. See Warren W. Smith Jr., *Tibetan Nation: A History of Tibetan Nationalism and Sino-Tibetan Relations* (Boulder, CO: Westview Press, 1996), 600n8, 607n27.

12. "The Development of Tibetan Culture" (Beijing: Information Office of the State Council of the People's Republic of China, 2000).

13. "Tibet's March toward Modernization" (Beijing: Information Office of the State Council of the People's Republic of China, 2001).

14. "Ecological Improvement and Environmental Protection in Tibet" (Beijing: Information Office of the State Council of the People's Republic of China, 2003).

15. "Regional Ethnic Autonomy in Tibet" (Beijing: Information Office of the State Council of the People's Republic of China, 2004).

16. "China's Public Relations Strategy on Tibet: Classified Documents from the Beijing Propaganda Conference" (Washington, DC: International Campaign for Tibet, 1993), 18.

17. "Tibet-Related External Propaganda and Tibetology Work in the New Era: Zhao Qizheng's Statement at the Meeting on National Research in Tibetology and External Propaganda on Tibet," Beijing, 12 June 2000, internal document translated and published by the International Campaign for Tibet, Washington, DC, May 2001.

18. "Jia Qinglin Inspects China Research Center for Tibetan Studies in Beijing 18 May," Xinhua, 18 May 2006, in Open Source Center CPP20060518506026, http://www.opensource.gov.

19. Phillip P. Pan, "In the Name of the Panchen Lama," *Washington Post*, 19 September 2003.

20. "China Protests Dalai Lama's US Trip," Agence France-Presse, 28 August 2003.

21. Eve Johnson, "China Says Tibetans Oppose Display of Dalai Photos," Reuters, 19 August 2004.

22. Robert Marquand, "Visit to a Potemkin Village," *Christian Science Monitor*, 27 August 2004.

23. "China Tibet Culture Festival to Celebrate Austria-China Ties," Xinhua, 16 October 2006, in Open Source Center CPP20061016042031.

6

Sino-Tibetan Dialogue

SINCE 1979, THE PEOPLE'S REPUBLIC OF CHINA (PRC) and representatives of the Tibetan exile community have engaged in a dialogue about Tibetan autonomy and a possible return of the Dalai Lama. For the Tibetan side, this dialogue has been about the political issue of Tibet and the nature of Tibetan autonomy. The Chinese side has denied that there are any unresolved political issues in regard to Tibet, however, including the nature of Tibetan autonomy, and has tried to confine the issue to the personal future of the Dalai Lama. Despite the Dalai Lama having abandoned the claim to independence, he maintains that Tibet was independent before 1950 and that there are still unresolved political issues; therefore, the Chinese believe, he has not given up the "idea of independence."

After the death of Mao Zedong in 1976 and the purge of the Gang of Four, Deng Xiaoping instituted more pragmatic policies in the PRC and attempted to finally resolve the issues of Taiwan and Tibet. The Third Plenary Session of the Eleventh Party Central Committee in December 1978 decided to initiate an economic and cultural liberalization in Tibet and to make overtures to Taiwan with regard to its "peaceful reunification." The Chinese Communist Party (CCP) hoped that liberalized economic and cultural policies in Tibet would resolve any remaining Tibetan discontent with Chinese rule and even convince the Dalai Lama to return, thus finally resolving the issue of China's legitimacy in Tibet. Liberalization in Tibet was also intended to impress Taiwan with the possibility of autonomy within the PRC.

In its overtures to Taiwan, the PRC promised a high degree of autonomy under what was later termed the "one country, two systems" formula. Far from denying the relevance of the Tibetan example for Taiwan, PRC officials suggested that the "peaceful liberation" of Tibet could serve as a model for peaceful reunification with Taiwan.[1] For the CCP, the salient characteristic of the "Tibet model" was the successful resolution of Tibet's status by means of the 1951 Seventeen-Point Agreement. The party offered as a model of autonomy not Tibet's history since liberation, during which the CCP admitted that it had made some "mistakes," but the new policy of liberalization in Tibet since 1979. The CCP was apparently confident that all problems in Tibet would be rapidly alleviated by its new "correct" policy and Tibet could therefore serve as a model of autonomy within the PRC sufficient to entice Taiwan to accept a similar status.

An opening for Sino-Tibetan dialogue had been created by the Dalai Lama's definition of the Tibetan issue as the "happiness" of the Tibetan people. In his annual 10 March statement in 1973, the Dalai Lama said, "If the Tibetans in Tibet are truly happy under Chinese rule then there is no reason for us here in exile to argue otherwise." This statement was repeated on 10 March 1978. In 1980, he said, "The core of the Tibetan issue is the welfare and ultimate happiness of the six million Tibetans in Tibet."[2] From his first 10 March address in 1961 until the late 1970s, the Dalai Lama had spoken of the issue of Tibet as independence or freedom. After 1978, he spoke of the issue as being the happiness of the Tibetan people and did not mention independence.[3] The Dalai Lama's definition appeared to relegate the issue of Tibet to one that China could claim to have satisfactorily resolved.

The date when the Dalai Lama actually abandoned the claim to Tibetan independence is the subject of some confusion. It is usually dated to the 1988 Strasbourg Statement, in which he officially announced that Tibet would accept autonomy under China. However, his representatives had discussed autonomy with Chinese officials in meetings in the early 1980s. In a statement in 2006, the Kalon Tripa (prime minister) of the Tibetan government-in-exile, Samdhong Rinpoche, said:

> For the past 27 years His Holiness the Dalai Lama and the Central Tibetan Administration did not demand for the restoration of Tibet's independence; rather, His Holiness the Dalai Lama implemented the Middle Way Approach, which demands genuine autonomy for Tibet, as enshrined in the Chinese Constitution.[4]

Presumably, Samdhong dated the Middle Way to 1979 because Dharamsala began talks with China at that time based upon an expansion of Tibetan autonomy. The Dalai Lama himself has recently said that he contemplated giving up the claim to independence and accepting autonomy under China as early as 1973. He was quoted as saying that his "spirit of Middle Way approach was developed around 1973/1974."[5] During his most recent visit to Washington, in October 2007, he said that the Middle Way policy dated from 1974. Presumably, this had something to do with the 1973 American rapprochement with China.

In fact, the Dalai Lama had been constrained in regard to the independence issue since late 1959, shortly after the revolt, when Tibet's case was appealed to the United Nations. In a letter that has only recently been revealed, the Dalai Lama appealed to U.S. president Dwight Eisenhower for help in the restoration of Tibetan independence. The letter, dated 26 May 1959, was written from Mussoorie, India. In it, the Dalai Lama asked the president to "please confer and plan whatever strategy is necessary in regard to giving Tibetans independence." The Dalai Lama also spoke of the Tibetans' desire for independence:

> I now wish to say for one purpose that the essential desire of all Tibetan people, central, north, south, east, west, Khamba, and Amdo, all having the same language, religion, and beliefs, and with one will, all together want independence of Tibet.[6]

The Dalai Lama's appeal to the United Nations, dated 9 September 1959, was also based on a claim that Tibet's sovereignty had been violated.[7] However, the United States, which took the lead in arousing support for Tibet at the UN, advised him that only a resolution about human rights violations could secure international support. Even though Tibet's political status remained the issue in theory, in practice even countries sympathetic to Tibet could raise only humanitarian or human rights issues since they recognized Chinese sovereignty over Tibet. In particular, India did not support Tibet's demand for a restoration of its independence. Tibet's legal status was also complicated by the Seventeen-Point Agreement of 1951, which the Dalai Lama and his government had accepted and lived under for some eight years.

To represent Tibet at the UN, the Dalai Lama sent his brother, Gyalo Thondup, who immediately encountered the reality that only a resolution about human rights could pass. Thondup was reportedly "distressed" at the lack of Asian support for Tibet and the "political facts of life at the UN," which prevented the political issue of Tibet being discussed.[8] While agreeing to downplay all but the human rights aspects of the Tibetan appeal, Thondup repeatedly questioned U.S. representatives, including Henry Cabot Lodge, head of the U.S. mission, whether "action on human rights basis would in some way affect adversely [the] cause of Tibetan independence." Thondup was assured that only on those grounds would the Tibetan issue be considered at all, but that even a resolution confined to human rights issues could be used as an entrance for the Tibetan issue into the UN, which could conceivably be expanded at some later date. Tibetan insistence that the UN consider the issue of Tibet's international political status, on the other hand, might close the door to any UN consideration of the Tibet issue at all.[9]

In conjunction with the Tibetan UN appeal, in November 1959 the United States, along with Taiwan, made a statement recognizing Tibet's right to self-determination. In supporting self-determination for Tibet, the United States did not commit itself to Tibetan independence, however, but only to the "concept that Tibetans have the right to decide for themselves whether or not Tibet is to be independent."[10] The U.S. position derived from its sympathy for Tibetans and its opposition to Communist China, but was constrained by its previous recognition of Chinese "suzerainty" over Tibet.

Thus, due to the exigencies of international support, the Tibetan exiles were never able to explicate an unambiguous policy with regard to Tibetan independence. While this was known to some of Tibet's international patrons and supporters, it was not made explicit to ordinary Tibetan exiles, most of whom imagined that their government-in-exile's policy was to demand the restoration of Tibetan independence. Thus, the Strasbourg Statement of 1988 came as a shock to many exiled Tibetans as well as to some international supporters.

China's post-Maoist overture to the Dalai Lama began with an invitation in December 1978 to Gyalo Thondup to meet with Deng Xiaoping in Beijing. Deng offered to hold discussions on the return of the Dalai Lama with the caveat that Tibet's political status as an integral part of China was not open to discussion. Deng was reported to have said: "The basic question is whether Tibet is part of China or not. This should be kept as criteria for testing the truth. . . . So long as it is not accepted that Tibet is an integral part of China, there is nothing else to talk about."[11] Deng's condition on talks was widely interpreted in the Tibetan community as meaning "anything but independence can be discussed." This interpretation has become virtually an article of faith in the Tibetan and Tibetan activist community.[12]

However, Deng's actual words do not support this interpretation. What Deng decreed as a precondition was not that any issue about Tibet except independence might be discussed but that the "idea of independence," past, present, or future, must be rejected before there could be any discussions. He apparently meant that no political issues could be discussed since all political issues of Tibet evolve from the Tibetan claim to independence. Thus, *nothing* about the political status of Tibet was to be open to discussion, including the nature of Tibetan autonomy and the territorial extent of the Tibet Autonomous Region (TAR). Subsequent events have demonstrated the validity of this interpretation. China's actual behavior in all talks has been to refuse to discuss any political issues of Tibet, including China's system of autonomy within Tibet.

In his meeting with Thondup, Deng agreed to permit Tibetan exile representatives to visit Tibet to see for themselves how conditions had improved. A subsequent series of Tibetan exile delegation visits revealed how loyal Tibetans remained to the Dalai Lama and how ignorant the Chinese were about Tibetans' actual sentiments. The delegations were mobbed by sobbing Tibetans, the Chinese were profoundly embarrassed, and the visits were terminated. The Chinese tried to save face by saying that the "frenzied welcome" accorded to representatives of the Dalai Lama in Tibet had no nationalist or political significance at all, but was merely a remnant of Tibetans' religious devotion.

Despite the unexpected results of the Tibetan exile delegations' visits, the Chinese continued their efforts to convince the Dalai Lama to return. In July 1981, Hu Yaobang conveyed to Thondup the CCP's assurances that a new era of political liberalization had dawned in Tibet. The Dalai Lama was promised that if he returned, his status and privileges would be the same as before 1959; he would also be appointed a vice president of the National People's Congress (NPC) and vice chairman of the Chinese People's Political Consultative Conference (CPPCC). He would be required to reside in Beijing, but would be allowed to visit Tibet "from time to time."

In April 1982, a delegation composed of three Tibetan government-in-exile officials, led by Lodi Gyari, was invited to Beijing to meet with Chinese officials. The Tibetan representatives proposed that all Tibetan cultural areas be reunited into a greater Tibetan autonomous region and that this unified TAR be accorded a higher degree of autonomy than that currently being offered to Taiwan. They suggested that Tibet was due a higher status of autonomy than Taiwan because Tibetans were a non-Chinese nationality.[13] The Chinese officials informed the Tibetans that the difference was that Tibet had already "returned to the Motherland" while Taiwan had not. Taiwan had to be offered concessions in order to secure its return, but the PRC had no reason to make any concessions to Tibet.[14] The proposal to reunite Tibetan cultural areas into one autonomous region was also rejected.

The same three Tibetan government-in-exile officials returned at the end of October 1984. As before, PRC officials refused to discuss any issue except the unconditional return of the Dalai Lama. The Chinese complained that "while the Dalai Lama expresses his wish of improving relations with the central authorities some of his followers carry out activities advocating Tibetan independence."[15] The Chinese were by this time apparently having second thoughts about the wisdom of reopening the Tibetan issue at all. They were increasingly uncertain about the potential effects of the Dalai Lama's return, even if he were to be confined to Beijing, since he was now a subject of international interest. In addition, the dialogue had opened the issue of Tibet's political status, an issue the Chinese had hoped was forever buried. Even though the Dalai Lama had indicated his willingness to accept a status of autonomy within China, the Chinese insisted that the Tibetans abandon not only their claim to Tibetan independence but also the claim that Tibet had *ever* been independent. The Tibetan claim to an independent status before 1950 called into question the CCP's anti-imperialist ideology and the legitimacy of Chinese sovereignty over Tibet.

By 1987, because negotiations with China had been entirely stalemated since the last negotiating team's visit in 1984, the Tibetan government-in-exile shifted its strategy to a campaign for international political support. In addition, the PRC's relatively liberal policies of the early 1980s had given way to a new "leftist wind," manifested by an Anti-Bourgeois Liberalization Campaign. In January 1987, Hu Yaobang was purged from his position as CCP general secretary, reportedly partly because of dissatisfaction with his Tibet policy.

In June 1988, in an address to the European Parliament at Strasbourg, France, the Dalai Lama attempted to revive negotiations with the PRC by formally accepting Deng Xiaoping's precondition that he "give up the idea of Tibetan independence." The Dalai Lama's proposal was the first official acknowledgment that he would accept Chinese sovereignty over Tibet in exchange for genuine and well-defined autonomy, although his representatives had already negotiated on that basis in the early 1980s. The Dalai Lama justified his change in policy with the rationalization that independence for Tibet was impossible to attain, whereas "genuine autonomy" was possible and was capable of preserving Tibetan culture.[16]

Despite his apparent acceptance of their conditions, China rejected the Dalai Lama's proposal as an attempt to "tamper with history, distort reality, and deny Tibet's status as an inalienable part of China's territory under Chinese sovereignty."[17] The Dalai Lama's Strasbourg Proposal did not fulfill the condition that he "give up the idea of independence" in the sense that the Chinese required: that Tibet had always been and would always be a part of China. He was required to admit that Tibet was an "inalienable part of China." The Dalai Lama's agreement to this version of reality was necessary in order to legitimate China's 1950 invasion of Tibet and to forever eliminate the possibility of Tibetan independence. The special autonomous status that the Dalai Lama demanded for Tibet was rejected by the Chinese as perpetuating the separate identity of Tibet and threatening the territorial integrity of the Chinese state. The Dalai Lama's demand for a democratic political system was regarded as an attempt to alter the PRC's system of national regional autonomy and to "negate the superior socialist system established in Tibet." The Dalai Lama's intention, the Chinese said, was "to transform China's internal affairs into a question between two countries and thus to lay the groundwork for an attempt to separate Tibet from the rest of China."[18]

In January 1989, the Panchen Lama died in Shigatse. The Dalai Lama was unexpectedly invited by the Chinese Buddhist Association to attend memorial services in Beijing. The Dalai Lama asked to also be allowed to visit Tibet, and when this was refused, he declined the invitation. The Tibetan government-in-exile reportedly suspected that this invitation was but another attempt to separate the issue of the Dalai Lama's personal status from that of Tibet and to negotiate directly with him without any Tibetan government participation. Some international and Chinese commentators have suggested that the Dalai Lama miscalculated in refusing this invitation. Had the Dalai Lama gone to China in early 1989, it is possible that the riots in Lhasa in March would not have occurred and martial law would not have been declared. However, the Tiananmen Square uprising in June 1989 would still have happened, with the subsequent hardening of China's policies on many issues, Tibet included. In fact, some of the officials who had proffered the invitation to the Dalai Lama were purged in the aftermath of Tiananmen.

After 1989, there were few signs of any Sino-Tibetan contacts or talks, even though China constantly expressed its willingness to talk with the Dalai Lama if he would really give up the independence of Tibet and stop his separatist activities. After the Tibet Work Forum of 1994, the Panchen Lama affair, and the subsequent Patriotic Education Campaign, the Dalai Lama was denounced in terms that made it seem unlikely that China was sincere about negotiating with him. The struggle with the "Dalai Clique" was said to be not about autonomy or religion but about preserving China's national unification. The Dalai Lama's proposals for "high-level autonomy" and "self-government of the greater Tibetan region" were condemned as being aimed at the realization of Tibetan independence and the splitting of the motherland.

> The type of national regional autonomy found in China is one that suits a unified, multinational country. Any place where nationality regional autonomy is practiced is an inseparable part of the People's Republic of China. It is neither "independent autonomy" divorced from the big family of the motherland, nor is it any kind of political autonomy of a semi-independent "autonomous state." The Dalai clique in exile abroad has concocted so-called new recommendations, such as "high-degree autonomy" and "autonomy of the greater Tibetan region," with the backing of the hostile western forces. Their real intention is to separate Tibet from the motherland. The issue between the CCP and the Dalai clique is not about autonomy but about safeguarding the unity of the motherland. . . . There is no room for bargaining over the fundamental issue of safeguarding the unity of the motherland.[19]

In 1998, Jiang Zemin, in a press conference with visiting U.S. president Bill Clinton, revealed that there had recently been some private contacts with the

Dalai Lama. This raised a flurry of excitement that perhaps another round of contacts and talks was being considered. However, no such talks took place, nor was it ever revealed what the contacts to which Jiang referred were or what, if anything, was discussed. Like China's often-repeated willingness to talk with the Dalai Lama, Jiang's remarks seem to have been solely intended to placate Clinton and other Western critics of China's Tibet policy, all of whom constantly suggested that China should talk to the Dalai Lama.

Revival of Sino-Tibetan Contacts

A revival of Sino-Tibetan contacts in 2002 once again raised the hopes of the exiles as well as of Tibetans inside Tibet. In June, the Dalai Lama's elder brother, Gyalo Thondup, made a visit to China and Tibet, ostensibly for personal reasons. His visit seems to have been in preparation for a revival of contacts. Then in September, a four-person Tibetan delegation representing the Dalai Lama made a visit to Lhasa. This was the first official contact between Dharamsala and the Chinese government since 1993 and the first visit of a Dharamsala delegation to Tibet since 1985 and to Lhasa since 1980.

The significance of the visit was unclear, but it predictably aroused hopes in the Tibetan exile community that China might be prepared to initiate talks with the Dalai Lama. These hopes, however, were dampened by China's insistence that its policy on Tibet remained unchanged. Chinese and Tibetan officials also continued their denunciations of the Dalai Lama. The Chinese government reiterated its policy that it was willing to begin talks with the Dalai Lama if he would give up his splittist activities and accept the legitimacy of Chinese rule over Tibet. However, Chinese officials insisted that any such talks would be about the Dalai Lama's personal future only, not about the future of Tibet.

The Dharamsala delegation was headed by Lodi Gyaltsen Gyari, the Dalai Lama's envoy in North America, and Kelsang Gyaltsen, the envoy to Europe. Both were officially designated by the Dalai Lama as his representatives in any negotiations with China. However, China described the visit as private, and Chinese and Tibetan officials pretended that they were unaware of any connection between the delegation members and the Dharamsala government. The Chinese Foreign Ministry spokesman was quoted as saying:

> There were some Tibetan expatriates allowed to come back to China in a private capacity. We welcome them back to see for themselves the development of Tibet and other Tibetan autonomous areas of China. . . . China believes that in recent years, with the support of anti-China forces internationally, the Dalai Lama has engaged in activities aimed at splitting China. To bring about better relations, the

Dalai Lama must cease these activities, recognize Tibet and Taiwan as part of China, and acknowledge Beijing as the sole legitimate government representing all of China. On that basis, China can have consultations with the Dalai Lama on his personal future.[20]

Legchok, the TAR deputy party secretary, said that he had met with the delegation, but that there had been no discussion about the Dalai Lama. Legchok described the delegation's visit as a personal one, to meet some relatives and to pay homage at some monasteries in Tibet. He said that he had briefed the delegation about Tibet's progress and economic development and that the delegation members had greatly appreciated the economic prosperity and the raising of the standard of living of the people of Tibet. Legchok denied that there was any change in Chinese policy on Tibet. In a revealing statement, he put the delegation's visit within the context of China's propaganda offensive about Tibet: "Maybe because we were too confident before, we didn't attach enough importance to the negative reports in the Western world about Tibet and we always believed that the facts and the truth lay on our side. We didn't attach enough importance to the work of the media, but we are now working on it."[21]

Upon the delegation's return to Dharamsala, Gyari described the visit as having been intended to establish direct contact with the Chinese leadership and to create a "conducive atmosphere" enabling direct face-to-face meetings on a regular basis in the future. He said it was also meant to explain to the Chinese leadership the Dalai Lama's Middle Way approach to resolving the Tibet issue. He said that the delegation had attempted to build confidence by dispelling mistrust and misconception. Gyari said that the delegation had been impressed by the economic development in Tibet, but added that they had emphasized the equal importance of preserving Tibet's unique cultural, religious, and linguistic heritage. He said that the delegation had had little opportunity to meet with ordinary Tibetans.[22] In fact, according to other reports, the delegation's visit was kept a secret in Tibet. Gyari has stated that his group was constantly surrounded by Chinese security personnel.[23]

The only positive aspect that the delegation had to report, besides the very fact of the visit itself, was that they seem to have been treated with more respect by Chinese and Tibetan officials than had been the case in the past: "The Chinese leaders listened to our explanation with keen interest and engaged in free and spontaneous exchanges. . . . What impressed us more this time was the much greater flexibility displayed by the current leaders in their mental attitude." This may have reflected a more relaxed style in China in general, rather than having any significance in relation to Tibet. Otherwise, both sides simply repeated their already known positions, without any new developments or breakthroughs.

The Tibetan government-in-exile was nevertheless encouraged by the resumption of its long-discontinued contacts with Beijing. Dharamsala felt that its envoys had been treated as equals for the first time by Chinese officials and expressed hope that Tibet could begin negotiations for greater autonomy. Samdhong Rinpoche, the prime minister of the Tibetan exile administration, said that the delegates had been encouraged by their discussions with the Chinese leadership, and he expressed hope that the visit would open a new chapter in the relationship with China and start a process of dialogue leading to negotiations toward resolving the issue of Tibet. Samdhong said that he hoped for a continuation of the dialogue before June 2003, until which time he suggested that Tibetans in exile should refrain from demonstrations against visiting Chinese officials in order to create an atmosphere conducive to talks.

The resumption of official contacts between Beijing and Dharamsala was undoubtedly significant. However, the actual significance may lie in Legchok's association of the visit to China's propaganda campaign about Tibet. His implication was that China intended no new initiative with regard to Tibet except to improve its image on the issue by seeming to be magnanimous and conciliatory. Beijing may also have hoped to impress Tibetan exile officials with the changes in Tibet since the Chinese occupation and with evidence of the firmness of China's control over Tibet and the permanence of its rule there. The Chinese may also have intended to play upon Tibetan hopes for dialogue and the usual Tibetan willingness to reduce its criticism of Chinese rule in Tibet in order to create the right atmosphere for such dialogue. If this was their hope, it had already been rewarded by Samdhong's appeal to Tibetans to suspend their demonstrations against Chinese officials.

The same group of Tibetan exile representatives made a second visit in late May and early June 2003, but were not allowed to visit Tibet. The four-man delegation visited a traditionally Tibetan area in Yunnan, but the majority of the visit was confined to Buddhist sites in Chinese provinces. The delegation leaders said that they were told that they could not visit Tibet because it was closed due to the SARS epidemic, although there were no reports of SARS in Tibet. The delegation therefore asked to go to Dechen Tibetan Autonomous District in Yunnan. They also met with officials of the CCP's United Front Work Department who were responsible for nationalities affairs.

Upon their return to India, the delegation leaders reported that they thought that they had improved relations with Chinese leaders, increased the Chinese officials' confidence in dealing with representatives of the Dalai Lama, and hopefully created conditions for a dialogue about Tibet. They had little evidence of this to justify their optimism, however, except the fact of the visit itself. In fact, China took the opportunity of the delegation's visit to issue an article stating that there was no issue of Tibet about which it should engage in dialogue with the Dalai Lama, that the Dalai Lama did not represent the interests of the Tibetan people, and that Tibetan resistance to Chinese rule was exclusively the product of American imperialist interference in Tibet.[24]

After the delegation's return, Lodi Gyari issued a statement to the press in which he said that he was impressed by the attention and candor of Chinese officials with whom the delegation had met. He said that the delegation felt encouraged by their exchange of views with their Chinese counterparts and, in the only statement that revealed anything about the substance of such talks, that Chinese officials had "explicitly acknowledged the positive efforts made by the Tibetan leadership to create a conducive environment for the continuation of the process."[25] Both sides suggested that further similar steps should be taken to create such an environment for contacts and to create mutual understanding and trust. However, in later statements, Gyari complained that there had been no actual dialogue and that, while the Tibetan side had tried to "create a conducive environment for the continuation of the process," China had taken no corresponding actions.[26]

The Chinese mention of "positive efforts" made by the Tibetan exile government was a reference to their attempts to limit criticism of China and to avoid embarrassing China about Tibet. In addition to Samdhong Rinpoche's suggestion against demonstrations, the Dalai Lama had also canceled a scheduled visit to Taiwan in order to avoid offending China. During a European visit, he had said that he was in agreement with the "One China" policy, implying his recognition that Taiwan was a part of China. After the latest visit, Samdhong expressed his determination to continue creating a conducive atmosphere for the process of dialogue.

Critics complained that the Chinese side had taken no corresponding steps. Since the first delegation visit in September, a popular Tibetan lama in eastern Tibet, Tenzin Delek Rinpoche, had been sentenced to death in what appeared to be an attempt to link Tibetan nationalism to terrorism. Also in eastern Tibet, Chinese authorities in the Ngaba Autonomous District of Sichuan closed a monastic school run by the Ngaba Kirti monastery.[27] This instance, and the previous closure of the Larung Gar monastic school in a nearby area, demonstrated Chinese intolerance for the teaching of Tibetan language, culture, and religion even when privately financed. Previously, it had been thought by some that the tolerance shown to Tibetan culture in areas outside the TAR demonstrated the possibility of Tibetan autonomy within China so long as it had no political implications.

China's intransigence led critics of the dialogue process to complain that China's purpose in engaging in the contacts was to discourage the anti-Chinese activities of Tibetans in exile, to silence the Tibetan government-in-exile by playing on its hope for negotiations, and to defuse international criticism of China regarding Tibet. Another apparent purpose of the Chinese was to impress the exiled Tibetans with how much China and Tibet had changed so that they would give up their futile attempt to separate Tibet from China.

The Dalai Lama's envoys returned to China for a third visit from 12 to 29 September 2004. They held discussions with officials of the United Front Work Department in Beijing and then traveled to the Kham Tibetan area of Sichuan. There they met with local Tibetan officials, to whom they emphasized "the importance of preserving and developing our heritage, namely the Tibetan language, culture and religion, while making economic progress." They "shared with the officials the vision and efforts that His Holiness the Dalai Lama is making in resolving the issue of Tibet."[28] They also visited Guangzhou and the special economic zones of Zhuhai and Shenzen in Guangdong Province and Chengde in Hebei Province, where the Manchu emperors had built replicas of the Potala and Tashilhunpo. In a statement released in Dharamsala after his return there, Lodi Gyari said:

> We had so far the most extensive and serious exchange of views on matters relating to Tibet. The discussions were held in a frank but cordial atmosphere. It was apparent from the discussions that there are major differences on a number of issues, including some fundamental ones. Both sides acknowledged the need for more substantive discussions in order to narrow down the gaps and reach a common ground. We stressed the need for both sides to demonstrate flexibility, far-sightedness and vision to bridge the differences.[29]

Envoys of the Dalai Lama next met with Chinese officials of the United Front Work Department at the Chinese Embassy in Bern, Switzerland, in June 2005. The meeting was described by the Tibetan side as the first session of the fourth round of their talks with the Chinese government, perhaps meaning that they expected this meeting to lead to the next invitation to visit China. The Chinese side described the talks in less formal terms, saying only that Chinese officials concerned with Tibetan issues had met with some Tibetans living abroad, some of whom were close to the Dalai Lama. The Chinese Foreign Ministry reiterated its policy that real talks could begin only when the Dalai Lama gave up his separatist activities and acknowledged both Tibet and Taiwan as inalienable Chinese territory. Only then could talks begin, and only concerning the Dalai Lama's personal situation.

While the Tibetan side tried to give as much substance to the meeting as possible, the Chinese side played down its significance. The Chinese Foreign Ministry spokesperson described the United Front officials who met with the Tibetans as being in Switzerland on a study tour, not specifically to meet with the Tibetan representatives. The spokesperson also said that Chinese officials routinely make arrangements for Tibetans residing abroad with regard to making visits to Tibet to see relatives or to make commercial investments. This implied that the Dalai Lama and other Tibetans in exile could return to Tibet, but only if they became patriotic to China, a reference to China's demand that Tibetans could return only if they gave up all separatist activities and pledged loyalty to China.

Lodi Gyari issued a statement in which he said that fundamental differences remained between the two sides. He criticized the Chinese for making no moves to create a "conducive atmosphere":

> Major differences on a number of issues, including some fundamental ones, continue to remain. . . . We reiterated our commitment to continue making every effort to create a better environment. At the same time we urged the Chinese side to join in this effort, and highlighted the absence of such obvious gestures from their side.[30]

According to Gyari, the Chinese officials sought to encourage the Tibetan side to continue the dialogue process despite the lack of any apparent progress. The senior Chinese official said that the Tibetans should not be pessimistic about the differences between the two sides and that it was possible to narrow those differences through more meetings and exchange of views.

> Despite the existing areas of disagreement, Vice Minister Zhu was pleased that our direct contact had now become stable and an "established practice." He also conveyed to us that the Central leadership of the Chinese Communist Party attached great importance to the contact with His Holiness the Dalai Lama. He stated that we need not be pessimistic about the existing differences and that it was possible to narrow down the gaps through more meetings and exchange of views.[31]

This ostensible expression of sincerity by the Chinese official was regarded by the hopeful as encouraging. However, it could equally be interpreted as revealing China's true strategy. A perpetuation of talks without any actual progress on the issues would serve China's purpose by satisfying its critics who were pressuring it to talk with the Dalai Lama. It would also allow China to delay until the current Dalai Lama passes from the scene. China had used this same strategy in its human rights dialogues with other countries. To avoid criticism by international organizations and at the United Nations, China established bilateral human rights dialogues with its more prominent critics. However, these dialogues resulted in little or no improvement in China's human rights practices.

Despite China's downplaying of the most recent contacts and the reiteration of its uncompromising conditions, the latest round of talks was greeted with relief in Dharamsala, which was under pressure to show some results of its Middle Path policy. The Dalai Lama issued a statement saying that Sino-Ti-betan dialogue had now become an established practice. Samdhong Rinpoche said that China had finally realized that the Dalai Lama was the solution to the Tibet issue, not the problem. He also said that he thought the Tibet issue would be resolved during the current Dalai Lama's lifetime. The U.S. State Department said that it was encouraging that the dialogue was continuing. The U.S. secretary of state, Condoleezza Rice, on a visit to China, told Chinese leaders that they should engage in dialogue with the Dalai Lama who, she said, was not a threat to China.

The Tibetan exile envoys went to China again, from 15 to 23 February 2006, shortly after Hu Jintao's first visit to the United States, for what Dharamsala described as the fifth round of talks with China. The delegation met with officials of the United Front Work Department in Guilin, Guangxi Zhuang Autonomous Region, as they had expressed an interest in looking at the situation of the different autonomous regions. Once again, Dharamsala said that the delegates were official envoys of the Dalai Lama, which China denied, saying that they were there in a private capacity. A Chinese Foreign Ministry spokesman said that the Tibetan delegation had close ties with the Dalai Lama but that the delegation leader, Lodi Gyari, and many other exiled Tibetans had returned to the Chinese motherland many times to visit their relatives and friends and to witness the development and changes in their motherland and their hometowns and to gain a clearer understanding of the Chinese government's policies.

Upon his return to Dharamsala, Gyari made a statement that indicated that the talks were essentially deadlocked:

> As a result [of the dialogue process and the latest visit], today there is a better and deeper understanding of each other's position and the fundamental differences that continue to exist in the position held by the two parties. This round of discussion also made it clear that there is a major difference even in the approach in addressing the issue. However, we remain committed to the dialogue process and are hopeful that progress will be possible by continuing the engagement. Our Chinese counterparts made clear their interest in continuing the present process and their firm belief that the obstacles can be overcome through more discussions and engagements.[32]

Gyari's phrase "there is a major difference even in the approach in addressing the issue" indicated that the visits had never actually reached the status of talks about Tibet. What the special envoy seemed to be saying was that there was no mutual understanding even about the definition of the issue that they should be discussing. Gyari said that the only understanding reached by the two sides was about their fundamental differences, a statement that revealed the lack of progress on any substantive issues. Although Gyari said that there was a deeper understanding between the two sides after the visits and that both sides remained committed to the dialogue process, his statements gave little hope to the proponents of that process.

Each of the visits thus far in the process seemed to have been more about tourism than talks, as China attempted to impress Tibetans with China's modernization. The Tibetan side had continually expressed its wish to talk about genuine autonomy for Tibet, while the Chinese had maintained that Tibet already had genuine autonomy under the Regional Ethnic Autonomy system, as it was now called. With regard to an expansion of the Tibet Autonomous Region to include all Tibetan areas, the Chinese again insisted that this was not open to discussion. From the Tibetan point of view, this left nothing to discuss, as the Chinese would talk about nothing except unconditional Tibetan acceptance of China's position. Basically, what China seemed to be saying was that all Tibetan exiles, with the possible exception of the Dalai Lama, would be allowed to return to China if they pledged allegiance to the Chinese government. Their former separatist activities would be forgiven, but no concessions would be made in China's policies toward Tibet. The itinerary of the delegation visits indicated that China hoped that the exiled Tibetan visitors to China would see that both China and Tibet had changed to an extent to be almost unrecognizable to the visitors, who therefore should give up their hopes for a return to a past that no longer existed.

Given the lack of any progress on any substantive issues in the latest round of talks, many Tibetans in exile and some of their international supporters questioned the wisdom of continuing the process. There seemed little to gain and perhaps much to lose from a process that had so far produced no results. There was little hope for progress on substantive issues if China refused to admit that there were any such issues. There was also some danger in continuing a nonproductive process. Despite its reluctance to acknowledge even that a dialogue was in progress, Beijing continually expressed its willingness to continue the process. Skeptics thought that this was because the contacts had allowed China to appear reasonable and conciliatory without actually conceding anything. The latest visit had come just after Hu Jintao's first visit to the United States, a visit marked by much dispute over protocol, and there was speculation that China allowed the subsequent Tibetan delegation visit only under pressure from the U.S. government.

Despite considerable opposition, Dharamsala expressed its intention to continue the process. Having committed itself to autonomy and dialogue, the Tibetan government-in-exile had little option, especially since the Middle Way policy had been decided upon by the Dalai Lama himself. Dharamsala was also under pressure from its international supporters, primarily the

United States, to continue the talks, since dialogue was the only policy the U.S. and other governments could support. Given the lack of any real results, Dharamsala was forced to cite the process itself as evidence of progress. Hence, Dharamsala described each delegation visit and the process as of more significance than Beijing did. The Tibetan government-in-exile kept the hope for dialogue alive by implying that talks with China had been more forthcoming than China officially acknowledged. Nevertheless, more candid statements by the Tibetan delegation leaders revealed no concessions on the part of the Chinese.

The danger for Dharamsala was that it would continue to pursue dialogue, even without any progress on the issues, simply to show that its dialogue policy was working. Dharamsala's almost desperate need to show some results from its policy was in fact a dangerous position to be in, since the need to produce results might lead to acceptance of a less than advantageous agreement, perhaps reminiscent of the 1951 Seventeen-Point Agreement. Another danger was that Dharamsala might give up its greatest negotiating strength in exchange for nothing. An apparent reason on Beijing's part for engaging in any contacts at all was to appear to be conciliatory in order to reduce international criticism. China was particularly sensitive to demonstrations against Chinese leaders on their international visits and had put pressure on foreign governments to prevent such protests. It had also put pressure on Dharamsala to discourage protests by exiled Tibetans and their supporters in exchange for promises to continue the contacts. Dharamsala had responded by suggesting to Tibetans and their supporters that any such protests against Chinese leaders might be harmful to the "conducive atmosphere" for dialogue that the Dalai Lama and the government-in-exile were trying to create.

Before the scheduled visit of Hu Jintao to the United States in late 2005, eventually postponed to early 2006, Dharamsala went so far as to send a public appeal to Tibetans and their supporters to avoid embarrassing him on his first U.S. visit. The appeal was sent in the name of the Kashag, the administration of the Tibetan government-in-exile:

> To the Tibetan people and Tibet supporters in the USA and Canada: Under the noble guidance of His Holiness the Dalai Lama's Middle Way policy, we have been striving for a genuine autonomous status for all the Tibetan people through negotiations. This policy has been adopted democratically by the Tibetan people in and outside Tibet, as well as the Assembly of Tibetan People's Deputies. In order to achieve this, the envoys of His Holiness the Dalai Lama have undertaken four rounds of talks with the concerned officials of the People's Republic of China since 2002. Particularly, in the third and fourth round of talks held in Beijing and Berne respectively, both sides were able to clear many doubts, and had the opportunity to provide clarifications and explanations on a number of issues

so that a meaningful negotiations can take place. Now that our efforts to bring about negotiations have reached a critical stage, a time has come for all the Tibetan people to employ every possible means to ensure the success of this process without creating any obstacles to it.

Soon after the reestablishment of our contacts in 2002, we have made an appeal for the creation of a conducive environment for our future negotiations, to which most of the Tibetans and Tibet supporters have responded positively. This has helped immensely in the ongoing process of dialogue. We, therefore, would like to thank all of you for your co-operation. At the same time, as you all know, the President of the People's Republic of China, Hu Jintao, will soon pay an official visit to the Americas sometime in September this year. We would like to take this opportunity to make an urgent appeal to all the Tibetans and Tibet Support Groups to refrain from any activities, including staging of protest demonstrations, which will cause him embarrassment. This is President Hu Jintao's first visit to the US as the President of the People's Republic of China and General Secretary of the Chinese Communist Party. Moreover of late, China has been showing a keen interest in and positive attitude towards our relations. Therefore, if the Tibetan people can demonstrate a new attitude this time, it will not only help bring about the fifth round of talks, but will also positively impact the future status of our negotiations. Conversely if we cause embarrassment to him, it will certainly have a negative impact on the process of negotiations, particularly on our existing contacts with the Chinese leadership. Therefore, irrespective of whether this is agreeable to the Tibetan people and Tibet supporters, we have dared to make this appeal. We hope that all of you will pay a close attention to this and lend us full co-operation.[33]

The Kashag appealed directly to Tibetans' loyalty to the Dalai Lama, saying that protests would also cause embarrassment to the Dalai Lama, who was also scheduled to be on a visit to the United States. The Kashag specified that it did not mean to prohibit nonviolent activities by Tibetans in exile, only violent activities, among which it included demonstrations because they were potentially violent in nature. The Kashag statement said that Tibetans and their supporters could still work on other political, social, educational, and economic initiatives that did not hamper the atmosphere for negotiations. Instead of demonstrations and protests, the Kashag emphasized the importance of enhancing the collective merit of the Tibetan people by means of merit-earning activities such as supporting rituals in monasteries.

At a time when the cause of Tibet is close to a resolution, owing to His Holiness the Dalai Lama's altruistic intentions and the unified force of the Tibetan people, the protective deities and highly-realized lamas have emphasized the importance of enhancing the collective merit of the Tibetan people. Accordingly, the Tibetans in and outside Tibet have been able to carry out a great deal of merit-earning activities throughout the last Tibetan Wood-Monkey year. This year also,

coinciding with the 70th birthday celebration of His Holiness the Dalai Lama, we
are performing a series of pujas at all the major monasteries and pilgrim sites by
collecting donations from the Tibetans in and outside Tibet.[34]

The Kashag statement about the need for Tibetans to accumulate merit reflected the religious mentality of the Kalon Tripa, Samdhong Rinpoche. This
is a particularly Tibetan mentality, one that imagined that China might be
moved by Tibetan prayers to negotiate with them. The former president of the
Tibetan Youth Congress, Lhasang Tsering, characterized this attitude with a
metaphor reminiscent of Deng Xiaoping's about the "white cat and black cat."
Tsering described Tibet as being like a cornered mouse, whose only strategy
when confronted by the hungry Chinese cat was to pray that the cat would become a vegetarian.[35]

The Kashag's statement was questionable in several other ways. The first
was whether Tibetans inside and outside Tibet had democratically chosen the
Middle Way policy. In response to surveys about what policy to choose, most
Tibetans said that they preferred to let the Dalai Lama decide—not that they
preferred the Middle Way policy, only that they trusted the Dalai Lama to
make the decision. As Dawa Norbu has written:

> The silent and innocent majority accept the Dalai Lama's middle path policy not
> because they understand the nuances and subtlety of his compromise politics,
> but because they believe him to be the living Buddha without a shadow of a
> doubt; they simply put their complete trust in him.[36]

Given the Dalai Lama's role in Tibetan society and his presumed infallibility,
it is logical that Tibetans would prefer that he make all the decisions with regard to Tibet's future. This is Tibetan tradition, but it is a particular form of
autocracy, not democracy. When this question was disassociated from the person of the Dalai Lama—that is, when Tibetans were asked whether they preferred independence or autonomy, without mention of the Dalai Lama's
policy—the majority invariably said that they would prefer independence.

Despite the Kashag's and Samdhong's belief that China would be led to negotiations if Tibetans refrained from demonstrations against Chinese leaders,
it was equally likely that China was willing to talk with Tibetan exile representatives only because they had been embarrassed by such demonstrations.
Assuming that it was demonstrations and other embarrassments that forced
China to talk about Tibet, not the absence of such embarrassments, it was not
logical to assume that China would be moved to dialogue or negotiate about
Tibet in the absence of any pressure from the Tibetan and international community. Therefore, critics complained, it might be unwise for the Tibetan side
to facilitate the Chinese goal by voluntarily abandoning the only leverage it

had with China. In addition, by telling Tibetans what to do based upon an appeal that they not embarrass the Dalai Lama by ignoring his wishes, the Kashag did little to further Tibetan democracy in exile.

There were rumors at the time of Hu Jintao's 2006 visit to the United States that the Chinese had told Dharamsala that if there were no demonstrations during Hu's visit, then *maybe* China would respond with an invitation for another delegation visit or even for a visit by the Dalai Lama to a Buddhist pilgrimage site in China. Indeed, another invitation was proffered, shortly after Hu's visit, despite the fact that not all Tibetans had respected the Kashag's appeal against demonstrations. At the time of the visit, the Chinese appeared confident that they had secured an agreement with Dharamsala to prevent demonstrations against Hu. They even went so far as to have Chinese dressed as Tibetans dancing in the streets of Washington to greet him. Some Chinese even reportedly confronted Tibetan demonstrators with the complaint that they were breaking an agreement not to demonstrate.

Another possible negative effect of the Middle Way policy was a general reluctance to criticize or offend China in any way that might jeopardize the dialogue. Some evidence of this came from the fact that Dharamsala ceased publishing responses to Chinese propaganda, including the White Papers. That role was taken up to some extent by the Tibetan Youth Congress. Another example involved Arjia Rinpoche, the abbot of Kumbum Monastery and a member of the CPPCC, who escaped from China in 1998 to avoid being named as tutor to the "fake Panchen." When Arjia met the Dalai Lama in New York in a private audience, he was advised to keep a low profile and avoid criticizing Chinese policies in Tibet so that the dialogue might not be affected by his defection. He was also asked to write Chinese leaders with whom he was familiar to persuade them in favor of dialogue—a request he found strangely unrealistic.[37] Some Western supporters of Tibet may also be presumed to have been restrained by Dharamsala's attempt to create a "conducive atmosphere" for dialogue. The effect of these restrictions was that China avoided exposure and criticism for some of the conditions inside Tibet—which was presumably the goal of China's strategy.

China's Strategy on Sino-Tibetan Dialogue

China's strategy with respect to contacts with representatives of the Dalai Lama was seemingly consistent with its overall strategy of dealing with the Tibet issue primarily by means of propaganda. The tactics seemed to be to appear conciliatory while making no actual concessions. The apparent goal of Beijing's strategy was to defuse international criticism of China about Tibet by displaying an appearance of willingness to resolve the issue. In addition, China apparently wanted to exploit Tibetan hopefulness for a resolution of the Tibet issue in order to convince them to cease all their splittist activities, including all the Dalai Lama's international travels and meetings and perhaps even the existence of the government-in-exile.

Besides allowing the delegation visits, China showed little evidence that it was in a mood to negotiate about Tibet or to alter its policies there in any way. China declared its Regional Ethnic Autonomy policy in Tibet both successful and unalterable. Beijing denied that the visits of representatives of the Dalai Lama to China constituted the opening of a dialogue on the issue. Chinese officials repeatedly said that if the Dalai Lama adhered to all of their conditions for dialogue, China would talk to him, but only about his own personal future—a position China had maintained since it initiated talks with the Dalai Lama's representatives in the early 1980s. The Chinese had never admitted that there was any issue of Tibet except the status of the Dalai Lama, since any "issue" of Tibet would imply that there was some unresolved question about Tibet's political status or the legitimacy of Chinese sovereignty over Tibet.

The visit of Zhu Xiaoming to the United States in January 2002 was, according to some sources, one of the precursors to the latest contacts.[38] Zhu was at that time the head of the nationalities and religion bureau of the United Front Work Department. He participated in a closed conference on Tibet at Harvard University aimed at the promotion of Sino-Tibetan dialogue. Some of what Zhu said to U.S. government officials during that visit confirms China's limitations on dialogue to the issue of the Dalai Lama's personal status:

> What is the nature of this negotiation? In my view, this negotiation is one between the Central Government of China and a religious figure in exile who is engaged in political activities. It is not a negotiation with the so-called "government in exile." . . . I think the negotiation should mainly discuss such questions as how the Dalai Lama and his followers should give up their stand for independence, stop carrying out separatist activities and contribute to the reunification of the motherland and national unity and progress, but not the question related to the legal and political status of Tibet. . . . What questions does the US Congress want the Chinese Government to negotiate with the Dalai Lama? The status of Tibet, a "high-level autonomy," or other questions? All these questions are not negotiable.[39]

China rejected the Dalai Lama's Middle Way proposal as simply a strategy to achieve independence in two stages: autonomy and then independence. A *China Daily* article at the time of the second delegation visit in June 2003 complained that when the Dalai Lama had felt that China was weak and his own position was strong, he had promoted independence. When he had felt that China's position was strong and his own was weak, he had talked about autonomy. This inconsistency, the article said, proved that the Dalai Lama was insincere in his acceptance of autonomy and that he secretly hoped for the restoration of Tibet's independence. The article denied that Tibet should have the same sort of autonomy as Hong Kong or Taiwan, both of which were at one time under foreign rule and needed the "one country, two systems" formula in order to reintegrate them into China. Tibet, it said, had always been part of China. It had already undergone liberation and democratic reforms, and the system of national regional autonomy had been implemented. Tibet had already been integrated and therefore did not need "one country, two systems."[40] The underlying rationale of this explanation was that any form of autonomy was a temporary expedient until ultimate integration and assimilation could be achieved.

The second delegation visit was also accompanied by an article by the Chinese State Council written in response to a U.S. State Department report to the U.S. Congress on the Tibet issue.[41] The State Department report was the first in response to a requirement by the U.S. Congress that the State Department report yearly on the status of the Tibet issue. The report urged China to engage in a dialogue with the Dalai Lama, saying that such dialogue would be in the interests of China and the people of Tibet, and it expressed the hope that this would lead to a negotiated resolution to the issue of Tibet.

The Chinese State Council article questioned how the United States could recognize Chinese sovereignty over Tibet while at the same time maintaining that there was some unresolved issue about Tibet's political status. It questioned how Washington could advise Beijing to negotiate with the Dalai Lama about the issue of Tibet when there was no such issue. It asked how the United States could demand that China allow Tibetans genuine self-rule when they already had such self-rule and why the United States would demand that Tibetans be allowed to preserve their culture and religion and exercise full human rights and civil liberties when they were already doing so. The State Council reiterated China's conditions for dialogue: that the Dalai Lama must abandon his claim for the independence of Tibet, halt any separatist activities, and declare that he recognizes Tibet and Taiwan as inalienable parts of China. It said that the Dalai Lama had fulfilled none of these conditions.

The article went on to condemn the history of U.S. interference in Tibet as well as current attempts to interfere by means such as the State Department report on Tibet. Much of the article was devoted to a recitation of the history of American interference in Tibet going back to the 1940s. U.S. interference was condemned for inciting the rebellion in Tibet, the flight of the Dalai Lama, and constant unrest and resistance, all of which had harmed the welfare of the Tibetan people. The Chinese maintained that all instability over the past half-century in Tibet was due to the disturbances and sabotage by Tibetan splittist forces backed by United States and other Western anti-China forces. The article maintained that there would be no Tibet issue if it weren't for Western imperialist interference in China in the past and at the present:

> The so-called "Tibet issue" essentially arose from the fact that for nearly a century western imperialist forces had fostered and supported Tibetan separatists attempting to separate Tibet from China. At present, the "Tibet issue" would not exist if the United States and other western countries don't support the Dalai clique, if the Dalai clique gives up its intention of seeking "Tibet independence" or independence in disguised forms and stops activities of splitting the country.

The Chinese article questioned the U.S. insistence that China negotiate with the Dalai Lama about Tibet. It said that the United States recognized Chinese sovereignty over Tibet, but at the same time maintained that the Dalai Lama was the legitimate leader of Tibet. This was equated to a U.S. denial that the Chinese government, or the government of the Tibet Autonomous Region, which was elected by the Tibetans themselves, represented the interests of Tibetans. The article said that the Dalai Lama did not represent the interests of the Tibetan people; instead, he had betrayed the Tibetan people when he fled Tibet and had done nothing but try to split Tibet from China ever since.

> The Dalai Lama betrayed his country and threw himself under the shield of foreign anti-China forces just because he was opposed to any change of the barbaric system. In exile, he has made no contribution to the development of Tibet nor to the happiness and benefit of the Tibetan Buddhism followers over the past 40-odd years. On the contrary, the so-called Tibetan "government-in-exile" led by the Dalai Lama has been involved in political activities aiming to split the country for years.

The Chinese State Council article maintained that the Tibetan people had voluntarily chosen the socialist system and national regional autonomy under the leadership of the Chinese Communist Party and that they would never reject this choice; that is, they would never return to the leadership of the Dalai Lama: "It is a historical choice made by all Tibetan people to follow the socialist road and the system of regional national autonomy under the leadership of the Communist Party of China, and they will never turn away from this choice." The article questioned why the United States ignored these facts and insisted upon interfering in China's internal affairs to the detriment of the interests of the people of Tibet. The article ended with the suggestion that the U.S. interest in Tibet, since it had nothing to do with the welfare of the Tibetan people, must simply be a means by which anti-China forces in the United States attempted to denigrate, weaken, and contain China.

While engaged in the latest round of contacts with the Tibetan exile representatives, China also continued to protest all the Dalai Lama's international activities in a manner that made it appear that the curtailment of these activities was one objective the Chinese hoped to achieve by offering the possibility of dialogue. The Dalai Lama's U.S. visit in September 2003 was accompanied by the usual official Chinese protests as well as a specific warning that such visits were not conducive to the dialogue process. Jampa Phuntsok, the chairman of the TAR government, said: "We resolutely oppose it [the visit], including Mr. Bush seeing the Dalai. I'm afraid these kinds of activities are not beneficial to the talks with the central government and the Dalai Lama's efforts to improve relations with our government."[42] He also portrayed the Tibetan delegation visits as representing only the Dalai Lama as an individual and the issue as one of the personal status of the Dalai Lama rather than of the political status of Tibet: "The sovereignty issue brooks no discussion. It is also inappropriate for the Dalai Lama to discuss human rights. We can only discuss the Dalai Lama's future."[43]

Jampa Phuntsok later went on the record in a 2005 interview with Xinhua with a claim that the Dalai Lama was increasingly unpopular in Tibet because of his attempt to split Tibet from China. He also said that there was no political issue of Tibet's status or about Tibetan autonomy. Any such issue was simply an invention of Western imperialists in the past in an attempt to split Tibet from China, he said. He claimed that Tibetans were loyal to the Chinese government, that they were enjoying unprecedented stability and prosperity, and that therefore they did not support any of the Dalai Lama's schemes to upset the stability in the region.[44] Jampa Phuntsok said that the Dalai Lama's proposal for a high degree of autonomy was inappropriate because it would change China's system of ethnic regional autonomy, which had been successful for more than two decades (perhaps an acknowledgment that there was no autonomy from 1965, when the TAR was granted autonomous status, until 1980) and was supported by the people.

Jampa Phuntsok also dismissed the Dalai Lama's proposal for a reunification of Tibetan areas in a greater Tibetan Autonomous Region. He said that such a unified Tibetan territory had existed only one time in history, more than a thousand years ago (during the Tibetan Empire period). The reunification of all Tibetan areas under current conditions was impossible, he declared. The Dalai Lama's schemes, no matter what they were called, were all aimed at splitting Tibet from China. His schemes were the same as those of Western imperialists in the past, and he was supported by those same imperialists at the present. Jampa Phuntsok said that the only issue of interest to Tibetans at the present time was economic development and that they would resist all attempts to raise other issues.

In an interview in Hong Kong, where he was attending a China Tibet Cultural Festival, Jampa Phuntsok later observed that the time was not ripe for the Dalai Lama to return.[45] He was quoted as saying that the Dalai Lama could not yet return because he had not given up his separatist activities, among which he mentioned the internationalization of the Tibet issue and the existence of a Tibetan government-in-exile. Jampa Phuntsok maintained that the Dalai Lama would not be allowed to return unless he abandoned his struggle for Tibetan independence. Should the Dalai Lama die in exile, his successor would be chosen according to Tibetan Buddhist traditions, the most important of which was approval by the Chinese central government. Jampa Phuntsok further suggested that the Dalai Lama should study Buddhism and not get involved in worldly affairs, by which he apparently meant that he should abandon all political activities.

China's 2004 White Paper on Tibetan Autonomy, "Regional Ethnic Autonomy in Tibet," further appeared to close the door on dialogue with the Dalai Lama about Tibetan autonomy.[46] It declared that China would not alter the system of autonomy in Tibet and envisioned no role for the Dalai Lama in Tibet's future. The White Paper said that the Dalai Lama's proposal that Tibet should enjoy autonomy like the "one country, two systems" or "a high degree of autonomy" as applied to Hong Kong was "totally untenable." Regional ethnic autonomy was declared to be unalterable; therefore, the Dalai Lama's proposals to change the system of autonomy in Tibet were unacceptable.

> The institution of regional ethnic autonomy in Tibet is the logical outcome of the Tibetan people's adherence to development along the road of Chinese-style socialism under the leadership of the Communist Party of China, and also the basic institutional guarantee for Tibetans to be true masters of their own affairs. . . . Regional ethnic autonomy is a basic political system of China, which, together with the National People's Congress system and the system of multi-party cooperation and political consultation led by the Communist Party of China, forms the basic framework of China's political system. The establishment of the Tibet Autonomous Region and the scope of its area are based on the provisions of the Constitution and the Law on Regional Ethnic Autonomy and decided by the conditions past and present. Any act aimed at undermining and changing the regional ethnic autonomy in Tibet is in violation of the Constitution and law and it is unacceptable to the entire Chinese people, including the broad masses of the Tibetan people.

China thus declared that it would not entertain the Dalai Lama's proposals for increased autonomy or an expansion of the territory, "the scope of its area," of the TAR. These were the two main items of the Dalai Lama's proposals: that Tibetans should enjoy "genuine autonomy" and that all Tibetan areas should be joined in a greater Tibetan Autonomous Region. The White Paper denied that the Dalai Lama had any authority to decide anything about Tibet's future, although it maintained a semblance of the policy that the Dalai Lama might be allowed to play some "patriotic" role:

> Since ancient times Tibet has been an inseparable part of Chinese territory, where the Central Government has always exercised effective sovereign jurisdiction over the region. . . . It must be pointed out that the local government of Tibet headed by the Dalai representing feudal serfdom under theocracy has long since been replaced by the democratic administration established by the Tibetan people themselves. The destiny and future of Tibet can no longer be decided by the Dalai Lama and his clique. Rather, it can only be decided by the whole Chinese nation, including the Tibetan people. This is an objective political fact in Tibet that cannot be denied or shaken. The Central Government's policy as regards the Dalai Lama is consistent and clear. It is hoped that the Dalai Lama will look reality in the face, make a correct judgment of the situation, truly relinquish his stand for "Tibet independence," and do something beneficial to the progress of China and the region of Tibet in his remaining years.

China thus denied that the future of Tibet could be decided by Tibetans alone; rather, it must be decided by all the Chinese people. The White Paper declared that the current system of autonomy was appropriate and successful; therefore, there was no need to talk to the Dalai Lama or anyone else about any alterations or improvements.

The White Paper's rejection of the Dalai Lama's negotiation points was echoed in 2006 in an article by "Yedor," of the China Tibet Information Center, published by Xinhua.[47] The article was written in reply to the Dalai Lama's 10 March 2006 statement in which he proposed to visit Buddhist sites in China on pilgrimage. Such a visit had also been proposed by his envoys during their February 2006 visit. The Dalai Lama said that he wanted to see for himself the changes and developments in the PRC and that he hoped to meet Chinese leaders so they could reduce their suspicion of him and come to believe that he had really given up Tibetan independence.

> I have stated time and again that I do not wish to seek Tibet's separation from China, but that I will seek its future within the framework of the Chinese constitution. Anyone who has heard this statement would realize, unless his or her view of reality is clouded by suspicion, that my demand for genuine self-rule does not amount to a demand for separation. . . . I have only one demand: self-rule and genuine autonomy for all Tibetans, i.e., the Tibetan nationality in its entirety.[48]

The Kashag of the Tibetan government-in-exile made a similar statement:

> His Holiness the Dalai Lama has adopted and pursued the Middle Way policy in which he does not seek independence for Tibet. This is in accordance with Deng

Xiaoping's assurance that except for independence all issues could be resolved through negotiations. Therefore, we believe that the fundamental differences between the two sides have already been resolved.[49]

The Chinese side immediately rejected the Dalai Lama's proposed visit as well as his claim that he had given up independence. The Yedor article by the China Tibet Information Center was a lengthy and detailed reply to the Dalai Lama and a rejection of his appeal for dialogue. It may also have been written in response to a series of incidents in Tibet in May and June 2006 that were unsettling for the Chinese leadership. The first incident was provoked by a message from the Dalai Lama delivered to Tibetans who had come to India for a Kalachakra ceremony in early 2006. In reply to Indian criticism of Tibetans who wore the fur of endangered species like the Indian tiger and the Himalayan snow leopard, the Dalai Lama called on Tibetans to cease the practice of using these skins. The response was dramatic: Tibetans within Tibet not only stopped wearing fur-lined garments but even organized bonfires of the skins and closed shops that sold them. This revelation of the Dalai Lama's influence within Tibet reportedly unnerved the Chinese leaders, who were at the same time claiming that the Dalai Lama was no longer popular and had no influence with Tibetans.

The second incident involved the Buddhist protective spirit, Shugden, whose worship the Dalai Lama had discouraged. China had tried to promote the worship of Shugden in order to oppose the Dalai Lama and to demonstrate that Tibetans did not follow the Dalai Lama's advice in regard to religion. Monks at the Ganden Monastery near Lhasa destroyed a shrine to Shugden, which the local officials interpreted as an expression of support for the Dalai Lama.

The third incident occurred in July, shortly after the vice chairman of the TAR had claimed that Tibetans would not welcome the Dalai Lama's return to Tibet since his splittist activities had adversely affected the economic prosperity and social stability there. Some ten thousand Tibetans of the Amdo region flocked to Kumbum Monastery in the hope of seeing the Dalai Lama, who was rumored to be planning to visit there. The source of the rumor may have been the Dalai Lama's March statement that he wanted to make such a pilgrimage. The rumor proved false, but the incident further served to demonstrate that China's claims that Tibetans no longer cared about the Dalai Lama were also false.

After the first of these events, the CCP called a meeting of local officials in Lhasa in mid-May to criticize the Dalai Lama and to increase vigilance against his influence. Chinese and Tibetan officials and the Tibetan population were encouraged to oppose the Dalai Lama and the hostile international forces of which he was accused of being the leader. The Dalai Lama was denounced as being the commander-in-chief of the splittist political clique plotting Tibet's independence, an agent of the international anti-China forces, and the main cause of social upheaval in Tibet. The goal of the Dalai Lama and the hostile Western forces was said to be to overthrow CCP leadership in Tibet, subvert the socialist system, reject the national regional autonomy system, restore the Dalai Lama's rule in Tibet, and once again condemn the Tibetan people to serfdom and slavery. The Dalai Lama was even accused of violating Tibetans' religious freedom by prohibiting the worship of Shugden. The struggle against the Dalai Lama was described as a matter of life and death, meaning that there could be no compromise. In order to counter the Dalai Lama, more patriotic education was recommended for all Tibetans, especially those in monasteries.

Gyalo Thondup, who was on a visit to China during May and June 2006, said that he noticed a dramatic change in the attitude of Chinese officials with whom he spoke. Never before had he heard such bitter personal criticism of the Dalai Lama from both Chinese and Tibetan officials. He also said that he found that Chinese officials now denied any understanding based on Deng Xiaoping's statement to him in 1979 that "anything but independence" could be discussed.[50]

The cumulative effect of the incidents demonstrating the Dalai Lama's continuing influence in Tibet in the spring of 2006 seems to have been almost as shocking to Chinese and Tibetan officials as the events of 1980, when the reception that the first Dharamsala delegations received in Tibet revealed that the local officials knew nothing about the true sentiments of Tibetans.

The Yedor article began by saying that the Dalai Lama had been telling the world in recent years that he had stopped seeking "Tibetan independence" and had turned toward a "middle way." By this, he said he meant "high-level autonomy" or "real autonomy" in Tibet and other Tibetan-inhabited areas within the framework of the Chinese Constitution. Yedor said that the Dalai Lama's words sounded reasonable at first: that he had given up the "independence of Tibet" and intended to work for the interest of the Tibetans. However, a closer look revealed that the Dalai Lama had just repackaged his previous Tibetan independence stand:

> People who know Tibetan history well know that the Dalai Lama stands for the "independence of Tibet" [since] when he has fled to India in 1959. On June 20, 1960, he held his first press conference in India, and vowed to "restore freedom and the special status Tibet enjoyed before the Chinese invasion in 1950." Thereafter, he made speeches on March 10 each year, vowing to win the "independence of Tibet." Moreover, the Dalai Lama set up his "government in exile" overseas and worked out a "Tibetan constitution." He built up a rebel army in Nepal for border harassments in the ensuing years. In the name of "organizing armed troops to fight their way back into Tibet," he collaborated with the Indian military

and American CIA to organize the "Indian Tibetan special border troops," set up "representative offices" in some countries, and organized the "Tibet youth congress," "Tibet national democratic party" and "Tibet women's federation." All these organizations have engaged in separatist activities overseas.[51]

Yedor claimed that it was only after the United States and India began working to improve relations with China, in the 1970s to the mid-1980s, that the Dalai clique came into difficulties and offered to "give up efforts seeking Tibetan independence and return to China." Thereafter, the Dalai Lama adopted his "middle way" policy. However, Yedor said, this policy "goes against the Chinese Constitution and law" in several ways. First, "the Dalai Lama still refuses to recognize the fact that Tibet is part of China." Second, he "attempts to refute the current political system followed in Tibet according to the Constitution which states that the socialist system is the fundamental system of the PRC." Third, "the Dalai Lama sticks to 'Large Tibetan Areas' that, however, do not exist in history." Fourth, he "distorts the meaning of the autonomous region."

With regard to the first point, Yedor complained that the Dalai Lama had often said that "Tibet was a completely independent state in 1949 when the PLA entered." He had also said that "Tibet is an occupied country under colonial rule." In recent years, the Dalai Lama had changed his tune by saying that the issue could be turned over to historians for discussion and that both sides should refrain from talking about the past and instead focus on the future. "We see that the Dalai Lama publicly refuses the fact that Tibet has since the ancient times been a part of China, and then says that he does not have to talk about this issue," Yedor said. "He does all these to impress the others he has made concession." He added, "It is an historic fact that Tibet has since the ancient times been an inalienable part of the Chinese territory, and the Central Government of China has exercised indisputable and effective rule over Tibet."

Yedor maintained that the Dalai Lama's ostensible concession on the historical issue was in reality an attempt to keep alive his claim that Tibet was an occupied country: "Legally speaking, the so-called 'Tibetan issue' will not then be an internal issue of China; it will then be related to 'colonial issues' whereby the Tibetans could enjoy the right to independence through 'national self-determination' according to international convention." This, he said, "goes against the historical fact that China enjoys sovereignty over Tibet and the principle set forth in the PRC Constitution that areas exercising national regional autonomy are inalienable parts of China." Yedor thus revealed China's sensitivity on the self-determination issue, which was why the Dalai Lama had to give up the idea that Tibet had ever been independent.

On the second point, Yedor wrote that, according to the Chinese Constitution, "no organization or individual is allowed to undermine the socialist system." The law of the PRC states that "national regional autonomy is the basic political system of the CPC to solve China's ethnic issues using Marxism-Leninism." However, the Dalai Lama had declared that "the autonomy China follows is not real autonomy," and that Tibet should have "high-level autonomy" or "real autonomy" according to the "one country, two systems" principle. The Dalai Lama had also said that Tibet should have a political system with some democratic characteristics, such as a legislature and an independent judiciary. What this meant, Yedor wrote, is that

> the CPC leadership, the socialist system, the people's congress system and the national regional autonomy in Tibet, which have been in place in Tibet for decades in accordance with the PRC Constitution, should all be refuted, and a whole new system introduced according to what he says is "real autonomy."

The author further claimed that what the Dalai Lama intended to do under a "one country, two systems" plan in Tibet was not to create democracy but to restore the feudal serf system.

Yedor addressed the third point by asserting that the Dalai Lama's plan to seek an "enlarged Tibet autonomous region" that "would cover one-fourth of Chinese territory" had no precedent in history and was but another part of the Dalai Lama's ulterior motive of eventually seeking Tibetan independence. Yedor cited the Yuan- and Qing-dynasty divisions of Tibet as evidence that the Lhasa government of the Dalai Lama had never directly administered all the Tibetan areas he now claimed ought to form part of one administrative region. Under the national regional autonomy system, he wrote,

> one ethnic group in China may be found in different administrative regions and one administrative region may be home to several ethnic groups. This is the result of historical changes and constitutes a salient feature of the relations between different ethnic groups in China.

As regards the fourth point—the Dalai Lama's "distortion of the meaning of the autonomous region"—Yedor quoted the Dalai Lama as saying that Tibet did not enjoy the autonomous rights supposedly guaranteed to it under the national regional autonomy system. The author criticized the Dalai Lama's "Zone of Peace" proposal, under which Tibet would be demilitarized, saying that this would violate China's right to station troops on its own territory. He also declared that the Dalai Lama's demand that Tibetans be allowed to exercise autonomy in the current TAR as well as in Tibetan autonomous districts outside the TAR was contrary to national regional autonomy under which all nationalities, including the Han, had equal rights in all areas of China. Thus, under national regional autonomy, Tibetans had no exclusive rights of the sort that the Dalai Lama demanded, particularly that Tibet should be an area where Tibetans had an exclusive right to habitation:

> Making non-Tibetans move away from where they have lived for many centuries so as to satisfy the Dalai Lama goes against the PRC Constitution and the Law on National Regional Autonomy, and shows that, once the Dalai Lama becomes leader of Tibet again, he will follow policies featuring national discrimination and national purge.

The Yedor article concluded with the claim that while the Dalai Lama talked about seeking a way out within the framework of the Chinese constitution, in fact his proposals were contrary to it: "This shows that what he pursues is a swindle and nothing stands between his 'high-level autonomy' and 'Tibetan independence.'" Tibetan exiles were quoted as saying that the Dalai Lama's acceptance of autonomy was only for the purpose of eventually seeking independence. Yedor accused the Dalai Lama of having changed his attitude with the changing tide in international affairs. He quoted international sources that reported that the Dalai Lama had expressed hope for Tibetan independence after the collapse of the Soviet Union in 1990 and threatened to return to an independence policy if China refused to negotiate with him. "Given the fact that the Dalai Lama gives out different signals at different times and even at the same time, one can hardly agree his 'middle way' is different from 'Tibetan independence.'"

> The Central Government has made public its views on the Dalai's "middle way" over the past 20 years, but the Dalai Lama still hates to say bye to his proposals which are "independence of Tibet" in nature. . . . If the Dalai Lama is sincere in improving ties with the Central Government, he needs, first and foremost, to have an objective understanding of the political reality in Tibet and, on this basis, re-think his political propositions. Only by truly giving up his "Tibetan independence" policy, can the Dalai Lama win the confidence of others and create conditions for him to do something in the interest of Tibet.

The 2004 White Paper and the China Tibet Information Center's Yedor article were the clearest and most detailed rejections of dialogue with the Dalai Lama. Meanwhile, China also continued its personal denunciations of him. China's new hard-line party chief in the TAR, Zhang Qingli, accused the Dalai Lama of engaging in activities unrelated to religion, saying he was an unworthy religious leader. Zhang said that the Dalai Lama was once a legitimate religious leader of Tibet and was appointed to China's National People's Congress and the Preparatory Committee for the TAR, which demonstrated

China's policy of religious freedom. However, the Dalai Lama had then betrayed his country, Zhang said, and since then he had allied himself with anti-China and separatist forces, which was contrary to his role as a religious leader:

> The Dalai Lama used to be an acknowledged religious leader, which is an undoubted fact, but what he has done makes him unworthy of the title. The Dalai Lama staged a failed armed rebellion against the Chinese government in the late 1950's and stirred social unrest in Lhasa in the late 1980's. By the end of the first half of this year he had paid 312 "official visits" to other countries, averaging six visits a year, while last year he made 12 overseas journeys. The goals of his "official visits" are to ally himself with anti-China forces and publicize his separatist beliefs, which deviate from the practice of religion.[52]

Zhang expressed his wonder that the Dalai Lama had been awarded the Nobel Peace Prize, saying that he had not done anything to promote peace. Zhang said that despite the Dalai Lama's past, he would be welcome to return to China if he would abandon his separatist ideas. He also said that the next Dalai Lama would be chosen by the traditional Tibetan practice of drawing lots from a golden urn.

Zhang's comments illustrate the wide gap between Chinese and Tibetan understanding of the political issue of Tibet. Zhang expressed the Chinese position that the only political activities allowable for a religious leader like the Dalai Lama were patriotic activities such as playing a role in Chinese political organizations. This assumes that China has a monopoly on political legitimacy in Tibet without any concessions to Tibetan autonomy. Zhang's comments were based on the belief that there was no political issue of Tibet's special status that the Dalai Lama represented. Zhang was formerly head of the Xinjiang Production and Construction Corps, the organization responsible for Chinese colonization in Xinjiang. His appointment in Tibet, in conjunction with the completion of the railroad to Lhasa, indicated that China's policy in Tibet would continue to deny Tibetan autonomy in favor of economic development and that this would be accompanied by Chinese colonization.

In response to China's rejection of all the Dalai Lama's proposals, and specifically in response to the Yedor article, the Dalai Lama's special envoy, Lodi Gyari, reiterated the Dalai Lama's position in a speech at the Brookings Institution in Washington, D.C., on 14 November 2006.[53] The speech was also apparently an attempt to stimulate a response from the Chinese, who had shown little willingness to talk since the last delegation visit in February 2006.

Gyari began by saying that he would for the first time publicly give the details of the dialogue process to date. He had previously refrained from giving any details, he said, because "China prefers to operate cautiously and free of scrutiny," and thus the Tibetan side felt that "to openly discuss the dialogue could adversely impact the process." However, the Chinese had been briefing foreign diplomats about the discussions, and some articles in the Chinese media, particularly the Yedor article, had "led to the circulation of speculative, uninformed, and one-sided information about some of the important issues at stake."

Gyari said that the five rounds of discussion so far had "brought our dialogue to a new level." There was a "deeper understanding of each other's positions and the recognition of where the fundamental differences lie." He claimed that despite the apparent lack of progress on these differences, "the very fact that the two sides have been able to explicitly state our differences represents a significant development." The Tibetan side was encouraged by the Chinese leadership's adoption of a new slogan about the creation of a "harmonious society" within China and a "peaceful rise" internationally. Gyari said that a resolution of the Tibet issue was essential to China's achievement of a harmonious society and "embracing its diversity and protecting the identity of the Tibetan people is integral to China's successful 'peaceful rise.'"

He then went on to explicate the primary issues involved in the dialogue with the Chinese leadership. These, he said, were based upon the Dalai Lama's "firm commitment to a resolution that has Tibet as part of the People's Republic of China." The essential issues were the unity of all Tibetans in one administrative entity and the genuine autonomy of the Tibetan people within the framework of China's constitution.

China's lack of trust in the Dalai Lama and the Tibetan people was one of the obstacles to the dialogue, Gyari said. He noted that one of the reasons for this lack of trust was the historical issue. The Dalai Lama had suggested that both sides avoid revisiting history, since they had different viewpoints of their past relations:

> Debates over Tibet's history, before we have reached mutual trust and confidence, are counter productive, making it more difficult for the Tibetans and Chinese alone to untangle this issue. . . . In 1979 Deng Xiaoping laid down the framework for resolving the issue of Tibet by stating that other than the issue of Tibetan independence anything else could be discussed and resolved. . . . The Middle Way approach represents the Dalai Lama's commitment to look to the future, instead of the past, to find a solution that will provide maximum autonomy for the Tibetan people and bring peace and stability to the PRC and the whole region.

Since the Dalai Lama had conceded on the issue of Tibet's political status, Gyari suggested that China should "reciprocate by acknowledging the legitimate needs of the Tibetan people." These were for a union of all Tibetan areas and a granting of "genuine autonomy" to all. On the territorial issue, "Just as the Chinese nation has sought to unify many different regions into one nation, the Tibetan people, too, yearn to be under one administrative entity so that their way of life, tradition, and religion can be more effectively and peacefully maintained." Gyari said that the Chinese had countered this proposal by saying that the present TAR corresponded to the territory actually administered by the Dalai Lama's government. The Chinese also suggested that since all of Tibet was a part of China then the administrative borders within Tibet were unimportant.[54]

Gyari contended that all the areas of Tibetan habitation were already designated as Tibetan autonomous regions or districts; therefore, their unification would be nothing more than an administrative change. Such unification would be consistent with the PRC's minority nationality laws, which specified that minorities should be grouped in autonomous areas according to "contiguous habitation" and without regard to previous historical boundaries. "The Tibetan people are striving for the right of a distinct people to be able to preserve that very distinctiveness through a single administrative entity."

Gyari implied that China did not allow Tibetans the autonomous rights provided to them in its constitution and according to the law on ethnic autonomy, namely, full political right of autonomy, full decision-making power in economic and social development undertakings, freedom to inherit and develop their traditional culture, freedom to practice their religious beliefs, and freedom to administer, protect, and be the first to utilize their own natural resources. He denied that the Dalai Lama's demand for autonomy meant that he intended to restore the serf system in Tibet; the only type of autonomy the Tibetans wanted was the kind that would allow them to be "able to survive as a distinct and prosperous people within the PRC."

Gyari denied that he or the Dalai Lama had suggested that Tibet should have a status as a special administrative region like Hong Kong, or that Tibet should have the same status as Hong Kong or as was offered by China to Taiwan. He did, however, assert that Tibet was due some status that acknowledged its special characteristics, citing the Seventeen-Point Agreement as evidence that the PRC had recognized Tibet's special status in the past and had promised it a large degree of political autonomy. The Dalai Lama had never demanded that Tibet be a territory of exclusive Tibetan habitation or that the People's Liberation Army (PLA) should be entirely withdrawn, Gyari insisted, although he noted that the large influx of Chinese to Tibet and the militarization of the plateau were problems that must be addressed.

The special envoy ended with an appeal to the Chinese to resolve the Tibet issue while the Fourteenth Dalai Lama was still alive:

> In the absence of the Dalai Lama, there is no way that the entire population would be able to contain their resentment and anger. . . . With His Holiness' unambiguous commitment to the integrity and sovereignty of the PRC, China's leaders must recognize the aspirations of the Tibetans to survive as a distinct people, a commitment that is already enshrined in China's laws. . . . In looking forward to finding a solution for Tibet, it is in China's best interest to have the Tibetan people accept their place within the PRC of their own free will.

The clarity of Gyari's assurances to the Chinese that the Dalai Lama wanted only the type of autonomy provided for in China's constitution was obscured by a Dharamsala official's statement in India shortly after the Brookings event. Tempa Tsering, the *kalon* (minister) in charge of the Department of Information and International Relations, told the International Conference of Autonomous Regions, organized by Dharamsala, that Tibetan autonomy would include a democratic system of government with an elected legislature and executive. He said that the PLA could remain in Tibet only until Tibet was transformed into a "zone of peace."[55] Such statements were likely to be used by the Chinese to bolster their contention that the type of autonomy the Dalai Lama demanded was just a step toward the ultimate goal of independence.

In January 2007, Zhang Qingli, in an article in *Quishi*, the official journal of the CCP Central Committee, urged a continuous struggle against the Dalai clique and its attempts to separate Tibet from China. Zhang said that social harmony was the essence of socialism with Chinese characteristics, that Tibet was an important and sensitive border area, and that development and stability were key to building a harmonious Tibet. He proclaimed that the separatist activities of the Dalai clique were the greatest obstacle to Tibet's stability and development and the creation of a harmonious society.

> Tibet's strategic position is extremely important; it is an important security screen in China's southwest. Tibet's special features in history, current state, environment, and geography determine that its development and stability are always closely linked to national sovereignty and security. Tibet is a focal point in our struggle with international anti-China forces. The desire of hostile forces to finish us is still alive, their desire to throw us into chaos has not changed, and they have all along tried to make use of the so-called Tibet question to contain and split China. Supported by international anti-China forces, the Dalai clique has continually changed its methods, frequently caused incidents, damaged social stability, and plotted so-called Tibet independence. It has all along been the greatest obstacle to Tibet's development and stability, and also the evil force sabotaging the unity of the motherland and ethnic solidarity. Our struggle against

the Dalai clique and the western hostile forces supporting it is long term, sharp, intense and complex.[56]

This makes it obvious that the chairman of the CCP in Tibet had no intention of being respectful toward the Dalai Lama and had received no instructions from Beijing to do so. There was nothing in Zhang's statement to indicate that China was in any mood to dialogue or negotiate with the Dalai Lama about Tibetan autonomy or Tibet's future.

The Yedor article was followed by one attributed to "Yan Zheng" (a pseudonym meaning "true speech") on the website of the China Tibet Information Center.[57] This article repeated the usual themes that the Dalai Lama had a history of seeking independence and of changing his tactics according to the international situation. His ultimate goal, however, had always been independence and his strategy of accepting autonomy was merely a subterfuge for this goal.

Yan Zheng accused the Dalai Lama of misinterpreting the situation of the early 1980s and of abusing China's conditions for dialogue:

> After the 14th Dalai Lama and his clique sent some people back to make an investigation and study, they came to a wrong conclusion, believing that they still had a market among the Tibetans and took advantage of the central government's policy of leniency to do many things in which they complied with the policy in public while opposing it in private.

The apparent meaning of this statement is that China continues to deny the reality that the delegation visits of that time revealed that Tibetans remained loyal to the Dalai Lama. The Tibetans were accused of violating the Chinese understanding of the conditions for dialogue, meaning that the Tibetans in negotiations had accepted Chinese sovereignty, while continuing to oppose it by claiming that Tibet had been independent and by other splittist activities.

The article went on to say that the Dalai Lama had used the period after the "instigated by Western forces June 4 political incident" to increase his separatist activities and had adopted his strategy of accepting Tibetan autonomy under China only after China survived that crisis and began to acquire greater economic and political influence. However, the article said, any good and honest person can see that "the essence of [the Dalai Lama's] 'true autonomy' is to strive for Tibetan independence in disguise."

The Dalai Lama's most deceptive and unacceptable claims were listed as: that Tibet was an independent country; that the PLA should withdraw from Tibet; that Tibet should have diplomatic relations with other countries; that all Tibetan areas should form one greater Tibet autonomous region; and that this region should be for the exclusive inhabitation of Tibetans. His demands, particularly that the status of Tibet should be the subject of international debate, that China should not have the right to station military forces in Tibet, and that Tibet should have diplomatic relations with other countries, were the equivalent of denying Chinese sovereignty over Tibet. "Therefore, the 'true autonomy' advocated by Dalai Lama is essentially aimed to change the legal status of Tibet and to negate that the central government of China has sovereignty over Tibet." This, the article said, was part of the Dalai Lama's three-stage strategy to "return to Tibet through negotiation," to "seize political power through 'true autonomy,'" and then to "have his dream of an independent greater Tibet come true through a 'general referendum.'"

The Yan Zheng essay condemned the proposal for a greater Tibetan Autonomous Region as an attempt to "overthrow the socialist system and the system of regional autonomy for ethnic minorities in Tibet and other areas inhabited by Tibetans and to put all Tibetan affairs under the control of the 14th Dalai Lama." The idea that all non-Tibetan peoples should be removed from Tibetan areas was compared to the "partition of India and Pakistan and the tragedy of the ethnic movements" that took place because of that political division.

This issue was the subject of further commentary that revealed much about Chinese psychology with respect to Tibet. One article by "Chinese Tibetologists and scholars of ethnic religion" accused the Dalai Lama of promoting ethnic conflict by characterizing the Tibet issue as one of conflict between two different ethnic groups and by demanding true autonomy in Tibet, the result of which would inevitably "incite the populist sentiments of the Tibetan people" and make them "regard the Hans as outsiders, to the extent that they will expel the Hans." The Dalai Lama's promotion of ethnic conflict was cited as evidence that he was insincere in his doctrine of nonviolence. This article also mentioned the Dalai Lama's warning that he could not guarantee that Tibetans would adhere to the path of nonviolence after he was no longer alive.[58] The Chinese seemed to interpret this as a threat to promote violence in Tibet and perhaps internationally if the Dalai Lama did not get what he wants.

Another commentary took up the issue of the Dalai Lama having said that the new railroad to Lhasa would result in cultural genocide in Tibet. It declared that this false claim by the Dalai Lama was a result of his mistaken understanding of the nature of culture. The Dalai Lama claimed that Tibetan culture and national identity are separate from that of China and that therefore China was eradicating Tibetan culture. However, the article said, Tibetan culture is just one aspect of Chinese culture, and the development of Tibetan culture within Chinese culture is a positive development that is not equivalent to eradication.[59]

A further commentary by yet another supposedly independent Chinese scholar condemned the Dalai Lama for having characterized the issue of Tibet as a dispute between two different ethnic groups. This author repeated the argument that ethnic conflict would result in Tibet if the Dalai Lama achieved his goal of genuine autonomy. He cited the example of what happened when the Soviet Union collapsed. The situation for many Russians in the non-Russian republics became difficult after these republics achieved their independence. This fact was used to argue that the independence of those republics had led to ethnic conflict.[60] According to this argument, the source of ethnic conflict is not the forcible inclusion of minority nationalities within an empire, like the Soviet Union or the PRC, in which one nationality dominates all others, but rather is the independence of nationalities, or their self-determination, upon the dissolution of such an empire.

A primary theme of the Yan Zheng article and its commentaries was that any semblance of real autonomy in Tibet would lead to a revival of Tibetan nationalism and the oppression of non-Tibetan nationalities, including the Han Chinese, by the Tibetans. This is an extraordinary perversion of the reality of Tibet's recent history of invasion by China and oppression of Tibetans by the Chinese. The essence of this argument reflects the Chinese belief that Tibetans are not loyal to China because they are not Chinese, and the fear that, if Tibetans had any real political authority, they would retaliate for the history of Chinese mistreatment. For these reasons, the Chinese seem to believe they cannot allow any real Tibetan autonomy, neither that demanded by the Dalai Lama nor that promised by themselves.

The Yan Zheng article advised that the Dalai Lama and his clique might be willing to "stoop to compromise and may come up with even lower conditions, but their doing so is all aimed at concealing the objective of Tibet independence. Good and honest people must never be confused and deceived by their flowery words and cunning statements." Therefore, China should not negotiate with the Dalai Lama even if he offered further concessions since his real aim would always be Tibetan independence.

Dharamsala's representatives responded to the Yan Zheng article by saying that China had misinterpreted the Dalai Lama's conditions, particularly that the PLA should be withdrawn from Tibet or that Chinese settlers should have to leave. However, the Dalai Lama had said that Tibet should be significantly demilitarized and that the problem of excessive Chinese migration to Tibet should be addressed. This exchange between the two sides revealed that the Tibetans did not comprehend the level of Chinese mistrust of the Dalai Lama and their intolerance of any degree of Tibetan autonomy.

Dialogue or Deadlock?

In its official statements, such as the 2004 White Paper and the Yedor article, as well as in statements by Chinese and Tibetan officials, China has consistently rejected the Dalai Lama's overtures point by point. China denies that the Dalai Lama's envoys represent anyone but themselves, that China has engaged with them in a dialogue about Tibet, or that there is any unresolved issue about Tibet except the Dalai Lama's personal future. Beijing also denies that there is any lingering historical issue of Tibet's status that it must resolve with Tibet's exiled religious leader. It rejects the Dalai Lama's proposal that all Tibetan areas be united in one administrative region. The White Paper on regional autonomy declared the PRC's national regional autonomy system inviolable and its application in Tibet appropriate and unalterable. The Chinese do not acknowledge any mutual understanding based upon Deng Xiaoping's 1979 statement that "anything but independence could be discussed."

Lodi Gyari's 2006 Brookings speech was an attempt to further the dialogue by dispelling China's mistrust of the Dalai Lama's intentions, establishing trust and confidence between the two sides, and creating as much as possible the "conducive atmosphere" required by the Chinese as a condition for discussions. Gyari explained that China had mistakenly interpreted the Dalai Lama's desire to look to the future rather than the past as meaning that he had "some sort of hidden agenda." Presumably the Chinese were suspicious that the Dalai Lama did not want to delve into the past because he did not want to abandon his claim that Tibet had once been independent. The Dalai Lama's conditions, from the Chinese viewpoint, were evidence that he did not fully recognize the legitimacy of Chinese sovereignty over Tibet.

The Dalai Lama's appeal to the Chinese to avoid "revisiting history" may have actually been based on the Tibetan understanding of Deng's 1979 conditions for dialogue. Deng at that time suggested that both sides should avoid history in order to address current issues within the context of a new era of post-Maoist Chinese politics. What Deng essentially proposed was that China would forgive the Dalai Lama's treason in 1959 if the Tibetans would forget about the repression of Tibetans and destruction of Tibetan culture since then. Deng also presumably wanted the Tibetans to give up any ideas related to a claim of Tibet's former independence, which is likely what he meant by his statement that there could be no discussions until the independence issue was dropped. However, the Chinese miscalculated in imagining that the independence issue was indeed dead or that Tibetans were reconciled to Chinese rule and would be forgiving of abuses of the past in the light of China's newly liberalized policies. China soon found that the historical issues were far from dead within Tibet.

China was suspicious of the Dalai Lama's current offer to ignore historical issues, since they regarded all his demands as being based on Tibet's former independence. For the Chinese, the historical issue could not be ignored. Tibet had to have been a part of China before 1950—and accepted as so by the Dalai Lama—so that China could not be accused, by the Dalai Lama or anyone else, of imperialist aggression against Tibet or lack of legitimate sovereignty over it. The issue of Tibet's former status could not be disregarded by China, because if Tibet had ever been independent, then the issue of Tibetan national self-determination might arise at any time in the future. This is what Chinese officials like Yedor meant when they accused the Dalai Lama of saying that Tibet was "once a country" or was now an occupied country in order to demand self-determination at some time in the future.

The Chinese were also adamant about the territorial issue. Gyari revealed that the Chinese had complained that if all Tibetan areas were combined in one autonomous region, it would constitute one-fourth of the total territory of the PRC. Presumably the Chinese fear that such a large territory united under one political administration would appear on the map much like a separate country. Having successfully divided Tibet, the Chinese were naturally loath to allow it to reunify, even under a Tibetan administration with only theoretical autonomy. They were deaf to appeals that the PRC's National Regional Autonomy law specified that autonomous territories should be established in "areas where people of minority nationalities live in compact communities." Tibetan areas were all contiguous and, according to China's own criteria, should constitute one unified autonomous territory, but the Chinese preferred to cite historical reasons why this could not be done.

Chinese spokespersons rationalized, for example, that although all Tibetan areas are contiguous, they have not been unified for a long time; thus, the subcultures have diverged. Furthermore, the economic relations of these areas are with the provinces into which they have been integrated. There would be no benefit, they claimed, in redirecting the economies and cultures of the autonomous Tibetan districts toward central Tibet rather than toward the more prosperous, and presumably more culturally advanced, Chinese provinces to which they were now attached. The divisive and assimilationist goals of this argument are obvious. The Chinese government also had to contend with the Chinese administrations of the provinces in which the Tibetan autonomous districts were included: Qinghai, Gansu, Sichuan, and Yunnan. All of these, particularly Sichuan, had their historical claims to parts of Tibet that they were reluctant to surrender.

Another extremely important factor had to do with water and hydropower resources. Water shortages loomed as one of China's major resource shortages, and plans had already been made to divert waters from the upper reaches of the Yangtze River to the Yellow River. The middle sections of the Yangtze in Sichuan (Jinsa Jiang or Dri Chu) have an estimated hydropower potential twice that of the Three Gorges Dam and were the site of major dam construction and planning. China's unexploited hydropower resources, a majority of which were on the edges of the Tibetan Plateau, mostly in the tributaries of the Yangtze in Sichuan and Yunnan, were four times that already exploited.

China's two major rivers have their sources in Qinghai, while the rivers within the TAR—the Brahmaputra (Tsangpo), Salween, and Mekong—all drain to other countries. The inclusion of the headwaters of the Yangtze and Yellow rivers in the "Chinese" province of Qinghai was not an accident of history. The Mongol Yuan and Manchu Qing dynasty divisions of Tibet intentionally placed the headwaters of the two rivers in administrative districts separated from central Tibet. The Qing, even though a conquest dynasty, were particularly intent upon discovering and claiming as Qing territory the headwaters of the Yellow and Yangtze rivers. Early in the Qing period (1709–1721), the K'ang Hsi emperor sponsored a Jesuit mapping expedition to Tibet and produced a series of maps showing Tibet as part of the Qing empire.[61] The Chinese Republican government in 1914 negotiated more forcefully about this division—keeping the rivers in "Inner Tibet"—than about the status of "Outer Tibet."

China has recently implemented a Three Rivers Source Protection Scheme involving the headwaters of the Yangtze, Yalong (a branch of the Yangtze), and Yellow rivers, all in the grasslands of Qinghai, in order to preserve China's water resources.[62] This has required the removal and settlement of most Tibetan nomads of the area, the richest grasslands in Tibet, with little regard for the consequent destruction of the important nomadic component of Tibetan culture. The headwaters of the Yellow and Yangtze were once an area of wetlands and lakes that acted much like a sponge, before being drained by the Chinese in the 1950s to create more pasture. The grasslands were subsequently degraded by Chinese policies for increased production. Nevertheless, the Chinese blamed the degradation of the grasslands on the nomads' "unscientific" lifestyles and decreed that they must settle and pursue other, more modern occupations. This project emphasizes China's proprietary interest in this area and demonstrates why China has rejected the Dalai Lama's proposal to reunite eastern Tibet with central Tibet in a greater TAR. China is not likely to give up the headwaters of China's major rivers to an autonomous Tibet, especially if that autonomy were to include any control of natural resources.

Ultimately, the most important reason that the Chinese were opposed to both a unified Tibetan autonomous territory and "genuine" autonomy may be the same reason that the Dalai Lama was for it: so that Tibetans might survive as a distinct culture and people. The Chinese cannot be assumed to share the Tibetans' desire that Tibet remain a distinct nation. The Chinese may be suspected of seeking the dissolution of Tibet's separate national distinctiveness as much as Tibetans want to preserve it. China naturally seeks to eradicate Tibetan national identity, because nations have the tendency to want national self-determination and are supported in that quest by international law. For China, the resolution of the Tibet issue had already been accomplished, in 1950 and 1959, through the elimination of a separate Tibetan political administration. China had done everything in its power to eradicate even the memory of a Tibet separate from China—except as an evil Hell on Earth. The Chinese were understandably reluctant to re-create any semblance of a separate Tibetan administration or allow it to control any territory at all, much less all the territory inhabited by Tibetans. They were unlikely to want to reopen a historical issue already resolved entirely in their favor. They had done so to some extent in 1957 and again in the 1980s with unanticipated results they did not wish to repeat.

The Chinese seemed to regard the Dalai Lama's claim that Tibetans did not enjoy genuine autonomy as equivalent to a denial of the legitimacy of Chinese sovereignty over Tibet. The Dalai Lama's challenge to the national regional autonomy system was thought to be based upon some presumed authority he and Tibet derived from a previous status of independence. For the Chinese, therefore, the Dalai Lama had to abandon any claim against China based upon Tibetan independence in the past. He had to accept that China had absolute authority over Tibet and that he had no standing upon which to even suggest that China should alter its administration of Tibet. Like the territorial issue, China considered the autonomy issue settled after Tibet's peaceful liberation and democratic reforms. China had experienced many ups and downs in its Tibet policy and had been unpleasantly surprised by the resilience of Tibetan nationalism in the 1980s. It had learned through trial and error that it could not allow genuine Tibetan autonomy. Tibetan autonomy might permit a distinct Tibetan cultural and national identity to survive, which was exactly what the Dalai Lama wanted but was exactly what China did not want, because a separate Tibetan national entity within a separate territory was seen as posing an intolerable threat to China's national unity and security.

Lodi Gyari's appeal to China's new Harmonious Society and Peaceful Rise policies was an unfortunate attempt to convince the Chinese of the Dalai Lama's adherence to current Chinese political culture and his willingness to repeat the CCP's slogans. The "harmonious society" and "harmonious world" slogans ("peaceful rise" was replaced after it raised international apprehensions) were conceived by Hu Jintao as his signature doctrine. The harmonious society ideal owes much to Confucianism and may be regarded as sharing that philosophy's emphasis on conformity to authority. The "harmonious world" slogan appeared to be intended primarily for propaganda purposes. What it seemed to mean, based upon China's actions in venues like the UN Human Rights Council, was that China or any other authoritarian country should be respected for its different political system and should be immune from criticism on that basis.

The best example of this doctrine was the unvarying Chinese Foreign Ministry response to any criticism of China as "baseless," "groundless," and "without foundation." Another example was the Chinese priority in the Sino-Tibetan dialogue of demanding that Tibetans create a "conducive atmosphere" for dialogue, especially by not demonstrating against Chinese leaders abroad. Gyari suggested that the acceptance of their inclusion within the PRC by the Tibetan people, "of their own free will," was essential for China to achieve a harmonious society. However, a skeptic might argue that given a truly free choice, Tibetans would choose independence, and knowing that, the Chinese would never allow sufficient autonomy for the Tibetans to have such a free choice.

Despite China's absolute rejection of any dialogue about the "issue of Tibet" and its constant denunciations of the Dalai Lama, Tibetan exile leaders continually reiterated their interpretation of Deng Xiaoping's comments in 1979, as this was the only basis for their hope for any discussions about the nature or scope of Tibetan autonomy. Dharamsala declared that, despite the lack of any progress, the Middle Way Approach—now dignified with its own abbreviation, MWA—would continue.[63] The Tibetan exile government organized educational sessions about the MWA in Dharamsala, New Delhi, and each of the Tibetan settlements in India. Dharamsala claimed that the Middle Way was democratically chosen by the Tibetans in exile and, by implication, those within Tibet as well, although the reality was that most Tibetans had simply expressed a typical willingness to pursue whatever path the Dalai Lama preferred. Tibetan exile leaders defended the policy as their only option, since any dialogue was arguably better than no dialogue, but many Tibetans criticized the policy for playing into China's hands.

Dharamsala's policy was determined not only by the lack of any perceived alternatives and, some would say, by wishful thinking but also by the realities of international support. The Dalai Lama won the Nobel Peace Prize in 1989 due to his conciliatory policy of accepting Tibetan autonomy within China (and the Nobel Committee's interest in making a statement about China after the June 1989 Tiananmen Square massacre). His international support since then has been substantially based on his Middle Path and dialogue policies. Were the Dalai Lama to suddenly admit the failure of this policy and demand Tibet's right to independence, his official welcome in many foreign capitals would probably be withdrawn. This was a lesson the exiled Tibetans had learned as early as 1959 when Gyalo Thondup was persuaded to pursue the human rights issue rather than Tibetan independence at the United Nations.

Dharamsala maintained that it had done what it could to meet China's conditions for dialogue, which were that the Dalai Lama give up his independence stand, accept the reality of China's sovereignty over Tibet (and Taiwan), and cease his splittist activities. Dharamsala repeatedly maintained that it had met China's conditions and that the only possible reason China did not accept this must be due to some misunderstanding. The Tibetans said that the Dalai Lama had given up independence and expressed mystification that the Chinese could not accept this fact. To this, the Chinese replied that if the Dalai Lama truly accepted the legitimacy of the Chinese administration in Tibet, then why did he maintain a government-in-exile? This confirms the opinion that the existence of the government-in-exile was one of the splittist activities that the Chinese insisted the Dalai Lama must abandon. Dharamsala's change of name from "government-in-exile" to "Central Tibetan Administration" (referring to the administration of Tibetan settlements in India) had failed to convince the Chinese that the Dharamsala government did not claim to represent Tibetans inside Tibet.

Tibetan attempts to convince the Chinese that the Dalai Lama had given up independence took some rather bizarre forms. After his last visit to China, Tibetan envoy Lodi Gyari said that the Chinese had complained that the Dalai Lama had said in a speech that Tibetans "deserved independence." However, Gyari denied the Dalai Lama had said this. Later, after making a search of the Dalai Lama's speeches to find to what the Chinese were referring, Gyari found that the Dalai Lama had said that Tibetans deserved "freedom," *rangwang,* not "independence," *rangzen.* The Tibetan envoy therefore thought that the Chinese were simply mistaken about what the Dalai Lama had actually said. However, more likely they interpreted freedom as being equivalent to independence. Perhaps the Chinese understood better than the Dalai Lama did that Tibetan freedom was not possible under Chinese rule.

Dharamsala also maintained that it had significantly adhered to China's conditions about splittist activities, given its suggestions to Tibetans and their supporters that they not demonstrate against Chinese leaders. Chinese officials had reportedly demanded that Dharamsala issue such a statement as a condition for a continuation of the dialogue, and Dharamsala had complied. However, the Chinese seem to have imagined that a word from the Dalai Lama would suffice to prevent all such embarrassments to Chinese leaders abroad. The Chinese were unrelenting in their contention that the Dalai Lama had not satisfied this or any of their conditions. They constantly complained about the Dalai Lama's international travels and his meetings with foreign leaders, all of which they apparently defined as splittist activities.

For the Dalai Lama and his envoys, the purpose of the Sino-Tibetan dialogue was to resolve the issue of Tibet. However, the Chinese admitted to no such issue and consistently refused to talk about it; therefore, there must have been some other reason for the Chinese willingness to engage in contacts. One obvious reason was to satisfy China's international critics, who were constantly suggesting that Chinese officials should talk with the Dalai Lama. Other reasons may be revealed by China's conditions. China demanded that the Dalai Lama recognize Chinese sovereignty over Tibet and refused to accept that this was satisfied by his acceptance of Tibetan autonomy under Chinese rule. China's conditions seemed to imply that the legitimacy of Chinese sovereignty over Tibet, past, present, or future, should be unchallenged by the Dalai Lama or anyone else. This condition apparently included not only Tibet's former political status but *all* political issues of Tibet, which the Chinese assumed to be founded upon Tibetan claims about Tibet's former status, including the "nature and the scope" of Tibetan autonomy. Therefore, for the Dalai Lama to fulfill Chinese conditions, he would presumably have to give up the idea that there were *any* issues of Tibet that China would discuss with him or make any concessions about.

China's goal also seemed to include the curtailment of all the Dalai Lama's international activities, including all his meetings with international leaders. The Dalai Lama should also presumably abolish the Tibetan government-in-exile, since the very existence of that government implied that the Dalai Lama did not accept the legitimacy of the Chinese government in Tibet. Fundamentally, what the Chinese required of the Dalai Lama was that he abandon his separatism, renounce his treasonous activities, and pledge allegiance to the CCP, after which he would, perhaps, be allowed to "return to the Motherland." Were the Chinese to achieve all this, and assuming they no longer really wanted the Dalai Lama to return to China, then they would have achieved all their objectives and would have no reason to dialogue, much less make any concessions.

For the Chinese, the resolution of the "issue of Tibet" would come about when the Dalai Lama and his international supporters stopped complaining about China's policies in Tibet, not by China making any changes in those policies to satisfy outside criticism. As the Tibetan filmmaker Tenzing Sonam has written:

> To the Chinese government, after all, the talks are not about discussing the Middle Way approach, but rather about how to neutralize the Dalai Lama's influence once and for all, both inside and outside Tibet. Gestures of goodwill on the part of the Kashag will ultimately mean nothing to China, other than to give its international image a public-relations boost. The only "conducive atmosphere," as far as Beijing is concerned, is one wherein the Dalai Lama ceases to exert influence of any sort in Tibet.[64]

China's duplicitous strategy toward the recent series of Tibetan delegation visits was revealed by a comment by Chen Yonglin, a Chinese diplomat who defected in 2005 from the Chinese embassy in Australia. He revealed that China had an extensive program of spying in almost every country of importance and that it was particularly interested in the activities of dissident overseas Chinese. Chen was an authority on nationalities affairs and had been assigned to monitor the activities in Australia of Tibetan and other dissident groups such as Falun Gong. While in Canada in 2007, in response to a question from a Tibetan reporter about the recent dialogue, Chen described the exercise as a "tactic by China": "There is no sincerity from the Chinese side; it is impossible for you to get any result from negotiations; the Dalai Lama has no bargaining chip at all."[65]

China's approach to the human rights issue was similar. The PRC had long countered criticisms about its human rights abuses with the argument that its interpretation of human rights was different from that of Western countries, but no less valid. China maintained that its overriding human rights concern was economic and that, until a certain level of economic security was achieved, it could not be as concerned as Western countries about individual rights and political rights. A fundamental assumption of Hu Jintao's new "harmonious world" slogan was that different countries had different conceptions of human rights and different levels of human rights development, and that such differences should be respected. What this apparently meant in practice was that China should not be criticized for its human rights practices. The PRC's role in refuting scrutiny for its human rights abuses at the former UN Human Rights Commission, and then playing a large role in the creation of a new downgraded Human Rights Council, is evidence of this strategy.

Another Chinese tactic was to advocate bilateral dialogue on human rights issues rather than bringing these issues up at international forums such as the United Nations. China successfully transformed almost all of its multilateral human rights dialogues into bilateral ones. These were convenient both for China and its critics, but they did nothing but obscure human rights issues and avoid international embarrassment to China for its abuses.

China's policy on human rights was illustrated by a recent human rights exhibition in Beijing, which was intended to demonstrate the improvement in the Chinese people's situation since their liberation by the CCP. However, the exhibition was closed to ordinary people, some of whom were arrested for trying to demonstrate there. Critics who were interviewed by Western reporters said the exhibition was a façade meant for foreign consumption while in reality the human rights situation remained unimproved.[66]

The recent history of Sino-Tibetan contacts reveals no Chinese willingness to compromise. The exiles and their supporters appeal to China that it is in China's interest to resolve the issue of Tibet, but China denies that there is any such issue. Why, indeed, one may ask, should China reopen a historical issue already resolved entirely in China's favor by the 1950–1951 "peaceful liberation" of Tibet? The exiles hope that international pressure will force China to compromise, but China has demonstrated its disdain for outside criticism. The exiles try to convince the PRC to adhere to its own laws on autonomy, but China insists that Tibet already has as much autonomy as any other of China's minority nationalities and will not have any more. For China to grant Tibet a special autonomous status would be to acknowledge Tibet's separate historical status.

The PRC's policies on national minority autonomy were never intended to allow for any of the minorities' permanently separate cultural or political existence. Instead, those policies were primarily meant to defuse the resistance of non-Chinese peoples to incorporation within the PRC, after which the assimilative effects of Chinese socialist culture were assumed to be capable of quickly alleviating the minorities' separatist tendencies. China abandoned its promises of the Seventeen-Point Agreement after it achieved military control over Tibet in the mid-1950s, and it abandoned all but the pretense of autonomy after it achieved political control as a consequence of the 1959 revolt. During the Democratic Reforms Campaign and the Cultural Revolution, there was virtually no respect for autonomy in Tibet even though the TAR was inaugurated in 1965 and Tibet was "granted" national regional autonomy. The experiment with allowing some autonomy in the 1980s met with essentially open revolt by 1987.

China's experience with autonomy in Tibet has been that very little can be allowed without arousing Tibetan resistance. Many Chinese officials cite the results of the liberalization policy of 1957, which they believe led to the 1959 revolt, and that of the 1980s, which led to the demonstrations and riots of 1987–1989, as evidence that hardly any Tibetan autonomy can be permitted. China has learned from long experience exactly how much autonomy it can allow in Tibet and still guarantee China's "unity and stability." Why then, Chinese leaders might ask, should China allow more autonomy in Tibet than its own experience dictates is appropriate? China was surprised after 1979 to find that the Tibetan political issue was still alive, and it has become increasingly intransigent as Tibetans have revealed their rejection of Chinese rule and the Dalai Lama has demonstrated his continuing ability to achieve international support.

The Dalai Lama continues to ask China to respect its own promises and laws that theoretically protect and perpetuate Tibetan culture. However, the Chinese have learned that a separate Tibetan cultural and national identity is incompatible with Chinese national unity and territorial integrity. China's traditional frontier policy of assimilation of frontier peoples offers a more certain solution to the Tibetan problem than does a perpetuation of Tibetan separatism by means of Tibetan autonomy. Traditional Chinese frontier policy was characterized by the establishment of indirect rule, or temporary local autonomy, followed ultimately by Chinese colonization and assimilation. Both traditional Chinese frontier policy and Marxist-Leninist nationalities policies aimed not at permanent autonomy but at eventual assimilation. The PRC's policy toward minorities has been relentlessly assimilationist. Assimilation, not autonomy, is dictated by both traditional Chinese frontier policy and Marxist-Leninist doctrine, and this is the pattern that China has followed in Tibet.

By mid-2007, there had been no delegation visit for eighteen months. Since the current series of dialogues began, in 2001, the visits have averaged about one a year. Therefore, by early 2007 another visit was due. China appeared to be demonstrating its displeasure at recent events within Tibet that revealed the continuing popularity of the Dalai Lama. Nevertheless, their overall strategy of using the "dialogue" as a part of the propaganda campaign about Tibet suggested that they would eventually issue another invitation. The Chinese appeared to be using the granting or withholding of delegation visits much like the ancient emperors had used the tribute system to grant or withhold trading privileges to barbarian tribes and states. The tribute system was actually tribute in reverse, since those offering tribute to China typically received goods far more valuable than those they offered in exchange for nominal recognition of Chinese pretensions to authority. The Chinese Communists seemed to be trying to control the behavior of the Tibetan exiles and their supporters in much the same way that the emperors had controlled the barbarians.

After the Chinese denunciations of the Dalai Lama in mid-2006, there appeared what critics of the MWA might regard as a glimmer of realism from Dharamsala. Samdhong Rinpoche withdrew his controversial request that Tibetans not demonstrate against the Chinese, saying:

> In the past we have asked the Tibetan people not to annoy the PRC by [engaging in] propaganda or campaigns against them. Unfortunately, since last year the PRC has not cared for our actions and they have attacked His Holiness the Dalai Lama. Under such circumstances we are not able to ask the Tibetan people to keep quiet.[67]

Samdhong said that this did not mean that he or the government-in-exile had abandoned the Middle Way or the policy of dialogue. It was unclear if his new policy on demonstrations was firm or if it would be abandoned as soon as the Chinese suggested another delegation visit. In contrast to Tibetan efforts to create a conducive atmosphere for dialogue, the Chinese had never relented in their propaganda campaign of denouncing the Dalai Lama and promoting their own version of Tibetan reality. They had furthermore revealed their frustration and defensiveness by reviving their most successful but also most duplicitous propaganda theme of denigrating pre-1950 Tibet as a feudal Hell on Earth. Mao's decree that the national issue is in essence a class issue, which had characterized the most intolerant periods of CCP nationality policy, was also revived.

Several notorious propaganda pieces from the past were dredged up. A new film, *Tibet in the Past*, was issued, with accompanying testimonials by Chinese Tibetologists and film footage from Tibet in the 1950s. The film was distilled from 900 hours of footage shot in Tibet before 1960 and was said to "describe the social situation in Tibet before 1959 with first-hand eye-witness accounts and precious historic video clips." Like several films of that earlier era, it portrayed the suffering of Tibetans under the feudal serf system and included scenes of downtrodden serfs and interviews with serfs who told of their suffering. Some of those serfs filmed in the 1950s were located for the new film, and they told of their much-improved life after liberation. Lhakpa Phuntsok, director of the China Tibetology Research Center, opined that "those who glorify the feudal serf regime and slander the positive changes that have taken place since 1959 will have to think again."[68]

This theme was continued with the republication of some of the infamous print publications of the past, including the book of photographs of the "Wrath of the Serfs" exhibition. Israel Epstein's *Tibet Transformed* was also reprinted, as were Anna Louise Strong's *When Serfs Stood Up in Tibet* and some fifty other "classics" of Western apologist literature, all of which were essentially sycophantic repetitions of Chinese propaganda. China's reversion to the discredited propaganda of the most repressive periods of its rule over Tibet revealed its frustration that its legitimacy in Tibet was still being questioned.

China's fundamental economic and political strategy for Tibet was confirmed by an announcement in early 2007 of the discovery of vast mineral resources on the Tibetan Plateau. Xinhua reported that Chinese geologists had discovered more than six hundred new sites of copper, iron, lead, and zinc ore deposits on the plateau, including twenty-four major deposits.[69] The finds were the result of a seven-year geological survey by more than a thousand experts from twenty-four geological survey teams. Even given the large number of personnel and the length of time involved, only half of the area of the Tibetan Plateau had been surveyed, which means that more resources were likely to be discovered. The highest and most remote areas of the plateau are yet to be surveyed. The iron ore sources near Nyainrong, north of Nagchuka, within the TAR, were said to be the largest and richest iron ore discovery in China. The iron ore there has a very high level of iron content, approximately

60 percent, much higher than any other site in China. The resources are also near the newly completed railway, so they can be relatively easily exploited.

Despite China's claims that the railway was intended solely to benefit Tibetans, the announcement of the discovery of these mineral resources confirmed its real purpose. Ever since China first gained control over Tibet, Chinese leaders have openly admitted that they coveted Tibet's mineral wealth. Mao told Tibetan leaders that Tibet would provide China with the mineral resources necessary for economic development, while China would provide Tibet with the people necessary to exploit those resources and to help Tibet develop. In other words, Tibet would give China its natural wealth while China would give Tibet its people. However, due to transportation difficulties, this Chinese dream of exploiting Tibet's mineral wealth had remained unrealized. Only now, with the completion of the railroad, have these heavy mineral resources of the Tibetan Plateau become economically exploitable.

With the completion of the railway, China's mining activities in Tibet are certain to increase to a very large extent. The creation of a large logistical center at Nagchuka, on the railway line, costing 1.5 billion yuan ($750 million), was announced, presumably intended to handle the logistics of the iron mine and other mining activities. As was the case with the construction of the railroad, the workers in this new town will probably be predominantly Chinese. The same will presumably be true of all of China's mineral resource exploitation activities in Tibet. This will increase the number of Chinese in Tibet and the proportion of Chinese relative to Tibetans. Chinese law specifies that all mineral resources are the property of the central state. Therefore, all of Tibet's resources belong to China, not to Tibet, and Tibetans will receive no payments or any other benefits from the exploitation of their resources.

The Chinese government recently announced that it would invest more than 100 billion yuan ($12 billion) in 180 projects in the TAR over the next four years.[70] The projects would involve infrastructure construction, education, social security, and environmental conservation. This is by far the largest amount of funds ever devoted for development in the TAR—three times the cost of the railway and more than the total Chinese investment in the TAR for the past ten years of 70 billion yuan, a figure that includes the cost of the railroad. On an annual basis, the level of Chinese investment for the next four years is planned to be almost four times per year more than the previous ten-year period, even including the enormous cost of the railroad. Although the announcement did not say so, presumably much of the funds will be devoted to mining and the roads necessary to take the mined minerals to the railroad. The extension of the railroad to Shigatse was presumably intended to facilitate the mining of a large copper deposit near there. China's new plan for an increased level of investment in Tibet demonstrates an almost unlimited willingness to devote whatever amount of funding is necessary in order to maintain political stability and Chinese control in Tibet. The TAR is now almost completely dependent upon funding from the central government.

The discovery of these vast new mineral resources in Tibet is a further reason why China is unlikely to negotiate with the Dalai Lama about Tibetan autonomy or allow any real autonomy in Tibet. The Dalai Lama has proposed that Tibet should have some control over its natural resources, which China refuses to allow since Tibet's resources are so essential to China's development. Any system of genuine autonomy in Tibet would presumably give Tibetans a measure of control over their own natural resources or at least some compensation. However, the current system is obviously preferable to China, since it does not have to acknowledge any Tibetan rights to Tibetan natural resources. China desperately needs Tibet's minerals, water, and hydropower resources and is not likely to give up any degree of control over their exploitation. With the completion of the railway, China now has the means to achieve its goal of making Tibet China's resource colony. Neither China's economic nor political strategy for Tibet would be served by allowing Tibetan autonomy.

In late June 2007, the Tibetan envoys were once again invited to China for what the Tibetans described as the sixth round of discussions, but which the Chinese in their usual fashion denied had anything to do with any discussions. In response to journalists' questions about the visit, a Foreign Ministry spokesman insisted, "Lodi Gyari and company are not so-called envoys of the Dalai." As was the case with previous visits, the Foreign Ministry described the visits as personal rather than official: "Every year, many Tibetan compatriots return for visits and to see relatives. Since 2002, Lodi Gyari and others came back many times and went to Tibet and many provinces on the mainland to see friends and relatives and for tours." The spokesman acknowledged that they were "relatively close to the Dalai," but, in a typically patronizing and condescending style, advised them to make the Dalai Lama recognize the present reality in Tibet and give up his splittism: "We hope they will treasure every opportunity to come back, seriously look around and give a factual account to the Dalai after they return [to India] to help the Dalai correctly understand the situation, understand the country's policies and thus make correct choices."[71]

The Tibetan envoys had three meetings with officials of the United Front Work Department in Shanghai and Nanjing. Upon their return to India, Gyari issued a press statement that was characterized by an almost complete lack of optimism: "The discussions were candid and frank. Both sides expressed in strong terms their divergent positions and views on a number of issues." He continued, "Our dialogue process has reached a critical stage. We conveyed our serious concerns in the strongest possible manner on the overall Tibetan issue and made some concrete proposals for implementation if our dialogue process is to go forward." Given this lack of results, the envoys were asked by the Dalai Lama to make a comprehensive analysis of the dialogue process.[72]

The wording of Gyari's statement indicated that the Chinese had been unwilling to make any compromises. Had there been any flexibility from the Chinese side, the Tibetans would undoubtedly have emphasized this as a positive development. Gyari said that he had made some proposals intended to further the dialogue, but gave no indication that the Chinese had responded. Before the latest visit, Dharamsala had announced that the Tibetan delegation intended to propose a visit to China by the Dalai Lama, perhaps a pilgrimage to some Buddhist site as had been suggested in the past. In conjunction with this, the U.S. State Department issued a statement saying: "The United States has long supported dialogue between China and the Dalai Lama and his representatives, and hopes this meeting leads to substantive progress on resolving longstanding differences. President Bush has urged Chinese leaders to invite the Dalai Lama to China."[73] However, Gyari's silence about any such visit upon his return to India presumably meant that the Chinese had declined this overture.

The latest Tibetan delegation visit was undoubtedly the most negative. Previously, all visits had produced at least some expression of optimism from the Tibetan side or at least an invitation from the Chinese to continue the dialogue. Even though it was presumably in China's interest to prolong the semblance of dialogue in order to appear conciliatory, especially in response to international pressure, during the latest meetings the Chinese side appeared to offer no hope to the Tibetans. The results of these discussions seemed to reveal that China was so rigid in regard to the Tibet issue that it would not even make concessions sufficient to continue the dialogue process, even if that process was thought to be to its own advantage.

After this latest delegation visit, Dharamsala undoubtedly felt more pressure from opponents of the Middle Path to abandon the policy of trying to conduct a dialogue with China. The Dalai Lama's call for an appraisal of the dialogue policy implied that he, too, was looking for alternatives. In the past, Dharamsala had said that there was no alternative to talking with the Chinese and that any dialogue with China was better than no dialogue at all. Now, however, the dialogue having produced no results, there would be greater pressure to find a new strategy. Opponents of the Middle Path policy had long maintained that China would never compromise over Tibet and was not sincere about its willingness to talk. They predicted that the Chinese would use the Tibetan hopes for negotiations to get concessions from the Tibetan side while giving none of its own. Now, Dharamsala would have to contemplate whether or not the opponents of the dialogue were also right in believing that

China would be more forthcoming in response to pressure than to appeasement.

The failure of the last round of dialogue was followed in August 2007 by an incident in the Kham area of Sichuan that demonstrated China's intolerance of any internal Tibetan support for the Dalai Lama. At the traditional horse festival at Lithang, a Tibetan nomad jumped on the stage and called for the return of the Dalai Lama. His outburst had apparently been provoked by a campaign in local monasteries to force monks to sign a statement saying they did not want the Dalai Lama to return. The nomad and several of his friends and relatives were arrested, and, despite promises by local officials to release them, apparently made to disperse an angry crowd, they were later charged with the crime of subverting the state. The area was flooded with thousands of People's Armed Police, local Tibetan officials were replaced by Chinese, and new measures were announced to address instability, including more aggressive gathering of intelligence, preemptive resolution of disputes, and increased criticism of the Dalai Lama as part of a "high tide of anti-splittist struggle." Ideological education was to be increased, using teams of officials who were to go from household to household carrying out propaganda and education to promote the rule of law. Officials involved in this work would include only those who had no "ideological problems related to the Dalai Lama and his separatist faction" and who could "hold to the Party line without faltering."[74]

In a further indication of Chinese rejection of the influence of the Dalai Lama and their intention to choose his successor, the Chinese government announced new regulations intended to control the selection of Tibetan Buddhist reincarnations (*tulkus*). The new rules were said to be meant to guarantee Tibetans' freedom of religion, to respect the Tibetan Buddhist system of reincarnation, and to regulate the management of reincarnations. According to the new guidelines, approved tulkus should respect and protect the unification of China, the unity of nationalities, and social harmony. They should not engage in any attempt to reestablish feudal privileges and should not be influenced by any foreign individual or organization.

The new regulations' prohibition of any foreign influence was apparently aimed at the Dalai Lama and his foreign supporters. It would also seem to apply to foreign supporters of any lama. Heads of other sects, such as the Sakyapa, Karmapa, and Ningmapa, all of whom are in exile from Tibet, would presumably be prohibited from approving reincarnations, as well. Thus the authority of all traditional leaders of Tibetan Buddhism would be replaced by that of the Chinese government.

The new ordinances furthermore seem to imply that already-chosen tulkus could be rejected by the Chinese authorities if they were chosen by the Dalai

Lama or without official approval. The regulations also permit the authorities to limit the number of tulkus, much as they previously limited the number of monasteries and monks. The Chinese government now requires that the selection of tulkus be reported to and approved, at different levels of government depending upon the importance of the reincarnation. The lowest level need be approved only at the provincial level, while higher reincarnations must be approved by the State Administration for Religious Affairs or even by the State Council.

Despite the announced purpose of protecting the freedom of religion in Tibet, the regulations' real purpose was clearly to secure Chinese government control over all religious affairs, especially the approval of high tulkus—a role formerly played by the Dalai Lama. In fact, the primary goal was obviously to eradicate the Dalai Lama's control or influence over the selection of tulkus and to replace his authority over Tibetan Buddhist affairs with that of the Chinese Communist Party. Ultimately, the purpose of the CCP's control over the process of choosing tulkus is to allow the party to choose the next Dalai Lama. This attempt to completely control all aspects of Tibetan Buddhism demonstrates that the priority of the Chinese government is political control, without any regard for the beliefs, opinions, or feelings of the Tibetans.

The "comprehensive analysis of the dialogue process" requested by the Dalai Lama after the last delegation visit was completed in mid-September by the Dialogue Task Force, composed of the delegation members and key exile government personnel. The recommendations of the task force were not made public, but international events had apparently convinced Dharamsala that the Middle Way policy should be continued. The Dalai Lama had just returned from a visit to Europe, where he had been officially received by the heads of government of Austria and Germany, and was about to depart for the United States to receive the Congressional Gold Medal. Despite its lack of success with the Chinese, the MWA was achieving remarkable success internationally, with several countries making dramatic shifts in policy toward Tibet by finally having official meetings with the Dalai Lama.

The policy change was begun by the governments of Australia and Austria, whose heads of government met officially with the Dalai Lama in June and September, respectively. Then, during the September European trip, the Dalai Lama was officially received by German chancellor Angela Merkel. The meeting with the German chancellor was an important change in that country's policy and occasioned a strong protest from China, including the cancellation of a scheduled human rights meeting. German officials and public generally approved of the chancellor's reception of the Dalai Lama and discounted any adverse repercussions in relations with China, including the human rights dialogues that were already regarded as essentially useless.

The remarkable upgrading of the Dalai Lama's international receptions may have been initiated by the award of the Congressional Gold Medal by the United States in September 2006, the actual award ceremony for which took place in Washington, D.C., in October 2007. The award, the highest civilian honor given by the United States, was presented in the Capitol Rotunda by U.S. president George W. Bush, marking the first official meeting between the president and the Dalai Lama, and was attended by the leaders of both parties of Congress. The award required the sponsorship of two-thirds of the members of Congress and therefore represented a high degree of U.S. support. The Congressional Gold Medal is the highest honor given to the Dalai Lama since the Nobel Peace Prize in 1989.

The Dalai Lama went from the United States to Canada, where he was also received officially for the first time. Canada is also distinguished for making the Dalai Lama an honorary citizen. The upgrading of many countries' receptions of the Dalai Lama was thought to signify their frustration with the lack of progress in Sino-Tibetan dialogue, which all of these countries have publicly supported. It may also signify international opposition to China's refusal to allow any meaningful autonomy within Tibet. All of these countries have important diplomatic and trade relations with China, which China threatened might be disrupted by their support for the Dalai Lama. Nevertheless, all were willing to defy China in order to express their support for the Dalai Lama and for Tibet.

China reacted with predictable scorn to the Dalai Lama's Congressional Gold Medal and attempted to prevent any celebrations within Tibet. The Dalai Lama was accused of "deviating from Buddhism" for all sorts of crimes, including murder of his opponents, supporting cults like Falun Gong, and betraying his motherland, meaning China, by instigating the revolt, fleeing into exile in 1959, and engaging in anti-China activities ever since. His proposals for genuine autonomy and an expanded Tibet Autonomous Region were denounced as "absurd," for being counter to China's constitution, and for ignoring historical facts of Chinese administration over areas of eastern Tibet from ancient times.

China's Foreign Ministry strenuously objected to the award to the Dalai Lama and his official meeting with the U.S. president, saying that the medal and its presentation in the presence of U.S. leaders had "severely trampled on the norms of international relations, hurt the feelings of the Chinese people, and are wild interference in China's domestic affairs." The Foreign Ministry spokesman added:

> China is strongly resentful of and resolutely opposes this and has made solemn representation to the US side. We seriously urged the US side to correct such

wrong doing and cancel relevant arrangement, and stop interfering in China's domestic affairs in any forms.[75]

China lodged a formal protest, summoned the U.S. ambassador, and said that the award had seriously damaged Sino-U.S. relations. As an unnamed "senior official" of the Foreign Affairs Committee of the NPC was quoted:

> To glorify the Dalai Lama for his so-called "contribution" to the advancement of human rights and call him a "fighter for human rights" not only distorts history but also makes a mockery of freedom, human rights and human dignity. . . . We urge the U.S. Congress and Administration not to forget the larger interests of U.S. relations with China, take speedy and credible steps to undo the damage caused by the above-mentioned wrong move, stop interfering in China's internal affairs, and refrain from making moves that are offensive to the Chinese people and impede the normal growth of China-U.S. relations. We would like to remind some individuals that the Chinese people stood up long since 1949. To uphold China's sovereignty and territorial integrity is the common resolve and firm determination of all the Chinese people, including the people in Tibet. No force can stop the progress of Tibet in the great family of the Chinese nation. All attempts to interfere in China's internal affairs and undermine China's fundamental interests are doomed to failure.[76]

Tibet's CCP chairman, Zhang Qingli, condemned the Dalai Lama as someone who "doesn't even love his own country." "How can someone who does not love, and even seeks to split, his own country receive a welcome in some countries and even get awards?" Zhang asked. "It's actually trampling on such awards."[77] "We are furious," he added. "If the Dalai Lama can receive such an award, there must be no justice or good people in the world."[78]

The Chinese state-controlled press further accused the Dalai Lama of being a pawn of the anti-China policy of the United States. The gold medal was described as "a lovely flower stuck in a dunghill." The Dalai Lama was denounced as the "scum of the Chinese nation," who "engineered a rebellion in Tibet."[79] The United States was advised to reject its Cold War attitudes and adopt new thinking toward China:

> The United States should first demonstrate such new thinking on the ideological level. The old ideological standards of human rights, freedom of religion, and freedom of the press are holdovers from the Cold War era. If the United States continues to use them to assess China, which is opening up and is building a market economy, then the US would clearly be out of tune with the times. Even minor trifles of no significance at all will be liable to upset Sino-US relations. In recent days, for instance, the United States gave an award to the Dalai Lama despite China's opposition. This move has seriously damaged Sino-US relations.[80]

The Chinese press went on to advise that, in light of China's "active coordination with US post-11 September global strategic plans," the United States and China should pursue the political cooperation necessary for harmony between the two countries. Obviously, what China meant by "harmony" would mean that the United States should cease criticism of China based on the "old ideological standards of human rights, freedom of religion and freedom of the press," which were just holdovers of a Cold War mentality.

This was not the reaction from China that the Dalai Lama or the U.S. leaders who spoke at his award ceremony had anticipated. The Dalai Lama said that he hoped China would achieve harmony by resolving the issue of Tibet. U.S. officials also echoed the language of harmony, without any apparent understanding of what China meant by the term. Several of the American leaders who presented the award, including President Bush and leaders of Congress, expressed the hope that China would take the opportunity presented by the Dalai Lama to resolve the issue of Tibet. The president spoke of the Tibet issue in exclusively religious terms, which, were it the case that the issue of Tibet was just about religion, could presumably be fairly easily resolved simply by allowing freedom of religion.

The Congressional Gold Medal award by the United States may have convinced Dharamsala that its Middle Path policy was achieving results, if not with China then at least with Western supporters, but it was also accompanied by an air of unreality. The events associated with the award were characterized by much talk, by the Dalai Lama and others, about nonviolence, dialogue rather than confrontation, and autonomy rather than independence. This type of language received an enthusiastic response from many in the U.S. audience but had very little to do with the reality in China or Tibet. These principles were all entirely compatible with Tibetan Buddhist traditions, but they also seemed to be tailored to suit the Western audience. Given that the West was the only venue in which the Dalai Lama's policy had received such a positive reception, this was understandable. However, there was considerable doubt expressed by some Tibetans and others about the efficacy of nonviolence against the brutality of the Chinese Communist regime, the sincerity of the Chinese regarding dialogue, and the possibility that China might ever allow autonomy sufficient to preserve Tibetan culture and national identity. Although all Tibetans and their supporters were gratified by the U.S. award to the Dalai Lama, many still harbored doubts about the wisdom of giving up Tibet's rightful demand for independence.

In fact, a dichotomy had emerged in Tibetan politics, with the Middle Path policy achieving great results outside China and almost none at all within. Since the mid-1980s, given the stalemate in dialogue with China at that point, Dharamsala had adopted a strategy of cultivation of foreign support—the "internationalization" of the issue, as the Chinese put it—with the hope that other countries would pressure China to resume negotiations. The strategy had resulted in the Nobel Peace Prize, tremendous popularity for the Dalai Lama, and now the Congressional Gold Medal, but if anything it had hardened China's refusal to sit down with the Dalai Lama or to resolve the Tibet issue to his or his Western supporters' satisfaction. There was an almost direct correlation between the increase in the Dalai Lama's international support and the virulence of China's denunciations of him.

China's sensitivity to any questions about the legitimacy of its sovereignty over Tibet meant that it could not be flexible on any issue related to that sovereignty, including the nature of Tibetan autonomy within the Chinese state. The Dalai Lama also found himself locked into his own policy, despite its lack of success with China, because of its popularity among his Western supporters. The Dalai Lama was winning the international propaganda war with China over Tibet, but he still had not gained any leverage sufficient to make China alter its policies there.

Notes

1. In its refutation of the "Tibet model" for Taiwan, the Asian People's Anti-Communist League of Taiwan referred to an article by Ngawang Jigme Ngapo in which he suggested that the liberation of Tibet could serve as a model for Taiwan, particularly that the problem could be resolved through a negotiated agreement similar to the Seventeen-Point Agreement of 1951, which he had negotiated and signed and which had resolved the status of Tibet; *The True Features of Chinese Communist "Tibet Model"* (Taipei: Asian People's Anti-Communist League, 1982), 2. Dawa Norbu also refers to a statement by Wang Bingnan, China's ambassador to Poland in the 1950s, that Tibet could be a model for Taiwan; Dawa Norbu, *China's Tibet Policy* (Richmond, Surrey, England: Curzon Press, 2001), 303.

2. *The Collected Statements, Interviews and Articles of His Holiness the Dalai Lama* (Dharamsala: Information Office of His Holiness the Dalai Lama, 1986), 41, 52, 60.

3. In 1973 and 1974, the Dalai Lama mentioned the freedom of the Tibetan people (Dalai Lama, *Collected Statements*, 42, 43). In 1975, he spoke of the freedom and independence of Tibet (46). In 1976, he spoke of "Tibetan freedom" and "national freedom of the Tibetan people" (48). And in 1977, he spoke, for the last time, of the independence of Tibet (51).

4. "Kalon Tripa: MWA Seeks Genuine Autonomy for Tibet," Tibet.net, 29 September 2006, http://www.tibet.net/en/flash/2006/0906/280906.html.

5. "Wen Plays Precondition Card, His Holiness Firm on Genuine Autonomy," Tibet.net, 26 November 2003, http://www.tibet.net/en/flash/2003/1103/261103.html.

6. Message from the Dalai Lama to the President and the Secretary of State, 17 June 1959, Central Intelligence Agency, Dulles Papers, http://www.foia.cia.gov/search.asp.

7. Warren W. Smith Jr., *Tibetan Nation: A History of Tibetan Nationalism and Sino-Tibetan Relations* (Boulder, CO: Westview Press, 1996), 493.

8. USUN to Secretary of State, 6 October 1959, National Archives, 793B.00/10–659.

9. USUN to Secretary of State, 8 October 1959, National Archives, 793B.00/10–859; Smith, *Tibetan Nation,* 492.

10. Department of State Outgoing Telegram, 6 November 1959, National Archives, 793B.00/11–659.

11. Quoted in Dawa Norbu, *China's Tibet Policy,* 316.

12. The Dalai Lama has recently said that his "Middle Way approach is based on the statement of the late Deng Xiaoping that except for the independence of Tibet all other questions could be discussed and resolved" ("Wen Plays Precondition Card"). Gyalo Thondup and Lodi Gyari, the Dalai Lama's special envoy in all subsequent Sino-Tibetan dialogues, have adamantly maintained that Deng meant that anything but independence could be discussed (Gyalo Thondup, public talk at International Campaign for Tibet, Washington, DC, August 2005; Lodi Gyari, personal communication, Washington, DC, 2006). In a policy statement published in 2006, Gyari called on China to adhere to its promise to conduct negotiations on the basis of Deng's conditions. He maintained that this understanding had been reiterated by Li Xianian of the United Front during the first delegation visit in 1979, to Thondup by Ding Guangen of the United Front in 1992, and again by a Chinese Foreign Ministry statement on 23 August 1993 (Lodi Gyari, "Seeking Unity through Equality: The Current Status of Discussions between His Holiness the Dalai Lama and the Government of the People's Republic of China: Remarks as Prepared for Delivery by Lodi Gyaltsen Gyari, Special Envoy of H.H. the Dalai Lama," Brookings Institution, Washington, DC, 14 November 2006). Interestingly, Gyari did not say that this understanding had ever been communicated to him by any Chinese officials during their official talks.

13. Dawa Norbu, "China's Dialogue with the Dalai Lama, 1978–90: Prenegotiation Stage or Dead End?" *Pacific Affairs* 64, no. 3 (Fall 1991): 357.

14. "Policy toward Dalai Lama," *Beijing Review,* 15 November 1982.

15. "Beijing Receives Dalai Lama's Envoys," *Beijing Review,* 3 December 1984, 9.

16. In his Strasbourg Proposal, the Dalai Lama defined Tibet's future status as a "self-governing political entity . . . in association with the People's Republic of China." The status of association proposed by the Dalai Lama was taken from UN resolutions on the means by which self-determination might be achieved, one of which is by "free association." Associative status is based upon a free choice by the people in question and a right to review that choice at any time. This freedom of choice also implies that independence might be chosen. Michael C. Van Walt van Pragg, *The Status of Tibet* (Boulder, CO: Westview Press, 1987), 201, 202.

17. "The Dalai Lama's 'New Proposal,'" *Beijing Review,* 1 August 1988.

18. "What Is behind the Dalai Lama's 'Plan,'" *Beijing Review,* 19 February 1990.

19. "Nationality Autonomy Key to Tibet's Success," Foreign Broadcast Information Service (FBIS), FBIS-CHI-95-205, 24 October 1995.

20. "AFP Cites PRC FM Spokesman: PRC Welcomes Tibetan Group, But Not Ready for Dalai Lama," Agence France-Presse, 10 September 2002, in FBIS CPP20020910000106.

21. Jeremy Page, "Dalai Lama Envoys Meet Tibet Government Chief," Reuters, 17 September 2002.

22. "Statement by Special Envoy Lodi Gyari, Head of the Delegation Which Visited China and Tibet," Dharamsala, 28 September 2002.

23. Lodi Gyari, personal communication, Washington, DC, October 2007.

24. "What Is the Real Intention of the United States?" Xinhua, 9 June 2003, in FBIS CPP20030609000063.

25. "Statement by Special Envoy Lodi Gyari, Head of the Delegation Sent by His Holiness the Dalai Lama to China," Dharamsala, 11 June 2003, http://www.tibet.net/en/prelease/2002/lodi_gyari_statement.html.

26. Statement by Lodi Gyari at the Light of Truth Award Ceremony, Washington, DC, September 2003.

27. "Ngaba Kirti Monastic School Closed, Patron Disappears," Tibetan Center for Human Rights and Democracy, Dharamsala, 30 September 2003.

28. International Campaign for Tibet, "Dalai Lama's Envoys Have 'Most Extensive and Serious' Discussions with Chinese Leaders," 13 October 2004, http://www.savetibet.org/news/newsitem.php?id=662.

29. Ibid.

30. "Statement by the Special Envoy of His Holiness the Dalai Lama," 7 July 2005, http://www.savetibet.org/news/newsitem.php?id=773.

31. Ibid.

32. "Statement by Special Envoy Lodi Gyari, Head of the Delegation Sent by His Holiness the Dalai Lama to China," Department of Information and International Relations, Dharamsala, 25 February 2006, http://www.tibet.net/en/prelease/2006/250206.html.

33. "Urgent Appeal to the Tibetan People and Tibet Supporters in the USA and Canada," Tibet.net, 6 September 2005, http://www.tibet.net/en/diir/wwtm/appeal.html#4.

34. Ibid.

35. "Think Like a Mosquito—Lhasang," Phayul.com, 25 February 2007, http://www.phayul.com/news/article.aspx?id=15653&c=0.

36. Dawa Norbu, *China's Tibet Policy*, 100.

37. Arjia Rinpoche, *Surviving the Dragon: The Autobiography of Arjia Rinpoche*, manuscript.

38. In an address to the European Parliament Forum on Tibet, Kelsang Gyaltsen, co-leader of the delegation that visited Tibet, said, "In January 2002 a first face-to-face meeting took place outside of China with Chinese officials responsible for China's Tibet policy. This meeting paved the way for the visit of a four-member Tibetan delegation to China and to the Tibetan capital Lhasa from September 9 to 25, 2002." "Address of Mr. Kelsang Gyaltsen, Envoy of H.H. the Dalai Lama to the European Parliament Forum on Tibet," Tibet.net, 12 November 2003, http://www.tibet.net/en/flash/2003/1103/261103.html.

39. Cheng Ran, "A Discussion on Tibetan Issue with American Experts on China," *China News and Report*, 17 September 2002.

40. "Dalai Lama Behaving Disingenuously by Pushing 'Middle Way,'" *China Daily*, 22 July 2003, in FBIS CPP20030722000010.

41. "What Is the Real Intention?" Subsequent unattributed quotes are from this article.

42. "China Protests Dalai Lama's US Trip," Agence France-Presse, 28 August 2003.

43. Christopher Bodeen, "At Dalai Lama's Former Palace, Reverence," Associated Press, 10 September 2003.

44. "Tibet Chairman Qiangba Puncog Tells Xinhua Dalai Lama More and More Unpopular," Xinhua, 31 May 2005, in FBIS CPP20050531000207.

45. "Tibet Chairman Qiangba Puncog Says Time Unripe for Dalai Lama's Return," *Ching Chi Jih Pao* (Hong Kong), 19 July 2005, in FBIS CPP20050719000077.

46. "Regional Ethnic Autonomy in Tibet" (Beijing: Information Office of the State Council of the People's Republic of China, 2004). Subsequent unattributed quotes are from this article.

47. Yedor, "Text of China Tibet Information Center Article on 'Middle Way' of Dalai Lama," *Beijing Xinhua*, 28 July 2006, in Open Source Center CPP20060728052027, http://www.opensource.gov. "Yedor" is apparently a pseudonym. Longtime Tibetan residents of Beijing said that there was no such Tibetan at the China Tibet Information Center (Jigme Ngapo, personal communication, Washington, DC, 2006). Interestingly, in this article published by the China Tibet Information Center in English, Yedor uses the older terminology of *National Regional Autonomy* rather than *Regional Ethnic Autonomy*.

48. "Statement of His Holiness the Dalai Lama on the 47th Anniversary of the Tibetan National Uprising," Office of His Holiness the Dalai Lama, Dharamsala, 10 March 2006.

49. "Statement of the Kashag on the 47th Anniversary of the Tibetan People's Uprising Day," Tibet.net, 11 March 2006, http://www.tibet.net/en/kashag/statements/10march/2006.html.

50. Gyalo Thondup, interview with Radio Free Asia, November 2006.

51. Yedor, "'Middle Way' of Dalai Lama." Subsequent unattributed quotes are from this article.

52. "Xinhua Cites Tibet's Party Chief: Dalai Lama Unworthy of Religious Leader," *Beijing Xinhua*, 8 August 2006, in Open Source Center CPP20060808318002.

53. Gyari, "Seeking Unity through Equality." Subsequent unattributed quotes are from this speech.

54. This point of view echoes that of Zhou Enlai as conveyed to Tibetan leaders, particularly Ngawang Jigme Ngapo, during the 1950s. See Smith, *Tibetan Nation*, 361n74.

55. "DIIR Kalon on Current Status of Negotiations on the Issue of Tibet," Tibet.net, 20 November 2006, http://www.tibet.net/en/flash/2006/1006/201106.html.

56. "Quishi: Tibet Party Leader on Building Harmony, Fighting Separatism," 17 January 2007, Open Source Center CPP20070117710006.

57. "China Publishes Article Slamming Dalai Lama for Seeking Tibetan Independence," 23 April 2007, Open Source Center CPP20070423001009.

58. "Tibetologists Comment on Dalai Lama's Article in *Der Spiegel*," 26 April 2007, Open Source Center CPP20070426138003.

59. "PRC Scholar Comments on Dalai Lama's Concern about 'Cultural Genocide' in Tibet," 26 April 2007, Open Source Center CPP20070426138004.

60. "China Daily 'Comment': Scholar Says Dalai Lama's Ethnic Fight to Harm Tibet," 26 April 2007, Open Source Center CPP20070426055037.

61. See Smith, *Tibetan Nation*, 122.

62. "No One Has the Liberty to Refuse: Tibetan Herders Forcibly Relocated in Gansu, Qinghai, Sichuan and the Tibet Autonomous Region," Human Rights Watch, 11 June 2007, http://hrw.org/reports/2007/tibet0607/.

63. "Kalon Tripa."

64. Tenzing Sonam, "Roadblock on the Middle Path," *Himal*, 20 December 2006, available at http://www.phayul.com/news/article.espx?id=15119&t=1&c=1.

65. "The Insider's Story Reveals Chinese Regime's Overseas Scheme," Phayul.com, 12 June 2007, http://www.phayul.com/news/article.espx?id=16815&t=1&c=1.

66. "China Holds Major Human Rights Exhibition in Beijing," Xinhua, 17 November 2006, in Open Source Center CPP20061117968163; "Beijing Police Arrest over 400 Mainland Petitioners at 'Human Rights Exhibition,'" *Ping Kuo Jih Pao* (Hong Kong), 25 November 2006, in Open Source Center CPP20061125704009; Lindsay Beck, "China Keeps Masses out of Human Rights Exhibit," Reuters, 23 November 2006.

67. "Tibet's Government in Exile Still Hopeful of an Amicable Solution with Beijing," Phayul.com, 25 January 2007, http://www.phayul.com/news/article.espx?id=15430&t=1&c=1.

68. "Documentary Portrays Tibet Situation before 1959," Xinhua, 7 February 2007, in Open Source Center CPP20070207968136.

69. "China Discovers 600 Sites of Copper, Iron Ore Deposits on Qinghai-Tibet Plateau," Xinhua, 13 February 2007.

70. "Chinese Government to Invest 100 Billion Yuan in Tibet," Xinhua, 26 March 2007, in Open Source Center CPP20070326968147.

71. "China Plays Down Trip by Dalai Lama's Envoys," Reuters, 3 July 2007.

72. "Sino-Tibetan Dialogue Process Has Reached a Critical Stage: Lodi Gyari," Phayul.com, 7 July 2007, http://www.phayul.com/news/article.aspx?id=17094&t=1&c-1.

73. "Statement by US Government on Meeting with Dalai Lama's Envoys," 29 June 2007, http://www.state.gov/r/pa/prs/ps/2007/jun/87562.htm.

74. "China Replaces Local Tibetans in Lithang after Protest," *Kanze Daily*, as reported on 6 September 2007, http://www.rfa.org/english/tibetan/2007/09/04/tibetan_protest_update/.

75. "China Strongly Urges the U.S. to Cancel Arrangement on Gold Medal Award to Dalai Lama," Xinhua, 14 October 2007, in OSC CPP20071014968121.

76. "Chinese Legislature on U.S. Congressional 'Award' to Dalai Lama," Xinhua, 18 October 2007, in OSC CPP20071018968195.

77. "Dalai Lama's US Award Not to Affect Tibet's Stability," Xinhua, 16 October 2007, in OSC CPP20071016968153.

78. "China Condemns Dalai Lama US Trip," BBC, 16 October 2007.

79. "Bush Meeting with the Dalai Lama Hurts Sino-US Relations," *Ta Kung Pao* (Hong Kong), 22 October 2007, in OSC CPP20071022710009.

80. "US Should Rid Itself of Arrogant Thinking toward China," *Ta Kung Pao* (Hong Kong), 18 October 2007, in OSC CPP20071018710006.

7

The Issue of Tibet

THE PEOPLE'S REPUBLIC OF CHINA (PRC) promised a greater degree of autonomy to Tibet in the 1951 Seventeen-Point Agreement than to any of the PRC's other "national minorities," none of whom required a similar treaty of incorporation. Tibet was promised not only all of the autonomous rights supposedly granted to all of China's national minorities under the National Regional Autonomy system, but much more, including no changes in the Tibetan government, the political role of the Dalai Lama, or the monastic system, even though all were based upon the "feudal serf system." However, the Seventeen-Point Agreement was contradictory in that it promised the preservation of the Tibetan political and religious systems and their replacement by an entirely different system. The Chinese Communists' promises were therefore either duplicitous and calculated to secure Tibet's "peaceful liberation" or, at best, overly optimistic, based upon the assumption that Tibetans would voluntarily accept the reform of their culture and society once they had experienced the superiority of Chinese culture and socialist society.

The Chinese Communists' promises of autonomy to Tibetans were contradicted by their intentions to integrate Tibet politically into the Chinese state. Tibet was meant to undergo "democratic reforms" and "socialist transformation," along with the rest of China, perhaps at a slower rate, but there was never any idea that Tibet or any other national minority should be permanently immune from such transformation. The only dispute in Chinese Communist policies toward Tibet has been between proponents of a gradual and voluntary (as much as possible) approach and those who preferred a more rapid assimilation.

The ultimate goal of Marxist-Leninist-Stalinist-Maoist nationalities doctrine was not autonomy, but assimilation. Autonomy in Marxist-Leninist theory and practice was a temporary tactic intended to reduce minorities' resistance to incorporation into Communist states. Autonomy was never, in Communist parties' or states' theory or practice, intended to be a permanent system, nor was the preservation of minorities' cultures and national identities an ultimate goal. Democratic reforms and socialist transformation were the minorities' future, not permanent autonomy. Assimilation of minority nationalities cultures to that of the majority nationality and their achievement of "socialist spiritual civilization" were assumed to be in their own best interests, as they themselves would eventually realize, while the retention of their traditional cultures would only hamper their economic and social progress.

Chinese Communist nationalities policies were entirely compatible with the equally assimilative doctrines of traditional Chinese frontier policies. The legitimacy of an assimilationist solution to China's nationality question, its inevitability, and even the voluntary and enthusiastic acceptance of Chinese culture by those being "allowed" to receive it have been virtually unquestioned in Chinese history.

The promises of the Seventeen-Point Agreement that the Tibetan political system would remain unchanged were abrogated within three years, in 1954, when preparations began for the creation of the Preparatory Committee of the Tibet Autonomous Region. The Chinese Communist Party (CCP) rationalized that this change was voluntary, the Dalai Lama and his government having agreed to it, and therefore was not a violation of the Seventeen-Point Agreement.

The PRC's nationalities policy began to go wrong in Tibet, and in other national minority areas, in 1956, when eastern Tibetan and other minority areas were subjected to the Democratic Reforms campaign. Revolt in eastern Tibet began as soon as democratic reforms were imposed. The PRC launched its first purge of "local nationalists" in 1957 after nationality cadres had the effrontery to demand the autonomy they had been promised. The future Tibet Autonomous Region (TAR) was granted a delay in reforms in 1957, but Tibetan areas outside the TAR were not. The 1959 Tibetan Revolt was precipitated by the CCP's refusal to allow eastern Tibet a similar delay in reforms, even though that area had already erupted in revolt. Had China been willing to treat eastern Tibet as "Tibet," rather than as parts of Chinese provinces where democratic reforms were to be implemented, then the Tibetan revolt might have been delayed, if not prevented.

After the revolt, all the promises of the Seventeen-Point Agreement were abandoned, with the excuse that the Tibetan government had violated its terms. This outcome was predictable, at least to Mao Zedong, who was quoted as saying that the Tibetans would either accept reforms or they would revolt, either result being favorable to China. Mao's plan was the socialist transformation of Tibet along with the rest of China, not adherence to the conditions of the Seventeen-Point Agreement or the preservation of Tibetan social, cultural, and political systems.

Despite having dissolved the former Tibetan government after the revolt and declaring the Seventeen-Point Agreement no longer valid, the Chinese government claimed that Tibetans had achieved their "final liberation" by overthrowing the feudal serf system and "self-rule" by means of the subsequent democratic reforms. Democratic reforms began the process toward the PRC's system of national regional autonomy, but in reality they were the means by which the Chinese identified and repressed opposition to Chinese rule. Thus, only eight years after promising extensive autonomy and no changes in the political system in Tibet, the Chinese Communists had eliminated Tibetan autonomy in all but theory.

Tibetans were granted an illusory status of national regional autonomy in 1965 with the establishment of the TAR, but even the pretense of autonomy was abandoned a year later when the Cultural Revolution began. For the next ten years, autonomy was ignored even in theory. Tibet's "special characteristics," the very justification for its autonomy, were the primary targets of the campaign against the "four olds." Just fifteen years after being incorporated within the PRC with promises of extensive autonomy, Tibet was subjected to an intensive assimilationist campaign in which all aspects of Tibetan culture were denounced as reactionary and counterrevolutionary and as such were repressed. Tibet's national wealth was looted from its upper classes and its monasteries and temples, and almost all cultural monuments were destroyed. Collectivization before and during the Cultural Revolution achieved almost total Chinese control over all aspects of Tibetans' lives, including their economic production.

When Mao died in 1976 and the Cultural Revolution finally ended, it was another four years before Tibetans saw any relief. The subsequent period of the 1980s saw a revival and resurgence of Tibetan culture and religion along with a rebirth of Tibetan nationalism. This came as a profound shock to the Chinese Communists, who imagined that Tibetan separatism was a dead issue and had initiated liberalization policies and overtures to the Dalai Lama based on that assumption. The subsequent demonstrations and riots in Lhasa from 1987 to 1989 reportedly convinced many Chinese officials that Tibetan autonomy could never be allowed.

Since 1989, the PRC has instituted a policy of repression of any and all aspects of Tibetan culture associated with nationalism, combined with economic development and colonization as a final solution to the Tibet problem.

Tibetans have been subjected to relentless and repeated "patriotic education" campaigns, and the Dalai Lama has been denounced in uncompromising terms. Current Chinese nationalist imperatives do not provide much hope that China will refrain from the "natural" and ever more feasible assimilationist solution to the Tibet issue.

The PRC has since 1979 maintained a policy of ostensible willingness to enter into dialogue with the Dalai Lama if he would abandon independence and his "splittist activities." However, it has been undeviating in its refusal to talk about or alter the system of autonomy in Tibet or the territorial boundaries of the TAR. China has been willing to discuss only the Dalai Lama's "personal status," and now even that seems unlikely since the Chinese no longer appear to want him to return. In their official statements and propaganda, they have said repeatedly that China will choose the next Dalai Lama according to "Tibetan Buddhist traditions," the most important of which is approval by the Chinese government.

Despite its often-repeated statements that there is no issue of Tibet's political status, that seems to be the *only* issue for China. The legitimacy of China's sovereignty over Tibet is so sensitive for Beijing that it cannot make any compromises that would allow any possibility for the survival of a separate Tibetan national identity and thus the perpetuation of the Tibetan separatist issue.

China's intransigence on the Tibet issue has only increased since the first overtures were made to the Dalai Lama in 1979. Chinese leaders at that time imagined that the only remaining issue to be resolved in regard to Tibet was that of the Dalai Lama. Deng Xiaoping was so confident that Tibetan separatism had been eradicated, that Tibetans were loyal to China, and that the Dalai Lama had lost his support from the United States when Washington had recognized the PRC, that the Dalai Lama could be persuaded to return, thus achieving the final legitimization of Chinese rule over Tibet. However, the Chinese were shocked to find that the Tibetans were not reconciled to the reality of Chinese rule and were still in fact loyal to the Dalai Lama. They were also surprised to find that the Dalai Lama could arouse popular international support based on human rights issues. The realization that the Tibet issue was far from being resolved and was still an international issue for China made the Chinese ever more resistant to any compromises.

China's current strategy in regard to the international issue of Tibet is primarily a propaganda policy, of which the dialogue process is apparently a part. Propaganda, both internal and external, has long been a fundamental aspect of Chinese policy toward Tibet, with huge amounts of propaganda being promulgated via every conceivable medium. Since 1989, the volume has only increased, and new venues have been developed, including the use of academic Tibetology and international Tibet cultural festivals. China's emphasis on propaganda and the dialogue process with regard to Tibet is consistent with its policy on other human rights issues. Beijing has shown no willingness to compromise on any issue in its bilateral human rights dialogues or in the recent Sino-Tibetan contacts. Nevertheless, the contacts allow China to appear conciliatory and to placate its international critics who are demanding that it talk with the Dalai Lama.

China has exploited Dharamsala's hope for dialogue in order to get it to promote a "conducive atmosphere" for such dialogue, including discouraging Tibetan demonstrations against Chinese leaders during their international travels. China's conditions for talks reveal a Chinese goal of elimination of the international Tibet issue without having to make any concessions on actual policy within Tibet. China's conditions include an end to the Dalai Lama's and Dharamsala's splittist activities, which seems to mean all the Dalai Lama's international activities and even the very existence of the Tibetan government-in-exile. Its other condition—that the Dalai Lama give up Tibetan independence—apparently means that he should abandon any claim that Tibet was ever independent of China. He should also abandon his complaints about the nature and extent of Tibetan autonomy.

Were China to achieve all its preconditions for dialogue, then there would truly be nothing left to discuss—as China has maintained all along—and the "so-called issue of Tibet" would be finally resolved. That this is China's goal in pursuing the dialogue is exposed in its own documents, officials' statements, and propaganda.

Despite Tibetan hopes that China will want to resolve the "issue of Tibet," the only issue that China appears to want to resolve is that of exile Tibetan and international criticism of China *about* Tibet. Beijing is not willing to reopen the historical issue of Tibet's status, even its autonomous status, since that issue was "finally resolved" in 1951. China has shown no willingness to alter any of its policies within Tibet, even if that would reduce international criticism. Presumably this is because China is neither able nor willing to change its policies there. The Chinese apparently believe that they cannot allow more Tibetan autonomy because this might permit the survival of a separate national and cultural identity. This is exactly what the Tibetans want, and what China fears because of the perceived ethnic unity and national security threat. Having achieved its goal of annexing Tibet, the legitimacy of Chinese sovereignty there is so sensitive for China that it cannot be flexible on any issue relevant to that legitimacy, including the nature of Tibetan autonomy within the Chinese state.

China is equally unwilling to expand the extent of the TAR to include all Tibetan areas. That issue was also resolved in 1951 with the partition of Tibetan areas into adjacent Chinese provinces. Despite some hints from Chinese leaders in the past that this issue might be revisited, many reasons preclude that possibility, including the fear of such a large territorial extent for any sort of Tibetan political entity. The need for China to control the headwaters of its two major rivers, the Yellow and Yangtze, is alone sufficient reason why China will not allow any expansion of the TAR.

The inadmissibility of this issue does not, however, mean that the other issue—the nature of Tibetan autonomy—might be resolved if the territorial issue were dropped. Genuine autonomy of the type the Dalai Lama demands is so unacceptable and is such a threat that China is unlikely to compromise on autonomy even if the territorial issue were removed.

There is, however, a possibility—in the unlikely event that Dharamsala should give up the territorial issue—that China might make a compromise. Beijing might, in that scenario, promise some increased level of autonomy in Tibet in order to achieve its goal of the elimination of the international Tibet issue. Dharamsala would then be in the predicament of deciding whether to accept a Chinese offer, knowing that China alone would decide whether or not to abide by its conditions. The situation could be much like that in 1951 when China made the promises of the Seventeen-Point Agreement in order to achieve the "peaceful liberation of Tibet" without any intention of honoring those promises. The Dalai Lama might imagine that he could still appeal to his international supporters, but the Tibet issue would be regarded as resolved and he might have difficulty finding much support. The Dalai Lama's access to the outside world would then be controlled by China.

Such was the situation after the Tibetan acceptance of the Seventeen-Point Agreement. Between the invasion of November 1950 and the Dalai Lama's return to Lhasa in August 1951, the United States made many offers of support to the Dalai Lama if he would go into exile. After the Dalai Lama's acceptance of the agreement, however, there was nothing the Americans or anyone else could do, and Tibet's ultimate appeal for support for its independence in 1959 was fatally compromised. The autonomy that China promised to Tibet in 1951 was violated by China at its will, while the autonomy that China supposedly guaranteed to Tibet in 1965 under the national regional autonomy system existed only in theory. The fundamental flaw in any system of autonomy is that the autonomy has no definition except that decided upon in practice by the ruling authority. Since the ostensibly autonomous entity has no ultimate authority, autonomy lacks any meaning in practice. No system of autonomy is capable of achieving Tibetan self-rule or self-determination because autonomy places all decision-making power, particularly about the nature of autonomy, in the hands of the Chinese, not Tibetans.

The system of autonomy that China has put into practice in Tibet purports to provide for the protection and preservation of Tibetan culture, but fails to do so in fact. The professed goal of autonomy—the preservation of a distinct culture—is utterly contradicted by the CCP's assimilationist doctrine. The essence of China's position is that autonomy has been bestowed upon Tibet by the Chinese Communist Party due to Tibet's ethnic distinctions from China's Han majority, not because of any national distinctions or past Tibetan political separation from China. China will grant Tibet whatever autonomy it sees fit, but will not admit that Tibet has any inherent right to autonomy on the basis of its non-Chinese national identity or its history as less than an integral part of China. China apparently believes that its control in Tibet is secure, and it does not fear Tibetan resistance even if the Dalai Lama dies in exile. Instead, China appears confident that it can control opposition within Tibet, resolve the internal Tibetan political issue by means of colonization, and eventually eliminate the international issue through coercive diplomacy and relentless propaganda.

Some proponents of autonomy and the dialogue process visualize China changing to such an extent that some future, perhaps democratic, Chinese government might not only negotiate about Tibet but even allow "genuine" autonomy. However, Tibet would pose the same threat to China's national unity and territorial integrity for any Chinese regime. Genuine nationality autonomy has been, and is likely to remain, an extremely doubtful prospect within China. Chinese political culture, even under a more democratic political system, is likely to retain much of its authoritarian, collectivist, and culturally and politically conformist character. Chinese political culture and nationalism, along with the political realities of economics and the educational and bureaucratic systems, would seem to preclude the possibility of meaningful nationality autonomy within the Chinese state. Tibetans' experience of an absence of any cultural or political autonomy in the past does not lead to confidence in the promises of any Chinese government to allow genuine autonomy in the future.

The issue of Tibet is a fundamental political issue arising from the existence of two national entities within one political state. This situation poses an existential dichotomy that can be resolved only by separation into two political entities or the assimilation of one nation to another. Beijing, if not Dharamsala, seems clear on this point. Although China claims that there is no issue of Tibet's sovereignty—Tibet having "always" been a part of China—it deals with Tibet as if that were the only issue. China is so sensitive to any questions about the legitimacy of its sovereignty over Tibet that it cannot allow any real autonomy out of fear that the sovereignty issue will reappear. Such is China's defensiveness on the Tibet issue that it reacts to international interest in Tibet as interference in its internal affairs and even accuses "hostile Western forces" of inventing and promoting the issue in order to denigrate and split China. Thus, as international criticism of China in regard to Tibet has increased, China's sensitivity, defensiveness, and unwillingness to compromise have also increased. China's reaction to any and all criticism about Tibet, including human rights issues, reveals that it interprets all such criticism as based upon the sovereignty issue.

The Dalai Lama's strategy for dialogue with China is based on convincing China that his acknowledgment of Chinese sovereignty over Tibet would eliminate the separatist threat in Tibet sufficiently that China could allow genuine autonomy. His acceptance of Chinese sovereignty would theoretically remove any Tibetan or international challenge to that sovereignty. However, China's insecurity in Tibet is due not so much to the Dalai Lama's nonacceptance as to the fundamental illegitimacy of Chinese rule over the non-Chinese Tibetans. China does not believe that the Dalai Lama has really accepted Chinese sovereignty, that is, "given up the idea of Tibetan independence," nor that all Tibetans have done so, and it does not believe that the Dalai Lama can convince them to do so. The Chinese at one time—in 1979, when they thought Tibetan separatism was no longer an issue—might have allowed the Fourteenth Dalai Lama to return. However, such is the animosity now to this Dalai Lama that the Chinese do not appear willing to allow him to return under any circumstances. In any case, they cannot make any concessions to the Dalai Lama's demands, since any compromise opens the door to admitting that there is an issue of Tibet that the Dalai Lama represents, based upon Tibet's former status as less than an integral part of China.

Because of the fundamental nature of the Tibet issue, China has apparently settled upon the traditional Chinese policy of assimilation as the only certain solution. For his part, the Dalai Lama has resorted to autonomy as a solution only because, with independence considered unachievable, it is the only way to prevent China's assimilationist solution. However, autonomy as a solution to a sovereignty issue has been successful only in the case of some small, usually territorially separate entities that have little relevance for the situation of Tibet.

A recent conference in Dharamsala, one of a series of events intended to give substance to the autonomy concept, illustrated this fact. The International Conference for Autonomous Regions for Tibet invited representatives of these "autonomous countries": Aaland Island, Bougainville, Quebec, Scotland, Catalonia, Greenland, Saami, Hong Kong, and South Tyrol. These are the best existing examples of autonomy in the world, and none represents a separatist threat to the state within which it exists. If one did, it would probably find its autonomy severely circumscribed, or in certain cases, it might achieve independence. None exists in a state so relentlessly assimilationist as the PRC, except Hong Kong, which has little autonomy in practice and is losing autonomous rights rather than gaining them. The PRC recently served notice to Hong Kong that its autonomy was an "authorized autonomy," not "complete autonomy"; that is, its autonomy was "authorized by the central government," rather than being "inherent in Hong Kong itself."[1]

The autonomy that Tibet enjoyed before 1950 was possible due to the characteristics of a former political era. In an era of vaguely defined states and empires, relationships between nations had a greater variety of forms, and borders were less clearly delimited. Tribute states, subject states, dependent states, protectorates, and even the Tibetan patron–priest relationship were arrangements that defined the association between empires and their territorial components. The archaic, feudal era of empires and indirect rule facilitated Tibetan autonomy relative to China. The non-Chinese empires that ruled China had neither the means nor the need to directly administer Tibet. Once China regained its sovereignty from the Manchu Qing and its claim to dominance over Tibet was threatened by a foreign imperialist rival, Britain, and by the simultaneous development of Tibetan nationalism, China attempted to replace the vague relationship of the past with definitive Chinese sovereignty over Tibet. The British attempted to perpetuate the already archaic and outdated system of Tibetan autonomy under Chinese "suzerainty" for their own interests. However, they were unable to define this relationship except by the use of an archaic terminology, and they were unable to substantiate it in practice.

Autonomy is a vague relationship of the type that existed in the former era but has little viability in the present. As Dawa Norbu has written:

> Empire-tolerated heterogeneity allowed considerable social space for different identities, cultures, languages, etc. to exist, whereas the nation-state, in the name of political centralization and cultural unification, does not tolerate the politics of differences; instead it melts minorities within the crucible of national integration. . . . By the late nineteenth or early twentieth centuries, the symbolic domination and ceremonial relations [between China and Tibet] fundamentally changed with the emergence of modern political ideas of Chinese nationalism and nation-state within which the Chinese Nationalists first and then the Communists sought to integrate Tibet, based upon a unitary conception of a Han-dominated state.[2]

When states became more centralized and defined, political frontiers and relationships also became better defined. The idea of nationalism arose along with that of national self-determination, with the result that nations either emerged as independent states or were absorbed into other states. The Marxists attempted to differentiate between "nations" that were large enough to be viable as independent states and "nationalities" that were not and should be absorbed. The CCP defined the Tibetans and all of China's other minorities as nationalities and scheduled them for assimilation.

Before 1950, Tibet was a nation that was developing a national identity sufficient to exist as an independent state and to qualify for the right of national self-determination. Unfortunately, Chinese nationalism was also rising with a determination to achieve the long-held goal of full Chinese sovereignty over Tibet. The PRC's "liberation" of Tibet terminated Tibet's attempt to achieve its legitimate right to self-determination. Having, in exile, failed to achieve international support for Tibetan independence, the Dalai Lama and his government now seem to want to return to a status much like Tibet's traditional relationship with China.

The Middle Way Approach (MWA) has many similarities to Tibet's former relationship with China of a former political era. The Dalai Lama's definition of Tibetan autonomy has many of the characteristics of the Tibetan conception of its relations with Yuan- and Qing-dynasty China. The "associative" status proposed by the Dalai Lama in his Strasbourg Statement was admitted to be similar to Tibet's traditional *cho–yon* relationship with China. Despite the Dalai Lama's stated intention to create a democratic system in an autonomous Tibet, his conception of an autonomous Tibet's relationship with China has much of the feudal "indirect rule" character. The autonomy concept, associative status, and "zone of peace" idea all have a vagueness about them typical of an earlier political era.

Both the Chinese and Tibetans agree that the real issue of Tibet is self-determination, even though they may not use that terminology. The Chinese claim that Tibetans achieved self-determination or "self-rule" by means of the liberation of 1950–1951 and by democratic reforms after the 1959 revolt, although they mean this in the class rather than the nationalist sense. China does not admit that there is any issue of Tibetan self-determination in the national sense. The Dalai Lama says that what he means by "genuine autonomy" is self-rule. However, he has been constrained in his demands by the realities of international support. He has been required to construe autonomy as capable of achieving "self-rule," or "internal self-determination," because true self-determination—that is, a free Tibetan choice as to their political status—is not considered feasible.

Dharamsala seems to be claiming that the MWA is in some sense an expression of self-determination by saying that Tibetans, both inside and outside Tibet, have democratically chosen this policy. However, what Tibetans have "democratically" chosen is to do what the Dalai Lama suggests, and they have done so because of the autocratic nature of his role, based upon his religious identity, rather than democracy. The weakness of the Tibetan political system is that Tibetans will not voluntarily choose their future for themselves as long as the Dalai Lama is there to choose for them. Much of Dharamsala's propaganda about Tibetans' democratic choice for the MWA is intended to convince the Chinese that the Dalai Lama has the authority to enforce a choice for autonomy upon Tibetans and that *only* the Dalai Lama has such authority.

Some have suggested that Tibetan self-determination might be achieved by a free choice of Tibetans both within and outside Tibet to accept autonomy. However, such a "free choice," like that in favor of the MWA, would likely be heavily influenced by the Dalai Lama's wishes. If Tibetans had a truly free choice, uninfluenced by either the Chinese or the Dalai Lama, all indications are that they would choose independence. Also, self-determination is not a one-time choice. Self-determination means having the freedom of choice at any time, which is why the Chinese will never believe that Tibetans have permanently given up their hope for independence.

All attempts to claim that the MWA is capable of achieving some semblance of Tibetan self-determination, even if only "internal self-determination," founder upon the fact that autonomy is not equivalent to self-determination. The idea of "internal self-determination" is contradictory to the fundamental definition of self-determination, which is that a nation of people decides for itself whether it is to be "internal" in relation to another state or independent of any other state. Besides being a contradiction in terms, "internal self-determination" represents a confusion over what the real issue of Tibet is. Is the issue of Tibet about individual rights or those of the collective? Is it the Dalai Lama's "happiness of the Tibetan people" or the survival of Tibetan national identity? Is it about religion or nation? Under an autonomous system, some freedom on the individual level might be possible for Tibetans in return for political allegiance to China. Collective freedom, on the other hand, is not possible for Tibetans under the conditions of Chinese rule.

The proponents of the autonomy strategy maintain that it will eventually produce results because of the international pressure on China. The strategy is indeed popular among Western governments, who repeatedly tell the Chinese government to "talk to the Dalai Lama." However, the policy may be too convenient, since foreign governments have only to ask the Chinese to settle their differences with the Dalai Lama without even taking any position on what those differences may be. The idea that the Tibet issue is some sort of "misunderstanding" that may be resolved by friendly talks between the Dalai Lama and the Chinese government greatly oversimplifies the complexities of the issue. China is able to defuse much of this international pressure, mild as it is, by claiming that it has always been willing to talk with the Dalai Lama if he would just give up his splittist activities—one of which is lobbying international governments to put pressure on China to talk with him.

The Dalai Lama remains incurably hopeful that the Chinese people will become more democratic and more respectful of Tibetan culture and religion. Many Chinese have in fact become more interested in Tibet and are flocking there in large numbers as tourists, especially after the opening of the Lhasa railroad. However, increased Chinese tourism can be interpreted as a negative sign for the survival of Tibetan culture. It will contribute to the dilution of the very Tibetan cultural differences that Tibetans hope to preserve and the tourists come to experience. It also means that Chinese people no longer have any fear of traveling to Tibet because China's position in Tibet is finally considered secure.

Many Chinese tend to respond to Americans' criticisms of China's role in Tibet by citing the example of the treatment of the Native Americans. The differences between these two situations are that the Native Americans did not have a political state structure and all the other requirements for national independence, as did the Tibetans, and that the Americans did not try to justify their conquest by claiming that it was actually a liberation. One similarity is that Americans became sympathetic to Native American culture only when it was practically eliminated and was no longer considered a threat, very much like the Chinese attitude toward Tibet.

The Dalai Lama and his supporters constantly express optimism that many Chinese are becoming more sympathetic to Tibet because of their increased interest in Buddhism. Chinese Buddhists are not necessarily sympathetic to the Tibetan political cause, however. Like their Western counterparts, who are notoriously more interested in their own enlightenment than in mundane politics and are even advised by some Tibetan lamas to avoid politics, Chinese Buddhists may be assumed to share this tendency to avoid political issues. Chinese authorities are also sensitive to this connection and have closed down Buddhist centers in eastern Tibet where there were Chinese students. Most recently, the Chinese People's Armed Police destroyed an almost-completed large statue of Guru Rinpoche, the historical figure who restored Buddhism in Tibet in the seventh century, at Samye, the monastery he founded. The statue's construction was sponsored by Chinese devotees from Guangzhou at a cost of some 800,000 yuan (more than $100,000).[3]

The Dalai Lama's hope that the Chinese people might become more sympathetic to the Tibetan political issue due to a renewed interest in Buddhism was called into question by a recent incident in the Indian state of Bihar in which a group of Chinese Buddhists visiting holy sites in India walked out of a film on Buddhism presented by the Bihar Tourism Ministry.[4] The film was on the history of Buddhism and the Buddhist holy sites in Bihar, including

Bodh Gaya, where the Buddha attained enlightenment. The film began with a scene in which the Dalai Lama appeared, at which point the Chinese tourists angrily left the theater, saying that the Dalai Lama was not their spiritual leader. This group of some 125 Chinese Buddhist tourists apparently believed their government's propaganda about him. Despite being Buddhists, they obviously felt a lot of animosity toward the Dalai Lama. If this incident is any indication, Chinese Buddhists are not necessarily sympathetic to the Tibetan political issue, at least as it is represented by the Dalai Lama.

The Tibetan optimism that the Chinese people, if not their government, are becoming more sympathetic to the Tibetan issue is also contradicted by the rise of nationalism among Chinese of all types, whether Buddhists or democracy advocates or those who have traveled to or worked in Tibet. Almost all Chinese are extremely sensitive to any criticism about China's role in Tibet for the same reasons that their government is—because it calls into question all their personal and collective legitimating ideologies. All Chinese have been taught about their country's liberating role in Tibet and the abject poverty and oppression to which Tibetans were subjected by their own exploitative upper class and religious institutions. To question this ideology is equivalent to questioning one's own identity and that of one's nation.

Most Chinese retain their anti-imperialist ideology, as inculcated by CCP indoctrination, along with its associated mentality of victimization, and are reluctant to see Chinese people or the Chinese state as the persecutors rather than the liberators of Tibetans. The most typical Chinese attitude toward Tibetans is resentment at their rejection of Chinese "assistance." This is accompanied by a feeling that Tibetans have no more right to Tibet than do the Chinese, Tibetans having marginalized themselves due to their rejection of China's assistance and Chinese culture. Most Chinese, even those with experience in Tibet, reject the idea of Chinese illegitimacy in Tibet, exploitation or oppression of Tibetans, or destruction of Tibetan culture. The usual defense against the last charge is that the defense of Tibetan culture represents a chauvinistic Tibetan resistance to modernization—a modernization that is of a universal rather than specifically Chinese type and has nothing to do with Chinese assimilation. Chinese often react to Western criticism of China's role in Tibet as their government does: with a rejection of all such criticism as a remnant of imperialist interference in China and an attempt to prevent China's rise. The attitude of righteous indignation in response to any criticism about Tibet is often shared by the Chinese people and their government.

Another tenet of Dharamsala's strategy is that the issue of Tibet is political, not cultural. This is the basis of the idea that the Tibetan and Chinese peoples could coexist peacefully within the same state if the political issues could be resolved. The Dalai Lama has often stated that Tibetans could benefit, at least economically, by being a part of the rapidly developing Chinese economy. However, this requires the coexistence of two nations within one centralized state—a state that has never allowed any autonomy of any type and that has an ancient and pervasive assimilationist ideology. The Dalai Lama imagines that Tibetan culture could be preserved within China if the political issues could be resolved. However, the political issue is characterized by Chinese intolerance of any non-Chinese "separatist" culture within the Chinese national state. The political issue of Tibet for China is the elimination of the separatist threat, which is based on the distinct Tibetan cultural and national identity. The solution for China then is the elimination of that distinct identity, the very thing that the Dalai Lama and Tibetans hope to preserve.

For China, there is no political solution that preserves Tibetan culture and, especially, Tibetan national identity. Despite the Dalai Lama's belief that the issue is not cultural, the nature of the Sino-Tibetan issue is as much cultural as it is political. The fundamental issue of Tibet is about the conflict between two nations and two cultures over territory, much as it was during the Tibetan Empire and Tang dynasty period. Now, however, China has the intention and ability to finally resolve the issue by the political and economic integration and the cultural absorption of Tibet within China, with methods that include the colonization of Tibet, the repression of Tibetan national identity, and the assimilation of Tibetan culture. Having originally promised autonomy, under the assumption that Tibetans would voluntarily give up their own culture, but having been surprised by the persistence of Tibetan culture and national identity, the Chinese have now reverted to Mao's more honest offer to Tibetans that Tibet should fulfill China's need for natural resources while China would fulfill Tibet's need for people.

A last-resort hope of the Dharamsala leadership is based upon the CCP's notorious factional conflicts. During the 1980s, there was indeed a faction within the Chinese leadership, led by Hu Yaobang and the Panchen Lama, that favored respect for China's own promises of autonomy for Tibet. However, since 1989 the hardline faction in Chinese politics has prevailed. Nevertheless, Tibetans continually hope for a resurgence of a more moderate faction that would allow expanded autonomy in Tibet and perhaps even pursue a resolution of the Tibet issue by means of negotiations with the Dalai Lama. These hopes seem unrealistic given the hardening of Chinese attitudes toward Tibet after the experience of the 1980s. There is a multitude of evidence that China has confidence in the capability of its current policy to achieve the final resolution of the Tibet issue. Were there any countervailing influences in Chinese politics with regard to Tibet, there would surely be some signs of them. Instead, there is a relentless denigration of the Dalai Lama, an intolerance of any aspects of Tibetan culture with nationalist implications, and overwhelming Chinese economic development and colonization projects in progress.

Similarly, Dharamsala prefers to regard Beijing's relentless anti–Dalai Lama, antidialogue propaganda as just that: propaganda, rather than actual policy. However, in Marxist and CCP doctrine, propaganda *is* the promotion of policy, without the negative connotation it carries in non-Communist countries. Dharamsala rationalizes Chinese propaganda about Tibet—none of which provides the slightest indication of any Chinese willingness to enter into dialogue—as simply a tactic in that nonexistent dialogue. China's 2004 White Paper on Tibet was thus characterized as "a negotiating tactic that underscores the resistance of hardliners to move forward in good faith."[5] Nevertheless, there is little but wishful thinking to indicate that China's propaganda about Tibet does not mean exactly what it says, especially since China's strategy in regard to the international issue of Tibet is to employ propaganda to convince the world of the correctness of China's policies in Tibet.

The Dalai Lama's Middle Way policy is a reflection not only of the politics of the situation but also, as the name implies, of Buddhist philosophy and traditions. Buddhism, as a universalistic religion, is essentially transnational and even antinationalist. The Dalai Lama has repeatedly said that national borders and national divisions are becoming less important in a globalizing world and that Tibet might benefit, particularly economically, from being a part of China. The MWA is presented as being a postnationalist model for the resolution of nationalist issues. However, far from being a visionary and practical strategy in international politics, it has primarily archaic and utopian characteristics; the archaism inherent in its wish to return to a premodern cho–yon relationship, and the utopianism in its idealistic view of the relations between individuals, nations, and states.

The utopian nature of the Middle Way truly makes it compatible, as the Dalai Lama has often said, with socialist or communist ideology. The wishful thinking imbued within this policy has taken on something akin to cultism, which is evident in the Kashag's call upon Tibetans to engage in prayer and religious rituals intended to move China to negotiate. There is also the willful dismissal of all historical and political factors that argue against the MWA. In the context of the lack of any progress in Sino-Tibetan dialogue, and China's constant and vociferous rejection of all the Dalai Lama's proposals and denunciations of him personally, the MWA has evolved into something akin to a cult of wishful thinking. This cult ignores all criticisms of its lack of realism and calls upon its proponents to increase their hopefulness as its only strategy. However, to repeat a common saying: hope is not a policy and wishful thinking is not a strategy.

Despite the Dalai Lama's statements that the issue of Tibet is the happiness of the Tibetan people, the most fundamental issue of Tibet is the survival of

Tibetan national identity. Despite his universalistic idea that national borders are not important, without borders there is no territory within which the nation can preserve its national identity. In order to imagine that the MWA is practical, the Dalai Lama and proponents of the autonomy strategy have to dismiss as irrelevant the history of China's assimilationist cultural and political policy, the evidence that autonomy is an inherent threat to China's national identity and territorial integrity, and the lack of any evidence that autonomy is capable of preserving Tibetan cultural and national identity. The MWA also has to assume that China would allow Tibetans to control their own economy and natural resources, despite the facts that economic development is an essential element of China's current strategy for strengthening its political control in Tibet and that Tibet's natural resources are essential for China's development and even survival.

The proponents of the MWA tend to reject the opinions of critics as negative and harmful to the possibility of achieving dialogue and a solution of the Tibet issue. This rejection often reaches the level of animosity of the type that critics of real cults receive. However, the MWA is also open to criticism for its negative effects. When the Dalai Lama formally gave up independence in his 1978 Strasbourg Statement, it had a confusing, disheartening, and demoralizing effect upon many Tibetans who imagined they had been fighting all along for independence and wondered why it had been given up. The lack of any definitive meaning of autonomy and doubts about its ability to preserve Tibetan identity within China have affected the morale of Tibetans and their supporters. The lack of any clear goal in the Tibetan struggle, which could no longer be characterized as a Tibetan freedom struggle, exacerbated the confusion and demoralization in the Tibetan community. The symbol of the change in strategy, and the confusion, was the adoption of a new slogan, "Save Tibet," which replaced the previous "Free Tibet" slogan in all of Dharamsala's and most Tibet support groups' campaigning.

The Strasbourg Statement had the opposite effect upon international support at the time, many non-Tibetan supporters having advised the Dalai Lama to announce an open policy of autonomy. After the Tiananmen Square incident of June 1989, China was very much out of international favor, and the award of the Nobel Peace Prize to the Dalai Lama in December of that year increased the profile of the Tibetan leader and his issue. The demoralizing effect of the strategy on many Tibetans could therefore be dismissed as the sentiments of traditionalists who could not understand the efficacy of the new strategy. However, the absence of any results for the next decade and a half has made Tibetans' qualms more salient.

Tibetans' spirits were revived by the resumption of Sino-Tibetan contacts in 2002. But, as the dialogue failed to produce any results, the dissatisfaction of many Tibetans increased. Dharamsala has attempted to arouse support for the policy by organizing seminars and conferences to promote the autonomy policy. However, its promotion of the strategy has reduced the impartiality and objectivity of its policy and further alienated opponents, with the effect of restricting the actual practice of democracy in exile. Official international interest in the Tibet issue was also negatively influenced because China was seemingly satisfying the demand that it talk with the representatives of the Dalai Lama. Thus, as many critics argue, the MWA has not only failed to achieve Tibet's goals but has even furthered those of China.

The MWA is often defended on the grounds that, independence being unachievable, there is no alternative. However, "genuine autonomy" capable of achieving the goal of the preservation of Tibetan culture and national identity within the PRC may be equally unachievable or even more so. Short of abandoning the Middle Way policy, there are alternatives to the way in which the MWA is being pursued. Much of the dissatisfaction within the exile Tibetan community would be eliminated if Dharamsala would be less subservient in its relations with China. In particular, acceding to China's demand that it discourage demonstrations has caused much resentment against Dharamsala, and many Tibetans have not honored the request. There is a sense that China's demands are essentially that the Dalai Lama and the exiles should kowtow to China, after which they might be forgiven, and that Dharamsala has been too ready to comply. Instead, some believe, the Tibetan issue should be presented with the forcefulness and dignity it deserves. The abandonment of a clear policy on self-determination has made this difficult since the autonomy strategy appears to have no goals except for Tibetans to be allowed to be good citizens of China with some allowance for cultural autonomy.

Rather than forever petition China to treat Tibetans better with little or no result, many Tibetans have expressed a preference for a more forceful policy, especially since China's strategy seems to be to stall until the death of the present Dalai Lama. There is also a sense that it was the very strategies that Dharamsala has discouraged—particularly those that have caused embarrassment to China's leaders—that forced China to openly deal with the issue at all, and that more such embarrassments are more likely to produce results with China than appeasement. China has indicated that it will not be satisfied short of a cessation of all the Dalai Lama's international activities and an elimination of his exile government. Given that this is unacceptable to the Tibetans in exile, many believe that Dharamsala should give up its attempts to create a "conducive atmosphere" for dialogue.

What the MWA lacks, besides realism, is a strategy with goals capable of inspiring Tibetans and defining the Tibetan issue in a clear and unambiguous way. Although the MWA aspires to achieve the preservation of Tibetan cultural and national identity, a rational analysis indicates that autonomy within the Chinese state is incapable of achieving that goal and that China is in any case unlikely to allow sufficient autonomy to even approach the Tibetan goal. Since the fundamental issue of Tibet is self-determination, the clearest and most unambiguous strategy is to demand Tibet's right to self-determination. This strategy is no more likely than the MWA to move China to resolve the Tibet issue, but at least it is capable of putting more pressure on Beijing to do so. Self-determination, unlike autonomy, is clearly defined and has the advantage of being regarded as a fundamental right—the foundation of all human rights—in international law.

The meaning of self-determination is that "peoples," defined as distinct nations, have the right to decide for themselves their political organization and affiliation. The potential results are not specified in international law, but, given a truly free choice without complicating factors, nations are assumed to prefer independence. No system of autonomy imposed by the majority state can satisfy the fundamental requirement of self-determination that political association and political system be self-decided. Autonomy has no definition, no basis in international law, and no reality except as determined by the majority government granting autonomy to a minority nationality. Under autonomy, the minority has no right to any political status except as defined by the majority state. No outside political authority, whether unilateral or multilateral, has any jurisdiction, since autonomy is entirely an internal affair of the state in question.

This is the status in which China would like to keep Tibet, since such status is entirely defined by China. All of China's actions and all of its propaganda about Tibet reveal that China is comfortable with an autonomy defined by itself but very uncomfortable with the idea of self-determination. China's denial that Tibet was ever independent is intended to eliminate the idea that Tibet was ever a nation that might be considered at any time in the past or the future to have the right to national self-determination. China denies all the Dalai Lama's suggestions about autonomy because it says they are based on the claim that Tibet was formerly independent, or the "idea of Tibetan independence," or "the idea that Tibet was a country." China's first response to the Dalai Lama's conditions as expressed in his Strasbourg Statement was to condemn them as an attempt to "internationalize" the Tibet issue.

It is obvious that China most fears the self-determination issue with respect to Tibet and fears the autonomy issue not at all. China can limit the reality of Tibetan autonomy as it wishes. The "Yedor" article condemned the idea that Tibet was independent in the past, or an occupied country in the present, since "the so-called 'Tibetan issue' will not then be an internal issue of China;

it will then be related to 'colonial issues' whereby the Tibetans could enjoy the right to independence through 'national self-determination' according to international convention."[6]

Further evidence is provided by China's propaganda book on Tibetan history, *The Historical Status of China's Tibet*, a chapter of which is entitled "Tibet Institutes National Regional Autonomy and Needs No Self-Determination." The book claims that the PRC's system of national regional autonomy eliminated the need for self-determination of Tibetans or any other minority nationality within the PRC: "Now, living in a big family of an independent and united multinational country and enjoying to the greatest extent more than 30 years of national regional autonomy, the Tibetan people really do not need self-determination or independence."[7]

Only self-determination makes Tibet an international issue. Autonomy is an internal issue of China, which is what China has always said about Tibet and why China so fears the "internationalization" of the Tibet issue. Only because of the denial of Tibet's right to self-determination do other countries have a reason to be interested in the Tibet issue. No doubt, most governments that are supportive of the Tibet issue would prefer to confine the issue to dialogue and autonomy. However, they respond to Tibet because of popular pressure; the self-determination issue is capable of arousing more popular support than is a vague indefinable autonomy. Most foreign governments that support Tibet have already said that they favor Tibetans having some form of decision-making capability, and the U.S. government went on record in 1959 in favor of Tibetan self-determination. In that statement, the United States committed itself to the concept that Tibetans have the right to decide for themselves whether or not Tibet is to be independent. Having adopted this policy at one time, the United States might do so again without abandoning consistency on the issue.

The self-determination argument is perhaps unlikely to result in Tibetan independence, but it is as likely as or even more likely than the MWA to pressure China to improve its treatment of Tibetans. A self-determination policy is as likely as and perhaps more likely than the MWA to result in "genuine Tibetan autonomy." The beauty of the self-determination argument is that it can be defined as a principle that people should be allowed to decide for themselves, without specifying what political arrangements the principle implies.

The Dalai Lama has often said that the autonomy he wishes for Tibet should be the equivalent of "self-rule," which has only served to confuse the issue since no form of autonomy is equivalent to self-rule, or even internal self-rule, because the state always has overriding authority. China has, of course, condemned such statements by the Dalai Lama as revealing that he really wants independence. The adoption of a self-determination policy by the

Dalai Lama would not change China's perception of the issue or its belief in what the Dalai Lama really wants. The only changes would be that Tibetans would have a much-needed clarity in their policy and China would be forced to respond to the reality of the issue.

It could be argued that there is nothing to lose and everything to gain by this change in terms of reviving the clarity and spirit of the Tibet issue. An essential part of Tibetan national identity is Tibet's right to determine its own political status, which would be lost by accepting autonomy under Chinese rule. By abandoning its right to national self-determination, Tibet would lose its status, even if only theoretical, of a distinct nation that deserves that right according to international law. Tibetans would then lose their national identity as Tibetans and become Chinese nationals with a Tibetan minority ethnicity, just as China now defines them. National identity is entirely self-defined; a nation is a group of people who regard themselves as such. To voluntarily give up this self-definition, to accept that Tibetans are Chinese, would be equivalent to abandonment of national identity—the very thing that the Dalai Lama hopes to preserve by means of his Middle Way policy. Tibetans' rejection of the legitimacy of Chinese rule over Tibet is all that remains of Tibet's independent national existence. The Dalai Lama has few bargaining advantages, but the one he has—his ability to deny the legitimacy of Chinese rule over Tibet—should not be so lightly abandoned.

There is some evidence that the Dalai Lama himself is coming around to the point of view that his return to Tibet is unlikely and perhaps not even advisable. He has recently said that autonomy is meaningless if Tibetans are a minority in Tibet.[8] And he has said that he might be more useful to the Tibetan cause at this point if he remains in exile.[9] Rather than fruitlessly attempting to satisfy China's conditions for dialogue or to create a "conducive atmosphere" for dialogue—none of which is apparently satisfactory or produces any results—Dharamsala and its supporters might achieve more results by pressing Tibet's best and most legitimate argument. Only political pressure on China is capable of producing any results, and the greatest political pressure available for Tibetans resides in the self-determination argument. If autonomy is incapable of achieving Tibetan cultural survival, then self-determination is a better option. As some Tibetans have said, if autonomy is 100 percent impossible and independence (or self-determination) is only 99 percent impossible, then independence is the better choice. Many Tibetans would accept this 1 percent chance rather than what they consider a certain elimination of Tibetan identity under any form of Chinese rule.

There may be no resolution to the Tibet issue other than the one that China chooses to impose. At the present time, the Chinese solution seems to be constant and relentless repression of any manifestation of Tibetan nationalism or separatism, autonomy limited to only those aspects of Tibetan culture that do not have nationalist implications, and economic development combined with and supportive of colonization. Since almost all aspects of Tibetan culture *do* have nationalist implications, the space for Tibetan autonomy will presumably remain very limited. The Dalai Lama and Tibetan exiles may be able to gain no concessions from China in its policy in Tibet. However, their best chance is surely to emphasize their most legitimate issue, which is certainly self-determination. China can pretend to already allow autonomy in Tibet, but it cannot pretend to have allowed Tibetans any semblance of national self-determination. This is why China is so sensitive to any Tibetan claim that raises this issue, including that Tibet was ever independent, that it is a separate nation deserving even of real autonomy, or that there is any reason the international community should be interested in Tibet.

In the absence of any resolution, or even any movement, the Tibet issue has now become substantially an ideological issue between the Tibetan exiles and their supporters and China. This is indeed how Chinese propaganda often defines it, as an issue that would not exist except as a tool for Western anti-Chinese forces to oppose, to denigrate, to weaken, and to split China. It may be difficult, especially for Tibetans themselves, to conceive of the issue of Tibet's fate as nothing more than an ideological struggle with China. And, of course, Tibetans every day are engaged in a struggle to preserve their way of life, in an exercise of the elemental right of self-determination, against the intentional assimilationism of Chinese policies and the unintentional assimilationism of modern culture. Nevertheless, as an international issue about Tibet's status, the struggle is now primarily ideological. In such an ideological struggle, self-determination is undeniably the best policy.

Unlike the current Tibetan exile leadership, the Uighur exile leadership has never believed in the possibility of autonomy under Chinese sovereignty and has therefore always maintained that the Uighurs are entitled to the right of self-determination.[10] The difference may lie in the Tibetan people's traditional hopefulness, the lesser degree (so far) of Chinese colonization in Tibet than in Xinjiang, and Tibet's greater international support, which has led Tibetans to believe that some "resolution" of the issue might actually be possible. However, the PRC has relentlessly pursued colonization and assimilation as its policy in Xinjiang, and there is no reason to assume that Tibet will be spared a similar fate.

Only a few years ago, at the time of the war in Kosovo, China greatly feared that self-determination was becoming the new norm in international relations. It worried that the doctrine of "humanitarian interventionism" was supplanting the doctrine of state sovereignty and thought that the doctrine might be used to justify international intervention in Taiwan, Tibet, or Xinjiang.

China therefore published a flurry of articles arguing against the doctrine of humanitarian interventionism and denouncing the idea that the principle of self-determination could override a state's sovereign rights or that the principle was applicable to Tibet.[11] Since then, China has exploited the war against terrorism to justify its repression in Xinjiang and even in Tibet. It has exploited its ostensible cooperation in the war against terrorism in order to lessen international, especially American, criticism of its policies in Tibet. Nevertheless, the principle of self-determination may again arise to challenge unrestricted state sovereignty in China and elsewhere.

China maintains that its rise is no threat to anyone in the world and that it intends to pursue a "harmonious world" policy. However, what it seems to mean by a harmonious world is one in which neither China nor any other authoritarian state is criticized about the nature of its political system or its actions internally or internationally. The Chinese doctrine implies that such states should be accepted by United Nations and other international organizations as they are, and that they should change those organizations to suit themselves rather than being required to alter their systems or practices to suit the existing international system.

China has already shown, with regard to international human rights organizations, that it will not integrate with an existing international system but will attempt to remake that system to be more compatible with its own political traditions. China's conflict with the existing international system, Western world traditions, and the United States is therefore inevitable. Sino-U.S. relations will almost inevitably become more competitive as China assumes a more assertive role in the world and demands more of its natural resources. China's slogans about its "peaceful rise," later altered to "harmonious world"—both of which were formulated to counter the "China threat theory"—illustrate the reality that China's economic, political, and military power is threatening to many in the world, particularly to the United States and, in Asia, to India.

Despite the argument that its best policy is self-determination, Dharamsala is unlikely to abandon the Middle Path policy, which is incompatible with the real meaning of self-determination. The popularity of the MWA with Western supporters and governments makes this almost inevitable. The Dharamsala government is reluctant to give up hope for a "solution" to the Tibet issue via autonomy, although they have already given up hope for independence or any solution capable of preserving Tibetan national identity. Western governments supportive of Tibet are comfortable with a policy of dialogue and a vague autonomy. They applaud the Dalai Lama's constant statements that he does "not want Tibetan independence," because this allows them to respond to popular support for Tibet without confronting China about the real issue of Tibetan self-determination. The Dalai Lama's policies of nonviolence, dialogue, and autonomy are popular with many Westerners who choose to think of Tibet as more a spiritual than a political issue. Dharamsala will keep hoping for a shift in Chinese politics that would bring a more liberal faction to power, or perhaps a greater Chinese respect for Tibetan Buddhism. However, there is no evidence of the existence of any liberal faction or any implication that Chinese interest in Tibetan Buddhism will translate into political support for Tibet.

The predominant phenomenon in Chinese politics at this time is the rise of China's "comprehensive national power," accompanied by a growing nationalism, which is promoted by the CCP in order to compensate for its lack of any other ideological legitimacy. China's new confidence and its rejection of foreign influence does not put it in any mood to compromise over Tibet. Chinese nationalism has become so defensive that any foreign criticism about Tibet is interpreted as a scheme to divide, weaken, or contain China. Beijing reacts to polite suggestions from the Dalai Lama or Western governments that it should respect its own laws on nationality autonomy with accusations that the real intention of the proponents is to achieve Tibetan independence. It would undoubtedly react no better to a demand from Dharamsala or anywhere else that Tibet should have the right to national self-determination. However, China already interprets all criticisms of its role in Tibet as based upon the fundamental issues of independence or self-determination. It would presumably respond no more defensively were the issue to be put in the terms of self-determination, which China is well aware is the actual issue.

The issue of Tibet is the denial by China of Tibet's right to national self-determination. China cannot allow or even talk about any real autonomy because to do so would raise the issue of the legitimacy of Chinese rule over Tibet. It cannot answer the question about its denial of Tibet's right to national self-determination. Self-determination as a principle of international law, although unenforceable, retains much of its moral and ideological legitimacy. Self-determination as a political policy has the advantage that it preserves Tibetan national identity, at least in the ideological sense, whereas autonomy is unable to preserve it in any sense at all.

Ultimately, the issue of Tibet will be decided by the other meaning of self-determination, which is that nations have not only the right to self-determination but also the responsibility to determine their fate as a nation. Self-determination must be self-determined. Tibetans are responsible for their own self-determination, the survival of their own national identity, and their national destiny. The final result of the Tibet issue will be that Tibetans themselves will determine their fate, or they will be unable to do so.

Notes

1. "Understand Authorized Autonomy, Respect the Central Government Power," *Wen Wei Po* (Hong Kong), 7 June 2007, in Open Source Center CPP20070607710009, http://www.opensource.gov.

2. Dawa Norbu, *China's Tibet Policy* (Richmond, Surrey, England: Curzon Press, 2001), 15.

3. "Colossal Guru Rinpoche's Statue Demolished in Tibet," Phayul.com, 5 June 2007, http://www.phayul.com/news/article.aspx?id=16719&article.

4. "When Dalai Lama Stopped a Patna Show for Chinese Pilgrims," *Indian Express*, 13 January 2007, available at http://www.phayul.com/news/article.aspx?id=15292&article.

5. International Campaign for Tibet, "Chronology of Sino-Tibetan Relations, 1979 to 2005," http://www.savetibet.org/news/positionpapers/chronology.php.

6. Yedor, "Text of China Tibet Information Center Article on 'Middle Way' of Dalai Lama," *Beijing Xinhua*, 28 July 2006, in Open Source Center CPP20060728052027.

7. Wang Jiawei and Nyima Gyaincain, *The Historical Status of China's Tibet* (Beijing: China Intercontinental Press, 2000), 282.

8. "Dalai Lama Denounces 'Cultural Genocide,'" Reuters, 9 October 2003.

9. The Dalai Lama was quoted as saying, "Some leader in a western country—I cannot tell you who—has told me it is very dangerous to return now. As soon as Chinese government begins to think about a new way of approach regarding Tibet issue then I think it's right time. Then I can make some contribution. Now, this is the best way to serve the Tibetan people. I can do more outside Tibet than inside Tibet." Older Tibetans long to see him return, he says, but the more politically minded Tibetans believe that he is better able to serve their cause in the West. Gillian Bowditch, "Peaceful Protest," Scotsman.com, 8 November 2003, http://www.scotsman.com/features/Peaceful-protest.2476715.jp.

10. Erkin Alptekin, president of the World Uighur Congress, personal communication, Washington, DC, 28 May 2004.

11. See Allen Carlson, *Beijing's Tibet Policy: Securing Sovereignty and Legitimacy* (Washington, DC: East-West Center, 2004), 34. Carlson quotes an article, "Discussion of Self-determination" by Yang Fan and Zhi Rong, two scholars from the International Relations Department of Beijing University: "In the last few years, with the drastic change in Eastern Europe, self-determination has been used to oppose communism and socialism and has taken on new characteristics. Under these conditions, anti-Chinese foreign forces and internal separatists have written many articles about "Tibetan self-determination" and stated that "the realization of Tibetan self-determination is the most reasonable, ideal, and peaceful method for solving the Tibetan issue in the future." . . . Actually, this trumpeting of the theory of self-determination is a distortion and misinterpretation of the theory of self-determination and a deliberate misunderstanding of Tibetan history and reality."

Bibliography

Alexander, Andre. *The Temples of Lhasa: Tibetan Buddhist Architecture from the 7th to the 21st Centuries.* Chicago: Serindia, 2005.

Bowles, Gordon T. *The People of Asia.* New York: Charles Scribner's Sons, 1977.

Carlson, Allen. *Beijing's Tibet Policy: Securing Sovereignty and Legitimacy.* Washington, DC: East-West Center, 2004.

Chang, Chih-i. *The Party and the National Question in China.* Trans. George Moseley. Cambridge, MA: MIT Press, 1966.

Chiang Kai-shek. "National Independence and Racial Equality." In *The Collected Wartime Messages of Generalissimo Chiang Kai-shek, 1937–1945*, comp. Chinese Ministry of Information. New York: John Day, 1949.

China's Public Relations Strategy on Tibet: Classified Documents from the Beijing Propaganda Conference. Washington, DC: International Campaign for Tibet, 1993.

Connor, Walker. *The National Question in Marxist-Leninist Theory and Strategy.* Princeton, NJ: Princeton University Press, 1984.

Cutting Off the Serpent's Head: Tightening Control in Tibet, 1994–1995. New York: Tibet Information Network, Human Rights Watch/Asia, 1996.

Dalai Lama. *The Collected Statements, Interviews and Articles of His Holiness the Dalai Lama.* Dharamsala: Information Office of His Holiness the Dalai Lama, 1986.

———. *My Land and My People.* New York: Potala Press, 1983.

Dawa Norbu. "China's Dialogue with the Dalai Lama, 1978–90: Prenegotiation Stage or Dead End?" *Pacific Affairs* 64, no. 3 (Fall 1991).

———. *China's Tibet Policy.* Richmond, Surrey, England: Curzon Press, 2001.

———. *Red Star over Tibet.* New York: Envoy Press, 1987.

———. *Tibet: The Road Ahead.* London: Rider, 1998.

Deng Xiaoping. "Report on the Rectification Campaign." In Robert R. Bowie and John K. Fairbank, *Communist China, 1955–1959: Policy Documents and Analysis.* Cambridge, MA: Harvard University Press, 1962.

Epstein, Israel. *My China Eye: Memoirs of a Jew and a Journalist.* San Francisco: Long River Press, 2005.

———. *Tibet Transformed.* Beijing: New World Press, 1983.

Gelder, Stuart, and Roma Gelder. *The Timely Rain: Travels in New Tibet.* London: Hutchinson, 1962.

Haarh, Erik. *The Yar-Lun Dynasty.* Copenhagen: Gads Forlag, 1969.

Han Suyin. *Lhasa, the Open City: A Journey to Tibet.* New York: G. P. Putnam's Sons, 1977.

Hollander, Paul. *From the Gulag to the Killing Fields: Personal Accounts of Political Violence and Repression in Communist States.* Wilmington, DE: Intercollegiate Studies Institute Books, 2006.

———. *Political Pilgrims: Travels of Western Intellectuals to the Soviet Union, China, and Cuba, 1928–1978.* New York: Harper Colophon Books, 1983.

International Commission of Jurists. *Tibet and the Chinese People's Republic: A Report to the International Commission of Jurists by Its Legal Inquiry Committee on Tibet.* Geneva: International Commission of Jurists, 1960.

Jampa: The Story of Racism in Tibet. Washington, DC: International Campaign for Tibet, 2001.

Khetsun, Thupten. *A Testament of Suffering: Memories of Life in Lhasa under Chinese Rule.* Published as Tubten Khetsun, *Memories of Life under Chinese Rule.* New York: Columbia University Press, 2007.

Kolas, Ashild, and Monika P. Thowsen. *On the Margins of Tibet: Cultural Survival on the Sino-Tibetan Frontier.* Seattle: University of Washington Press, 2005.

Lamb, Alastair. *The McMahon Line: A Study in the Relations between India, China and Tibet, 1904–1914.* 2 vols. London: Routledge & Kegan Paul, 1966.

Ling Nai-Min, comp. *Tibet, 1950–1967.* Hong Kong: Union Research Institute, 1967.

Mao Zedong. "On the Correct Handling of Contradictions among the People." In Robert R. Bowie and John K. Fairbank, *Communist China, 1955–1959: Policy Documents and Analysis.* Cambridge, MA: Harvard University Press, 1962.

———. "On the Policies of Our Work in Tibet." In *Selected Works,* vol. 5. Beijing: Foreign Languages Press, 1977.

News Review: Reports from Tibet, 2001. London: Tibet Information Network.

Palden Gyatso. *The Autobiography of a Tibetan Monk.* New York: Grove Press, 1997.

Paljor, Kunsang. *Tibet, the Undying Flame.* Dharamsala: Information Office of His Holiness the Dalai Lama, 1977.

Panchen Lama. *A Poisoned Arrow: The Secret Report of the 10th Panchen Lama.* London: Tibet Information Network, 1997.

Richardson, Hugh. "Tibetan Precis." In *High Peaks, Pure Earth: Collected Writings on Tibetan History and Culture,* 517–666. London: Serindia, 1998.

Smith, Warren W., Jr. *Tibetan Nation: A History of Tibetan Nationalism and Sino-Tibetan Relations.* Boulder, CO: Westview Press, 1996.

Stalin, Joseph. *Marxism and the National-Colonial Question.* Moscow: Proletarian Publishers, 1975.

Stein, R. A. *Les Tribus Anciennes des Marches Sino-Tibetaines.* Paris: Imprimerie Nationale, 1959.

Strong, Anna Louise. *Tibetan Interviews.* Beijing: New World Press, 1959.

———. *When Serfs Stood Up in Tibet.* Beijing: New World Press, 1960.

Thomas, F. W. *Ancient Folk Literature from North-Eastern Tibet.* Abhandlungen der Deutschen Akademie der Wissenschaften zu Berlin. Berlin: Akademie Verlag, 1957.

———. *Nam: An Ancient Language of the Sino-Tibetan Borderland.* Publications of the Philological Society, no. 14. London: Oxford University Press, 1948.

Tibet under Chinese Communist Rule: A Compilation of Refugee Statements, 1958–1975. Dharamsala: Information and Publicity Office of His Holiness the Dalai Lama, 1976.

The True Features of Chinese Communist "Tibet Model." Taipei: Asian People's Anti-Communist League, 1982.

Tulku, Rinbur. *The Search for Jowo Mikyoe Dorje.* Dharamsala: Office of Information and International Relations, 1988.

Van Walt van Pragg, Michael C. *The Status of Tibet.* Boulder, CO: Westview Press, 1987.

Wang Jiawei and Nyima Gyaincain. *The Historical Status of China's Tibet.* Beijing: China Intercontinental Press, 2000.

Wrath of the Serfs: A Group of Life-Size Sculptures. Beijing: New World Press, 1976.

Index

activists, 36, 47, 55, 56, 80, 95
agriculture, 80–82
Akseter, Matthew, 163n4
Alexander, Andre, 163n4
Altan Khan, 7, 172
Ama Adhe, 115, 117
amban, 7, 8, 9, 138, 172
Amdo, 8, 11, 19, 23, 24, 32, 39, 45, 67,
    88–90, 117, 119n9, 134, 146, 238
Andrutsang, Gompo Tashi, 106
Ani Tsamkhung, 118
Anti-Bourgeois Liberalization
    Campaign, 218
Anti–Local Nationalist Campaign, 41,
    43, 44
Anti-Rightist Campaign, 41, 42, 43
Arabs, 4
Arjia Rinpoche, 168, 231
Army of Bodhisattvas, 101, 103, 109,
    110, 155
Asian Relations Conference, 11
Asoka, 67
Assam, 2
Assembly of Tibetan People's Deputies,
    228

assimilation, 25, 26, 28, 33, 42, 43, 44,
    48, 94, 95, 124, 128, 233, 258, 259,
    275, 276, 278, 281, 281, 282, 284, 288,
    290, 295
Australia, xviii, 265
Austria, xviii, 265
autonomous districts, 24, 36, 245, 251
autonomy, ix, xii, xv, xvi, xvii, xix, 6, 8,
    10, 11, 12, 13, 16, 21, 23, 26, 27, 28,
    28–36, 39, 40, 42, 48, 51, 67, 95, 96,
    124, 127, 128, 152, 153, 165, 166, 167,
    170, 181, 187, 195, 196, 198, 203, 206,
    213, 214, 216, 217, 218, 219, 232, 233,
    235, 236, 245, 259, 262, 275, 276, 277,
    279, 280, 291, 294; genuine, 236, 237,
    239, 241, 242, 244, 245, 247, 248, 249,
    252, 253, 262, 266, 281, 284, 291. *See
    also* National Regional Autonomy,
    Regional Ethnic Autonomy

Bapa Phuntsok Wangyal, 67
Barkor, 145, 149
Beijing, 9, 19, 20, 21, 30, 31, 34, 45, 66,
    116, 125, 201, 289
Bethune, Norman, 159

About the Author

Warren W. Smith Jr. has more than twenty-five years of experience in Tibetan studies. From 1970 to 1981 he was a resident of Nepal. In 1982 he was one of the first Westerners allowed in Tibet. In 1994 he received a Ph.D. in international relations from the Fletcher School of Law and Diplomacy, with a dissertation on Tibetan nationalism. He is the coauthor, with Manabajra Bajracharya, of *Mythological History of Nepal Valley from Svayambhu Purana* (1977) and the author of *Tibetan Nation: A History of Tibetan Nationalism and Sino-Tibetan Relations* (1996) and numerous articles on Tibetan politics. Since 1997 he has been a researcher and writer with the Tibetan Service of Radio Free Asia, where he has written more than seven hundred short programs on all aspects of Tibetan history and politics, Sino-Tibetan relations, Chinese politics, and Sino-U.S. relations.